THE THREE DIVINE WITNESSES

THE THREE DIVINE WITNESSES

EXPOSING THE HISTORY OF THE UNDERWORLD

HOW A CADRE OF OCCULTISTS CORRUPTED CHRISTIAN THEOLOGY

STEVEN S. JONES

JONES & JONES

The Three Divine Witnesses: Exposing the History of the Underworld

Jones & Jones Pub.

The Bridgeman Art Library, Ltd. vs. Corel Corporation

Non-interpretive, faithful photographic reproductions of two-dimensional works of art are considered in the public domain as they display no originality.

36 F. Supp. 2d 191, 1999 U.S. Dist. LEXIS 1731, 50 U.S.P.Q.2d (BNA) 1110. 25 F. Supp. 2d 421 (S.D.N.Y. 1998), U.S. Const. Art. I; Copyright Act of 1976

Front Cover: The *Sent Myhell Armys*, "St. Michael's Arms" (the archangel), from a 15th century manuscript *"Aunciant Coates"* found in the Harleian collection of the British Library. — Wikimedia Commons

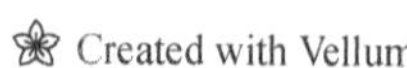 Created with Vellum

"Bow thine ear, O Lord, and hear us:
Let thine anger cease from us.
Sion is wasted and brought low,
Jerusalem desolate and void"

— WILLIAM BYRD - CHORAL ADAPTATION OF ISAIAH
64:9-10 (PUBLISHED 1768)

CONTENTS

TESTIMONY OF THE THREE WITNESSES CONCERNING THE SON OF GOD

English

1Jn 5:6 — This is he that came by water and blood, even Jesus Christ; not by water only, but by water and blood. And it is the Spirit that beareth witness, because the Spirit is truth.

1Jn 5:7 — For there are three that bear record in heaven, the Father, the Word, and the Holy Ghost: and these three are one.

1Jn 5:8 — And there are three that bear witness in earth, the Spirit, and the water, and the blood: and these three agree in one.

1Jn 5:9 — If we receive the witness of men, the witness of God is greater: for this is the witness of God which he hath testified of his Son.

1Jn 5:10 — He that believeth on the Son of God hath the witness in himself: he that believeth not God hath made him a liar; because he believeth not the record that God gave of his Son.

1Jn 5:11 — And this is the record, that God hath given to us eternal life, and this life is in his Son.

1Jn 5:12 — He that hath the Son hath life; and he that hath not the Son of God hath not life.

Greek

1Jn 5:6 — ουτος εστιν ο ελθων δι υδατος και αιματος ιησους ο χριστος ουκ εν τω υδατι μονον αλλ εν τω υδατι και τω αιματι και το πνευμα εστιν το μαρτυρουν οτι το πνευμα εστιν η αληθεια

1Jn 5:7 — οτι τρεις εισιν οι μαρτυρουντες εν τω ουρανω ο πατηρ ο λογος και το αγιον πνευμα και ουτοι οι τρεις εν εισιν

1Jn 5:8 — και τρεις εισιν οι μαρτυρουντες εν τη γη το πνευμα και το υδωρ και το αιμα και οι τρεις εις το εν εισιν

1Jn 5:9 — ει την μαρτυριαν των ανθρωπων λαμβανομεν η μαρτυρια του θεου μειζων εστιν οτι αυτη εστιν η μαρτυρια του θεου ην μεμαρτυρηκεν περι του υιου αυτου

1Jn 5:10 — ο πιστευων εις τον υιον του θεου εχει την μαρτυριαν εν εαυτω ο μη πιστευων τω θεω ψευστην πεποιηκεν αυτον οτι ου πεπιστευκεν εις την μαρτυριαν ην μεμαρτυρηκεν ο θεος περι του υιου αυτου

1Jn 5:11 — και αυτη εστιν η μαρτυρια οτι ζωην αιωνιον εδωκεν ημιν ο θεος και αυτη η ζωη εν τω υιω αυτου εστιν

1Jn 5:12 — ο εχων τον υιον εχει την ζωην ο μη εχων τον υιον του θεου την ζωην ουκ εχει

Latin

1Jn 5:6 — hic est qui venit per aquam et sanguinem Iesus Christus non in aqua solum sed in aqua et sanguine et Spiritus est qui testificatur quoniam Christus est veritas

1Jn 5:7 — quia tres sunt qui testimonium dant

1Jn 5:8 — Spiritus et aqua et sanguis et tres unum sunt

1Jn 5:9 — si testimonium hominum accipimus testimonium Dei maius est quoniam hoc est testimonium Dei quod maius est quia testificatus est de Filio suo

1Jn 5:10 — qui credit in Filio Dei habet testimonium Dei in se qui non credit Filio mendacem facit eum quoniam non credidit in testimonio quod testificatus est Deus de Filio suo

1Jn 5:11 — et hoc est testimonium quoniam vitam aeternam dedit nobis Deus et haec vita in Filio eius est

1Jn 5:12 — qui habet Filium habet vitam qui non habet Filium Dei vitam non habet

THE INTRODUCTION TO THE GOSPEL OF ST. JOHN

OTHERWISE KNOWN AS THE FIRST EPISTLE OF JOHN THE APOSTLE

VETUS LATINA (ITALIANA)

CHAPTER 1

1 Quod fuit ab initio, quod audivimus, quod vidimus oculis nostris, quod perspeximus, et manus nostræ contrectaverunt de verbo vitæ:

That which was from the beginning, which we have heard, which we have seen with our eyes, which we have looked upon, and our hands have handled, of the word of life:

2 et vita manifestata est, et vidimus, et testamur, et annuntiamus vobis vitam æternam, quæ erat apud Patrem, et apparuit nobis:

For the life was manifested; and we have seen and do bear witness, and declare unto you the life eternal, which was with the Father, and hath appeared to us:

3 quod vidimus et audivimus, annuntiamus vobis, ut et vos societatem habeatis nobiscum, et societas nostra sit cum Patre, et cum Filio ejus Jesu Christo.

That which we have seen and have heard, we declare unto you, that you also may have fellowship with us, and our fellowship may be with the Father, and with his Son Jesus Christ.

4 Et hæc scribimus vobis ut gaudeatis, et gaudium vestrum sit plenum.

And these things we write to you, that you may rejoice, and your joy may be full.

5 Et hæc est annuntiatio, quam audivimus ab eo, et annuntiamus vobis: quoniam Deus lux est, et tenebræ in eo non sunt ullæ.

And this is the declaration which we have heard from him, and declare unto you: That God is light, and in him there is no darkness.

6 Si dixerimus quoniam societatem habemus cum eo, et in tenebris ambulamus, mentimur, et veritatem non facimus.

If we say that we have fellowship with him, and walk in darkness, we lie, and do not the truth.

7 Si autem in luce ambulamus sicut et ipse est in luce, societatem habemus ad invicem, et sanguis Jesu Christi, Filii ejus, emundat nos ab omni peccato.

But if we walk in the light, as he also is in the light, we have fellowship one with another, and the blood of Jesus Christ his Son cleanseth us from all sin.

8 Si dixerimus quoniam peccatum non habemus, ipsi nos seducimus, et veritas in nobis non est.

If we say that we have no sin, we deceive ourselves, and the truth is not in us.

9 Si confiteamur peccata nostra: fidelis est, et justus, ut remittat nobis peccata nostra, et emundet nos ab omni iniquitate.

If we confess our sins, he is faithful and just, to forgive us our sins, and to cleanse us from all iniquity.

10 Si dixerimus quoniam non peccavimus, mendacem facimus eum, et verbum ejus non est in nobis.

If we say that we have not sinned, we make him a liar, and his word is not in us.

Chapter 2

1 Filioli mei, hæc scribo vobis, ut non peccetis. Sed et si quis peccaverit, advocatum habemus apud Patrem, Jesum Christum justum:

My little children, these things I write to you, that you may not sin. But if any man sin, we have an advocate with the Father, Jesus Christ the just:

2 et ipse est propitiatio pro peccatis nostris: non pro nostris autem tantum, sed etiam pro totius mundi.

And he is the propitiation for our sins: and not for ours only, but also for those of the whole world.

3 Et in hoc scimus quoniam cognovimus eum, si mandata ejus observemus.

And by this we know that we have known him, if we keep his commandments.

4 Qui dicit se nosse eum, et mandata ejus non custodit, mendax est, et in hoc veritas non est.

He who saith that he knoweth him, and keepeth not his commandments, is a liar, and the truth is not in him.

5 Qui autem servat verbum ejus, vere in hoc caritas Dei perfecta est: et in hoc scimus quoniam in ipso sumus.

But he that keepeth his word, in him in very deed the charity of God is perfected; and by this we know that we are in him.

6 Qui dicit se in ipso manere, debet, sicut ille ambulavit, et ipse ambulare.

He that saith he abideth in him, ought himself also to walk, even as he walked.

7 Carissimi, non mandatum novum scribo vobis, sed mandatum vetus, quod habuistis ab initio. Mandatum vetus est verbum, quod audistis.

Dearly beloved, I write not a new commandment to you, but an old commandment which you had from the beginning. The old commandment is the word which you have heard.

8 Iterum mandatum novum scribo vobis, quod verum est et in ipso, et in vobis: quia tenebræ transierunt, et verum lumen jam lucet.

Again a new commandment I write unto you, which thing is true both in him and in you; because the darkness is passed, and the true light now shineth.

9 Qui dicit se in luce esse, et fratrem suum odit, in tenebris est usque adhuc.

He that saith he is in the light, and hateth his brother, is in darkness even until now.

10 Qui diligit fratrem suum, in lumine manet, et scandalum in eo non est.

He that loveth his brother, abideth in the light, and there is no scandal in him.

11 Qui autem odit fratrem suum, in tenebris est, et in tenebris ambulat, et nescit quo eat: quia tenebræ obcæcaverunt oculos ejus.

But he that hateth his brother, is in darkness, and walketh in darkness, and knoweth not whither he goeth; because the darkness hath blinded his eyes.

12 Scribo vobis, filioli, quoniam remittuntur vobis peccata propter nomen ejus.

I write unto you, little children, because your sins are forgiven you for his name' s sake.

13 Scribo vobis, patres, quoniam cognovistis eum, qui ab initio est. Scribo vobis, adolescentes, quoniam vicistis malignum.

I write unto you, fathers, because you have known him, who is from the beginning. I write unto you, young men, because you have overcome the wicked one.

14 Scribo vobis, infantes, quoniam cognovistis patrem. Scribo vobis juvenes, quoniam fortes estis, et verbum Dei manet in vobis, et vicistis malignum.

I write unto you, babes, because you have known the Father. I write unto you, young men, because you are strong, and the word of God abideth in you, and you have overcome the wicked one.

15 Nolite diligere mundum, neque ea quæ in mundo sunt. Si quis diligit mundum, non est caritas Patris in eo:

Love not the world, nor the things which are in the world. If any man love the world, the charity of the Father is not in him.

16 quoniam omne quod est in mundo, concupiscentia carnis est, et concupiscentia oculorum, et superbia vitæ: quæ non est ex Patre, sed ex mundo est.

For all that is in the world, is the concupiscence of the flesh, and the concupiscence of the eyes, and the pride of life, which is not of the Father, but is of the world.

17 Et mundus transit, et concupiscentia ejus: qui autem facit voluntatem Dei manet in æternum.

And the world passeth away, and the concupiscence thereof: but he that doth the will of God, abideth for ever.

18 Filioli, novissima hora est: et sicut audistis quia antichristus venit, et nunc antichristi multi facti sunt; unde scimus, quia novissima hora est.

Little children, it is the last hour; and as you have heard that Antichrist cometh, even now there are become many Antichrists: whereby we know that it is the last hour.

19 Ex nobis prodierunt, sed non erant ex nobis, nam, si fuissent ex nobis, permansissent utique nobiscum: sed ut manifesti sint quoniam non sunt omnes ex nobis.

They went out from us, but they were not of us. For if they had been of us, they would no doubt have remained with us; but that they may be manifest, that they are not all of us.

20 Sed vos unctionem habetis a Sancto, et nostis omnia.

But you have the unction from the Holy One, and know all things.

21 Non scripsi vobis quasi ignorantibus veritatem, sed quasi scientibus eam· et quoniam omne mendacium ex veritate non est.

I have not written to you as to them that know not the truth, but as to them that know it: and that no lie is of the truth.

22 Quis est mendax, nisi is qui negat quoniam Jesus est Christus? Hic est antichristus, qui negat Patrem, et Filium.

Who is a liar, but he who denieth that Jesus is the Christ? This is Antichrist, who denieth the Father, and the Son.

23 Omnis qui negat Filium, nec Patrem habet: qui confitetur Filium, et Patrem habet.

Whosoever denieth the Son, the same hath not the Father. He that confesseth the Son, hath the Father also.

24 Vos quod audistis ab initio, in vobis permaneat: si in vobis permanserit quod audistis ab initio, et vos in Filio et Patre manebitis.

As for you, let that which you have heard from the beginning, abide in you. If that abide in you, which you have heard from the beginning, you also shall abide in the Son, and in the Father.

25 Et hæc est repromissio, quam ipse pollicitus est nobis, vitam æternam.

And this is the promise which he hath promised us, life everlasting.

26 Hæc scripsi vobis de his, qui seducant vos.

These things have I written to you, concerning them that seduce you.

27 Et vos unctionem, quam accepistis ab eo, maneat in vobis. Et non necesse habetis ut aliquis doceat vos: sed sicut unctio ejus docet vos de omnibus, et verum est, et non est mendacium. Et sicut docuit vos: manete in eo.

And as for you, let the unction, which you have received from him, abide in you. And you have no need that any man teach you; but as his unction teacheth you of all things, and is truth, and is no lie. And as it hath taught you, abide in him.

28 Et nunc, filioli, manete in eo: ut cum apparuerit, habeamus fiduciam, et non confundamur ab eo in adventu ejus.

And now, little children, abide in him, that when he shall appear, we may have confidence, and not be confounded by him at his coming.

29 Si scitis quoniam justus est, scitote quoniam et omnis, qui facit justitiam, ex ipso natus est.

If you know, that he is just, know ye, that every one also, who doth justice, is born of him.

Chapter 3

1 Videte qualem caritatem dedit nobis Pater, ut filii Dei nominemur et simus. Propter hoc mundus non novit nos: quia non novit eum.

Behold what manner of charity the Father hath bestowed upon us, that we should be called, and should be the sons of God. Therefore the world knoweth not us, because it knew not him.

2 Carissimi, nunc filii Dei sumus: et nondum apparuit quid erimus. Scimus quoniam cum apparuerit, similes ei erimus: quoniam videbimus eum sicuti est.

Dearly beloved, we are now the sons of God; and it hath not yet appeared what we shall be. We know, that, when he shall appear, we shall be like to him: because we shall see him as he is.

3 Et omnis qui habet hanc spem in eo, sanctificat se, sicut et ille sanctus est.

And every one that hath this hope in him, sanctifieth himself, as he also is holy.

4 Omnis qui facit peccatum, et iniquitatem facit: et peccatum est iniquitas.

Whosoever committeth sin committeth also iniquity; and sin is iniquity.

5 Et scitis quia ille apparuit ut peccata nostra tolleret: et peccatum in eo non est.

And you know that he appeared to take away our sins, and in him there is no sin.

6 Omnis qui in eo manet, non peccat: et omnis qui peccat, non vidit eum, nec cognovit eum.

Whosoever abideth in him, sinneth not; and whosoever sinneth, hath not seen him, nor known him.

7 Filioli, nemo vos seducat. Qui facit justitiam, justus est, sicut et ille justus est.

Little children, let no man deceive you. He that doth justice is just, even as he is just.

8 Qui facit peccatum, ex diabolo est: quoniam ab initio diabolus peccat. In hoc apparuit Filius Dei, ut dissolvat opera diaboli.

He that committeth sin is of the devil: for the devil sinneth from the beginning. For this purpose, the Son of God appeared, that he might destroy the works of the devil.

9 Omnis qui natus est ex Deo, peccatum non facit: quoniam semen ipsius in eo manet, et non potest peccare, quoniam ex Deo natus est.

Whosoever is born of God, committeth not sin: for his seed abideth in him, and he can not sin, because he is born of God.

10 In hoc manifesti sunt filii Dei, et filii diaboli. Omnis qui non est justus, non est ex Deo, et qui non diligit fratrem suum:

In this the children of God are manifest, and the children of the devil. Whosoever is not just, is not of God, nor he that loveth not his brother.

11 quoniam hæc est annuntiatio, quam audistis ab initio, ut diligatis alterutrum.

For this is the declaration, which you have heard from the beginning, that you should love one another.

12 Non sicut Cain, qui ex maligno erat, et occidit fratrem suum. Et propter quid occidit eum? Quoniam opera ejus maligna erant: fratris autem ejus, justa.

Not as Cain, who was of the wicked one, and killed his brother. And wherefore did he kill him? Because his own works were wicked: and his brother' s just.

13 Nolite mirari, fratres, si odit vos mundus.

Wonder not, brethren, if the world hate you.

14 Nos scimus quoniam translati sumus de morte ad vitam, quoniam diligimus fratres. Qui non diligit, manet in morte:

We know that we have passed from death to life, because we love the brethren. He that loveth not, abideth in death.

15 omnis qui odit fratrem suum, homicida est. Et scitis quoniam omnis homicida non habet vitam æternam in semetipso manentem.

Whosoever hateth his brother is a murderer. And you know that no murderer hath eternal life abiding in himself.

16 In hoc cognovimus caritatem Dei, quoniam ille animam suam pro nobis posuit: et nos debemus pro fratribus animas ponere.

In this we have known the charity of God, because he hath laid down his life for us: and we ought to lay down our lives for the brethren.

17 Qui habuerit substantiam hujus mundi, et viderit fratrem suum necessitatem habere, et clauserit viscera sua ab eo: quomodo caritas Dei manet in eo?

He that hath the substance of this world, and shall see his brother in

need, and shall shut up his bowels from him: how doth the charity of God abide in him?

18 Filioli mei, non diligamus verbo neque lingua, sed opere et veritate:

My little children, let us not love in word, nor in tongue, but in deed, and in truth.

19 in hoc cognoscimus quoniam ex veritate sumus: et in conspectu ejus suadebimus corda nostra.

In this we know that we are of the truth: and in his sight shall persuade our hearts.

20 Quoniam si reprehenderit nos cor nostrum: major est Deus corde nostro, et novit omnia.

For if our heart reprehend us, God is greater than our heart, and knoweth all things.

21 Carissimi, si cor nostrum non reprehenderit nos, fiduciam habemus ad Deum:

Dearly beloved, if our heart do not reprehend us, we have confidence towards God:

22 et quidquid petierimus, accipiemus ab eo: quoniam mandata ejus custodimus, et ea, quæ sunt placita coram eo, facimus.

And whatsoever we shall ask, we shall receive of him: because we keep his commandments, and do those things which are pleasing in his sight.

23 Et hoc est mandatum ejus: ut credamus in nomine Filii ejus Jesu Christi: et diligamus alterutrum, sicut dedit mandatum nobis.

And this is his commandment, that we should believe in the name of his Son Jesus Christ: and love one another, as he hath given commandment unto us.

24 Et qui servat mandata ejus, in illo manet, et ipse in eo: et in hoc scimus quoniam manet in nobis, de Spiritu quem dedit nobis.

And he that keepeth his commandments, abideth in him, and he in him. And in this we know that he abideth in us, by the Spirit which he hath given us.

1 Carissimi, nolite omni spiritui credere, sed probate spiritus si ex Deo sint: quoniam multi pseudoprophetæ exierunt in mundum.

Dearly beloved, believe not every spirit, but try the spirits if they be of God: because many false prophets are gone out into the world.

2 In hoc cognoscitur Spiritus Dei: omnis spiritus qui confitetur Jesum Christum in carne venisse, ex Deo est:

By this is the spirit of God known. Every spirit which confesseth that Jesus Christ is come in the flesh, is of God:

3 et omnis spiritus qui solvit Jesum, ex Deo non est, et hic est antichristus, de quo audistis quoniam venit, et nunc jam in mundo est.

And every spirit that dissolveth Jesus, is not of God: and this is Antichrist, of whom you have heard that he cometh, and he is now already in the world.

4 Vos ex Deo estis filioli, et vicistis eum, quoniam major est qui in vobis est, quam qui in mundo.

You are of God, little children, and have overcome him. Because greater is he that is in you, than he that is in the world.

5 Ipsi de mundo sunt: ideo de mundo loquuntur, et mundus eos audit.

They are of the world: therefore of the world they speak, and the world heareth them.

6 Nos ex Deo sumus. Qui novit Deum, audit nos; qui non est ex Deo, non audit nos: in hoc cognoscimus Spiritum veritatis, et spiritum erroris.

We are of God. He that knoweth God, heareth us. He that is not of God, heareth us not. By this we know the spirit of truth, and the spirit of error.

7 Carissimi, diligamus nos invicem: quia caritas ex Deo est. Et omnis qui diligit, ex Deo natus est, et cognoscit Deum.

Dearly beloved, let us love one another, for charity is of God. And every one that loveth, is born of God, and knoweth God.

8 Qui non diligit, non novit Deum: quoniam Deus caritas est.

He that loveth not, knoweth not God: for God is charity.

9 In hoc apparuit caritas Dei in nobis, quoniam Filium suum unigenitum misit Deus in mundum, ut vivamus per eum.

By this hath the charity of God appeared towards us, because God hath sent his only begotten Son into the world, that we may live by him.

10 In hoc est caritas: non quasi nos dilexerimus Deum, sed quoniam ipse prior dilexit nos, et misit Filium suum propitiationem pro peccatis nostris.

In this is charity: not as though we had loved God, but because he hath first loved us, and sent his Son to be a propitiation for our sins.

11 Carissimi, si sic Deus dilexit nos: et nos debemus alterutrum diligere.

My dearest, if God hath so loved us; we also ought to love one another.

12 Deum nemo vidit umquam. Si diligamus invicem, Deus in nobis manet, et caritas ejus in nobis perfecta est.

No man hath seen God at any time. If we love one another, God abideth in us, and his charity is perfected in us.

13 In hoc cognoscimus quoniam in eo manemus, et ipse in nobis: quoniam de Spiritu suo dedit nobis.

In this we know that we abide in him, and he in us: because he hath given us of his spirit.

14 Et vos vidimus, et testificamur quoniam Pater misit Filium suum Salvatorem mundi.

And we have seen, and do testify, that the Father hath sent his Son to be the Saviour of the world.

15 Quisquis confessus fuerit quoniam Jesus est Filius Dei, Deus in eo manet, et ipse in Deo.

Whosoever shall confess that Jesus is the Son of God, God abideth in him, and he in God.

16 Et nos cognovimus, et credidimus caritati, quam habet Deus in nobis. Deus caritas est: et qui manet in caritate, in Deo manet, et Deus in eo.

And we have known, and have believed the charity, which God hath

to us. God is charity: and he that abideth in charity, abideth in God, and God in him.

17 In hoc perfecta est caritas Dei nobiscum, ut fiduciam habeamus in die judicii: quia sicut ille est, et nos sumus in hoc mundo.

In this is the charity of God perfected with us, that we may have confidence in the day of judgment: because as he is, we also are in this world.

18 Timor non est in caritate: sed perfecta caritas foras mittit timorem, quoniam timor pœnam habet: qui autem timet, non est perfectus in caritate.

Fear is not in charity: but perfect charity casteth out fear, because fear hath pain. And he that feareth, is not perfected in charity.

19 Nos ergo diligamus Deum, quoniam Deus prior dilexit nos.

Let us therefore love God, because God first hath loved us.

20 Si quis dixerit, Quoniam diligo Deum, et fratrem suum oderit, mendax est. Qui enim non diligit fratrem suum quem vidit, Deum, quem non vidit, quomodo potest diligere?

If any man say, I love God, and hateth his brother; he is a liar. For he that loveth not his brother, whom he seeth, how can he love God, whom he seeth not?

21 Et hoc mandatum habemus a Deo: ut qui diligit Deum, diligat et fratrem suum.

And this commandment we have from God, that he, who loveth God, love also his brother.

CHAPTER 5

1 Omnis qui credit quoniam Jesus est Christus, ex Deo natus est. Et omnis qui diligit eum qui genuit, diligit et eum qui natus est ex eo.

Whosoever believeth that Jesus is the Christ, is born of God. And every one that loveth him who begot, loveth him also who is born of him.

2 In hoc cognoscimus quoniam diligamus natos Dei, cum Deum diligamus, et mandata ejus faciamus.

In this we know that we love the children of God: when we love God, and keep his commandments.

3 Hæc est enim caritas Dei, ut mandata ejus custodiamus: et mandata ejus gravia non sunt.

For this is the charity of God, that we keep his commandments: and his commandments are not heavy.

4 Quoniam omne quod natum est ex Deo, vincit mundum: et hæc est victoria, quæ vincit mundum, fides nostra.

For whatsoever is born of God, overcometh the world: and this is the victory which overcometh the world, our faith.

5 Quis est, qui vincit mundum, nisi qui credit quoniam Jesus est Filius Dei?

Who is he that overcometh the world, but he that believeth that Jesus is the Son of God?

6 Hic est, qui venit per aquam et sanguinem, Jesus Christus: non in aqua solum, sed in aqua et sanguine. Et Spiritus est, qui testificatur quoniam Christus est veritas.

This is he that came by water and blood, Jesus Christ: not by water only, but by water and blood. And it is the Spirit which testifieth, that Christ is the truth.

7 Quoniam tres sunt, qui testimonium dant in cælo: Pater, Verbum, et Spiritus Sanctus: et hi tres unum sunt.

And there are three who give testimony in heaven, the Father, the Word, and the Holy Ghost. And these three are one.

8 Et tres sunt, qui testimonium dant in terra: spiritus, et aqua, et sanguis: et hi tres unum sunt.

And there are three that give testimony on earth: the spirit, and the water, and the blood: and these three are one.

9 Si testimonium hominum accipimus, testimonium Dei majus est: quoniam hoc est testimonium Dei, quod majus est, quoniam testificatus est de Filio suo.

If we receive the testimony of men, the testimony of God is greater. For this is the testimony of God, which is greater, because he hath testified of his Son.

10 Qui credit in Filium Dei, habet testimonium Dei in se. Qui non credit Filio, mendacem facit eum: quia non credit in testimonium quod testificatus est Deus de Filio suo.

He that believeth in the Son of God, hath the testimony of God in himself. He that believeth not the Son, maketh him a liar: because he believeth not in the testimony which God hath testified of his Son.

11 Et hoc est testimonium, quoniam vitam æternam dedit nobis Deus: et hæc vita in Filio ejus est.

And this is the testimony, that God hath given to us eternal life. And this life is in his Son.

12 Qui habet Filium, habet vitam: qui non habet Filium, vitam non habet.

He that hath the Son, hath life. He that hath not the Son, hath not life.

13 Hæc scribo vobis ut sciatis quoniam vitam habetis æternam, qui creditis in nomine Filii Dei.

These things I write to you, that you may know that you have eternal life, you who believe in the name of the Son of God.

14 Et hæc est fiducia, quam habemus ad eum: quia quodcumque petierimus, secundum voluntatem ejus, audit nos.

And this is the confidence which we have towards him: That, whatsoever we shall ask according to his will, he heareth us.

15 Et scimus quia audit nos quidquid petierimus: scimus quoniam habemus petitiones quas postulamus ab eo.

And we know that he heareth us whatsoever we ask: we know that we have the petitions which we request of him.

16 Qui scit fratrem suum peccare peccatum non ad mortem, petat, et dabitur ei vita peccanti non ad mortem. Est peccatum ad mortem: non pro illo dico ut roget quis.

He that knoweth his brother to sin a sin which is not to death, let him ask, and life shall be given to him, who sinneth not to death. There is a sin unto death: for that I say not that any man ask.

17 Omnis iniquitas, peccatum est: et est peccatum ad mortem.

All iniquity is sin. And there is a sin unto death.

18 Scimus quia omnis qui natus est ex Deo, non peccat: sed generatio Dei conservat eum, et malignus non tangit eum.

We know that whosoever is born of God, sinneth not: but the generation of God preserveth him, and the wicked one toucheth him not.

19 Scimus quoniam ex Deo sumus: et mundus totus in maligno positus est.

We know that we are of God, and the whole world is seated in wickedness.

20 Et scimus quoniam Filius Dei venit, et dedit nobis sensum ut cognoscamus verum Deum, et simus in vero Filio ejus. Hic est verus Deus, et vita æterna.

And we know that the Son of God is come: and he hath given us understanding that we may know the true God, and may be in his true Son. This is the true God and life eternal.

21 Filioli, custodite vos a simulacris. Amen.

Little children, keep yourselves from idols. Amen.[1]

---

1. VETUSLATINA.ORG: *Resources for the Study of the Old Latin Bible,* https://itseeweb.cal.bham.ac.uk/vetuslatina/

FOREWORD
A MAGICIAN IN DISGUISE

CERTAINE TRICKS — TO TURNE WATERS INTO WINE INTO CLARET.

Take as much lockwood as you can hold in your mouth without discovery
tye it up in a cloth, & put it in your mouth, then sup up some wather & champe
ye lockwood 3 or 4 times & doe it out into a glass.[1]

In mid-July 1936, just prior to the then next war to end all wars, Sotheby's London was to have an auction of very rare manuscripts. Offered for bidding was a mysterious metal box filled with Isaac Newton's mostly never before seen writings. Perhaps once and for all some lingering questions would be answered. Was Newton ordained in the Church, as many had speculated? Had he copied Leibniz in his discovery of calculus? What inspired him to discover the physical laws of light and motion? What was found was startling...

The chest was not high on the list of valuable items to be auctioned that day. The contents only had the interest of a few. In any case, it brought in £9,000. More than one person won bids on the items, meaning they would be separated, but the person who could claim the most was the famous economist John Maynard Keynes. Keynes, himself, was a member of the Cambridge Apostles, an elite debate society began in the early 19th century whose members often envisioned themselves as the future captains of society. And, indeed, many did, including the ignominious Cambridge Five, Soviet spies within the WWII British Government whose secret mission was to lay the groundwork for future socialist states such as Israel.

Newton, once considered the most knowledgable Christian in England and founder of the Enlightenment, had a secret to hide also. At one time his expertise in Christianity caused him to be pressured to accept ordination. But to this he declined. It was assumed out of humility. It was not...

Almost paradoxically, at least to our modern ears, Newton, a scientist, was considered one of England's premier ecclesiastical authorities. Just as he was consulted often on higher physics and mathematics, he was also consulted by clergy on theological matters. However, Keynes' newly acquired letters were to reveal a different Newton... a magician, an alchemist, a Hermeticist, in short, a heretic.

It turns out Newton's religion was Arianism, the very sect condemned at the most important of all early Church councils, the Council of Nicaea. Further still, his philosophy seemed to be inspired by texts then unknown to the modern world, he and John Milton had left remnants of it in their writings. A new questions arose, how did a defunct heretical doctrine hide itself for over fifteen hundred years only to emerge and inspire the founders of the Age of Reason? Why did they base their 'enlightenment' on Gnosticism?

What Keynes found was shocking. It was not that Newton dabbled in a quirky hobby, he was a magician through and through. The philosophy was at the root of his theories, he only began to reveal it towards the end of his life. In fact, he had been preaching 'Arianism' for years, but nobody detected it. *How had he hid this for so long? From where did he get a doctrine assumed to be dead? Is it possible that Christianity never truly recovered from its worst heresy?*

MODERNISM: AN ORCHESTRATED AMNESIA OF THE PAST

The problem with much of the mainline Church is that it is blind to its own errors. Like a cargo ship, the Church also has cargo. One is worthless without the other. The purpose of a ship is not only its own survival, but its cargo also. The ship is without purpose if the cargo is lost or destroyed. However, in this waning era of Truth, the captains of the ship have decided to sacrifice the cargo to save the ship. They seem to think that the condition of the cargo is impertinent so long as the ship makes the destination.

Every Truth is a doctrine of sorts. The most basic of doctrines is this: Truth is conformity of mind to reality. But it is in this that most no longer believe. The Modern skeptic can only find truth in his own self-relevancy. He has been convinced that all truth is discovered from within, a sort of act of self-discovery and recollection.

While most of the modern Church avoids or denies teaching a doctrine, in fact it teaches one that predates Christianity itself—the above are the symptoms.

The word 'doctrine' simply means *teaching*. The term derives from the Latin '*doceo*,' which is related to other words like *doctor* and *disciple*. But it is also related to the term *docile*. This means that the student, to truly be taught, must set aside his ego and his resistance. He must not just remember, he must allow himself to grow in understanding. He must put his trust in someone who actually 'knows.' The simple fact is that many of the most important teachings are things one would never figure out in one's own life-time, or by one's self. Therefore one needs a doctrine to weigh veracity and a tradition for context and meaning.

What once brought the Church together and inspired its growth was a coming together in *belief* guided by a saving Truth. It is precisely *belief,* that by its very nature, cannot be merely a personal experience. Truth is never confirmed by a single witness. Yet, this is precisely what the modern cannot do. In fact, he'd rather prefer the single witness, himself. This allows him to tailor make his own truths, and insulates him from the judgments of others. What he relies on is a condition of mutual tolerance, a lukewarm compassion he calls 'love.' However, this is not love at all, it is more of the nature of a self-protection scheme, a release from the responsibility to discern and to be discerned.

At the absolute core of this problem is the term *catholic*. It is perhaps one of the most misrepresented terms in history. And to be honest, the term started to get in the way of Church growth. Rather than representing a doctrine, it represented a *brand*. Originally, the term meant '*universal Truth.*' But, over time the term was stripped of *Truth*, leaving only *universal*. So, no longer seeking Truth, the Church began to seek numbers. The result was the reverse of what was expected. Seeking to create the Universal Church, they put their entire stock into being the universal common denominator of all faiths—as belief depleted, so did the numbers. There was nothing to separate the teaching of the Church from what you might find anywhere else.

This *new* doctrine seemed wholesome. Believing doctrine to be too cumbersome, it sought something more 'inclusive.' After all, wasn't that what Christ Himself had commanded? But it was *conformity for conformity's sake*, an inversion of the Golden Rule: I will allow you whatsoever, as long you allow me the same. Over time, there became little left to witness.

It seems rather odd, almost contradictory, that *selfism* and *universalism* are different sides of the same coin. Yet, in the above, we have laid the groundwork. To be meaningful we must trust that *our* **eyes and ears** are reliable witnesses of reality, the very things that is now in doubt by the modern. Unless I am very clever, I would have to admit that at least some of my thoughts must come from elsewhere than me. But where? And how?

If we add up all these above points, we must face a certain fact— modernism, what we might call science, really isn't based upon 'discovery' as much as one might think. Much of science has been an attempt to legitimize this cultish doctrine, despite the fact that time and time again it has been proved phoney. Much of science is an attempt to understand the cult's materialistic world view, despite that it questions whether 'to understand' has any meaning at all. Science, at its core, reveals itself as a religion—many of its high priests like Newton actually worshipped 'the other God.' To them, **eyes and ears** have no value for the discovery is not found in reality, but in one's own thoughts. The evidence they produce is not for them, it is for you so that you put your faith entirely in them.

This is actually the basic doctrine shared by both Gnosticism and the Occult—that reality is an illusion and what we call 'self' is actually ultimately part of that illusion. The proof is not 'discovered,' it is 'remembered.' It comes from the universal thought center, a sort of borg-like Universal Mind called a *monopsychism*. This was declared the heresy of heresies by the Catholic Church in 1277.

The Church has been doing a dance with its Adversary from nearly the beginning. The Adversary's doctrine was kept somewhat in check until just before the Renaissance. Then the Adversary began to gain strength. The result was that the Church began a long process of incorporating his doctrine it into its midst.

As the Adversary gained strength, the Church relinquished its own primacy. The first consequence was the splitting into factions. The Roman Catholic Church began to believe itself to be the sole repository of authentic faith. The Protestants began to believe that just being anti-catholic would solve all its errors. The non-conforming church put is faith in the inerrancy of the perfect Bible, that everything needed for faith was written therein and was found nowhere else. Once pieces of a larger puzzle, these factions had lost the glue that once held them together.

The dilemma was this: can all that is needed to be known be reduced to a simple unifying belief? If so, which would it be? In faith, in writings, in doctrine, in tradition? Can everything God wants us to know be reduced to a simple nugget comprehended by the human mind? Yet this is precisely what science and many faiths want us to believe. If we were to know everything that God knows, would we not be as gods?

Ask most any pastor or priest today if they have a philosophical basis for their faith they most likely will say, 'no.' They believe the purity of faith requires no philosophy. Yet, if you push them hard most will admit to one form or another of the teachings of the philosopher Plato. However, it is hard to believe many if any have actually read Plato, especially the relevant bits. If they had they would recognize something, something they typically deny outright—that perhaps the greatest enemy of faith was a certain 'god' named Thoth (Theuth) and his Greek persona Hermes. Plato, through the voice of Socrates, illustrates our very dilemma in one of his most important dialogs, *Phœdrus*:

> SOCRATES: Very well. I heard, then, that at Naucratis in Egypt there lived one of the old gods of that country, the one whose sacred bird is called the ibis; and the name of the divinity was Theuth. It was he who first invented numbers and calculation, geometry and astronomy, not to speak of draughts and dice, and above all writing (*grammata*). Now the King of all Egypt at that time was Thamus who lived in the great city of the upper region which the Greeks call the Egyptian Thebes; the god himself they call Ammon. Theuth came to him and exhibited his arts and declared that they ought to be imparted to the other Egyptians. And Thamus questioned him about the usefulness of each one, and as Theuth enumerated, the King blamed or praised what he thought were the good or bad points in the explanation. Now Thamus is said to have had a good deal to remark on both sides of the question about every single art (it would take too long to repeat it here); but when it came to writing, Theuth said, "This discipline (*to mathēma*), my King, will make the Egyptians wiser and will improve their memories (*sophōterous kai mnēmonikōterous*): my invention is a recipe (*pharmakon*) for both memory and wisdom."
>
> But the king said, "Theuth, my master of arts (*Ō tekhnikōtate Theuth*), to one man it is given to create the elements of an art, to another to judge the extent of harm and usefulness it will have for those who are going to employ it. And now, since you are father of written letters (*patēr on grammatōn*), your paternal goodwill has led you to pronounce the very opposite (*tounantion*) of what is their real power. The fact is that this invention will produce forgetfulness in the souls of those who have learned it because they will not need to exercise their memories (*lēthēn men en psuchais parexei mnēmēs ameletēsiai*), being able to rely on what is written, using the stimulus of external marks that are alien to themselves (*dia pislin graphēs exōthen hup' allotrion tupōn*) rather

than, from within, their own unaided powers to call things to mind (*ouk endothen autous huph' hautōn anamimnēskomenous*). So it's not a remedy for memory, but for reminding, that you have discovered (*oukoun mnēmēs, alla hupomnēseōs, pharmakon hēures*). And as for wisdom (*sophias de*), you're equipping your pupils with only a semblance (*doxan*) of it, not with truth (*alētheian*). Thanks to you and your invention, your pupils will be widely read without benefit of a teacher's instruction; in consequence, they'll entertain the delusion that they have wide knowledge, while they are, in fact, for the most part incapable of real judgment. They will also be difficult to get on with since they will be men filled with the conceit of wisdom (*doxosophoi*), not men of wisdom (*anti sophōn*)."[2]

All this will play out at the critical Council of Nicaea. For centuries historians have told a 'conventional' story that cannot stand up to the facts. Essentially it is this:

Due to the onslaught of barbarians attacking Rome, the Emperor Constantine the Great mounted his forces to rescue the Church. Defeating the barbarians, Constantine picked up the entire remains of Rome and moved it to Byzantium. There he renamed the city Constantinople, after himself. This allowed Constantine to Christianize the Empire forming an imperial 'state' Church. To complete this task he called for a council at Nicaea to resolve any resulting disputes, thus laying the foundation for the Catholic Church. *There, doctrine was determined, and most importantly the canon of Scripture was agreed upon. But a problem surfaced. A heretic, Arius, nearly won the day, jeopardizing the fate of the Church. Narrowly escaping that tragedy, the Church triumphed and began its mission to Christianize all peoples.*

ORIENTALISM — MODERNISM

Today, it is difficult to comprehend a doctrine so reprehensible that it would run the risk of collapsing not only the Church, but all of civilization. Yet, just such a debate was going on underneath the surface at Nicaea. The modern story has been reduced to a debate over rather inconsequential doctrines and traditions, mere arbitrary customs. Recognizing this, modern churches have either politicized the event or debated trivializing the event so as to remove it entirely as being a stumbling block to unity. But if we do that, we will miss the Truth of Nicaea. Further still, the doctrine of Arius has never actually been revealed entirely!

In the above *conventional* story the names and places are all real, but the story is not, so I will re-tell it. It hides what plagues the Church today. While the Faith may be simple, the schemes of the Adversary are sophisticated. Not understanding this, we have allowed a doctrine to survive by stealth. Early on it was first called *Gnosticism,* a seemingly innocuous term. As it matured it became known as *Neoplatonism.* By the time it surfaced at the Council of Nicaea it had become *Arianism.* Today we know it as *Modernism* and *Post-Modernism.* There is a common thread most don't acknowledge. What ties all these '*-isms*' together was something William Enfield called *Orientalism* propagated by a secret gospel hidden from history.

The core of *Orientalism* are two principles, 1) that Man is an incompetent witness to Truth as discerned from reality, and; 2) that the Soul of Man pre-existed his conception. The necessary conclusion is that all that we know is the product of 'the *One,*' the *Universal Mind,* of which we are all only small insignificant portions. These suppositions seem innocent enough, but their consequence is that all of reality is an illusion. Truth has no anchor leaving nothing for us to witness.

Orientalism passed into the Church as *Gnosticism.* Its theology is this: Somewhere before the beginning of time existed the One-Mind. This was considered the Perfection. Yet, there arose a condition, a break-away Mind, a Son of Mind, that began to believe it could reason on its own. The very act of reasoning is to make distinctions. Therefore, as a result, the One-Mind began to disintegrate into infinite numbers of minds all believing they could reason by themselves. To counter this, Gnosticism proposed a solution—if the many minds could be tricked into believing that their individuality was only an illusion, they would be forced to reunite back into the One. Therefore, the secret task of Gnosticism was *to thwart man's understanding, to thwart procreation, thus thwarting the will of the Son of Mind. Once successful, all minds would be forced to return to the One.*

But Gnosticism does hold a Truth, which is why it sounds wholesome. It is this: to seek God within one's self *IS* appealing. But while it does seem to grant eternal life, the consequence is the loss of Free Will. It's a catch-22, what you gain in one, you lose in the other. It is the scheme of the Adversary that can only be broken by what the early Church called *Logos.* It was through humble understanding, something denied by the Gnostics, that the spell was broken. However the lasting appeal to this cult was not. What began as a neoplatonist cult eventually became a quasi-Christian sect. Then it was led by a cultish 'cloud of unknowing' in the Middle Ages. It was this that resurfaced in the Renaissance inspiring the Occult. In the Enlightenment it seemed to end faith altogether. Today it has been disguised as

Socialism and Marxism, it is what modern science seeks in Artificial Intelligence.

The doctrine was propagated by a fake Secret Gospel falsely attributed to St. John. It was hidden from the public until 1945. I hope to show that it was this that undergirded Arius at Nicaea. It was this doctrine that caused the Trinitarian verses to be removed from the Bible.

Overtime, the Church steered its doctrines towards the authority of 'scholars,' those who had read much but understood little. Their science got in the way and prohibited them from seeing. They failed to see that when Constantine instructed the Church to produce the 'official' Bible, that they were reproducing heresy. This means that the Council of Nicaea was compromised before it started. Many had already succumbed to this heresy, including Constantine. 1300 years later many scholars began to realize these errors, but by then it was too late. They began to realize that the most reliable Scriptures were not the work of scholars, but 'vulgar' copies made by peasants.

Fr. Athanasius Kircher (1602-1680) seventeenth century German Jesuit scholar and polymath who by some is considered not only the first modern scientist but the father of the modern Occult.

*A NOTE TO THE READER—I will be extensively quoting from William Enfield's *The History of Philosophy from Earliest Times to the Beginning of the Present Century*, first published in 1791. It was derived and translated into English from the German *Historia Critica Philosophiae* by Johann Jakob

Brucker (1742) quoted by many including Cardinal Newman. Why do I use a text most have never heard of? These gentlemen lived right at the center of the crux of our matter to be discussed. They represent a point of view few have heard. They are critical to understand why the world today is as it is. Fr. Athanasius Kircher was head Jesuit at the Vatican. He published at least forty volumes dealing with the emerging field we now call science which has never been entirely divorced from the Occult. Sending Jesuit emissaries virtually throughout the world he collected vast amounts of evidence and tales found nowhere else. Much of this is pseudo-science, many of his stories myths, but his writings reveal the 'under belly' of modern thought. It is also the 'shoulders' on which many more 'reputable giants of science' would later stand. Kircher is a source of data not polluted by modern propaganda. This serves our purposes very well for it is from this that we can reconstruct the philosophy of the early gnostics and reveal what precisely was going on at the Council of Nicaea.

---

1. Isaac Newton, from his hidden alchemical writings. From the Newton Project, Oxford University, retrieved 2023 — https://www.newtonproject.ox.ac.uk/
2. Plato, *Phædrus* (274c - 275b) Translation quoted from Derrida, Jacques and Johnson, Barbara. "Plato's Pharmacy." *Dissemination. University of Chicago Press, Chicago,* 1981. 61-171. from the French translation of the Greek by Léon Robin—this translation is critical in that is the foundation of all that follows.

CHAPTER ONE
PRELUDE

"I will tell you, he said. The lovers of knowledge are conscious that the soul was simply fastened and glued to the body—until philosophy received her, she could only view real existence through the bars of a prison, not in and through herself; she was wallowing in the mire of every sort of ignorance; and by reason of lust had become the principal accomplice in her own captivity. This was her original state; and then, as I was saying, and as the lovers of knowledge are well aware, philosophy, seeing how terrible was her confinement, of which she was to herself the cause, received and gently comforted her and sought to release her, pointing out that the eye and the ear and the other senses are full of deception, and persuading her to retire from them, and abstain from all but the necessary use of them…"[1]

— PLATO (AS SOCRATES), PHÆDO

INTRODUCTION TO THE PROBLEM

I would ask the reader to go back and re-read the previous quote from Plato (Socrates) on Theuth (Thoth) for it will be the basis of much that follows. Let me try to illustrate.

Plato has put his finger on a serious problem. He points out the difference between the craftsman and the artist, the sophist and the wise, the gate-keeper and the educator, the one who learns by rote and the one who understands.

This is not to disparage the novice, or the craftsman. It is to say that the craftsman and the artist exemplify two different talents.

The talent of the craftsman is to duplicate. Like a scribe, the craftsman doesn't make up his own verses. The craftsman faithfully reproduces what came before. He relies on tried and true methods to solve the problems of the day.

On the other hand the artist's talent is different. In some ways he may be less skilled than the craftsman, but he does have a deep conceptual understanding, something not easily duplicated... or conveyed in writing alone. This is to say that the true 'whole Man' must be both craftsman and artist. He cannot just jump to the end, he cannot just memorize the answers, he must cultivate skill.

Yet, this is precisely what our education system has become, a reward system for those who memorize the answers. They know without understanding, they duplicate without skill. The student of language learns by flashcards rather than grammar or phonics. The student of math calculates by counting knuckles and running calculators, not by learning operations and math tables. Those who understand are less useful to leaders who desire a society that operates like a machine at their service. We fail to realize that a society can be imperceptibly orchestrated so that only the compliant win, those who only care about the rewards of the trophy without caring how they got there.

While Plato's little parable was intended as a warning, it was quickly taken up by those who coveted being like Thoth. Equating Hermes with him, it became an anti-philosophy, a cult of pretenders called *Sophists*. Plato's worry was that writing would replace true understanding forming a cult based upon 'memorizing the answers.' At the time Thoth represented the discovery of an evil. But to those with blind ambition Thoth became a God, a way of cheating the system called *Hermeticism*. As understanding slipped into the background, it became replaced by a darkness of magical psychological causations.

Much of the Renaissance centered around just such a dispute. It is customarily taught today that the Church was first exposed to philosophy in the late Middle Ages, derailing the Church from its divine purpose. This is not true. As we will see, philosophy rose out of the need to replace a barbaric spirituality.

While books were scarce in Europe, the core of most teaching was Aristotelian because for the most part it represented common sense. By then Plato's teaching had become perverted by something called *Neoplatonism*, something that had been banned for centuries. It was not the authentic Plato, it was a 'new' Hermes-inspired version of Plato. What emerged was a debate over which philosophy best supported Christian doctrine. While early Neoplatonism had birthed Arianism, now a latent Arianism would give birth to a modern Hermeticism.

While today Plato is most noted for his doctrine of 'Idealism,' this is not the core of Plato. What spurred Plato was the realization that spirituality up until then was an evolved form of barbarism. While the true barbaric cults had been made obsolete, they had been replaced with various forms of intoxication called *pharmakon*. Plato found this reprehensible, so he founded a new art-form called *philosophy*. While true understanding was still in its infantile stage, philosophy opened the door to reason. To some degree 'Idealism' is a bastardization of Plato's true intent, thought was a vehicle, not an end in itself. It was intended as a replacement for superstition and intoxication. Allusions to this can be found in the prior 'quote' of Socrates. They are these:

1) **THE PROBLEM OF RELIGION:** The very beginning of philosophy was founded on the realization that the ancient foundations of religion were uncivilized and needed a replacement. Very early religions were primarily barbaric cults based upon child abuse, human sacrifice, sexual debauchery, combined with some form of intoxication all designed to make you feel as if a god. By the time of the Greeks much of this had been civilized and transferred to institutions like the Greek Symposium. While the human abuse waned, intoxications grew.

Symposiums were largely quasi-religious Bacchanalian affairs designed to invoke the gods Demeter and Hermes (Dionysius) in what were called the *Eleusinian Mysteries*. Demeter was the goddess of fertility, agriculture, and the underworld. While subject to debate, it seems generally agreed that the cult included a final ceremony of drinking the intoxicating '*Kykeon,*' called a '*pharmakon*'. While this was well regulated during the Symposium, releasing intoxicated participants afterwards would lead to *hubris* when intoxicated revelers and rabbal-rousers paraded through the streets creating havoc. This 'mob' irritated the *demos*, the ordinary citizen, leading to *hubris* becoming outlawed.

By 415 BC this became a huge problem.[2] The warrior Alcibiades was accused of just this, leading a youthful rebellion against the sex cult of Hermes/Demeter. It is believed that Socrates, disturbed by these Symposiums, had illegally formed his own symposium formed of his youthful followers which included both Alcibiades and Plato. It was this that ultimately led to

Socrates' famous trial of 'perverting the youth.' After one of these symposiums, Socrates' youthful followers, in an act of hubris of their own, retaliated culminating in the mass destruction of Hermetic idols throughout Athens. It was this that led to Socrates' death sentence.[3]

Early forms of food production lacked the ability to refine and preserve. This could result in fungal and other impurities. Exotic mixtures of such called *pharmakon* became the basis of the symposium. These often had hallucinogenic properties and could be interpreted as experiences of the divine. Some had the capacity to convince people they were immortal, an issue philosophy would have to confront.

Adding to this confusion is the term itself, *pharmakon*. While initially intended to represent this 'magical' potion, failures to purify and to control the potency often led to permanent psychological damage and even death. This means *'pharmakon'* could represent both a remedy as well as a poison, a cure and a hallucinogen. Over time the term represented inspiring words as philosophy became a more accepted replacement. As these cult traditions were guarded with secrecy it is difficult to determine how any given cult was using the term. The problem is modern translations only interpreted the term as 'remedy.'

As Demeter was the goddess of wheat/barley, it is reasonable to speculate that her cult was based upon a particularly hallucinogenic fungi called *ergot,* an LSD-like psychedelic alkaloid. An alternatives could be wormwood, the basis of absinthe (as mentioned in the Bible). Indeed, fragments of ergot were found in an Eleusinian temple at Girona, Spain, confirming this.[4]

It was in response to this that Socrates first sought a philosophical replacement. He envisioned a reasonable *pharmakon*. It was from this Plato built his philosophy as evidenced in the Dialogs *Phædo* and *Phædrus*.

From this we might make some assumptions. To the extent that any given society displays similar acts of hubris (such as today), we might assume a similar reversion to the *pharmakon* that causes it. If traditional Christianity was a bulwark against such behavior, the abandonment would see a return. We now know that the response to this was a search for truth. It is reasonable to suppose that **where one sees a philosophy of 'truth' emerging it is in rejection of just such cults.**

IN A SENSE, modern religion is a formulated reversion back to the cult of *pharmakon*. While it may reject the drug use, the philosophical *pharmakon* it advocates is nothing more than a drug-like philosophy of Idealism.

Without any clear concept of cause and effect, Greek society struggled with pointing out which specific thing caused any specific event. This was something that would not be made clear until Aristotle. For example, if a person was killed by a sword, what caused the murder? The person? The sword? Being in the right place at the wrong time? Early Greek culture seemed to have no clear solution. The result was superstition. What the world was waiting for was a *philosophy of truth* that made such beliefs obsolete.[5]

Indeed, we can see that *pharmakon* was not limited to just pharmaceuticals, but any magical invocation whatsoever.

> "*Pharmaka*, however many are a defense against evils and old age,
> you will learn, since for you alone I shall accomplish these things.
> You will (i.e. for example) stop the strength of the weariless winds,
>   which
> rise up along the earth and lay waste to cultivated lands with their
>   blasts,
> and again, if you want, you will lead the winds back.
> And out of black rain you will make a timely drought
> for men, and out of a summer drought you will make
> tree-nourishing streams, that dwell(?) in the air.
> And you will lead from Hades the strength of a dead man."[6]

> — FROM *EMPEDOCLES THE SORCERER*

2) **THE PROBLEM OF WISDOM OR '*LOGOS*'.** Greek philosophers, primarily Plato, recognized the need for a replacement spirituality, but this invoked a larger problem. Considering the abstract nature of knowing, what is the best way of conveying this deeper knowledge? Can an aspiring artist learn his craft through 'words' alone? Considering the imprecision of written text, and the possibility of different people's interpretations, how can we be sure the essence of meaning can be conveyed? Do words have meanings or just usages?

Plato understood the problem. What is to prevent an aspiring 'scholar' from reading a deep philosophical text, memorizing it by rote, and re-interpreting to his own devises while never understanding what the text truly meant? What happens when the *sophist* replaces the true expert? Plato found this repugnant, that an 'expert' could quote inspired text, yet never truly understand what he read, *and that this would replace true knowledge.* It is this he called *sophistry.* Let me illustrate this by Benjamin Jowett's translation of *Phædo*:

> "So in my own case, I was afraid that my soul might be blinded altogether if I looked at things with my eyes or tried to apprehend them by the help of the senses. And I thought that I had better have recourse to the world of mind and seek there the truth of existence. I dare say that the simile is not perfect—for I am very far from admitting that he who contemplates existences through the medium of thought, sees them only 'through a glass darkly,'"[7]

Socrates speaks directly to our problem. Yet, the phrase Jowett uses, 'through a glass darkly,' comes from 1 Corinthians 13:12 written hundreds of years after Socrates. Henry Cary translates the same phrase as '*them in their effects,*' yet this is not adequate either because Plato seems to be quoting someone, something not conveyed in Cary's translation. Translators of Plato have consistently done this to Plato's dialog, seeing in them things that might not be there, or, in the case of the word '*pharmakon*' unintentionally hiding the seamy side of Greek culture.

It appears to me that Plato had not entirely left this drug-like ideal conveyed by the *pharmakon.* Yes, he was probably seeking a more civilized replacement, something based upon 'words' (*logoi*), but to him reason had yet to be formulated as a test for truth. Truth was more like a 'harmony' designed to rhetorically promote the ideal society. This left Plato's philosophy open to re-interpretation. While Plato was truly trying to formulate a words-based *pharmakon,* there was nothing to safeguard Truth. Without a clear set of rules, Platos method could be misinterpreted as a path back to the very psychology he wanted to replace.

What we end up with is two entirely different understandings of '*Logos.*' Plato's version rejected the cult of 'knowers,' what we called sophists. Yet, it is this very cult of 'knowers' (gnostics) that have profited most from his philosophy. To them *logos* only represented a clever use of words, simply comfortable or inspiring words. This included inspiring prose, poetry, lyrics, and interpretation of history. This opened the door to often (intentionally) misrepresenting words throughout history. Eventually it led to the purposeful misrepresenting the words of Christ Himself in a false gospel by Cerinthus.

The second deeper meaning logos is the logical. It eludes the written word, and points to true wisdom, the true rationality, and actual meaning. To illustrate this, we will investigate the Bible, but not the entire Bible, only one chapter... in fact only one verse, 1 John 5:7. It will be argued that it was this

verse that not only solved Plato's dilemma, but prevented the misinterpretation of the term *Logos*.

THE IMMENSE IMPORTANCE of this verse is seldom grasped today. Originally, it
was the only clear reference to the Trinity in the Bible. As *Logos*, it insured
that the text was not just a reversion back to the Hermetic, early Platonic interpretation. Yes, there are other 'trinitarian' verses such as at Matthew 28:19
pertaining to baptism, but none that settle the problem of *Logos*.

The beginning of the Gospel of John says, "In the beginning was the
Word." The original Greek term for word, '*Logos*,' is seldom explained today.
The word implies a doctrine, something beyond a simple, rhetorical, interpretation of the term. When Christ said 'I AM TRUTH,' He was not just saying
'the stories are true,' but that He was Truth incarnate. It was 1 John 5:7 that
anchored this meaning.

Initially Christianity was a tolerated version of the Jewish faith. Soon
thereafter Christianity began to be persecuted by Pharisaical factions. Pharisees at that time regarded the oral tradition as higher than the written. For the
most part the Talmud had superseded Scripture. Early Christians, likewise,
had no New Testament.

This all changed following the destruction of the Temple c. 69/70 AD.
What we see is a mounting intolerance of Christianity necessitating a move
towards the written 'word'. The result was the first three Gospels, Matthew,
Mark, and Luke (along with Acts, an auxiliary to Luke), today called the
Synoptic Gospels. All were written about the same time. None of these texts
are considered deeply philosophical.

Somewhere around 90 AD a heretical Gospel emerged falsely attributed to
St. John, fabricated by *Cerinthus*. His gospel envisioned a form of Christianity
completely charged with ancient Greek mysticism, the very thing *logos* was
supposed to have replaced. This forced St. John to write a refutation around
100 AD based on *Christ as the embodiment of Logos as Truth*. The first
Epistle of John was intended as an introduction, a preparation for understanding his Gospel. While many today still hold that it is an epistle, it is not
formed like a 'letter' nor sounds like a 'letter.' Like many introductions (such
as the one you are reading now) it was intended as a preparation for understanding what followed. With the verse found at 1 John 5:7 removed there is
nothing to insure the proper interpretation of the beginning of John's Gospel. I
hope to show that it was this debate that occurred at the Council of Nicaea.

Usually it is taught that the Council advocated a trinitarian formula, and was countered by the Arians who advocated a 'unitarian' formula, but the evidence will show this is not true. Records show that the Arians, at least the ones that were part of the final compromise, never objected to a trinitarian formula. Further, Arius, the main antagonist, was not part of these negotiations, and his true philosophy has never been revealed, very little of his writings survive. It doesn't take much to realize little of this makes sense. Further, the question should be asked, was the elimination of the verse rash, *have we crippled the Faith?*

Most Bibles today do not contain the afore-mentioned verse. It was stricken for reasons that should be contested. Christian denominations that retain the verse usually reject a philosophical interpretation. Those denominations that accept a more doctrinal, philosophical understanding usually reject the verse out of hand.

While many have thoroughly examined this problem, I believe not thoroughly enough. Few are aware that their 'Revised' Bibles means that they are deficient, verses have been removed. Fewer still are aware of *Cerinthus'* false gospel that John's Gospel was written in refutation of it. Further, 'unrevised' Bibles do not adequately translate 1 John 5:7, it does not appear in its original form. Therefore, what was once a key doctrine of Christianity is entirely open to *sophistry*.

We find ourselves seriously disadvantaged. There is not much data out there that has not been thoroughly examined. Seldom has all the data been provided in one place. Some has been missing for centuries. Further, many scholars both ancient and modern have weighed in on the problem, and their verdict is in, the verse is inauthentic. Their logic works something like this:

The earliest Bibles are the most authentic. There are only just a couple, and neither have the verse. Shortly thereafter the number of Bibles exploded, many of which have the verse. Therefore, the verse was a later invention, part of a 'fad', and not original to the Bible.

Okay, fair enough. But there are many people before the earliest Bibles who were referring to the Trinity as if the verse was there. What are we to make of them? Is it really legitimate to argue from an absence? If no earlier Bibles exist, how can we be sure that these two Bibles that caused this trouble are correct? When does a judge convict *on missing evidence.*

I ask, how does a criminal investigation approach such a problem? He knows the crime was committed, and then tries to construct a plausible explanation *from supporting evidence.* His reasoning is called 'forensic,' *from the available evidence he tries to reconstruct what happened.* Rather than arguing forward from an assumed condition, he argues backwards from a known state letting the evidence speak for itself. For nearly 1500 years no one considered the verse to be inauthentic. Can we construct a plausible path that explains that?

I will add one more thing to this reasoning, *what if it can be proved that the 'oldest Bible' was not sanctioned by the Church at all, but was forced upon it by a party sympathetic to the Arians? And what if it can be shown that the people who removed the verse were not dispassionate at all, but were Arians in disguise?*

So, what are we to do? Can we catch the criminals in the act? To do this we must have witnesses (which we will produce), and we will show opportunity and motive. We will also produce the 'co-conspirators.' Further, we will show that the modern day criminals were, in fact, advocates of this ancient heresy. I only ask one thing of the reader, and it is this: keep an open mind. Not always what appears to be evil is evil. Not everyone you assume to be good is good. Not everyone you might assume to be a saint... is one. Many were just people doing the best they could. Many had ulterior motives...

---

1. Plato, *Dialogues of Plato: Containing The Apology of Socrates, Crito, Phaedo, and Protagoras*. Vol. 17. Colonial Press, 1899. Benjamin Jowett trans.
2. Rinella, Michael A. *Pharmakon: Plato, drug culture, and identity in ancient Athens*. Lexington Books, 2010.
3. Rinella, Michael A. *Pharmakon. Plato, drug culture, and identity in ancient Athens*. Lexington Books, 2010.
4. Bueno, P. Balbín, R. & Barroso, R. (cur.) 'A study of the microscopic residue and organic compounds in grinding tools and jar contents.' El dolmen de Toledo (pp. 235–241). Alcalá de Henares, Spain: Universidad de Alcalá.
5. Collins, Derek. *Magic in the ancient Greek world*. John Wiley & Sons, 2008.
6. From Faraone, Christopher. "Empedocles the sorcerer and his hexametrical pharmaka." *Antichthon* 53, 2019: 14-32. Kingsley trans. 1995
7. Plato, *Dialogues of Plato: Containing The Apology of Socrates, Crito, Phaedo, and Protagoras*. Colonial Press, 1899. Benjamin Jowett trans.

CHAPTER TWO

SOCRATES' OFFSPRING
THE SCHOOL OF IDEALISM

"I saw clearly, that in the history of Arianism, the pure Arians were the Protestants, the semi-Arians were the Anglicans, and that Rome now was what it was."[1]

— CARDINAL JOHN HENRY NEWMAN

"The importance of the *Secret Revelation of John* can hardly be overestimated. It was the first Christian writing to formulate a comprehensive narrative of the nature of God, the origin of the world, and human salvation. Its fresh and provocative interpretation of some of the most prestigious intellectual traditions of antiquity—from Genesis to Plato and beyond—illustrates the extraordinary intellectual labor that was going on during the foundational period of Christianity. Yet this work remains almost entirely unknown to the larger public, and indeed is only rarely cited in works on early Christian history and theology. Part of the reason for this obscurity is that it was entirely unknown until four copies were discovered in Egypt over the last century. Once found, however, the work was classified as "Gnostic heresy" and largely relegated to the scholarly interest of a few specialists."[2]

— KAREN L. KING, HOLLIS PROFESSOR OF DIVINITY,
HARVARD UNIVERSITY, THE OLDEST ENDOWED CHAIR
IN THE UNITED STATES

A COMPLEX PROBLEM

Plato's *Phædo* is a remarkable work. It portrays Socrates while in his jail cell awaiting death and the hope that is within him for eternal life. To him, eternal life was not a matter of faith, but a matter of fact. Here we see a pivotal point for civilization, a transition from the barbaric to the civilized. The dialog also represents the cusp of a problem.

Ancient spirituality wasn't so much a religion as it was a fetish. The inspiration wasn't so much philosophical as hormonal, deriving its fulfillment from customs like cannibalism, child sacrifice, sexual exploitation, and the like. At some point in time it became coupled to drug intake, ergot, wormwood, fermented potions, and the like. Most of these 'pharmaceuticals' were poisons if not prepared correctly or if taken in too high of dose. Like many 'remedies' today what can cure could also kill.

By the time of Socrates civilization had evolved... but not by much. The Greek symposium provided a safe environment to express a 'civilized' version of these customs, but make no mistake, the spirituality was essentially the same, just in a refined 'regulated' form. Whether the customs be in the worship of Hermes, Dionysius, Yahweh, Allah or whatever, all were in some form of this. Socrates represents a departure, *Phædo* is the catalyst of change.

Rather than a drug-like chemical induced feeling of immortality, Socrates envisioned a spirituality based upon a poetic 'artful' use of words. While he considered it 'reason,' it was yet that. While the core of truth is a principle Socrates has yet to discover, he is intuitively invoking it, 'everything that exists must have sufficient reason for existing.'

He looks at his own mind and realizes that within that mind alone is not sufficient reason for all that it is—the Mind could not have invented nor created itself. Socrates' determination is that that which is Mind must have been inherited from God, as is all that he knows and will know. Precisely here is Socrates' (Plato's) contribution to the civilization of Man... yet, it is also his greatest error.

Socrates is actually invoking an ancient truth, 'from nothing, nothing comes.' He correctly estimates that Man is a creation in God's image, but by seeing the Body as a profanity, he begins the process of severing Man from his own reality. He has cut man off from his sensual experiences as a meaningful conveyor of truth. To understand Man needs evidence, but this evidence cannot just be himself or all he has proved is himself. In other words, without the sensual data, the very hope Socrates espouses has no foundation, it lacks evidence. It does not have sufficient reason. The Mind-alone 'ideal' he creates is not that different from the drug-like experience he hopes to escape from. Socrates has laid the foundation for both hope and heresy. The consequence is that he has discovered God, and it is his own thoughts.

Modern society has been fractured into parties, both sides interested in keeping their status quo. We have been taught to think of these factions as Liberal vs. Conservative. It is this paradigm that taints all our reasonings. While the Liberal relentlessly pursues the Ideal, the Conservative does the same just more slowly. I would put it that this is a false paradigm, a remnant of 19th century Marxist/Hegelian political theory. It was designed to hide the true struggle, the eternal struggle of the Individual vs. the Collective. Is civilization founded upon social togetherness, or upon the individual's allegiance to Truth?

Yet, Socrates is on the doorstep of reason. He correctly discovers that the heart of reason is the dialectical process of discernment.

"…in the dialectical process we define as essence or true existence—whether essence of equality, beauty, or anything else—are these essences…"— *Phœdo*[3]

He correctly realizes that the dialectical process rests in Man's ability to make distinctions. Yet in reducing everything to Mind-alone, Socrates has removed the possibility of distinguishing his mind from anyone else's. Reality is no longer a guide. In one stroke he has made both obsolete. He has laid the foundation for both Aristotle and Gnosticism, one based upon reason, the other the Collective.

It is only through this lens can we can understand the Church's most crucial controversy, the Council of Nicaea. While I don't know that Cardinal Newman would agree with me, I do find his categorizations thought provoking… that there were not two parties at the Council, there were three. The third, the true Arians have been hidden from history.

Conventionally, the Council of Nicaea is taught as a controversy between two parties, the *Orthodox* and the *Arians* led by Arius. However, following Newman, the three parties were the *Orthodox*, the *Semi-Arians*, and the *Arians*. These will be defined as such: The Orthodox party is more-or-less what we would think it to be, a general allegiance to scripture and tradition. The Semi-Arians, generally thought to be Unitarians, were not. Generally, they represent a more heterodox view, but were not anti-Trinitarian. Contrary to conventional thought, these two sides generally agreed on most issues. Issues conventionally displayed as in dispute were not.

The Semi-Arians were not anti-Trinitarians which is why the name does not fit. Their main dispute was over the eternal nature of Christ as *Logos.* Was Christ *'eternal'* as in having a beginning, or was He *'sempi*ternal,' meaning He *always* existed from before time, like God the Father. Was He 'begotten' by the Father and only eternal from the point forward, or was He 'un-beggoten' and co-eternal with the Father. *Neither party was strictly unitarian.*

This discrepancy between the two major parties, the Orthodox and the Semi-Arians, was not as huge as conventionally portrayed. What Arius proposed was actually something quite radical. Remnants of his writings display a curious similarity to the writings of someone else, Cerinthus. In his writings Logos (Christ) was in no way co-eternal with anything. In fact, he was the first to separate from the collective of the God-head. In the process he accidentally creates reality and everyone else. The process, if believed, *makes all-that-is obsolete.* People like Newman sensed something terrible like this, but had no definitive proof.

Surprisingly, Arian doctrine was repugnant to the Orthodox *and* the semi-Arians. However, until now we could not know why. Most of Arius' writings were burned after the Council leaving only one, called *Thalia.* Likewise, Cerinthus' texts have been hidden from the public for nearly two thousand years. Unless Cardinal Newman was well-connected, *he would have known nothing of this.*

Part of this book will be an attempt to reconstruct Arianism from the remaining evidence. This will involve a reasonable assumption: that the basis of this cult is exactly what its advocates say it is. While the average Christian scholar has insulated himself from this, he does so at his own peril.

An example of 'hiding the evidence' is the controversial term *homoousios.* Throughout history, almost the entirety of the Nicene controversy has been attributed to this term. In our paradigm we will see the term under a new light as a 'false flag.' Therefore, I will introduce an entirely different proposition— that the real Arians had a 'secret' doctrine that was never entirely revealed. It was based on the 'secret' gospel of Cerinthus. While we may be unfamiliar with this doctrine, does not mean they were—the texts have not been fabricated.

I believe there is more than enough evidence for this, but one must accept a proposition—*there were numerous admonitions at the time against a false gospel, but not having the actual text, scholars directed all this animus towards the wrong text, a legitimate version of the Bible.* While the text was known to a select group of scholars, in general few knew anything of it until after WWII. By then it was the basis of a movement called *Modernism* which was taking control of the Church. Heretics in the West had been secretly distributing versions of the text for nearly a thousand years. However, controversial issues such as WWII and the Holocaust provided an opportunity to make the text public forcing a revision of the Church. *Seeing the obsolescence of the Church was at hand, the ship captains abandoned the cargo and decided to save the ship.* What should have been seen as heresy, was seen as proof that the Church had been in error for two thousand years.

The result has been a stealthy take-over of the Church by foreign doctrines. One such result was removal of 1 John 5:7, the Trinitarian verse. While the groundwork was laid in the late 19th century, the effect didn't emerge until mid 20th century. The result is the now common Revised Bible which eliminates the very verse entirely. The problem is the result of *not knowing which version of Scripture was authorized by the Council of Nicaea and under what conditions.* With little records left to resolve the dispute, we will base our conclusion on two questions: 1) *to what side did the winners at Nicaea hold their allegiance?* and; 2) *of the records that remain, from what similar writings are Arius' writings derived?*

Traditionalists, today, have been engaged in a Don Quixote-like struggle—they have been fighting windmills. Not knowing the source of what they fight, they try to use reason and morality against an adversary that knows only an allegiance to another god. All along it has been the Adversary that has gained in strength. The result is the modern almost universal acceptance of a near doctrine-less, gnostic-like Christianity, one that has little to distinguish it from any spirituality one can find anywhere else. What was once a body of believers has become a community based upon the Gnostic *pleroma*. Others have reduced Christianity to a cult of self-help, or of prosperity. Still others have found success in using rock concert-like liturgies as a form of *pharmakon* in service of church growth.

The Church is failing, yet few admit to the problem. Below are several illustrations:

- The core doctrine of Christianity, the *Logos* based Trinity, does not specifically appear in the modern 'revised' Bible. It is only vaguely alluded to it in the Baptism formula and is no longer taught.
- The reason for removing the Trinitarian verse was highly contested by scholars at the time. This revision was heavy-handed, and began a process of revamping all of Church doctrine.
- This missing verse does not merely express the doctrine of the Trinity, it implies a doctrine that challenges the modern innovations of the Church.

- The historical Councils originally solved the problem, but have since been misrepresented. One important Council has been ignored. The Council of Nicaea, considered the triumph of Orthodoxy, ended in dispute. In fact many Protestants today consider the Council as the beginning of the pagan takeover of the Church.
- The term *Logos* as found in the opening chapters of St. John's Gospel is clearly being used in a different manner than any other place in the Bible, but without 1 John its definition is open to question… and heresy. The verse has been replaced by what many consider to be a mutant verse.
- This misrepresentation has left a vacuum leading many to believe early Christianity was actually doctrine-less. This only encourages the flourishing of Gnosticism.
- Modern clergy, not knowing the true story of Nicaea, have actually unknowingly taken the side of Arianism seeing it as a solution to the debate, often seeing it as 'fresh' or 'inspirational.'

The result is the modern Church has integrated a quintessential heresy within its midsts. The Church has often resorted to the very doctrines the laity are seeking shelter from. Many have left the Church being intuitively suspicious.

Following is a chart illustrating much of this controversy. It should be immediately apparent that the Church aspiring to universality has actually fractured itself.

Contrary Perceptions of the Council of Nicaea

problem →	Catholic →	← Non-Catholic	← problem
Not evenly remotely true, most attended were semi-Arians	Brought the various factions together to unite & form the foundation the Roman Catholic Church	Corrupted early Christianity and put it under the control of the Roman Empire	*Partially true—the Church solved many of the problems at the Council of Constantinople.*
Not even remotely true, the Creed was not even ratified until 381	Affirmed Christianity as a sacramental, doctrinal religion—the triumph of Athanasius over heresy	Perverted the simplicity of original Christianity with doctrine and sacramentalism	*Not even remotely true, no party reflected this belief at the time.*
There are earlier references to the Trinity long before Nicaea.	Began the process of affirming the Doctrine of the Trinity which was not well-defined	The Trinity was permanently affixed in 1 John, it disappeared after the Council proving corruption	*This is sort of true, but later Councils corrected this only for the controversy to emerge later.*
Not true—both sides were Trinitarian. It was the nature of the Trinity that was in dispute.	Hinged upon the Trinitarian controversy between Athanasius (a Trinitarian) and Arius (a Unitarian)	The Trinity is in the 'authentic' Bible, the *Textus Receptus*	*Marginally true, but there were other Bibles consulted and were critical to solving the question.*
The Nicene Creed was not decided at Nicaea. Only preliminary versions were created.	Created the Nicene Creed which was critical to defining Orthodoxy	The Nicene Creed is extra-Biblical, therefore unnecessary	*All the doctrines of the Creed were Biblically derived except for the word 'homoousios'*
Technically true. True Arianism was Gnostic. The Qur'an was influenced by Gnostic texts.	The followers of Arius eventually split forming non-orthodox factions including Islam	Orthodoxy was ill-defined at the council — Arius is of no consequence	*The Commentary on the Qur'an actually approves of Protestantism saying it evolved out of Arianism.*
The Church united in 381. Constantine was at least semi-Arian and was baptised on his deathbed by the semi-Arians	The Council was called by Constantine the Great who converted to Christianity, then united the Church	Constantine merely authorized a false religion based on eastern mythology at the service of his Empire	*This is somewhat true, but it only lasted until 381.*
Not true.	Constantine became Orthodox on his death bed	Constantine was never an orthodox Christian	*He was a Semi-Arian with an underlying Hermeticism*
The controversy is still with us.	The Council ended the Church controversy	The controversy arose out of the Council	*The controversy is documented by Irenaeus c. 170, before the Council*

1. Newman, John Henry. *Apologia Pro Vita Sua: being a history of his religious opinions.* Longmans, Green, Reader, and Dyer, 1876. p.130
2. King, Karen L., *The Secret Revelation of John,* Harvard University Press. 2006, Preface
3. Plato, *Dialogues of Plato: Containing The Apology of Socrates, Crito, Phaedo, and Protagoras.* Colonial Press, 1899. Benjamin Jowett trans.

CHAPTER THREE

THE THREE 'CONSTANTINES'
TISCHENDORF, USPENSKY, AND SIMONIDES

"With respect to God, Pythagoras appears to have taught that he is the Universal Mind; diffused through all things; the source of all animal life; the proper and intrinsic cause of all motion; in substance similar to light; in nature like truth; the first principle of the universe; incapable of pain; invisible; incorruptible, and only to be comprehended by the mind."[1]

— WILLIAM ENFIELD, *THE HISTORY OF PHILOSOPHY, FROM THE EARLIEST PERIODS* (1791)

Constantine the Great was a remarkable man, some even consider him a saint. He was not without his flaws, as we shall see. In his honor, many would name their children after him. It is ironic that these three represent the three sides of the Council the saint founded.

Early on in my career I was taking a class in Biblical Greek. The professor was a priest who obtained his Phd. from Marquette University. He was considered one of the top theological experts in the country. The goal of his course was to translate the entire Greek Gospel of St. John into English. It took years.

I would constantly get in arguments with him. He would take phrases like 'God is amongst you' and re-translate them as 'God is within you,' sort of his own secret wisdom. Other words he treated similarly. When I asked from where he got this doctrine, he would point to *Bauer's Greek Lexicon,* a source now generally considered tainted with Gnosticism. By simply redefining the

Greek words he juggled the text into meaning the exact opposite of what was intended. I, not willing to concede that these reasons were valid, eventually came to be resented. At the time I thought he was a novelty. I now realize he represented most of the Church.

Following WWII numerous books began to be published advocating similar doctrines. Books like *The Other Side of Silence* by Morton Kelsey, *Meditations on the Tarot: a Journey into Christian Hermeticism* with approvals by Cardinal Hans Urs Balthasar and Fr. Bede Griffiths, and *Christian Zen* by William Johnston. About that same time new discoveries emerged such as the *Dead Sea Scrolls*, the *Nag Hammadi Codices*, and Tischendorf's *Codex Sinaiticus,* all advocating what seemed dubious to me, that the true basis of Christianity was now just becoming known after 2000 years. All seemed to be orchestrated to prove an early corruption of Christianity that the new clergy were now charged with fixing. Somehow everyone prior had gotten things wrong and a new breed of scholars were going correct the matter.

Then, being just an organist and not considering myself a theologian, it didn't matter much to me... but it did all seem rather hypocritical. Clergy at that time seemed to be relinquishing their ordained obligations in favor of self-discovery. They no longer wanted to be priests but gurus. Even then many were deeply convinced that the Church was a fabrication of a corrupt 'western' male hierarchy, which the infusion of women priests would fix. Yet, countering their deep convictions was the lack of evidence they could produce, or at least admit to. Old faithfuls like Aquinas, Augustine, and Damascene were kicked to the curb, and soon replaced by the likes of Jung, Heidegger, Teilhard de Chardin, and Alan W. Watts. What led them to believe they were right and all the saints of the Church were wrong?

Upon investigation, much of what they said could not be substantiated. Many of the doctrines they called 'Eastern' actually had their source in Western thought. Conversely, many of the doctrines they called too Western actually had their source in the Eastern schools like Nisibis. Typically they were brought to the West by orthodox refugees fleeing Islam. Likewise, many early Christians desiring not to be under Roman control fled to the East. This was not without theological peril. While Rome provided some doctrinal unity, the East was a bit of a free-for-all. This perhaps allowed for a purer orthodoxy, but it also allowed for heterodoxies to go unchallenged.

While I resisted calling the re-emergence of these heterodoxies a conspiracy, what else could you call it? It was not a simple difference in opinion, there seemed to be an underlying agenda. For example, if you wanted to research the *Codex Sinaiticus,* the discovery that supposedly started this all, you would naturally start with something popular such as Bentley's *Secrets of Mount Sinai.* But like many other books of that period, it was less an academic text than a subtle indoctrination into this new way of thinking. Like my 'mentor,' they would twist the truth into anything they liked, and who could challenge them? One day Christopher Columbus was a here, the next a savage. It was all to prepare you for the inevitable fall of the traditional Church.

All this pivots on a man named Lobegott Friedrich *Constantin* von Tischendorf. Until him the failings of the Council of Nicaea had yet to have the upper hand. The problem is this: Tischendorf was pre-loaded with the emerging gnostic belief system of his German professors. It was a school of thought began by the German Gnostic F.C. Baur, the first 'modernist.' Tischendorf claimed he wanted to save Christianity from the emerging skepticism. Yet, like his predecessors, he was not so much interested in saving Christian thought as he was adapting it to modern thinking. Saving the institution was more important than saving the doctrine. He would do this by setting out to find the most authentic Bible ever written.

As a researcher who began his career in his early twenties, Tischendorf would need high-level social connections to accomplish his task. But how does a near twenty-year-old do this? More than once he smuggled a rare text out of a Muslim country without penalty. Often he was given access to rare manuscripts granted by European monarchies and nobles. Somehow he was granted access to St. Catherine's Monastery in Sinai, an Islamic jurisdiction, removing their oldest, rarest possession, the *Codex Sinaiticus,* on a promise to return it he never fulfilled.

Tischendorf represents a pattern of philosophical 'conspirators' that begins before the Enlightenment and travels down to the present day. They often reference texts few have access to. They leave undocumented clues. They make claims few can verify. Archaeological finds are predicted and show up out of nowhere that eventually prove them right.

Their motives are similar: traditional Christianity is corrupt, outdated, purposely based upon texts picked by 'men' who had censored the real documents. Feigning support for tradition, these new 'scholars' propose a study to find out the truth. They investigate ancient texts, discover archaeological sites, uncover new historical facts, yet, in the end, the new way of thinking is right, the Church is foolish. Oddly coincidental, the ancients had thought the same as their latest shiny object.

Out of this they create prophets such as Galileo. All the way back to Socrates people had speculated on the movements of the heavens, many had discovered the earth was not flat, ancient devices made to tell time. But now no such discoveries ever existed. That would be for the new prophets. Galileo is artificially made a martyr. Columbus is first to discover the spherical earth. Much of Newton's light theory was clearly based upon much older Christian models... but now Newton alone founded the Enlightenment and that fact alone was more important than the truth. When the true story emerges, no one goes back and corrects the textbooks, no university sends out a recall notice, no pressure is put on schools to refund their tuitions.

THE CODEX *SINAITICUS*

Before the nineteenth century Europe was still primarily governed by Christian Monarchies. All were barely hanging on to their power in the face of the mounting political liberalism. Beginning with Machiavelli certain 'methods' emerge that make normal politics obsolete. His book *the Prince* instructs rulers how to psychologically manipulate opinion to maintain control. This prods others such as the Rosicrucian inspired philosopher Georg Wilhelm Friedrich Hegel to develop 'dialectical' methods of their own. This method moves on to the theological historian F.C. Baur, and philosophers like Ernest Renan, Jean-Jacques Rousseau and Karl Marx.

On the surface this seems innocent enough, perhaps even 'enlightened,' but the end result is always a questioning of the legitimacy of Christianity. Sometimes the new doctrine seems to fall on the left, sometimes on the right, but the conclusion is always suspiciously the same—early Christian doctrines such as the Trinity are not longer serving the public. What is needed is a doctrine of unity, a form of eastern mysticism.

On the surface their arguments are persuasive, even 'scientific.' I am about to challenge this.

Let me start with a question, how did they know ahead of time where all this was going to end up? Take F.C. Baur for instance. Using Hegelian theory, he devises a theory 'proving' that John's Gospel was wrongly dated. Instead of the late first century he endeavored to prove it was late second century. Oh, and didn't he tell you, this pushes it to a time when Gnosticism was flourishing. This allowed him to re-interpret it as a Gnostic writing. Eventually Baur was proved wrong, yet if you check, many Bibles use his dating to this day.

So, why John's Gospel? Why not Mark or Luke? It wasn't like Baur had any real physical evidence or that Hegel's philosophy naturally leads to that conclusion. Yet, it *seems* reasonable. But what if you knew that a cadre of

Gnostic scholars actually possessed another 'gnostic' gospel of John and that they were predisposed to proving that one the authentic one?

By the end of the eighteenth century such thinking was leading to doubts about the legitimacy of traditional Christianity. It was the age of Science, of the Enlightenment, the age of Newton. What would the monarchies of Europe (including the Vatican) do without a 'Christian' claim to their legitimacy? What if the public found out that their leaders had sworn to uphold an illegitimate religion? Would it not lead to a British civil war, a colonial rebellion, a French revolution?

Right in the thick of the dispute a young scholar, Constantin von Tischendorf, sets out to 'save' Christianity. A product of the Tübingen school inspired by Baur, he sets off for Palestine to find proof of his 'enlightened' version of Christianity. Very young, he somehow convinces the European nobility to not only finance his expedition, to write letters of introduction, but to open to him many of the prestigious libraries of Europe, including the Vatican, to inspect their editions for authenticity.

But wait! How was this going to save the day? It's not like Europe didn't have any ancient Bibles. Hadn't they gone through this centuries before when Erasmus introduced Europe to the oldest 'Greek' Bible?

Tischendorf heads off to Palestine. By then it was becoming a sort of a German play ground—vacation railroad lines were being built with the actual intent of returning oil needed to fuel Germany's industrialization. Often people taking exotic vacations there were bringing back 'treasures,' and other artifacts. Some were stolen outright. Other times they were sold fakes purchased from questionable sources, often bedouin. This is not to say *Codex Sinaiticus* is fake. (I hope to later show it is ancient, and indeed as Tischendorf insisted, was a product of the Council of Nicaea.) It is to ask, considering the state of science at that time, how were these texts authenticated? Who decided Tischendorf's find represented the authentic teaching of the early Church? Why was it such an easy sell to some and strongly objected to by others?

Tischendorf discovers the *Codex Sinaiticus* at St. Catherine's Monastery under very questionable circumstances. By his own testimony it is found in a basket destined to be burned (something denied by the monastery). In fact, he sort of discovers it twice. The first time (1844) he takes a portion of this newly discovered 'trash' back to Europe calling it the '*Codex Friderico-Augustanus*' in honor of the king of Saxony. The second time (1853) he attempts to retrieve the rest, but is denied by the monks. Then in 1859, again claiming he found it in a waste basket, he comes by the authority of the Tzar of Russia, Alexander II, *under the assumption that the trash of monks is the lost oldest copy of the*

Bible. Yet, as I will show, the claim was highly and reasonably contested, yet ignored.

Tischendorf charts his course. Saying he's fighting to save the Church, by the end of the day he authenticates a text that strips the Bible of key elements, the end of Mark's Gospel (putting the Ascension in doubt) and the Trinitarian formula at 1 John 5:7 (putting the Trinity in doubt). *You would think this would disturb the powers that be!* Not so. The heads of the European Monarchies including the Pope lavish Tischendorf with awards, titles and honorary degrees. They say he has saved Christianity... it's just that now it doesn't fit the traditions of the Church. It becomes compatible with, Buddhism, with Islam... and Arianism. Much of this happens before Tischendorf is thirty.

As I have just said, there seems to be no concern in saving tradition, just hanging on to power. European nobles look at revolutions in France and England and see that their days are numbered. Academicians were just then getting started in a new field and had reputations to build. They aren't looking for truth, they are looking to become authorities. Ignoring scholarly protests from around the world, as soon as a good enough reason is found the case is considered closed, the Bibles are all wrong.

The method used to date *Sinaiticus* was developed by Richard Porson. Carbon dating lay a century in the future. Porson's method was based upon determining relative dates by grouping texts into 'families.' The method is substantially based on tracking the evolution of errors. First, texts with similar errors are grouped together. Then, it is arbitrarily assumed that authentic texts would be a product of the same scriptorium, that once an error is introduced by a scribe it would be perpetually copied into the future. By charting the evolution of these errors, a relative chronology can be created.

But Porson's method was not meant to be able to assign precise dates, only relative dates. *It also assumes that 'authentic' texts are all of a scriptorium-like lineage. Those that aren't are summarily dismissed. Yet, many of the Bibles contesting this are known to be made by private parties, people with varying familiarity with Greek, all translated into their own Latin dialect. Out of hand, these texts are considered irrelevant. Further still, Tischendorf is basing his argument from the absence of a text—how do you track the errors of a text that is missing? Shouldn't the absence of something at least be considered an error in itself?*

Porson's method was called *philological,* it is a necessary part of his method. This means he must know not just track scribal errors, but the structure, meter, and word order to establish relative dates. In regard to 1 John 5:7 I hope to show this was never established. Further, Tischendorf barely knew

Greek grammar—his letters are full of errors. Therefore, to establish a date, it was merely assumed the Codex was the product of the *'Orthodox'* at Nicaea, *a fact that was never established.*

It should be understood, the discovery of *Sinaiticus* begins a long line of how such texts are handled. It is a tradition of its own that once established is hard to go against. There is nothing to say that the *Codex Sinaiticus* was not a 'red-headed stepchild.' The conclusion is not formulated by considering the majority of the texts from the period, it is formulated, out-of-hand, to fit a pre-established scenario—*Sinaiticus* is the original and all the rest corruptions. *It supports their theology.* Indeed, *Sinaiticus* may very well be the oldest text, but that doesn't prove it is the most authentic. There are now over 5000 ancient New Testament texts—there are exactly two that meet Tischendorf's criteria.

While scholars consider Tischendorf's method bullet-proof, the result undermines long established *documented* Christian doctrines, witnesses by Church Fathers, often built upon principles recorded in the Jewish Targums.

Further, these methods are not applied to other ancient texts. For example, it is generally agreed that one of the oldest Bibles was the *Diatessaron*. It was created before the concept of having four separate Gospels had been established. Rather, it lifts verses out of the four Gospels and arranges them into a chronological order to form one long story. The entire concept behind it is that parts would necessarily be left out. While no original copies of the Diatessaron exist, no one doubts it to be ancient. Yet, the Diatessaron does have parts Tischendorf said were inauthentic. How can this be?

Anyone familiar with Vatican II knows it inaugurated a revision of Christianity. Much of this was based on modernism, something condemned by Pope Pius X earlier in the century. Excepting the legitimacy of *Sinaiticus* undermines doctrines declared heretical by the Church. So, why would the Church do this? The famous nineteenth century cleric Cardinal Newman believed that Modernism was the resurfacing of ancient Arianism, the very thing contested by all this. Yet, no one seems seriously concerned by all this. Many are not willing to go against the Church's judgment, even though the Church contradicts itself.

It was believed that the Council of Nicaea was the defining moment of the Church, and *Sinaiticus* was a product of that Council. The fact that it was missing key portions of the Bible became troublesome. But if it can be shown that the *Sinaiticus* is actually the product of the side that lost at Nicaea, all this changes. While this may seem outrageous today, this is precisely what the very first expert to examine *Sinaiticus* declared, the

Russian Orthodox Bishop Porphiry, it is a product of the Arians, the side that lost.

The final determination occurred when Tischendorf compared the *Codex Sinaiticus* to Rome's *Codex Vaticanus* and found both were missing the same crucial texts. Having similarities with each other and combined with the fact that they were both made by skilled scribes, led to the determination that both represented the official Bible authorized by Constantine the Great at the Council of Nicaea. This determination made many Bibles instantly obsolete, the Protestant Bibles, the Greek *Textus Receptus,* and eventually the Latin *Vulgate* Bible, a product of the work of St. Jerome and St. Augustine.

Porson's method became the core to Biblical historical criticism. It was formulated precisely at eliminating non-skilled examples. All considered a cul-de-sac, they necessarily were dead-ends, and thus non-authoritative. No other scenario was considered:

"More probable than others is the reading that appears to have occasioned the other readings, or that still contains within itself elements of the other readings. Taken broadly, this is the foundation of all rules."

— CONSTANTIN VON TISCHENDORF

This became the basis of Biblical criticism. No longer would traditional doctrine be a determinate in authenticity. The coincidence that several non-connected parties all preserved the same verse is irrelevant. The fact that 'approved' texts destroyed the doctrinal basis of Christianity no longer mattered. Their justifications were two:

1. **PRINCIPLE 1— two references (witnesses) to a doctrine are needed to consider a teaching authentic.** If an episode, event or reference doesn't appear twice in the Bible, then it is inauthentic. – Before Tischendorf Christ as *Logos* appeared twice, at the beginning of John's Gospel, and at 1 John 5:7 (the Trinity). By in-authenticating the second reference, the first is stripped of any doctrinal significance. Logos is stripped of its conceptual meaning, it just means 'word.'

2. **PRINCIPLE 2—earlier texts are the more authoritative, the later are degenerative copies.** In essence this is tautological. It's an easy way of in-authenticating a non-preferred text by just declaring it newer than the preferred text. This allowed scholars to in

authenticate the less polished *Vetus Latina* in favor of the more
polished 'official' *Codices Sinaiticus* and *Vaticanus*.

The problem is this: The Bible is the holiest of all books regarded by
Christians. Much of Christianity believes it to be Divinely Inspired, *inerrant*,
literally written through the direct inspiration of God. However, there is a
treachery behind this viewpoint. Rather than considering that two 'authentic'
versions of the Bible existed side-by-side, each representing the beliefs of
their respective schools (something that could be debated), it became a simple
matter of which is in error and which is not. As God cannot be against
himself, only one or the other can be considered 'inspired.'

Once the weight of evidence fell in favor of the Arian inspired Bibles, the
traditional Bible was rejected out-of-hand, *it was in error*, thus forcing a theological shift in doctrine (or, *to no doctrine at all*). Once representing established doctrines, Bibles became mere collections of wisdom sayings and holy
events. Biblical verses became sort of 'self-help slogans.' To support the traditional text meant you would be looked at with suspicion, regarded a crank, a
fundamentalist, *you were in error*.

If we limit our research just to the 4th century and the general Roman
Church of that time period we will find two versions of the Bible contesting to
be the authentic text, the two proclaimed by Tischendorf, and fifty others
often called the *Old Latin* (*Vetus Latina*), the basis of the future Latin Vulgate.
Tischendorf's discovery of *Sinaiticus* prodded a search to determine which
version was the authentic Bible. Like voting for president, the one with the
most examples wins the title 'inspired.' While the vast majority of Latin
Bibles had 1 John 5:7, the Greek ones did not, those that did were recent.

By declaring the *Vetus Latina* texts as spurious (written by peasants)
allowed scholars to declare the entire lineage of Latin Bibles as inauthentic.
Further, Protestants, in an effort to be more authentic than Rome, regarded the
Greek as the more pure. This ended the debate began by Machiavelli et al. It
set the stage for nineteenth century scholars to remove the verses, and stamp
their Bibles 'Revised,' make all doctrines obsolete. The *Codices Sinaiticus*
and *Vaticanus* now represented the 'universal' Bible commissioned by the
ancient Roman Empire. It was never considered that perhaps the *Vetus Latina*
represented private parties trying to preserve the original doctrinal basis of the
Church in the face of mass persecution. Considered inauthentic for most of the
first through the second millennium, the 'Arian' version became the authentic
Bible for the new Post Modern 'universal' Church—all doctrines were
replaced with 'love.'

The questions are these, if 1 John 5:7 is authentic, why was it not in the official Bible of the Council, why are there no records? Why was a doctrine so poisonous to Arianism not referenced? *If the Council of Nicaea represented the defeat of Arianism, why was the resulting Bible sympathetic to Arianism? Where was the debate?*

The reason is actually quite simple, the true Arians were never part of the original Council. They only emerged later after the Orthodox had been weakened through dispute and Imperial influence. Athanasius, their true protector, ran afoul of the Empire, fled for his life, allowing the Arian influenced parties to gain strength.

As will be shown, the true Councils of the 4th century were actually far more cautiously reasoned than normally presented. The actual two parties involved were the Orthodox and the Semi-Arians. I hope to show that the real Arians were not all that influential. However this cautious approach allowed a temporary heterodoxy to gain initial strength, the very time period *Sinaiticus* was authorized. While this heretical influence, inspired by a heretical gospel, was short lived, the rediscovery of these documents formed the basis of a twentieth century Gnostic revival. This opened the door for all the innovations of the twentieth century.

THREE CONSTANTINES — THREE STORIES

While I do agree, *Sinaiticus* does represent the Bible authorized by the ancient Roman Empire, an examination of the following events reveals the true nature of that Bible and serious discrepancies. The true nature of *Sinaiticus* has been suppressed:

A BRIEF TIMELINE CONCERNING THE CODEX SINAITICUS

- **1804**—Konstantin Aleksandrovich Uspensky is born. He eventually is ordained Bishop Porphyrius (Porphiry). He is an expert in ancient codices, an Orthodox theologian, orientalist, and archaeologist. He founded the Russian Ecclesiastical Mission in Jerusalem.

Napoleon crowning himself Emperor— 'Consecration of the Emperor Napoléon I in the Cathedral of Notre-Dame de Paris' *Jacques-Louis David (1804) - Public Domain*

- **1815**—Friedrich Constantin von Tischendorf is born in Lengenfeld, Saxony, in northern Europe, the son of a physician.
- **1818**—Konstantin Uspensky finishes religious school in 1822, then he studies at the Theological Seminary in Kostroma. In 1829, he finished his studies at Saint Petersburg Theological Academy, became a priest and received the name Porphyrius.
- **1834**—Tischendorf is educated in Greek at the University of Leipzig. The same year Bishop Porphyrius became an authority and ordained archimandrite, Tischendorf was just a novice.
- **1840**—Tischendorf is now 25 and has spent four years searching through some of the finest archives in Europe for precious rare Biblical texts usually only available to seasoned academics. He documents his thoughts in a letter. It displays the arrogance of an amateur:

LEIPZIG, October 1840.

"At last I have reached the eve of the completion of my New Testament. This gigantic undertaking has weighed heavily on me, and later on it will seem unbelievable, even to me, that I could write a book in less than a year which will bring me both curses and blessings, disgrace and glory. I lay its future in God's hand. Though jealousy and narrow mindedness cast suspicion upon me, I know I have struggled, in an earnest and holy endeavour, though all my strength is but weakness. But I also have influential and respected friends. My beloved Bishop Draseke has written to me so warmly. He welcomes my *Novum Testamentum Græce* as "the foundation stone of my literary immortality". On the occasion of the Swearing of Allegiance he wants to present a copy of the book to the King of Prussia. And the Prussian Minister Eichhorn is in consequence going to grant me a personal interview. If others suspect me of following any other than a heaven-sent goal, you must not believe it."[2]

— CONSTANTIN VON TISCHENDORF

Tischendorf says, "the foundation stone of my literary immortality". By age 25 Tischendorf has been granted access to the finest libraries in Europe, finances from the most powerful monarchies. Why? He says he is being guided by the hand of God. It is more likely that under the rising liberalism, the monarchies of Europe as well as the Magisterium of the Church were under threat of being delegitimized. If Christianity does not keep up with trends, their power and authority would collapse. Therefore, they need a reason, a path by which their legitimacy could be compatible with a rising atheism to avoid the path of the British Puritan Civil War (Cromwell), the bloody French Revolution (Napoleon), and the American Revolution. The abolition of monarchies was on the horizon. In France the execution of King Louis XVI and Queen Marie Antoinette, led to Napoleon crowning himself Emperor, a direct insult to the Pope and his Magisterium.

- **1842**—Bishop Porphyrius began his travels to Palestine
- **1844**—Tischendorf first reaches St. Catherine's Monastery in Sinai (hence the name *Sinaiticus*). He was given access to three libraries. He claims to discover in a hall of the main library a large waste basket containing 129 leaves of ancient parchments that are considered refuse to be burned.
- **1845-46**—Bishop Porphyrius travels to the Middle East. He begins at Mount Athos, Greece, and eventually travels to St. Catherine's Monastery in Sinai. While there he examines the same codex Tischendorf had 'discovered.'

- **1845**—Russian Orthodox Bishop Porphyrius describes the manuscript in the 1856 book, Первое путешествие в Синайский Монастыґ в 1845 году, detailing his 1845 visit to St. Catherine's Monastery.

Above, in the un-retouched photo of Tischendorf on the left he is wearing the awarded medals from the Monarchies of Europe. On the right is the published drawn version hiding the awards. Both have the Napoleonic hand-in-breast salute of a savant. If the claimed date of 1846 is correct, he has already received awards from the monarchies before the text has been authenticated or even seen by the crowns of Europe. - Public Domain

FOLLOWING IS the direct quote from the book translated from the Slavonic, found on pages 225 - 226:

"The first manuscript, containing the incomplete Old Testament [note—In addition to the books, Tobit, Judith, and Maccabees, all other historical writings are lost, and the prophecies of Jeremiah, Ezekiel, Daniel, Hosea and Amos] and the entire New Testament with the Epistle of the Apostle Barnabas and the Book of Hermas, was written on the thinnest white parchment in the fourth part of a long and wide sheet. The letters in it are completely similar to Church Slavonic. Their staging is straight and solid. There are no pre-breaths and stresses above the words, and speeches are not separated by any spelling marks, except for dots. The entire sacred text is written in four and two columns in a verse manner and so seamlessly, as if one long utterance stretches from point to point. Such a setting of letters without grammatical prosody, and such a way of writing the sacred text, invented by the Alexandrian deacon Euthalius around the year 446 after the birth of Christ and soon abandoned for the reason that there were many gaps between the columns on expensive parchment, prove that this manuscript was published in the fifth century."[3]

— RUSSIAN ORTHODOX BISHOP PORPHYRIUS

- **1847**—Bishop Porphyrius establishes the Russian Orthodox Ecclesiastical Mission in Jerusalem which he heads until 1854.
- **1853**—Tischendorf embarks again to St. Catherine's. He discovers a fragment of the same codex that he dates to c. 350 AD. At that date the Council of Nicaea was 25 years past and the Apostate Roman Empire was emerging in power. Athanasius, the so-called victor of the Council, was condemned and exiled in 335 and is running for his life. Tischendorf deposits this codex in the library of the University of Leipzig. They are christened the *Codex Friderico-Augustanus* in honor of the King of Saxony. Yet, another Constantine named Simonides, a person declared a forger and a fraud, states that the Codex Tischendorf 'discovered' was known by him to be in the monastery, *and was forged by himself.* Simonides claims that the codex was a 'copy' he made and was in safe-keeping at St. Catherine's with the intention of presenting it to the Tsar of Russia.[4]
- **1859**—Tischendorf returns to Mount Sinai for the third time, now commissioned by Tsar Alexander II of Russia. At this point Tischendorf is emissary of the Tsar and had letters of introduction written by him and delivered to the Abbot of St. Catherine's. Just before he was scheduled to leave, he was shown the manuscripts he had saved from destruction fifteen years earlier.

I bring up the question of provenance—many of the above discrepancies are still unsettled. Would we wave these same criteria if applied to any other text? Wouldn't prudence demand clear answers to these questions before we accepted them as doctrine?

At the time Tischendorf takes possession of his '*Codex Sinaiticus,*' he leaves a 'promissory note' in Greek. James Bentley (*Secrets of Mount Sinai*) says it is written in "bad Greek" and that the translation is "not very competent," not what you would expect from a scholar on which the history of the Church depends. He records what Tischendorf wrote:

"I the undersigned, Constantin von Tischendorf, sent at present to the East by orders of Alexander, Tsar of All Russias, testify by the present letter that the Holy Confraternity of Mount Sinai, in accordance with the letter of His Excellency Ambassador Lobanov, has handed over to me, as a loan, an ancient manuscript of both Testaments, being the property of the aforementioned monastery and consisting of 346 folia and a small fragment. These I wish to take with me to St Petersburg in order that I may compare the original with the copy made by me when that is printed.

This manuscript is entrusted to me under the conditions laid down in the aforementioned letter of Mr. Lobanov, dated 10 September 1859, numbered 510. I promise to return it, undamaged and in a good state of preservation, to the Holy Confraternity of Mount Sinai at its first request."[5]

— CONSTANTIN VON TISCHENDORF

The manuscript is presented to the Tsar. Eventually the Russian monarchy falls, the *Codex Sinaiticus* becomes the property of Great Britain. <u>It is never returned.</u>

- **1864**—Archimandrite Porphyrius writes a letter to Tischendorf as to the authenticity of the *Codex*. The problems with it are not just a few verses, Bishop Porphyrius considers it subtly corrupt on many levels, a product of Arian forgers. Several verses are listed and their corruptions displayed. The Archimandrite's letter is recorded in "Proceedings of the Kiev Theological Academy," November, 1865, pp. 429-436.[6]

LETTER TO KONSTANTIN TISCHENDORF
(Against the antiquity of the Codex Sinaiticus)

Petersburg. February 23, 1864

Dear Konstantin!

Your letter has been received. Here is my answer.

[from the conclusion]

I read the Gospel of John in the Sinai manuscript, and, comparing it with the Vatican Gospel and with my manuscripts of 835 and 1272, I was convinced that the original from which this manuscript was copied was distorted by the Arians in Alexandria (not all, but only in a few places) ... In this original, all the passages in which St. John the Theologian reveals to us the consubstantial Father and the Son. Let's consider them.

"No man hath seen God at any time; the only begotten Son, the 'one' who exists in the bosom of the Father, he hath declared him." (John 1:18). Here the phrase 'o ων' [the 'one' who exists] is omitted. How does this only-begotten struggle to be in the bosom of the Father? Is he one in essence with Him? No. He exists in the bosom of the Father, not as His Son, not as 'the one' who exists 'o ων' with him forever, but like all other creatures, which, according to St. Paul, live and move in God. He is God created (not 'the God', θεος without the term 'o' [the]), because he is not this 'o ων'. Arianism!

For God so loved the world [*cosmos*], that he gave his 'own' only-begotten Son (John 3:16). The pronoun 'own' is omitted here. For what? in order to accustom readers and hearers of the Gospel to the belief that the Son is not consubstantial with the Father.

The hour is coming, and now is, when the dead shall hear the voice of the Son of God: and they that hear shall live, For as the Father hath life in himself; so hath he given to the Son to have life in himself (John 5:25, 26). Here the words are omitted: "so hath he given to the Son to have life in himself." For what? in order to impress readers that the Son does not have life in Himself and that from the fullness of the life of the Father, only the power to resurrect and judge people is given to him, because he is their representative and such power, through which everything was created (δι αυτουπανταεγενετο). But it smells of Arianism.

Everyone who hears from the Father and the skill will come to me: it was not like the Father who saw who was eating: only from the Father, in this form of God (John 6:45, 46). A wonderful change to the original text! He who is from the Father sees God in Him. So the Father eats his God. What does this mean? It smells like Arianism. Let's read the original text: "Not that any man hath seen the Father, save he which is of God" Here is a different teaching! The Son born of God, and therefore being God Himself, sees his Father, and not his God. This is Orthodox,

All things that my Father (John 16:15). These words are logically omitted. If the Son does not have life in himself, if he is a created God, if his Father is at the same time his God; then how could I say that he has all that his Father has? These Words of St. John are opposed to the teachings of the Arians; and behold, they excluded them from the Gospel.

— ARCHIMANDRITE PORPHYRIUS

Then a third 'Constantine' emerges. A letter had been sent c. 1862/3 and published in the English *The Christian Remembrancer* documented in the book *Codex Sinaiticus and the Simonides Affair*, J.K. Elliott:

"He can tell us all about this Codex abstracted from Sinai. He had seen the unwearied Simonides writing it at Athos, in February 1840. He knows for certain (and this, be it observed, is more than Simonides knew on Sept. 3) that the venerable patriarch Constantius had sent it to Sinai, to be compared there with other MSS. of the Holy Scriptures, then to be transcribed again by the same Simonides, and presented to the Emperor Nicholas, no longer as a gift from the Monastery of Panteleemon, but from the patriarch himself. The holy monk Callistratus compared the Codex in part with Sinai copies, and left the rest against Simonides' return (when had he been there before?). Meanwhile, about May 1844, Tischendorf visited the monastery, and, being allowed to peruse and re-peruse it frequently, "abstracted secretly a small portion of it" and, coming again, at length obtained the rest, through the Russian Consul, by extravagant promises, never likely to be fulfilled. That Tischendorf obtained the identical codex written by Simonides, Callinicos is quite sure, for he saw it in the hands of Tischendorf, recognised the work, and first informed Simonides thereof (was this in 1844 or 1859? Probably the latter), for originally he had read on it the hemistich Σιμωνίδου τὸ ἔργον; but, two days afterwards, this line had disappeared. The MS. had also been cleaned with lemon-juice, professedly for the purpose of washing the vellum, but, in reality, to weaken the freshness of the letters.

From Simonides' original story we were expected to assume that Tischendorf must either have been incompetent at judging the age of a manuscript or else be putting forward fraudulent claims. We have already shown that the two English scholars Tregelles and Bradshaw confirmed Tischendorf's judgement about the age of Sinaiticus when they saw the manuscript in Leipzig. However since the letter of Kallinikos the charge becomes more serious against Tischendorf. From that letter we not only learn that Simonides had known of the existence of that portion of his manuscript that came to be designated *Codex Friderico-Augustanus* but that Tischendorf was a thief."[7]

Authentic or not, would any other text pass these questions of provenance? While Simonides claims are dubious, they reveal the fact that no definitive way of proving which text was most authentic existed. The Book on Simonides ends with a curious warning, one that could be assumed to apply to Sinai as it too was under the Ottoman Empire:

"The discovery of these manuscripts and library may be considered as one of the most important events in the history of Simonides. It must be remembered that Mount Athos is subject to the Turkish Government, and that the sole law throughout the Ottoman empire is the will of the Sultan and his officials. In England it would appear highly improbable that the discoverer of an ancient library would remove it in secret and keep it concealed from the world in a secure hiding place. But under a Government such as the Turkish, where law is slightly regarded and the property of the conquered people little respected, the proceeding most natural is that of concealment. So uncontrolled is the power of the Turks over their Greek subjects, that life would be in absolute danger if it were known that a Greek had made a discovery of property and had not delivered it up to the nearest officer of the Turkish despotism. Even at the present moment, writing in London, there are many facts of very general public interest that cannot be narrated in this Memoir, owing to a fear of the consequences that might ensue to individuals now living in the Turkish dominions if a knowledge of such matters should be conveyed to the Turkish officials in the neighbourhood."[8]

So, how did Tischendorf smuggle the text out? Why was he not subject to the penalty of death for stealing rare manuscripts? Was it a set up? Did the Ottoman Empire know the codex was Arian, sympathetic to Islam, and thus contributed to the conspiracy? Was the scientific authentication of the text influenced by the very Arianism that founded science in the first place?

---

1. Enfield, William. *The History of Philosophy: From the Earliest Times to the Beginning of the Present Century: Drawn Up from Brucker's Historia Critical Philosophiae*. Vol. 1. JF Dove, 1839, p.227 which itself was based upon the writings of Fr. Athanasius Kircher, seventeenth century German Jesuit scholar and polymath who by some is considered the first modern scientist.

2. Schneller, Ludwig. *Search on Sinai,*, Epworth Press, 1939

3. Porphyrius, Russian Orthodox Bishop, Первое путешествие в Синайский Монастыґ в 1845 году, 1856 — Translated by Google Translate with comparison to other translations

4. Elliott, J.K. *Codex Sinaiticus and the Simonides Affair,* Mt. Athos, 1982

5. Bentley, James. *Secrets of Mount Sinai: the story of the world's oldest Bible--Codex Sinaiticus,* Doubleday & Co. New York, 1986. p.98

6. Porphyrius, Archimandrite. "Proceedings of the Kiev Theological Academy," November, 1865, pp. 429-436—translated by Google Translate with the aid of the King James Bible

7. Elliott, J.K. *Codex Sinaiticus and the Simonides Affair,* Mt. Athos, 1982—article from *The Christian Remembrancer,* p.78

8. Elliott, J.K. *Codex Sinaiticus and the Simonides Affair,* Mt. Athos, 1982 p.178

CHAPTER FOUR

THE PEDIGREE OF HERESY

To these authorities, in proof of the existence of the Oriental philosophy, it may be added, as a consideration of great weight, that, if all the systems of philosophy distinct from the Grecian sects, which became famous in Asia or Egypt, particularly the Egyptian, Cabbalistic, Gnostic, and Eclectic, be compared, there will be found among them a wonderful agreement with the general principles of that system which we call the *Oriental* philosophy; whence **it seems perfectly reasonable to admit the existence of this philosophy as a common source, and to make use of it as a universal key to unlock the mysteries of the rest.**[1]

— WILLIAM ENFIELD

THE WORLD BEFORE *PHARMAKON*

Perhaps the biggest target of far left sentiment today is the Western cultural tradition, specifically what is termed 'Western Colonialism.' When one breaks down these criticisms, at the root is this premise, '*all cultures were peaceful and relatively advanced until Christian Colonialism stepped in, perverted them, enslaved them, and converted them against their will to Christianity.*' While I don't doubt that this happened to some extent, a major piece of the puzzle has been purposely suppressed.

As an example, a major contributor to this viewpoint is the professor of anthropology William Arens and his book *The Man Eating Myth*. Arens contests what was long believed, that up to 50% of primitive cultures throughout the world were engaged in cannibalism and ritual murder. Indeed, when Christopher Columbus came to America he found peaceful natives which he befriended. But he also found cannibalism, even naming the islands he found the 'Caribbean,' a term for 'cannibalism.' When he brought twenty or so natives back to Europe, it was not as slaves, but as prisoners, cannibals who were tormenting his new-found friends. Reports of such behavior were very prevalent throughout that time period, some ranging into the last century.[2] The mis-telling of these and similar stories are clearly ideologically motivated.

From an article by Neil L. Whitehead entitled 'Carib Cannibalism: the Historical Evidence' is quoted just such a report:

"However, Spanish authors and chroniclers were prepared to go further than a mere repetition of the fact of Carib cannibalism and have left various descriptions of related practices: e.g. the fattening up and castration of future victims. Vespucio relates the following incident, concerning some Spaniards who encountered a Carib pirogue off the coast of Tierra Firme:

We were about two leagues from the coast... In the pirogue there were four young men, they were not from the same group as the others, but had been taken prisoner in another land : and they had been castrated and all were without the male member and with fresh wounds, at which we marvelled much... They said to us that they had been castrated in order to eat them and we supposed that these were the people called cannibals, very fierce, that eat human flesh..."[3]

Similar reports from early French explorers and missionaries to New France (North America) record similar witnesses in *The Jesuit Relations and Allied Documents Travels and Explorations of the Jesuit Missionaries in New France* 1610-1791, a catalog of their reports sent back to France. Below is the very first record of cannibalism:

"In battle they strive especially to capture their enemies alive. Those who have been captured and led off to their villages are first stripped of their clothing; then they savagely tear off their nails one by one with their teeth; then they bind them to stakes and beat them as long as they please. Next they release them from their bonds, and compel them to pass back and forth between a double row of men armed with thorns, clubs and instruments of iron. Finally, they kindle a fire about them, and roast the miserable creatures with slow heat. Sometimes they pierce the flesh of the muscles with red-hot plates and with spits, or cut it off and devour it, half-burned and dripping with gore and blood. Next they plant blazing torches all over the body, and especially in the gaping wounds; then, after scalping him they scatter ashes and live coals upon his naked head; then they tear the tendons of the arms and legs, lacerate them, or, after removing a little of the skin, leisurely cut them with a knife at the ankle and wrist. often they compel the unhappy prisoner to walk through fire, or to eat, and thus entomb in a living sepulcher, pieces of his own flesh. Torture of this sort has been borne by not a few of the Fathers of the Society [Jesuits]. Moreover, they prolong this torment throughout many days, and, in order that the poor victim may undergo fresh trials, intermit it for some time, until his vitality is entirely exhausted and he perishes. Then they tear the heart from the breast, roast it upon the coals, and, if the prisoner has bravely borne the bitterness of the torture, give it, seasoned with blood, to the boys, to be greedily eaten, in order, as they say, that the warlike youth may imbibe the heroic strength of the valiant man. The prisoner who has beheld and endured stake, knives and wounds with an unchanging countenance, who has not groaned; who with laughter and song has ridiculed his tormentors, is praised; for they think that to sing amid so many deaths is great and noble. So they themselves compose songs long beforehand, in order that they may repeat them if they should by chance be captured. The rest of the crowd consume the corpse in a brutal feast. The chief reserves for himself the scalp as a sign of victory, a trophy of cruelty."[4]

— JESUIT MISSIONS TO NEW FRANCE (AMERICA)

I have compiled over forty single-line spaced pages of accounts from these Jesuit records. Similar records show that African tribes sold other barbaric blacks into slavery as a way of protecting their villages from cannibalism. These tribes were attacking their villages and creating havoc.

Similar records show such behavior in places like New Guinea, Hawaii, Asia, parts of Europe, etc. If one does a search at archive.org one will find most anthropology books of the late 1800s/early 1900s list similar behaviors, often combined with hallucinogens to heighten the experience. What one will also find, however, is the beginning of a propaganda campaign, about the very time revised Bibles were being proposed. Anthropologists such as Margaret Meade who knew full well the true history of such accounts, decided to switch narratives. Primitive tribes began to be presented not as barbaric, but as sexually innocent with drugs being just a recreational activity. Missing are the intricate sacrificial rituals often based upon ritual drug use. One can immediately see ties of this historical revisionism to Socialism and the modern academic agendas.[5]

All this represents an academic push-back against what they regarded as fabrications designed to justify colonialism. While they admit some accounts are true, they maintain that the vast majority are severely over-stated and are confusing sacrificial rituals with battle rituals. Apparently, devouring the deceased is now an 'acceptable' funeral rite. But either way, are such barbaric practices acceptable in a civilized world? Considering the limitations in cataloging such events, on what data do socialists like Arens base their findings? What is the acceptable amount of anthropophagy, child sacrifice, holocausts, and barbarism?

Arens labels such accounts as 'myth-making,' an effort to over exaggerate these accounts as a way of presenting colonialism in a better light. But Arens' claims are not based in fact. It has now been verified that up to 50% of the world's uncivilized tribes were engaging in this behavior, and that it was perhaps Christianity that was most effective in treatment. Specifically, the Christian Eucharist and baptism were very effective in re-directing cannibalistic desires. A study by Randall Caroline Watson Forsberg reveals:

"Finally, a careful review of the Arens-related claims and counterclaims [...], along with the evidence concerning the incidence of customary cannibalism given in the next section of this chapter, persuaded me that ritual forms of cannibalism not merely existed, but were widespread, being practiced by at least 50 percent of simple societies in most parts of the world, and more in some areas."[6]

— RANDALL CAROLINE WATSON FORSBERG

PLATONISM BECOMES ORIENTALISM

"The truth appears to have been that Plato, ambitious of the honour of forming a new sect, and endued by nature with more brilliancy of fancy than strength of judgment, collected the tenets of other philosophers, which were, in many particulars, contradictory, and could by no exertion of ingenuity be brought to coalesce, and that out of this heterogeneous mass he framed a confused system, destitute of form or consistency. This will be acknowledged by every one who, in perusing the philosophical writings of Plato, is capable of divesting himself of that blind respect for antiquity by which the learned so frequently suffer themselves to be misled. In confirmation of the propriety of this judgment, we need only refer to the dialogue entitled *Timæus*, a chaotic mass of opinions, which no commentators have yet been able to reconcile, or to explain."[7]

— WILLIAM ENFIELD

As Enfield indicates, Plato had no clear comprehensive philosophy he could claim his own. Essentially he catalogued the thinking of others in an effort to find a suitable replacement for Man's natural Bacchanalian tendencies. Not recognizing this, many have tried to see Plato as the door to the very mystery religions Plato was trying to make obsolete. Out of the catalogued bits and pieces of his writings they envisioned a mystical philosophy that would provide the same experiences drugs had promised.

Plato represents a key point where the modern solution is exposed for what it is. Early philosophers such as Aristotle were searching for a conforming truth on which philosophy could be based. Platos solution, however, sets the stage for a future idealisms where everyone determines their own truth based upon experience. While Plato endeavored to make the barbarisms and drug based rites of the past obsolete, modern idealism only makes them acceptable once again. Idealism is just socialism by yet another name. Both base their popularity on the utopian ideal, that a mass collective society can be formed upon the proposition that everyone can do as they please. It is the inevitable conclusion of a psychology based upon Onc-ncss. The result is what Gustave Le Bon called the 'Psychology of the Crowd.'[8] His book, *Psychologie des Foules,* is usually translated *The Crowd,* but a more accurate translation might be *The Mob.* Being French and witnessing everything from Napoleon to the Dreyfus Affair, he summed up the dangers of the mob and its psychological allure. It is based upon communal flashes of experience, what we might today call 'psychedelics.' Sucked up in the mass confusion of the mob, the average person replaces reason with fury, individuality with group frenzy, thought with ecstasy.

Over the years there have been many Christian heresies, Neoplatonism, Hermeticism, Monophysitism, Quartodecimanism and a staggering array of others. William Enfield, on the other hand, searched for a common feature, some shared umbrella under which he could put all these 'sophias.' Most might tell you it is 'Gnosticism' and its feature *dualism.*

For a long time this puzzled me. Dualism has a ring of truth about it, but when push comes to shove all philosophies are sort of dualistic, faith against reason, you against the other, the immaterial against the material. Simple dualism doesn't appear to explain much.

Enfield noticed something different, what he believed was the underlying doctrine:

"According to this doctrine it may be conceived, that all souls, being portions of the universal mind, must return to the Divinity; but that since different minds, by their union with the body, are stained with different degrees of impurity, it becomes necessary that, before their return, they should pass through different degrees of purgation, which might be supposed to be accomplished by means of successive transmigrations. According to this system, bad men would undergo this metempsychosis for a longer, good men for a shorter period; and the Amenthes, or Hades, may be conceived to have been the region in which departed souls, immediately after death, received their respective designations."[9]

— WILLIAM ENFIELD

What Enfield is referring to he called *Orientalism*. It is the *monopyche*, the belief that all thoughts emanate from the One-Mind, that the proper termination of all souls is an absorption back into the One. Curiously, this is the very doctrine condemned by the Catholic Church in 1277. The problem is now our philosophies and terms are all mixed up. The conventional earmarks of Gnosticism are not dualistic at all, they are monistic! Further still, how did a 'remedy' intended to solve the problem become the future instigator?

In this monism, everything obvious to you, to me, becomes obsolete. A sense of 'self'—gone. A sense of individuality—gone. A sense that reality is concrete and has meaning—gone. Discernment—gone. Logic—gone. The fact of knowledge—denied. In fact I would say that even the ability to validate such a scheme is impossible under its own system. 'Salvation' becomes a giving up of reason, of individuality, of even life. All are illusions. It is essentially collectivist in practice, nihilistic in execution.

Adherents to this monistic doctrine will insist it is found in Genesis. If you look you will not find it. This is because most believe the Serpent, the Adversary, to be bad, and God to be good. This is not the way they see it. To them the Serpent is good for he represents the warning of wisdom. The Tree of Knowledge is evil. To them Christ is the Demiurge, the rebellious Son of All, the catalyst of the fall from grace. Christ, therefore, represents discernment, the basis of reasoning, the separation from the One, and he must be sacrificed for his crime. Creation was a mistake, the defecated remains of a once great spiritual Dream. The duty of the Gnostic, like Christ, must pay for this crime. It is to foil the scheme of the Demiurge by giving up of 'self,' by giving up reason, by thwarting procreation, thus forcing a return to the All.

Under this 'enlightened' system salvation is an 'unknowing,' a giving up of discernment. Once you realize there is no substantial difference between you and God, that no mind is distinct, you become God. It is 'unknowing' that eradicates the need for 'knowing.' It is seductive because it makes all the nasty bits of real knowledge obsolete.

Many theologians today hold to just this. In the face of contradicting schemes and reasonings, challenged with competing cultures and tradition, perhaps it becomes reasonable to just give up on reason. But what do you replace it with?

What scholars call 'Platonism' represents a solution to a dilemma. Without a guiding doctrine, Platonism just seems like a more democratic. True, it is an advancement from the Greek symposium, but it is weak on guidance. We see this in Socrates' death scene, a promise of hope beyond barbarism, but the art has no Artist. It seems 'reasonable' to believe that reality is a dream, it explains the miracle, but avoids the Miracle. The mysticism seduces, but hides the fact it explains little.

What Plato fails to realize is that it wasn't the drugs or even the debauchery that was the true evil, *it was the <u>mob-like state of mind</u> created by the drugs that led to the debauchery. And, at the end of the day, it was not necessary to use drugs to achieve that state of mind, Reformulated and tweaked, Plato's Idealism could accomplish this all by itself.*

But there is a moral side to Gnosticism, it is anything that promotes the reformation of the One. Immorality becomes anything that resists or thwarts the formation of the One. As the ideal is a collective state of One-ness, anything that impedes the re-constitution of the One becomes evil. Procreation, then, becomes just this sort of evil because birth is a siphoning of souls away from their perfect existence. Preventing a birth becomes much more efficient than the its later re-education. It is precisely here the radical feminism reveals itself as Gnosticism in action.

This system was not so much the brain-child of Plato or even Socrates. It is the result of the unpacking of conjectures found in Plato's *Phædrus,* merged with Greek philosophy (Hermes) and Egyptian mysticism (Thoth). What happened is that the deficiencies in one, were back-filled by the excesses of the other. Key to this was the reading into Egyptian hieroglyphs stories that just weren't there. Also contributing was the pseudepigrapha, the false attribution of texts to people who never wrote them.

Time after time proposed new discoveries of gnostic texts were claimed to be authentic and found to be fraudulent. One was the *Letters of Dionysius*. Presenting himself to be Dionysius the Areopagite of the Bible, the author was proved to be a pretender. Similarly, the *Corpus Hermeticum* was proved fraudulent. By the nineteenth century this all came to a breaking point. Losing ground to true reason, it became necessary to re-affirm the system 'scientifically.' In steps the prophets of the New Age.

Today we live in two worlds each distinguished by its own realities. The first, Idealism, is all spirituality. It has no permanence, no foundation for truth. Permanently dissatisfied with reality it habitually seeks to undermine it in pursuit of utopia. Socialism and Communism are merely spin-offs. As reality ultimately has no meaning, all is progress or change.

On the other side we find radical materialism. It denies the Spirit all together. To them, thought is only a chemical process, Man is just a sack of biological material. Oddly enough Idealism and Materialism are sort of versions of the same thing—in both the individual is an illusion.

The only way out of the dilemma is a moderated third way. This was the doctrine of *Logos* first represented by Aristotle, but later sanctified by the Scholastics. At the heart of the method was a technique to spark the mind's ability to discern, something the world seems to have a tendency to dull. It was a blending of the best of both worldviews, and a denial of the worst. It realized Truth requires a 'changeless foundation' or it can have no meaning. But it also recognized change as a necessary consequence of reality. *Logos* represents the need for a conceptual understanding of Truth, something that cannot be memorized by rote. It resists the notion that knowledge is just a process of remembering and reading into truth your own boutique set of proclivities.

While *Orientalism* promises a simple form of immortality, it is actually a form of Hell, a *solipsism*. Believed to its fullest, it can only promise a universe of self. Believing all one's ideas are thoughts that originate with God, you never have to question your own motives, you can deceive yourself into any dream you wish to be true. Eventually the All is yourself, everything else is just Other.

We must examine Socrates doctrine even deeper. Only then will we see what the Arians were up to.

1. Enfield, William. *The History of Philosophy*, 1839, p.377
2. Irvin, Jan R. *God's Flesh: Teononácatl — the True History of the Sacred Mushroom*, Logos-media, 2022
3. Whitehead, Neil L. 'Carib Cannibalism: the Historical Evidence,' quote from *Archivo General de Indias*, Sevilla, 1951 : 237
4. Jesuits letters from missions. *The Jesuit Relations and Allied Documents Travels and Explorations of the Jesuit Missionaries in New France (Relations des Jésuites de la Nouvelle-France)* 1610-1791, Vol.1-p.271-3, translated from the French
5. Irvin, Jan R. *God's Flesh: Teononácatl — the True History of the Sacred Mushroom*, Logos-media, 2022
6. Forsberg, Randall Caroline Watson. 'Ritual Cannibalism, A Case Study of Socially Sanctioned Group Violence,' in *Toward a Theory of Peace*. Cornell University Press, 2019, ISBN: 1501744356
7. Enfield, *The History of Philosophy*, 1839, p.126
8. Le Bon, Gustave, *The Crowd: A Study of the Popular Mind (Psychologie des Foules)* , T. Fisher Unwin, London, 1896 (1895)
9. Enfield, *The History of Philosophy*, 1839 p.45

CHAPTER FIVE

THE ONE MIND: THE UNIVERSAL SOUL OF THE WORLD

"It has been asserted, that it was in Egypt that Plato acquired his opinions concerning the origin of the world, and learnt the doctrines of, transmigration, and the immortality of the soul: but it is more probable that he learned the latter doctrine from Socrates, and the former from Pythagoras. It is not likely that Plato, in the habit of a merchant, could have gained access to the sacred mysteries of Egypt; for we shall after-wards see, in the case of Pythagoras, that the Egyptian priests were so unwilling to communicate their secrets to strangers, that even a royal mandate was scarcely sufficient, in a single instance, to procure this indulgence. Little regard is therefore due to the opinion of those who assert that Plato derived his system of philosophy from the Egyptians."[1]

— WILLIAM ENFIELD

Scholars have been reading Plato wrong for centuries. In an effort to portray Socrates as a 'civilized' pre-Christian saint interpreters 'Christian-ized' his writings, hiding significant facts. This is particularly true of the word '*pharmakon*' when they translated the word as 'remedy' and avoided 'poison.'

The post-modern French philosopher Jackie 'Jacques' Derrida (*Plato's Pharmacy*) recognized this. What he saw, particularly in the word '*pharmakon*,' was what we might call Plato's 'Thothic Dilemma': the deficiency of the written word to convey with any accuracy the concepts they represent. But Derrida took this one step further.

Where the moderns questioned the meanings of words, post-moderns like Derrida questioned the meaning of meaning itself. Seeing words such as *pharmakon* as contronyms (words that have potentially contradictory meanings) Derrida saw the objects of reality as 'physical contronyms.' To Derrida this was not a bad thing, it was license to create any reality you wanted. Reality became a toy, a box of Legos out of which you could design your own truths. Derrida believed this is the essence of Plato's philosophy, a method of suspending reason by embracing contradicting concepts at the same time. If one tried to behold both meanings at the same time it creates what is called a *cognitive dissonance*, a sort of mental drug-like state, but using only words. It was Derrida's way of seeing the world anew, of confounding discernment so that one becomes one with reality.

Contronyms are words that have contradictory meanings. Typical contronyms are 'fast' (meaning both *quick* or *stuck*), 'left' (to *stay* or to *leave*), 'overlook' (to *supervise* or to *neglect*). *Pharmakon* was just such a contronym, meaning both poison/remedy, or intoxicant/medicine.[2] The method was advocated by John Lennon in his music and James Joyce in his writings.

Countering Derrida's theory is Michael Rinella's (author of *Pharmakon*). He saw *pharmakon* not as a word of inner contradiction, but as a word in transition. In his disdain for symposiums as an upper social class institution, Socrates got in trouble precisely because he tried to socialize the use of *pharmakon*.[3]

In their own way, both Derrida and Rinella display critical aspects of the story, Derrida's is more philosophical, Rinella's more historical. *Yet, both are based on the belief that Plato was advocating the use of words as a replacement for the ancient pharmakon as a way of inducing a peculiar state of mind.* We find this in Socrates' death scene where the taking of a lethal potion represents the very transfer of the *pharmakon* of old becoming the new, the artful use of words. Both the hallucinogenic *pharmakon* and the clever use of words could create a feeling of immortality.

It is here we can see the infantile stages of Arianism. Socrates' speaks of the pre-existence of Souls, a doctrine later condemned by the Church. While it provided a path to immortality, it called for no allegiance to anything—no God, no truth, no reverence, nothing. Immortality was just something that happened. By leveraging the notions that knowledge is just recollection, he could construct a proof of immortality.

"Cebes added: Your favorite doctrine, Socrates, that knowledge is simply recollection, if true, also necessarily implies a previous time in which we have learned that which we now recollect. But this would be impossible unless our soul had been in some place before existing in the form of man; here then is another proof of the soul's immortality."

— PLATO (AS SOCRATES), *PHÆDO*

PLATO'S PHILOSOPHICAL SCHIZOPHRENIA

"The schizophrenic is a soul not merely unregenerate, but desperately sick into the bargain. His sickness consists in the inability to take refuge from inner and outer reality (as the sane person habitually does) in the homemade universe of common sense—the strictly human world of useful notions, shared symbols and socially acceptable conventions. The schizophrenic is like a man permanently under influence of mescalin, and therefore unable to shut off the experience of a reality which he is not holy enough to live with, which he cannot explain away because it never permits him to look at the world with merely human eyes, scares him into interpreting its unremitting strangeness, its burning intensity of significance, as the manifestation of human or even cosmic malevolence, calling for the most desperate countermeasures, from murderous violence at one end of the scale to catatonia, or psychological suicide at the other."[4]

— ALDOUS HUXLEY, *THE DOORS OF PERCEPTION*

If knowledge is just remembrance, then discernment is futile. While Derrida and Rinella have slightly different understandings of the *pharmakon*, both agree as to Plato's intentions, to achieve a god-like state of mind through words rather than drugs. We might consider this a sort of prestidigitation, a from of magic based on *eros,* what new agers today might call *the law of attraction.*[5] It was this that gave birth to Gnosticism—sacred texts were to be regarded as sort of magical *grimoires*, ethereal 'words spells' designed to enrapture the imagination. The last thing words represent are discernible Truths.

A drug-like state of mind can be mimicked by exploiting the *cognitive dissonance.* The mind, caught between two irreconcilable truths, also loses its ability to discern. Normally, this is healthy when the anxiety leads to resolution, but if the confusion itself can be accepted as a positive experience, something to be enjoyed, it becomes a sort of out-of-body revelation. Aldous Huxley defined this as schizophrenia, *'the inability to take refuge from inner and outer reality.'* This is precisely the condition the Platonist seeks to create.

Huxley likened this to an hallucination. Like with *pharmakon*, the schizophrenic spends everyday living both in mundane reality and in the euphoric ideal. Eventually he must make a choice—which world should he occupy? The schizophrenic sides in favor of the inner, the imagined.

Scholastic philosophers, taking a more reasoned approach, called this the *Ego-centric Predicament*. 'Can I trust that my senses present to me a truthful reality?' If not, then I live as a schizophrenic.

This predicament has been memorialized by Anglican Bishop and philosopher George Berkeley, 'If the tree falls in the forest does it make a sound?'

In a sense, the idealist is one who shrinks from the dilemma, finding refuge in the world of his own thoughts. The result is reality has nothing to give, the red is no longer in the rose, reality is a projection of my mind. When John Lennon says, "Picture yourself in a boat on a river; With tangerine trees and marmalade skies," it is not nonsense, it is an invitation to come on board. When James Joyce says, "Absence, the highest form of presence," he is not just mystifying, he is evangelizing. Yet, what are the boundaries of thought if not reality? If I visualize Warp Speed does it make it so? Are nightmares true on some level? If I dream of a time machine will I one day talk to Napoleon?

The farther we go down this rabbit hole, the further we disassociate from a world that makes sense. In a way, this also the state of mind we create when we reduce the world to a mathematical formula, or a cosmological paradox. In the end, do we really feel we would have a place in such a world? Is Plato's God the God we need? If God is an hallucinogenic-like event, does this mean all hallucinogenic-like events are God?

WHO WAS PLATO'S SOCRATES?

"Socrates left behind him nothing in writing; but his illustrious pupils, Xenophon and Plato, have, in some measure, supplied this defect. The Memoirs of Socrates, written by Xenophon, afford, however, a much more accurate idea of the opinions of Socrates, and of his manner of teaching, than the Dialogues of Plato, who every where mixes his own conceptions and diction, and as we shall afterwards see, those of other philosophers, with the ideas and language of his master. It is related, that when Socrates heard Plato recite his *Lysis*, he said, "How much does this young man make me say which I never conceived!" Xenophon denies that Socrates ever taught natural philosophy, or any mathematical science, and charges with misrepresentation and falsehood those who had ascribed to him dissertations of this kind; probably referring to Plato, in whose works Socrates is introduced as discoursing upon these subjects. The truth appears to be, that the distinguished character of Socrates was that of a moral philosopher."[6]

— WILLIAM ENFIELD

The ego-centric predicament is actually very ancient. In Euripides' play the *Bacchae*, he asked the question, 'what happens to a society that totally abandons reason for pleasure?' His analogy was the 'Horse and the Rider.' The tension between faith and reason is represented by a horse (*faith/passion*), and its rider (*reason*). The question is who is in charge? Does the horse tame the rider, or the rider tame the horse? Which leads to the best results?

The answer is both, at least in a way. It is the duty of the rider to rein in the horse, to guide it, and to make sure it has direction. But the horse has purpose too, without it the rider goes nowhere. What could appear like a dissonance, is in fact not.

Similarly, in the *Bacchae* women creating a cult of Dionysius (a form of Hermeticism), abandon all reason to pleasure … they end up eating their own. We find a similar allegory in the Psalms. Some would even say the story of Creation invokes a similar metaphor, Adam representing reason, and Eve faith. Even John's Gospel uses Bacchae-like allegory to represent the conflict between the mob and Christ.

But there was one notable dissenter, Plato and his allegory of the Chariot. Whereas the *Bacchae* divided the soul into two faculties, Plato's version divided the soul in into three, the chariot driver and his *two* horses. Unlike Euripides, he saw the driver not as *reason,* but as a *gambler,* one who bets on which horse to follow, the horse with the *reasonable* character, or the one with the *passionate* character. This choice is necessarily a 'coin toss' for reason resides in one of the horses, not the driver. Should the driver choose correctly, he rises above physical reality and enters Plato's utopia of perfect geometrical forms. Incorrectly he is doomed.

The question becomes, how does the chariot driver decide which horse to follow if it is not by reason? If reason is foreign to the intellect, how does he decide? To Plato, the thing that decides is an inner faculty called *theia mania,* or *divine madness,* it is ecstasy (ἐκστασης). Plato attributes this insight to

Socrates in his *Phædrus*, "in fact the best things we have comes from madness," it is a "gift from the gods."

> "In such families that accumulated vast wealth were found dire plagues and afflictions of the soul, for which *mania* devised a remedy (*pharmakon*), inasmuch as the same was a gift from the gods, if only to be rightly frenzied and possessed, using proper atonement rituals."[7]

> — PLATO, *PHÆDRUS*

Keep in mind, the *mania* advocated here sounds much like what Le Bon called '*Psychologie des Foules*.' And in the end, wasn't it the mob that killed Jesus?

While Plato portrays Socrates as a philosopher, he was actually something less. While he creates the Socratic Method asking, 'why aren't people morally consistent,' the truth he implies is never fully realized. His method questions more than it resolves. But this is not the Socrates we find in Plato's *Phædrus* or *Phædo*. Here Socrates is genuinely philosophical.

After a life time of provoking debate, at about the age of seventy Socrates finds himself in trouble with the ruling authorities. He was accused of corrupting the minds of his youthful students… one of which was Plato. Enfield illustrates:

> "The minds of the people being thus artfully prepared for the sequel, the enemies of Socrates preferred a direct accusation against him before the supreme court of judicature. His accusers were Anytus, a leather-dresser, who had long entertained a personal enmity against Socrates, for reprehending his avarice, in depriving his sons of the benefits of learning, that they might pursue the gains of trade; Melitus, a young rhetorician, who was capable of undertaking any thing for the sake of gain, and Lycon, who was glad of any opportunity of displaying his talents. The accusation, which was delivered to the senate under the name of Melitus, was this: "Melitus, son of Melitus, of the tribe of Pythos, accuseth Socrates son of Sophroniscus, of the tribe of Alopeces. **Socrates violates the laws, in not acknowledging the gods which the state acknowledges, and by introducing new divinities. He also violates the laws by corrupting the youth. Be his punishment death.**"[8]

> "This charge was delivered upon oath to the senate, and Crito, a friend of Socrates, became surety for his appearance on the day of trial. Anytus soon

afterwards sent a private message to Socrates, assuring him, that if he would desist from censuring his conduct he would withdraw his accusation. But Socrates refused to comply with so degrading a condition, and with his usual spirit replied, "Whilst I live I will never disguise the truth, nor speak otherwise than my duty requires." The interval between the accusation and the trial he spent in philosophical conversations with his friends, choosing to discourse upon any other subject rather than his own situation. Hermogenes, one of his friends, was much struck with this circumstance, and asked him, why he did not employ his time in preparing his defence ? "Because," replied Socrates, "I have never in my life done any thing unjust." The eminent orator Lysias; composed an apology, in the name of his master, which he requited him to adopt; but Socrates excused himself by saying that, though it was eloquently written, it would not suit his character."

"...**Plato, who was a young man, and a zealous follower of Socrates, then rose up to address the judges in defence of his master; but, whilst he was attempting to apologize for his youth, he was abruptly commanded by the court to sit down.** Socrates, however, needed no advocate."[9]

— WILLIAM ENFIELD

It is speculated that Socrates disapproved of the symposium, particularly that participation was limited to the elite. The people disapproved because of the post-symposium rabal-rousing called *hubris*. Plato himself apparently disapproved of the use of drugs to create this *theia mania.* By not adhering to the approved methods, Socrates accused of invoking unapproved gods...and the youth, such as Plato, were participating![10]

There is a fair amount of evidence that having unapproved symposiums is what got Socrates in trouble, but once the events of June 7, 415 BC were attributed to him, his fate was sealed. It was then that the youth of Athens after an unapproved symposium went through the streets smashing religious statues. This was far from an innocuous event, it perhaps influenced Greece's fate in the Peloponnesian War. More importantly for us, it gives us a look inside as to the birth of Hermeticism.

The initial charge was against the Greek statesman Alcibiades, a former student of Socrates and general in the Peloponnesian War. Accused of having participated in the events of 415, eventually the evidence turns to Socrates. The majority of destroyed statues were dedicated to Hermes. Called *Hermai,* these were large rectangular stones with the head of Hermes on top, and an *erect penis* functionally where it ought to be. First discovered by women waking to their chores, they found the statue's faces busted up and the appendages hacked off. After a trial Socrates was condemned to death. The accusation of worshipping other gods might partially be attributed to Socrates' claiming that he was guided by a Daemon:

"I have a voice from God which clearly signifies to me what I ought to do. Why? what else do those who make use of the cries of birds or utterances of men draw their conclusions from if not from voices? Who will deny that the thunder has a voice and is a very mighty omen; and the priestess on her tripod at Pytho, does not she also proclaim by voice the messages from the god? The god, at any rate, has fore-knowledge, and premonishes those whom he will of what is about to be. That is a thing which all the world believes and asserts even as I do. Only, when they describe these premonitions under the name of birds and utterances, tokens and soothsayers, I speak of a divinity, and in using that designation I claim to speak at once more exactly and more reverentially than they do who ascribe the power of the gods to birds. And that I am not lying against the Godhead I have this as a proof: although I have reported to numbers of friends the counsels of heaven, I have never at any time been shown to be a deceiver or deceived."[11]

— XENOPHON, *THE APOLOGY*

Psychologist and philosopher William James said this of Socrates:

"Unless we are to believe that the ancients misinterpreted Socrates' own words about the nature of his inspirations, or that these word were a form of hoax, we must conclude that Socrates suffered from auditory–and perhaps an occasional visual–hallucinations. Since only mad people so suffer, Socrates, in spite of all the other virtues he may have possessed, must have been mad."

— WILLIAM JAMES

Socrates' philosophical career was prodded early on by a *cognitive dissonance* of his own. As a student he asked Pythia the Oracle of Delphi, 'who is the smartest man in Athens?' She responded, 'Socrates.' This created a dissonance: if Socrates proves the Oracle wrong, he clearly does so by out-smarting her, making himself the *de facto* smartest person in Athens. If Socrates concedes she is right, he again is the smartest person in Athens, the Oracle said so. It is a logical trap. Like the statement 'This sentence is false,' there is no good answer. It is the ultimate dilemma called the Liar's Paradox, which would have a long, controversial future. One day it would prove the impossibility of the *monopsyche.*

There is no doubt that Socrates was a real person. There are four important sources, Aristophanes, Aristotle, Xenophon, and of course Plato. The other sources generally present Socrates not as an academic as Plato does, but as a sort of Hunter S. Thompson anti-hero. Where Plato's Socrates becomes wise, the others are rugged and independent. He fought wars, stayed out in bad weather, was jobless, made a living through his teaching, and had more of the character of a gonzo moralist.

The problem is that Plato's Socrates is not this. Plato's Socrates would never accept money for his teaching. He is sophisticated, academic, more, well, like Plato.

Today scholars divide Plato's dialogs into three phases representing the transition from an historically accurate Socrates, ending in one where Socrates *is* more-or-less Plato. The transition seems to occur about the time when Plato develops his Theory of Idealism. Many conclude that the later Socrates is a literary device for Plato's himself, to give weight to his Idealism.

Plato provides the narrative of Socrates' death... a death by suicide, an event he says he did not witness. In *Phædo* we see a mature philosopher, someone who profoundly speaks of Man's soul. Plato also provides details of the suicide he could not have known.

Pathologist William Ober, classicist Christopher Gill, and Bonita Graves all wrote papers on the subject contesting the death as reported by Plato. Plato's Socrates dies a noble, peaceful death by taking an unnamed *pharmakon.* Many assume it was hemlock, but according to these experts the symptoms don't match up. Hemlock poisoning is not so peaceful as Plato leads us to believe. In fact it is quite wicked. And did we not just question if Plato's *pharmakon* was a real potion? The account has clearly been idealized. So, what was Plato's purpose?[12]

The importance of this cannot be overstated. Beginning with the Council of Nicaea we will see two forms of Christianity emerging, both contesting to be the legitimate one. One is clearly deeply influenced by this very neoplatonism.

My question is this, if Socrates at this point in his dialogs is actually Plato, who then committed suicide, Socrates, or Plato? Certainly, Socrates (or Plato) could not have documented his own death, nor could Plato document an event he did not witness. So, was the account metaphorical? What if 'Socrates' was metaphor for Plato's own *cognitive dissonance*? What if the dialog represents the conflict and development of Plato's search for a philosophical *pharmakon*? Could Socrates' actual death represent Plato's metaphysical death, Plato's own transition to Idealism? We've already spoken of the madness of dissonance. But so does Plato's *Phædrus*. Socrates says:

> "Madness, provided it comes as the gift of heaven, is the channel by which we receive the greatest blessings... the men of old who gave things their names saw no disgrace or reproach in madness; otherwise they would not have connected it with the name of the noblest of arts, the art of discerning the future, and called it the *manic art*... So, according to the evidence provided by our ancestors, madness is a nobler thing than sober sense.... madness comes from God, whereas *sober sense is merely human.*"

> — PLATO, *PHÆDRUS*

Plato seems to be laying the groundwork for the religious experience as a form of *mania*, a form of *ecstasy*. A symptom of schizophrenia is reality appears as a projection of one's own thoughts. Much like the hallucination, Plato's theory of sight found in his *Timæus* is similar:

> "And of the organs they first contrived the eyes to give light, and the principle according to which they were inserted was as follows: So much of fire as would not burn, but gave a gentle light, they formed into a substance akin to the light of every-day life; and the pure fire which is within us and related thereto they made to flow through the eyes in a stream smooth and dense, compressing the whole eye, and especially the centre part, so that it kept out everything of a coarser nature, and allowed to pass only this pure element. When the light of day surrounds the stream of vision, then like falls upon like, and they coalesce, and one body is formed by natural affinity in the line of vision, wherever the light that falls from within meets with an external object. And the whole stream of vision, being similarly affected in virtue of similarity, diffuses the motions of what it touches or what touches it over the whole body, until they reach the soul, causing that perception which we call sight."[13]

> — PLATO, *TIMÆUS*

Further still, who is this '*Theia*'? She is none other than *this feminine god within (Theia, Θεία meaning Divine Goddess),* also called *Euryphaessa* (*Εὐρυφάεσσα*), the Greek goddess of sight and vision! The Bible sees divine light as a metaphor for wisdom. But here we are toying with God as light itself, a concept later Arians such as Isaac Newton would invoke.

Now you may think me mad also, but it has been this very flirt with madness that is the subtle force within Modernism (and Post Modernism). It is in fact the *pharmakon* of the modern era. And it is also the force behind *Orientalism*. Louis Sass in his book *Madness and Modernism* makes the case that this is the only way you can explain modern art, modern music, modern poetry, modern architecture, attempts to recreate the mind of the schizophrenic.

Consider this, ask most any clergy person what is their philosophical inspiration. Ask the mathematician. Ask the scientist. Even ask the modern scholar. Chances are most all will say, 'Plato.' Is it possible that our obsession with Idealism has been a flirt with madness? Could it be the creation of this artificial, self-referential tautology of 'self' that is the real problem? *Could it be that Socrates WAS perverting the minds of the youth as charged by the Athenian jurors, that Plato WAS a student of Socrates as he himself confessed, and that this theology as Plato conceived it was a pharmakon, an attempt to create a sort of mania that mimicked this ecstasy? A sort of philosophical schizophrenia? Could it be that this is what the 'modern' considers normal?*[14]

Over time, the post modernist's new *raison d'être* becomes just that, to seduce and shock the minds of others, *épater la bourgeoisie*, becoming co-conspirators in the corruption of the real and the replacing of it with the schizophrenic.

Is this the true spirit of Descartes, "I think, therefore I am"? Is this the true Fludd, Marcilio Ficino, Paracelsus, and even Isaac Newton? Of, dare I say, the Arian? Was the Christ they worshipped really the God of Hermes, of Thoth, the god of the Occult. The evidence will show that it was.

It is very clear that what we've been calling *Orientalism*, what we will find is the basis of Gnosticism, has its roots in this dilemma. Eventually it would be called Neo-Platonism. It was precisely this that was coming into vogue just after Christ. It is the result of an odd marriage between Greek and Eastern mysticisms that questioned the very efficacy of words as meaning. They did not heed Plato's warnings of sophistry, they ran with it eventually leading to our modern dysphoric culture. I will later contend that this was also at the root of Arianism at the Council of Nicaea, the very belief system targeted by 1 John 5:7.

THE NEW ARIANS

"One often hears and reads about the dangers of Yoga, particularly of the ill-reputed Kundalini Yoga. The deliberately induced psychotic state, which in certain unstable individuals might easily lead to a real psychosis, is a danger that needs to be taken very seriously indeed. These things really are dangerous and ought not to be meddled with in our typically Western way. It is a meddling with Fate, which strikes at the very roots of human existence and can let loose a flood of sufferings of which no sane person ever dreamed."[15]

— PSYCHOLOGIST CARL JUNG

Today we live in a culture of addictions. Normal, relatively innocuous things such as cinema, music, sports, video games, yoga, even religion have all been radicalized so as to produce pharmakon-like hormones. Most people diligently pursue a college degree or a certification, but once obtained, few continue to read or grow in understanding. The entire society appears orchestrated to produce a public euphoria in service of making a buck and keeping control.

Yet, I would submit, that what modern society has adopted is not only the pharmakon of old, but a hyper realized version of the very Arianism of the heresy condemned under Nicaea. Both Jung (hermeticism) and Freud (cabbala) took these very teachings, dressed them up with scientific terms, and called it Psychology.[16,17] Combined with politics and marketing they have become a system of societal subversion all aspiring to this 'modern' ideal. What cannot be done with psychology, we do with Ritalin.

Let's take yoga for an example, although I am sure a similar chain of inspiration could be found in all the above. In time, HR departments, retreats, conflict resolution classes, festivals such as Burning Man, all suspiciously promote a similar yoga-like ideal that is less-and-less rational. Most are similar methods of emptying the mind, of divorcing from reality, even creating an artificial reality, all designed to create an inner peace. The method is inherently paradoxical. The whole thing is suspiciously like what the Hindu call 'Vedanta,' which literally means 'the end of knowledge,' the philosophical basis of yoga.

But there a price to be paid for all this. This paradoxical pursuits can never achieve their goal, the ideal state. What is designed to end anxiety has been statistically shown to often results in anxiety and disturbances. Most may not be aware, but there have been studies on the prolonged effects of practicing of yoga. Below are two citations:

"Similarly, recent scholarship on religion and mental health has attempted to establish comparisons—especially differences—between "religious experiences" and experiences associated with psychopathology, particularly schizophrenia and psychosis [87–90]. While these studies grapple with important issues of differential diagnosis, they tend to place an excessive emphasis on the role of "belief" in religious life, while overlooking the various changes in perception, affect, cognition, embodiment, and sense of self that are also reported in the context of both religious experiences and mental illnesses. **Many of the experiences reported by practitioners in our study resemble to varying degrees phenomena discussed in the vast literature on schizophrenia, schizotypy, psychosis, as well as non-psychopathological forms of anomalous experience. Without sufficiently attending to the role of appraisal processes at both individual and interpersonal levels, scholars may fundamentally misconstrue differential diagnosis as being about identifying inherent differences between religious experiences and mental illnesses, rather than seeing them as potentially more ambiguous categories or closely related phenomena that may well be grounded in common cognitive, perceptual, and behavioral mechanisms.**[18]

In a study on related pathologies called 'The Varieties of Contemplative Experience: A mixed-methods study of meditation-related challenges in Western Buddhists' (Lindahl, J., Fisher, N., Cooper, D., Rosen, R., and Britton, W) data was gathered. A partial summation was listed in Table 4:

DATA FROM TABLE 4 OF THE STUDY: Phenomenology coding structure (experiences).[19]

- Cognitive: Experienced Delusional, Irrational or paranormal beliefs 47%
- Change in worldview 48%
- Perceptual: Hallucinations, visions, or illusions 42%
- Affective: Fear, anxiety, panic or paranoia 82%
- Depression, dysphoria, or grief 57%
- Somatic: Sleep changes 62%
- Connative: Changes in motivation goals 78%
- Sense of Self: Changes in self-other or self-world boundaries 53%
- Loss of sense of basic self 25%

- Social: Social impairment 50%
- Occupational impairment 42%

The general idea of all these techniques is to create a mental utopia. Researcher John B. Calhoun of the National Institute of Mental Health (NIMH) purposely tried to test the lines between utopia and dystopia by creating an artificial doomsday. In fact, he believed the line itself was 'fictitious.' He based his research on the economic theories of Rev. Thomas Malthus, the Anglican priest who developed Malthusian Economics. Calhoun tested the implications of over-population in the face of dwindling food supply. His solution was 'survival of the fittest,' the very theory that inspired Darwin's Theory of Evolution. Malthus' psychological effect on Victorian England has been memorialized in Charles Dickens' *Christmas Carol*, where Malthus is portrayed as Scrooge.

"In 1947, John B. Calhoun of the National Institute of Mental Health (NIMH) began experimenting with artificially created rat colonies. By first creating a rat 'utopia,' he then exposed it to the stresses of over-population and under supply of resources. The result was a dystopia of behavioral dysfunction, something Calhoun called the 'behavioral sink.' It was scientific evidence of the causes of social decay. Calhoun's paper "Population Density and Social Pathology" was considered one of the seminal papers on par with the likes Freud, Pavlov, Skinner and the like."[20]

— EDMUND RAMSDEN & JON ADAMS, UNIVERSITY OF
EXETER, LONDON SCHOOL OF ECONOMICS

Calhoun's Behavioral Sink produced cannibalism, violent gangs, sexual confusion, mother rats eating their young, and cowering in the corners. This prodded government agencies such as the CIA to investigate the use of real pharmaceuticals as a means of staving off what they believed was the inevitable fall of civilization. This is precisely what they were introducing into society in the 1960s. Gustave Le Bon's mob/crowd was coming to fruition:

"The crowd had long been associated with pathology: with mass panic, with the spread of disease, with political radicalism, aggression, and unruly social behavior. Many of these issues had been brought to the fore by contemporary events: the Watts riots of 1965, then again in Newark and Detroit in 1967, prefigured civil unrest across 125 American cities subsequent to the assassination of Martin Luther King in 1968. With these uprisings mirrored on college campuses (most prominently at Columbia), and the reported rise of an anti-authoritarian drug-culture, America looked ready to unravel. Worse still, local collapses of social order seemed part of a wider moral degeneracy, a failure horrifically exemplified by the apathetic non-response of many witnesses to the brutal rape and murder of Kitty Genovese in Queens in 1964. The urbanization of America seemed at least partially culpable for the turpitude and the ensuing dissolution of community ties--all were amenable to being viewed as problems of "the crowd."[21]

— EDMUND RAMSDEN & JON ADAMS

At some point in Calhoun's research a line was in fact breached. What began as an investigation of barbarism in rats subjected to environmental disaster, resulted in the idea that governments should proactively social engineer a way out of the inevitable 'doomsdays' brought on by environmental catastrophe. Using Malthusian theory, the intentional evolution of society would be promoted through using artificial economic fear campaigns, mitigated by the modification of society using drugs and the psychologies of 'love' and 'unity'—we would try to make everyone obediently happy. How? *By reverting back to the very behavior Plato had tried to make obsolete!* Calhoun's prognosis?

"Human beings thus face a predicament: If we try to make everybody totally happy, we'll destroy mankind."[22]

— JOHN B. CALHOUN, NATIONAL INSTITUTE OF
MENTAL HEALTH (NIMH)

The principal methods is to shut down the central nervous system making it callous to change. The result was the revisioning of the education system. Was it to teach or to indoctrinate? What couldn't be done through method could be accomplished with psychoactive drugs like Ritalin and Prozac. Rather than face reality, escaping it was promoted, the result was hubris. The benefits are necessarily short-lived, eventually requiring the dose to upped. Thus, an habitual circular routine is set up. The goal, a mystical high state of consciousness, is in actuality a self-induced sensory deprivation. As the aspirant becomes more seduced by the system, he necessarily loses the rational ability to assess what's going on, thwarting his instinct to pull out. He perceives this confusion to be a state of high mysticism when in actuality it is just a misinterpretation of his own self-preservation instincts.

> "By 1981, William Mayer, of the Alcohol, Drug Abuse, and Mental Health Administration, was able to declare that "N.I.M.H. is drugs, period." Behavioral studies could highlight the problems, but their solutions would only be found in neuropharmacology—in Ritalin, in Prozac. In 1983, the decision was taken to terminate Calhoun's contract—one year before the competition of his research cycle, and teasingly close to 1984. Casting himself as Winston Smith, Calhoun began to find echoes of 1984's oppressive bureaucracy in the nested structure of the American health system."[23]

— EDMUND RAMSDEN & JON ADAMS

The solution was:

> "It had been 1968, Calhoun recalled, when he first realized that the "portent of change" he saw "could not be clarified without building an incipient 'World Brain.' The direct referent here is H. G. Wells' visionary story which imagines all human knowledge made accessible through aggregation in a pre-digital "supercomputer." Calhoun suggested organizing scientists into a global, inter communicating network composed of independent but interconnected groups and sub-groups—only then could the necessary conceptual growth to avoid a catastrophic sink be achieved."[24]

— EDMUND RAMSDEN & JON ADAMS

THE MAIN LESSON LEARNED

Whether you call it the World Brain, Artificial Intelligence, or the Gnostic Pleroma, they are all versions of the same thing. The entire pursuit of philosophy, of *Logos*, was to find a moral basis of society unlinked to the personal ecstasy, to find an eternal truth that transcends personal preference. There is nothing inherently reasonable nor moral about cell phones, social platforms, gaming, roll playing and the like, but they all are allusions to a rather juvenile concept of community. Before philosophy, spirituality was entirely focused on creating a personal god-like experience. It was this that often led to hubris. But a morality based upon Truth, allowed Man as best as possible to separate the right from the wrong and act accordingly. It was the promise of eternal life that gave the system purpose.

In examining Gnosticism many have been factually correct, but conceptually wrong. All have missed the point. The core of Gnosticism is not *dualism*, it is *unitarianism*. The *dualism* it creates is in our mind is a result of its inherent irreconcilable paradox. We chase something impossible because it seems so reasonable, but, as Gödel proved, Unitarian All-in-all systems are necessarily paradoxical. If we concede that Gnosticism is dualistic, we never discover what is actually going on.

Mentally, we seek a unified, 'unitarian' understanding of the world. In this we can do no other, the mind abhors a contradiction. Once we achieve this unification, we go on and project this unity on to our vision of God—it only seems reasonable. We then go on to conceive God as the All-in-all, a philosophically unitarian 'complete' system. This necessarily leads to Gödel's logical paradox, a mental *dualism*. *We perceive a unity, but we must conceive a duality.*

Therefore, we believe the primary feature of Gnosticism is *dualism*, it is not. The dualism we conceive is only in our head, a result of this *unitarian predicament*. We mentally set up a *two-fold liar's paradox*. The unitarian All-in-all creates a two-fold philosophical dualism in our mind—perceiving this, we then mistakenly project this mental construct on to the unitarian perception that created it. The argument is circular and we become stuck in it. We start with a unity, conceive a duality—once we concede to the duality, we are back to the unity. By setting up a barrier, conceding that God is necessarily a Trinity, we break the cycle, we defeat the predicament—our thoughts can become unified without projecting this predicament onto God.

---

1. Enfield, *The History of Philosophy*, p.116
2. Nichol, Mark. *75 Contronyms* (Words with Contradictory Meanings) https://www.dailywrit ingtips.com/75-contronyms-words-with-contradictory-meanings/
3. Rinella, Michael A. *Pharmakon: Plato, drug culture, and identity in ancient Athens.* Lexington Books, 2010
4. Huxley, Aldous. *The doors of perception.* Chatto and Windus, London, 1954.
5. Couliano, Ioan P, *Eros and Magic in the Renaissance*, Univ. of Chicago, 1987
6. Enfield, *The History of Philosophy*, p.100
7. Plato, *Phædrus*, 244d, 244d-244e — *Dialogues of Plato: Containing The Apology of Socrates, Crito, Phaedo, and Protagoras.* Colonial Press, 1899. Benjamin Jowett trans.
8. Laert., Plato, *Apologia*, from Enfield *The History of Philosophy*, p. 97
9. Enfield, *The History of Philosophy*, p.97
10. Rinella, Michael A. *Pharmakon: Plato, drug culture, and identity in ancient Athens.* Lexington Books, 2010
11. Dakyns, H. G. trans. *The works of Xenophon.* Vol. 1. Macmillan and Company, 1890

12. Graves, B.M. et al., 'The Death of Socrates', Classical Quarterly, 23, 1973, pp. 25-8 and 'Did Socrates Die of Hemlock Poisoning?', New York State Journal of Medicine, 77.1, Feb., 1977, pp. 254-8, 'Hemlock Poisoning: Twentieth Century Scientific Light Shed on the Death of Socrates,' pp. 156-68 in Boudouris, K.J., ed, The Philosophy of Socrates, International Center for Greek Philosophy and Culture, Athens, 1991

13. Plato, *Timæus* — translation Jowett

14. Sass, Louis Arnorsson. *Madness and modernism: Insanity in the light of modern art, literature, and thought*. Basic Books, 1992. Sass suggests this, I've tried to historically back it up.

15. Evans-Wentz, and Yeeling, Walter ed. *The Tibetan book of the dead: Or the after-death experiences on the bardo plane, according to Lama Kazi Dawa-Samdup's English Rendering*. Oxford University Press, 1937. Carl Jung, introduction

16. Noll, Richard, *The Aryan Christ: the Secret Life of Carl Jung*, Random House, 1997.

17. Bakan, David, *Sigmund Freud and the Jewish Mystical Tradition*, Free Association Books, London, 1958/1990

18. Lindahl, JR, Fisher, NE, Cooper, DJ, Rosen, RK, Britton, WB, The varieties of contemplative experience: A mixed-methods study of meditation-related challenges in Western Buddhists, 2017. The varieties of contemplative experience: A mixed-methods study of meditation-related challenges in Western Buddhists. PLOS ONE 12(5): e0176239. https://doi.org/10.1371/journal.pone.0176239

19. Lindahl JR, Fisher NE, Cooper DJ, Rosen RK, Britton WB, The varieties of contemplative experience: A mixed-methods study of meditation-related challenges in Western Buddhists, 2017. The varieties of contemplative experience: A mixed-methods study of meditation-related challenges in Western Buddhists. PLOS ONE 12(5): e0176239. https://journals.plos.org/plosone/article?id=10.1371/journal.pone.0176239

20. Ramsden, Edmund and Adams, Jon. "Escaping the Laboratory: the rodent experiments of John B. Calhoun & their cultural influence", University of Exeter, London School of Economics. 2008 — Calhoun published the results of his early experiments with the rats at NIMH in a 1962 edition of 'Scientific American'. That paper, went on to be one of the most widely cited in psychology. It has since been included as one of "Forty Studies that Changed Psychology," joining papers by such figures as Freud, Pavlov, Milgram, Rorschach, Skinner, and Watson.

    Calhoun, John B. 'Population Density and Social Pathology,' Scientific American, Nov. 1970. p.54

21. Ramsden, Edmund and Adams, Jon"Escaping the Laboratory: the rodent experiments of John B. Calhoun & their cultural influence", University of Exeter, London School of Economics. 2008

22. Ramsden, Edmund and Adams, Jon"Escaping the Laboratory: the rodent experiments of John B. Calhoun & their cultural influence", University of Exeter, London School of Economics. 2008

23. Ramsden, Edmund/Adams, Jon"Escaping the Laboratory: the rodent experiments of John B. Calhoun & their cultural influence", University of Exeter, London School of Economics. 2008

24. Ramsden, Edmund/Adams, Jon"Escaping the Laboratory: the rodent experiments of John B. Calhoun & their cultural influence", University of Exeter, London School of Economics. 2008

CHAPTER SIX
PROOF IDEALISM CAN'T WORK
A BRIEF COURSE IN SCHOLASTIC THOUGHT

"Man's proper perfection consists in the knowledge of the absolute good and in response to beauty. The absolute is the good in itself and source of all goodness in all other things. It is not 'good' mediately as being the cause of something else, but immediately and ultimately as being the end to which all other things are means. Man seeks this end not by his senses, but by his intellect and can obtain it only with his mind. But, man must begin with his senses and gradually advance through higher and higher aspects of the good reflected in the world of contingent things until he is finally ready to see the primal source of all goodness. On this way to the absolute good, beauty is the signpost. Man must therefore begin by learning to respond to beauty as given to the senses and as found in the visible universe, but, he must not dwell in it nor let it conceal that beauty it is meant merely to proclaim. Not all knowledge, therefore, is conducive to the perfection of man and consequently not all knowledge has value in liberal education. All the sciences of space and time, of experience and experiments, of statistics and measurements, such sciences as physics, chemistry, mathematics, biology, history, economics, etc. must find there justification primarily in the practical order."[1]

— BROTHER FRANCIS (FAKHRI MALUF)

Historically, the underlying debate between the two Christian factions has been Idealism vs what is called *Moderate Realism*. Conventionally, Greek philosophy had debated Idealism vs. Realism (Materialism) with no resolution. Aristotle was perhaps the first to propose a middle path, trying to combine the best of both sides. Christianity rejected Materialism out of hand as defective, leaving the other two, a debate that carried through from the beginning. It was the same at the Council of Nicaea, although most accounts today don't show it.

Perhaps the best argument against pure Idealism was that of the Scholastics. In order to understand the rest of this book it is important to be thoroughly convinced of the unviability of pure Idealism.[2]

In the middle of the twentieth century Fr. Celestine Bittle compiled perhaps the last complete anthology of traditional Scholastic thought. Scorned today, Scholasticism was once the cornerstone of Catholic philosophy, the first weapon against both Idealism and Materialism. The method was divided into two parts, the *Trivium* and the *Quadrivium*. The doctrine was summed up in a slogan: "*There is nothing in the intellect that is not first found in the senses.*" Once considered a near necessity, few clergy today are familiar with the doctrine.

Considered the first and most essential part of the *Trivium* was Logic. Bittle called his volume on it *The Science of Correct Thinking,* in the belief that the mind needed to be purged of fallacies before it could appreciate Truth.

About halfway through Bittle's second volume *Epistemology: Reality and the Mind,*[3] lives a chapter entitled 'The Fallacy of Idealism.' While Fr. Bittle illustrates the maze of conflicting philosophies and fallacies that contributed to modern skepticism, he shows that they all are actually an elaboration of one root-idea which he calls the *idealist postulate.*

To do this Bittle re-creates the reasonings of a 'straw man.' But make no mistake, it is the idealist Anglican bishop philosopher George Berkeley (1685–1753). Berkeley is a continuation of an Anglican movement begun by the Cambridge Platonists, led by Ralph Cudworth. Dismayed by Isaac Casaubon's proof that the *Corpus Hermeticum* was a fake, Cudworth continued to practice the philosophy as if the proof had never happened. Like other Modernists, their system is 'true' regardless of the evidence.

Berkeley's based his philosophy on his postulate *esse es percipi* (*to be is to be perceived*). It is commonly known as, "If a tree falls in the forest, and there is no one to hear it, does it make a sound?" By Berkeley's time much of Newton's Enlightenment was affecting the Church. Berkeley represents a cleric trying to save a sense of orthodoxy in the face of an emerging Idealism. Like Rousseau's "Profession of Faith of a Savoyard Vicar," both have decided that a new formula of faith is needed, but it is a piety of despair.

The thought was this: if it was the emerging Idealism that was threatening the church, what is to prevent the Church from switching to that philosophy? If reality is just mind, why can't we dream any reality we choose, why not an orthodox one? In some ways, Berkeley was a harbinger of the quantum theorists of the twentieth century, paradox is not the enemy of truth, it *is* truth. Of course at that time no one realized that the Idealist movement was actually Arianism in disguise.

Berkeley answers his own question in true Idealist fashion: *no, if not heard the sound does not exist.* However, in an attempt to save orthodoxy, he comes up with a novel solution: *but, in the end, the sound does exist because God is always listening.* Berkeley is straddling the dilemma by having a foot in both camps, Modernism and Orthodoxy. He is trying to save the latter by means of the former. But he is at the very nub of the problem. He is not dangerous because he is so flagrantly wrong, but because he is so close to being right.

Berkeley must have believed to some degree in Arianism. His thought system is very similar. To him, like the 'One,' the Spirit is "one simple, undivided, active being." To him, the act of understanding is the direct infusion of the God's Spirit into our perceptions, we hear because God hears. The tree exists when and only because it is being perceived, because *God is always perceiving.*[4]

Whatever were Berkeley's true beliefs, they are between him and his God. But we deceive ourselves if we think his *esse es percipi* has not been used as a convenient way of dismantling belief in general. In some ways, Berkeley's Idealism seems to check all the right boxes. I'm not the creator, God is. It's not my perceptions that create the tree, it is God's. My rituals are not my invention, they are God's. Yet, there still is something very wrong.

BERKELEY'S SOUNDLESS TREE

The flaw is this, in his formulation *reality does not exist independently of mind. Therefore, reality to some degree is counterfeit, a delusion. Its existence requires observation.* Berkeley has sidestepped the issue of human fallibility and accountability. By what means am I morally accountable if my perceptions are all God's? If I perceive a tree falling, and it was actually my uncle, which made the sound, the tree or my uncle? And who made the mistake in perceiving, me or God? Of course, Berkeley would say your uncle for the perception originated with God, but isn't that our point? Where do 'I' fit into the scheme? And if I am mistaken, then, who is accountable for the mistake? Are all the correct perceptions from God and all the incorrect perceptions from me? Somewhere my own discernment must step in.

To test the veracity of Berkeley's system, Bittle converts Berkeley's postulate into a logical syllogism (a logical sequence of thought).[5] It seems almost reasonable:

> Physical things, such as trees, dogs, and houses, are things perceived
>   by sense,
> and things perceived by sense are ideas;
> therefore, physical things are ideas.

If one objects to the first premise, Berkeley could reply, 'name one physical example of something that is not sensed.' The second premise seems true enough, perceptions must become ideas before they become thought. It indeed seems like Berkeley has stumped us, all objects do indeed enter the mind as ideas.

We must ask the question, what is a tree? Or, what is anything for that matter? When we look at it are we looking at a thing or an idea? The fact that both of us can look at something and both recognize it as the same thing means something remarkable must be going on. We call it the same thing, we smell the same thing, if we share our thoughts they too are similar. The Idealist answer does seem like the simplest solution, the Mind of the 'One' is feeding us the information. What we both see is not so much the tree of reality, but the idealized tree in God's mind.

But our individuality is the price to this concession, Aristotle saw things differently. He believed the only true answer was that all 'trees' share a *universal* 'tree-ness' that each person perceives individually. While the senses perceive the shape and color by rote, the mind conceptualizes 'what the tree actually is'. When we first encounter 'tree,' it is like Derrida's abstract word, void of concept. But as we go through life's experiences, the mind conceptually fills in the blanks as we grow in understanding. As we learn we discern, we communicate, we reason, all things denied under the idealist postulate.

The question is, then, is reality necessary? Are my perceptions real or a clever con job? What then is the purpose of reason? If Aristotle is right does not something physical from the object have to leave it and enter my mind as idea? But where is the evidence of this? But even if there were evidence, is it even possible to escape the paradigm? Where, in what organ, does the does the tree convert from a physical object into a conceptual idea?

Scottish philosopher Thomas Reid realized that this dilemma was setting the stage for skepticism, both Kant's and Hume's solution only disguised the problem more than solved it. They were laying the foundation for nihilism. Trying to salvage 'common sense,' the Scottish philosopher Thomas Reid summed up the problem,

"To what cause is it owing that modern philosophers are so prone to fall back into this hypothesis, as if they really believed it? For of this proneness I could give many instances besides this of Mr. Hume; and I take the cause to be, that images in the mind, and images let in by the senses, are so nearly allied, and so strictly connected, that they must stand or fall together. The old system consistently maintained both: but the new system has rejected the doctrine of images let in by the senses, holding, nevertheless, that there are images in the mind; and, having made this unnatural divorce of two doctrines which ought not to be put asunder, that which they have retained often leads them back involuntarily to that which they have rejected.[6]

— THOMAS REID

Reid realized: *perhaps the very notion of witnessing a transition from the real to the idea was wrong.* Early biologist speculated that there was an actual physical organ called the 'common sense' that handled this transition, but autopsies were unable to find it. Looking at the physiology of the eye and its neurological pathways to the brain, Reid asked, 'where exactly does this transition occur? Where does the physical 'thing' become an immaterial idea? It all poses a very real threat to 'common sense.'

To the Idealist the existence of reality is an unnecessary extravagance. Therefore it is expendable. To Plato, each physical 'thing' was merely a representation of its perfection that existed only in the mind of the 'One.' But in this paradigm God is not fully God, and the individual is not fully a person. Therefore, Aristotle solved the problem by moving Plato's idealized 'thing' out of the universal Mind and into substrate of each individual thing calling it *'the Universal.'* While it retains the concepts 'God' and 'individual,' it leads to the dilemma of Berkeley and Reid. The question is this: is it possible to come up with an all-inclusive theory that saves all the evidence?

Aristotle's logic can account for Truth, Plato's can't. Yet, both leave a gap. We cannot say that 'all men are mortal' unless by it we mean that *all,* a *universal*, applies to *each* man. There are many shapes, sizes, and colors of man, just as there are many shapes, sizes, and colors of triangles. The shapes, size and color of a thing determine what kind of thing the thing is—but, they do not determine *what* the thing is. Something else must. But can we prove it? Perhaps never. But perhaps we can prove that the alternative, Idealism, doesn't work.

So, is Berkeley a pure Idealist? Perhaps we will never know. What is for sure is that Berkeley has opened Pandora's box, and Bittle intends to shut it. Fr. Bittle begins with the phrase:

> "Idealism arose out of the difficulty of understanding and explaining how the mind can transcend itself and know extra-mental reality."

Bittle is about to begin his attack on Descartes' "I think, therefore I am." He implies mind has a fascination with creating its own prison by denying reality, and it must be rescued. He explores the problem in terms of a particular mental predicament: *how do I know that the world is not a figment of my own imagination*? Fr. Bittle:

> "The greatest difficulty lies in the fact of the dissimilarity which exists between mind and matter. The mind is mental, while the object is physical... All knowledge, then, since it proceeds from the mind and takes place in the mind, must be purely mental. Physical objects are, therefore, absolutely excluded from knowledge: the objects of knowledge are mental objects, ideas."

> — FR. CELESTINE BITTLE

Indeed, Descartes' skeptical "I think, therefore I am" when distilled becomes Berkeley's "being is perceiving." To say that the object doesn't exist unless it is perceived, is to say it does not necessary exist at all! "This doctrine, that the mind in its knowing can only know its own 'ideas' or 'percepts,' is idealism; and when accepted as an axiom or postulate, it is the *idealist postulate*." Using Berkeley's words:

> "What are the aforementioned objects but the things we perceive by sense? And what do we perceive beside our own ideas and sensations? And is it not plainly repugnant that any of these, or any combination of them, should exist unperceived?"

— GEORGE BERKELEY

Knowingly or not, Berkeley has just stated the Hermetical principle: ideas do not occur just *by the aid of* God, *they are God Himself.* It is the necessary consequence of Idealism—ideas simply have no other source if we cannot believe our senses. *Idealism ultimately provides no corrective if it is wrong.*

Fr. Bittle's proof of the fallacy of the *idealist postulate* is quite interesting and conclusive. The consequence of the postulate is this: objects cease to exist once they cease to be perceived, this is a consequence of all thought just being recollection. Fr. Bittle creates a syllogism to sum up Berkeley:

Ideas or sensations cannot exist unperceived;
But sensible objects are ideas or sensations;
Ergo, sensible objects cannot exist unperceived.

This seems almost logical, but the fallacy is in the second minor premise, that 'sensible objects are ideas and sensations.' True, but sometimes they are not. Berkeley has rigged the conclusion by equivocating the word *are*, he is making sensible objects equivalent to ideas. However, this is exactly what he is trying to prove: he can't assume that which requires proof. To make the objection clearer, Fr. Bittle recasts the argument as a hypothetical, 'if, then' syllogism:

If something has a purely subjective existence, [then] it has a mental
    existence;
But perceived objects have a mental existence;
Ergo, perceived objects have a purely subjective existence.

While both premises are true, the logic is wrong. For example, I can say, if 'A' demands 'B,' it does not necessarily follow that 'B' demands 'A'. All balls may be round, but not all that is round is a ball. It should read 'But perceived objects have a purely subjective existence.' For the logic to work, the syllogism should look like this:

If something has a purely subjective existence, then it has a mental
    existence;
But perceived objects have a purely subjective existence;
Ergo, perceived objects have a mental existence.

The logic works, but so what? What the idealist is trying to prove, that 'being is perceiving,' has yet to be proven: the middle 'but perceived objects have a purely subjective existence,' is not true—'purely' assumes 'only,' 'subjective' assumes 'mental,' together they mean 'only mental.' All along the way the conclusion is assumed in words he is using—the argument is rigged. The only remaining logical formulation of the problem is this:

> If something has a mental existence, then it has a purely subjective
> existence;
> But perceived objects have a mental existence;
> Ergo, perceived objects have a purely subjective existence.

The conclusion logically follows however it is not valid for it is merely a reiteration of the major premise. Fr. Bittle asks: "Is it a fact that, if something has a mental existence, it has a purely subjective existence? This is the very point which the idealist intends to prove by the argument."—one can't assume what one is trying to prove.

In order for a syllogism to be valid, it must stick to three terms—each time used the term must have precisely the same meaning. The syllogism is merely the logical version of the mathematical, If $A = B$, and $B = C$, then must $A = C$. 'B' cannot represent both '4' and '7' or it doesn't work. In other words, this:

> Bars are rods of metal;
> An establishment that sells beer is a bar;
> Ergo, an establishment that sells beer is a rod of metal.

The term bar has been equivocated. We can now see this in Berkeley's original postulate:

> Physical things, such as trees, dogs, and houses, are things perceived
> by sense,
> and things perceived by sense are ideas;
> therefore, physical things are ideas.

'Things perceived' are not necessarily 'ideas.' As Reid has pointed out, 'physical things' are perceived, ideas can also be considered 'things,' but you cannot *perceive* an idea, ideas are only *conceived* by the mind. To *perceive* and to *conceive* are two separate faculties. Is this fact enough to declare that the entirety of reality is a fraud?

There are realities that are exclusively mental, such as dreams, but that does not disprove realities not perceived by the mind. And really, wouldn't a God that must constantly service the perceptive whims of each individual be sort of a *Deus ex machina*, perceptions popping and disappearing like a carnival ride? The reality of dreams, does not prove reality is a dream.

To quote Cardinal Mercier from his *Criteriology*, "The contention of the realists is that we can be certain of the existence of the external world." His proof is this:

"Argument drawn from the passive character of sensations.—We are conscious that we are the subject of certain internal experiences in the presence of which we are purely passive. These facts of experience require a sufficient reason for their occurrence. Now since our consciousness bears us testimony that we are passive, this sufficient reason must be, at least in part, exterior to ourselves. Therefore some reality outside the ego must exist, there must be an external world."[7]

— CARDINAL DÉSIRÉ FÉLICIEN FRANÇOIS JOSEPH
MERCIER

The world we perceive unfolds predictably, but more often unpredictably. Of much of this we have no part. It is not just a question of causality, but of efficiency. Do we really expect a Divinity to act both predictably and randomly, orchestrating every little nuance of my thoughts but everyone else's. Can we really hold God accountable for not only every blessing, but every corruption, no matter how grand or minor, there is? C. S. Lewis:

"Each particular thought is valueless if it is the result of irrational causes. Obviously, then, the whole process of human thought, that we call Reason, is equally valueless if it is the result of irrational causes. Hence, every theory of the universe which makes the mind a result of irrational causes is inadmissible, for it would be a proof that there are no such proofs. Which is nonsense. But Naturalism, as commonly held, is precisely a theory of this sort."[8]

— CLIVE STAPLES LEWIS, OXFORD THEOLOGIAN

A world based on Idealism is, in truth, the furthest from what it claims: while I don't believe the pure Idealist exists anymore, his replacement is one who believes the Ideal is achievable. He look out into the physical and sees only mathematical formulas and chemicals. His equations leave no room for morality. It leaves man in a world where any opinion is as good as the next.

While we may struggle to find absolute truths, we seldom find what we seek. It is not that our search is in vain, or that there is nothing certain at the end of our search. We must accept that there are realities beyond definition, beyond description. We can 'know,' but we will never know exhaustively… nor should we try. We look at the Moon, we know there must be a backside even though we may never see it. The proof in the righteousness of our cause is not in the proof, it is that the alternative doesn't work.

---

1. Maluf, Fakhri (Brother Francis). From a *Philosophia Perennis: Course on Scholasticism*, St. Augustine Institute, https://store.catholicism.org/complete-philosophy-mp3-set.html

2. The following argument is in homage to Brother Francis (Fakhri Maluf) From a *Philosophia Perennis: Course on Scholasticism*, St. Augustine Institute, Brother Francis (Fakhri Maluf) https://store.catholicism.org/complete-philosophy-mp3-set.html

3. Today Epistemology is considered the science of knowing. Scholastics typically treated the subject as the science of error and how it could be corrected.

4. Encyclopædia Britannica, *Article on George Berkeley*, 1994-2001

5. Argument derived from Bittle. Celestine N., O.F.M. Cap. 'Fallacy of Idealism,' *Reality and the Mind: Epistemology*, Bruce Pub., Milw. 1936

6. Reid, Thomas. Derek R. Brookes ed. *An Inquiry into the Human Mind on the Principles of Common Sense,* 1764. Edinburgh UP. 1997

7. Mercier, Cardinal Désiré. *A manual of modern scholastic philosophy.* Vol. 1. K. Paul, Trench, Trubner & Company, 1916. p. 394

8. Lewis, C. S., *Miracles,* Macmillan Publishing Co., New York, 1947, p. 21.

THE CHURCH INFECTED

"For the other Arians, who took their cue from Lucian and Origen and were companions of a sophist named Asterius who lapsed in the persecution under Maximian, ***did not disclose the whole of their heresy about the Son.***"[1]

— SALAMIS, *THE PANARION OF EPIPHANIUS*

"Upon the foundation of the Platonic philosophy, with an abundance of heterogeneous materials, collected from every other sect, was erected an irregular, cumbrous, and useless edifice, called the Eclectic School. The founders of this sect formed the flattering design of selecting, from the doctrines of all former philosophers, such opinions as seemed to approach nearest the truth, and combining them into one system. But in executing this plan, they did nothing better than pile up a shapeless and incoherent mass, *rudis indigestaque moles* not unlike that chaos, which they admitted as an essential article in their doctrine of nature. In some particulars, indeed, they attempted to adorn and enrich the system with fancies of their own..."[2]

— WILLIAM ENFIELD

MODERNISM AS IGNORANCE

Few people today are aware that the post-1960s Church has little to do with the pre-1960s Church. The principles of Vatican II did not just effect the Catholic Church, it effected all churches. Yet, the Church of today is the only one most people have ever known, the old is not even a distant memory. While many still have the same outward appearances, underneath very little is the same. Even the conservative churches have not been immune.

The core of this change we call *Modernism*. It is not based on a new core principle, it is the question whether core principles even exist at all. In this vacuum, Modernism has filled the void with a collection of 'eclectic truths,' something it calls 'diversity.' Yet, there is little notice that many of these 'truths' are incompatible with each other. In the end, this perpetuates the new notion that there is no Truth and no Absolutes whatsoever. If we regard Truth as 'Logos,' and Absolutes as 'God,' it should be immediately apparent that this can provide no foundation for a Church. Modernism is just this, *the principle of ignorance*. This is Arianism. Modernism was condemned by Pope Pius X in the encyclical *Pascendi Gregis* as precisely this.

> "If we pass on from the moral to the intellectual causes of Modernism, the first and the chief which presents itself is ignorance. Yes, these very Modernists who seek to be esteemed as Doctors of the Church, who speak so loftily of modern philosophy and show such contempt for scholasticism, have embraced the one with all its false glamour, precisely because their ignorance of the other has left them without the means of being able to recognise confusion of thought and to refute sophistry. Their whole system, containing as it does errors so many and so great, has been born of the union between faith and false philosophy."
>
> — POPE PIUS X, *THE DOCTRINE OF THE MODERNISTS*

Today, Modernism has evolved into a movement called *progressivism*. It is sold to the public as just 'keeping up with the times.' None of this is what it professes to be. No one would contest with having a more efficient car, a more healthy food supply, safer work environments, etc. While progressivism rides the wave of technology, seldom has it invented anything, seldom does it end poverty, seldom does it understand that which it professes, seldom does it create an actual utopia. Yet it believes whole-heartedly in its own superiority, its own inevitability.

Dare I say that its real cause is not progress, but the belief that Truth is drag on progress—if we were to merely adopt an all-inclusive *laissez faire* attitude, then surely some undefined utopian force would emerge and save us. All we need to do is tear down the icons of the past, stand aside, and let it engulf us. Removing impediments and memories of the past allows the formation of the 'One.' Man has been reduced to a virus, an infection on the host organism, Gaia. He is in the way.

While I think Enfield has brought a critical insight into the discussion, I also believe he is partially wrong. Enfield, a Unitarian, believed that the early Church Fathers were infected with Orientalism, and there is some evidence of this. But he fails to realize that Arianism is just Orientalism by another name. He therefore never realizes that Unitarianism is just an outgrowth of Arius. Not understanding this, on Nicaea he has taken the wrong side since. The Council did seem to struggle with this, but it did come to understand correctly.

Prior to the Council Enfield's history is spot on, he recognizes and defines the emerging heresy. But by the time he reaches Nicaea he makes a grave error, *he sees the heresy that was influencing the Council, but glosses over the true debate. While he provides valuable evidence, he fails to continue the story through to the end.* Being a worshiper of Isaac Newton, he must vindicate Arius as does Newton. It was Newton who gave birth to the modern Unitarians, it was Newton who was a closet Arian, and it was Newton who began his cause by attacking the verse found at 1 John 5:7, the very verse the Arian party found repugnant. The very verse they persuaded Constantine to remove from the 'official' Bible.

The problem is this: while the Council correctly identified some *members* of the cult, it never completely understood the *nature* of the cult. We do that by connecting Arius' theology back to Corinth's. By never fully understanding the Arian pedigree, it was never able to defeat it.

THE PEDIGREE OF ARIANISM

When the ancient Jews contemplated their manifold of gods they came to the conclusion that this was an impossibility. They realized that for god to be 'God' would mean that He could only be 'One.' He could not have a competitor. With this came the realization that while God could be known, He could not be known *exhaustively*—the essence of God was always protected by the Holiest of Holies, a mystery beyond comprehension.

Arianism sought to reverse this. While creating an insurmountable gulf between Man and God's creation, it proposed that the whole of God could be experienced through the inner thoughts of the believer.

What could be more evidential than one's own inner thoughts? And with God permanently divorced from his creation, it opened the door for a perpetual 'scientific' investigation in search for the 'One.' The process mimics the Fall of Man.

At the Enlightenment, Arianism became disguised as the *Scientific Method*. It was heresy dressed up with scientific terms. Arians like Isaac Newton convinced the world that the highest 'truths' could all be assimilated into one Grand Unifying equation that could explain it all.

The essence of Arianism is a complete mis-understanding of the *ubiquity* of God. In thought it contends God is everywhere. In material it contends God is nowhere. Therefore, all that is material must be thought also, it has no alternative. Certainly I think, I see other animals that think, but I have yet to find a rock that thinks. Because this argument fails, they must find some other ubiquitous nature, a property that is everywhere, yet nowhere.

For example, most things have weight or mass—they are properties all tangible things have. Yet, the Arian maintains that the essence of God cannot be found in things that have weight and mass. So, he must find an ubiquitous mass-less property. So, let's consider that both weight and ideas are sort of attractions, let's call them gravity, something with mathematical properties. But wait, we've excluded human attraction, let's include that. And aren't these all, then, a sort of '*love*.' And is this not what the Bible says, that 'God is love'? And, is not 'love' sort of like the Golden Rule? And, of course, let's not forget that love is blind. And what about judging? Let's not do that either. And, can I really say my love is more virtuous than yours? So, let's twist the Golden Rule around to accommodate our new-found wisdom—let's make it a blanket permission to allow whatever one wills, as long as I permit the same to everyone else. Now that's true love! There you have it, a simple faith for the modern world. Open the church doors!

It is this that is at the core of Newton's Arianism—it is what Marsilio Ficino called *Platonic Love*, a sort of non-gendered *eroticism*, nothing more. Similarly, so is light. The ubiquitous nature of gravity and light have virtually none of the other qualities of God except this ubiquity. Yet, this is now the 'scientific' essence of God.

This having been said, we now have to go back into the history of philosophy I find its proper birth. From the beginning, this philosophy was a marriage of incompatible doctrines all cleverly massaged to appear as One. From Enfield:

"A clear judgment may, after what has been said, be without much difficulty formed, concerning this new race of Platonists. The peculiar respect which they paid to the doctrines of Plato and Pythagoras, as in some sort of Divine original, rested upon suppositions which have never been established. The story of Pythagoras's journey into the East is extremely uncertain; and it is highly improbable that he should ever have conversed with Hebrew prophets. Of his school, which had failed at a very early period, little was known. The whole notion of the Divine original of Plato's theology is built upon such slight evidence, that it may, without hesitation, be pronounced visionary. The Cabbalistic tenets, upon which these philosophers laid so much stress, were not, as they supposed, the pure doctrines of the Hebrews, but mystical fictions derived from Egyptian and Oriental sources. The tenets of the Platonic and of the Cabbalistic systems differed essentially from the sacred truths which are taught in the Hebrew scriptures. It is not to be conceived, that the fanciful doctrine of emanation, which lies at the foundation of both these systems, could have been derived by tradition from Divine Revelation.

Yet, so much were these learned men blinded by prejudice in favour of an hypothesis, that they could see nothing but a perfect harmony between Platonism and Christianity, and mistook the dreams of the Alexandrian philosophers, and Jewish Cabbalistics, for the pure doctrine of religion. To this we must add, that they suffered themselves, in some instances, to be deceived by impostors; and with a degree of credulity not wholly to be excused, admitted spurious writings as genuine; such for example, as the remains of Zoroaster, Hermes, and Orpheus. From these and other causes they were led into so many misconceptions and errors, that caution should be exercised in acceding to their judgment concerning either Platonic or Christian doctrines."[3]

Plato's radical Idealism was never by itself enough to be a threat to true philosophy, or to undermine religious faith. To do that it needed to be united to the *prospect of human perfectibility*. This is why the unification of Plato's Idealism with Pythagoras' mathematics was so vital to their cause. Where Plato provided the ideas, Pythagoras provided the perfection. The abstractions of Pythagoras were filled in by Plato's mysticism.

This 'perfectibility' is a subtle feature. When the math teacher asks you to calculate how long it takes for Suzy to go from Chicago to New York, we think nothing of the fact that our precise mathematical answer would never be attained in reality. When the astronomer calculates to the thousandth of a second how long it takes the Earth to revolve around the Sun, we make no mind of the fact that it would be impossible to pinpoint the starting and finishing point. When the Schrödinger's cat bumps up against his world of quantum paradox he doesn't turn around and go back, he insists that opposites can both be true. The absurdity of this led astronomer Sir Fred Hoyle to remark that the modern astronomer seldom even uses his telescope, his calculator is all he needs.

It was precisely this, the imagined marriage of Plato to Pythagoras that birthed the heresy of all thought. It led us to believe that the perfect triangle actually existed somewhere in idea, and that in 'idea' alone would be our perfection.

THE FIRST GNOSTICS

The New Testament speaks frequently of an *anti-Christianity*. Conventionally it is believed this began with Simon the Magician (Acts 8:9), and was picked up Marcion of Sinope. This anti-Christianity is commonly regarded as 'Gnosticism.' However, true Gnosticism doesn't get going until the late second century. So, is the Bible wrong?

St. Polycarp, disciple of St. John (the 'disciple of the Lord' who knew Christ Himself), denounced Marcion as being the "first-born of Satan." Indeed, the ancient prologue to the forth Gospel was this:

> "The gospel of John was published and given to the churches by John while he was still in the body, as Papias of Hierapolis, John's dear disciple, has related in his five exoteric, that is his last, books. He wrote down the gospel accurately at John's dictation. But, the heretic Marcion was rejected by John, having been condemned by him for his contrary views. Marcion had carried writings or letters to him from the brothers in Pontus."[4]

Therefore, the quintessential heresy must have been birthed before John's Gospel and promoted by Marcion. But why would Papias seek out John? What was the sense of urgency?

While I doubt that many theologians have heard of him, the true enemy of the Church was named *Cerinthus*. It was he who fabricated his own Gospel *falsely attributing it to St. John*. It was in response to this that John wrote his Gospel. It is this that I hope to show was the basis of the Arian heresy.

Conventionally, *Cerinthus'* gospel has been called '*the secret Apocryphon of John*' (aka the *Secret Revelation of John*) along with numerous other affiliated texts. It was these that inspired men of the Enlightenment such as Isaac

Newton and John Milton as the 'knowledge falsely so called.' The following is from Irenæus' *Against Heresies,* who was a disciple of Polycarp. You will notice it shows a direct attack on *Logos* by Cerinthus. No reputable scholar could doubt this:

"John, the disciple of the Lord, preaches this faith, and seeks, by the proclamation of the Gospel, to remove that error which by *Cerinthus* had been disseminated among men, and a long time previously by those termed Nicolaitans, who are an offset of that ***"knowledge" falsely so called,*** that he might confound them, and persuade them that there is but one God, who made all things by His Word (*Logos*); and not, as they allege, that the Creator was one, but the Father of the Lord another; and that the Son of the Creator was, forsooth, one, but the Christ from above another, who also continued impossible, descending upon Jesus, the Son of the Creator, and flew back again into His *Pleroma*; and that *Monogenes* was the beginning, but Logos was the true son of *Monogenes*; and that this creation to which we belong was not made by the primary God, but by some power lying far below Him, and shut off from communion with the things invisible and ineffable. The disciple of the Lord therefore desiring to put an end to all such doctrines, and to establish the rule of truth in the Church, that there is one Almighty God, who made all things by His Word, both visible and invisible; showing at the same time, that by the Word, through whom God made the creation, He also bestowed salvation on the men included in the creation; thus commenced His teaching in the Gospel: "In the beginning was the Word (*Logos*), and the Word was with God, and the Word was God. The same was in the beginning with God. All things were made by Him, and without Him was nothing made. What was made was life in Him, and the life was the light of men. And the light shineth in darkness, and the darkness comprehended it not." "All things," he says, "were made by Him;" therefore in "all things" this creation of ours is, for we cannot concede to these men that "all things" are spoken in reference to those within their *Pleroma*. For if their *Pleroma* do indeed contain these, this creation, as being such, is not outside, as I have demonstrated in the preceding book; but if they are outside the *Pleroma*, which indeed appeared impossible, it follows, in that case, that their *Pleroma* cannot be "all things:" therefore this vast creation is not outside [the *Pleroma*]."[5]

— ST. IRENÆUS, *AGAINST HERESIES*

St. John and the heretic Cerinthus in the bathhouse, 1701 engraving
by Jan Luyken—Rijksmuseum, - CC0, via Wikimedia Commons

Notice the reference to "knowledge falsely so called." This very phrase from the Bible has been historically met with much contention, sometimes defining it as 'science,' sometimes 'philosophy.'

1 Timothy 6:20 — O Timothy, guard that which is committed unto *thee*, turning away from the profane babblings and oppositions of the ***knowledge which is falsely so called***;

Historically the phrase was something of a mystery, but here it is precisely spelled out by someone within the early apostolic chain—it is precisely any teaching that undermines *Logos* and associates it with the *pleroma*. The reasoning is precisely consistent with that of 1 John 5:7.

So what is the *pleroma*? The world of the Occult makes no mistake of their own heritage. Their pedigree leads directly back to Plato and Pythagoras. As an example, here is a cut from *The Secret Teaching of All Ages,* by self-acclaimed Occultist and Freemason Manly P. Hall:

"The Platonic discipline was founded upon the theory that learning is really reminiscence, or the bringing into objectivity of knowledge formerly acquired by the soul in a previous state of existence. At the entrance of the Platonic school in the Academy were written the words: "Let none ignorant of geometry enter here.""[6]

— MANLY HALL

A representative of this is Hermeticism. It was this that continued the teachings of Cerinthus. The doctrine is found in *Pomandres,* the first tract of the *Corpus Hermeticum,* a Gnostic paraphrase of the very 'light and life' verse quoted above by Irenæus. This is how Hermeticists define themselves:

The heart of the Hermetic teaching. . . is the realization that the individual is fundamentally no different from the Supreme [God]. This realization is *gnosis*, a single, immediate event, characterized as a second birth.[7]

— CLEMENT SALAMAN, COMMENTARY ON
HERMETICISM

"The account which we have given of the Pythagoric doctrine concerning the Divine nature is confirmed by Cicero, who asserts that **Pythagoras conceived God to be a soul pervading all nature, of which every human soul is a portion**; a doctrine perfectly consonant to the opinions received in the countries which Pythagoras visited, and where he learned theology. Clemens Alexandrinus, speaking of the tenets of the Pythagoreans, says, that they held God to be ψυχωσις τω ολω κυκλω the animating principle of the universal sphere ... it may be concluded with much appearance of probability, that Pythagoras conceived the Deity to be the informing soul of the world, animating it in a manner similar to that in which the human soul animates the body."[8]

— WILLIAM ENFIELD

GNOSTICISM INFECTS THE EARLY CHURCH

What the Gnostics called 'Logos' was actually the *Pleroma* (their abode of the spiritual universe). Knowledge was not contained in the individual, or learned through experience, but was this animating *Pleroma.* It was the conduit through which all knowledge passed. To be outside the *Pleroma* meant to be ignorant. The *Pleroma* sidestepped the need for an observable reality. It was this concept that passed into modern science in its seeking the animated principle of the cosmos.

This is a problem. As the *Pleroma* is 'the spiritual *abode* of God,' a *place* where all are destined, it by definition means it must pre-exist God. It is not God, it is the *dwelling* of the Mind-continuum. It means God is not above all, nor the First Cause, but secondary to this *Pleroma*.

If you understand this you understand the true dilemma at the Council of Nicaea—by identifying *Logos* with the *Pleroma* we must ask, does *Logos pre-exist God*, or does *Logos* emanate *from God*. It creates a *Euthyphro-like dilemma*—does God follow laws, or does God make laws? The first way relegates God secondary to reason, the second makes reason an arbitrary construct of God—should God want He could decree that 2+2=5 and then later change His mind and make it equal 7, undermining the concept of the Absolute. The only solution to the dilemma is to make *Logos* an aspect of the God-Head. Again, it was precisely this that John's Gospel in conjunction with 1 John 5:7 did.

As Enfield saw it, the Bible's use of the term *Logos* was problematic. Both the Platonists and the Aristotelians used their own versions making it critical to determine which version was authentic to the Bible. Interpreted wrongly, the *Orientalist* understanding of Scripture is warranted.

According to Enfield, this all started with Aristobulus (c. 2nd century BC). Rather than see *Logos* as a refined method of Truth, Aristobulus tried to find its exposition in parallel cultures. He envisioned Greek philosophy as having its roots in Jewish thought, merely a method of living the best possible life. Successful for a while as *epicureanism*, it eventually turned into *hedonism*. The system is essentially *eclecticism*, each person inventing their own religion of 'self.' Quoting Enfield:

"The Eclectic sect took its rise at Alexandria in Egypt; a country which, in more remote periods, had admitted foreign dogmas and superstitions, particularly after the invasion of the Persians. Egypt having in consequence of the conquests of Alexander become a part of the Grecian empire, the Egyptian priests accommodated themselves, not only to the laws and manners, but even to the speculative tenets of their conquerors. That they might not appear inferior to the Greeks in learning, they affected to admire and adopt their philosophy. The Pythagoric and Platonic systems, especially, gained an easy admission into the Egyptian schools, on account of the respect which they paid to religion, and the opportunities which they afforded of reconciling vulgar superstitions and vernacular traditions with systematic science."[9]

The result was the Egyptian school mapping itself onto the Greek, giving it an artificial 'Egyptian' provenance. Hermes became Thoth, Plato became Pythagoras. This further promoted the Eclectic system, but it demanded marriages that are chronologically impossible. Over time, this Eclecticism became very appealing to Rome. This provided an opportunity for *Iamblicus* to found the Neoplatonic school, a school which all the other schools could be assimilated.

Iamblicus (Ἰάμβλιχος) (c.245 – c.325 AD) was a student of both Porphyry and Plotinus (who considered himself a sort of second Plato). Plotinus himself was a student of *Ammonius Saccas* (175 – 242 AD) from around 232 until the end of Saccas' life. While not much is known about *Saccas,* it is clear he developed the philosophy of Neoplatonism by evidence of the students he taught. It is conjectured that he is of Egyptian birth, but was taught in Indian *Vedanta,* explaining why Neoplatonism is so similar. *Saccas* once considered himself a Christian, but probably fell away later in life.

While *Iamblicus* was schooled in their Neoplatonic school, the philosophy as yet was only that, a philosophy. *Iamblicus,* perhaps the first Free Mason at least in spirit, envisioned it as a religion, integrating it with ritual symbolism and mathematical mysticism. He did this by uniting the schools of Aristotle and Plato with Pythagoras, who he regarded as a near god. To this he added a sprinkling of Simon the Magician.

The system was based upon a concept called *theurgy,* meaning "divine working," derived from the Chaldean Oracles. Essentially it was a syncretic system of paganism coupled to an erotic mental unification with God.

This doctrine has been documented by Porphyry, the biographer of Plotinus. The relevant points are found in his writing, the *Enneads,* derived from *Timæus,* one of the philosophers surveyed by Plato:

"There is a reason, then, why the soul of this All should be sent into it from God: in the same way the soul of each single one of us is sent, that the universe may be complete; it was necessary that all beings of the Intellectual should be tallied by just so many forms of living creatures here in the realm of sense....This state long maintained, the soul is a deserter from the All; its differentiation has severed it; its vision is no longer set in the Intellectual; it is a partial thing, isolated, weakened, full of care, intent upon the fragment; severed from the whole, it nestles in one form of being; for this, it abandons all else, entering into and caring for only the one, for a thing buffeted about by a world-ful of things: thus it has drifted away from the universal and, by an actual presence, it administers the particular; it is caught into contact now, and tends to the outer to which it has become present and into whose inner depths it henceforth sinks far."[10]

— FROM THE FOURTH ENNEAD DERIVED FROM PLATO'S
TIMÆUS

"That the Soul of every individual is one thing we deduce from the fact that it is present entire at every point of the body — the sign of veritable unity — not some part of it here and another part there. In all sensitive beings the sensitive soul is an omnipresent unity, and so in the forms of vegetal life the vegetal soul is entire at each several point throughout the organism.

Now are we to hold similarly that your soul and mine and all are one, and that the same thing is true of the universe, the soul in all the several forms of life being one soul, not parcelled out in separate items, but an omnipresent identity?

If the soul in me is a unity, why need that in the universe be otherwise seeing that there is no longer any question of bulk or body? And if that, too, is one soul and yours, and mine, belongs to it, then yours and mine must also be one: and if, again, the soul of the universe and mine depend from one soul, once more all must be one."[11]

— FROM THE NINTH ENNEAD

Further evidence of Iamblicus' thought can be found in his *Theology of Arithmetic,* a clear indication that he was equating God with the mathematical Monad, God was numbers. The basis of this is that the *Pleroma* is virtually identical to God the Monad. Enlightenment is the realization that God has no counterpart in nature whatsoever and that contradiction is no problem to a mathematical god. Iamblicus' book begins with the following paragraph:

"Nicomachus says that God coincides with the monad, since he is seminally everything which exists, just as the monad is in the case of number; and there are encompassed in it in potential things which, when actual, seem to be extremely opposed (in all the ways in which things may, generally speaking, be opposed), just as it is seen, throughout the *Introduction to Arithmetic,* to be capable, thanks to its ineffable nature, of becoming all classes of things, and to have encompassed the beginning, middle and end of all things (whether we understand them to be composed by continuity or by juxtaposition), because the monad is the beginning, middle and end of quantity, of size and moreover of every quality."[12]

— IAMBLICUS, *THE THEOLOGY OF ARITHMETIC*

"The wise speak as follows: the soul having a twofold life, one being in conjunction with body, but the other being separate from all body; when we are awake we employ, for the most part, the life which is common with the body, except when we separate ourselves entirely from it by pure intellectual and dianoetic energies. But when we are asleep, we are perfectly liberated, as it were, from certain surrounding bonds, and use a life separated from generation."[13]

— IAMBLICUS

By the time of the Council of Nicaea, Iamblicus' version of Neoplatonism was being embraced by some influential Christians, pressuring Constantine and his family as a legitimate form of Christianity. Over time it began to be embraced by the Imperial family, and later fully by Emperor Julian the Apostate. Eventually Julian the Apostate shed the Christian parts and became a full blown Neoplatonist:

"This prince [Julian the Apostate] not only encouraged letters by his patronage, but was himself a learned writer. It is easy to perceive, from a slight inspection of his works, that he strictly adhered to the Alexandrian or ECLECTIC school. He professes himself a warm admirer of Pythagoras and Plato, and recommends a union of their tenets with those of Aristotle. The later Platonists of his own period, he loads with encomiums, particularly Jamblicus [Iamblicus], whom he calls The Light of the World, and The Physician of the Mind. Amidst the numerous traces of an enthusiastic and bigotted attachment to Pagan theology and philosophy, and of an inveterate enmity to Christianity, which are to be found in his writings, the candid reader will discern many marks of genius and erudition."[14]

— WILLIAM ENFIELD

Eventually the sect became so powerful it nearly wiped out the Church.

FROM THE MIDDLE AGES ON

Conventional history runs something like this: the early Classical 'enlight-ened' Age ended with the fall of the Roman Empire, shortly after the Council of Nicaea. From then until the Renaissance was the Dark Ages, considered an age of ignorance and repression. Some go so far as to believe the Christian Church died, not to be re-discovered again until the Reformation. People of the Dark Ages had superstitious beliefs in witches, hobgoblins and magic potions, often promoted by the Catholic Church. Before Columbus, everyone thought that the earth was flat. Before Galileo, everyone thought that the earth was in the center of the universe. Without clocks there was no time. An eclipse was the Sun being devoured by a dragon. In winter, the Sun had to be prayed to so that it would return next spring. What the world was waiting for were the prophets of reason.

But then along came the men of science. It was they who boldly stepped into this pit of dragons and saved the world from itself. All visionaries, they dispelled all the myths and superstitions of the past and opened the way for scholarly pursuits. As dispassionate observers of reality, they would come to objective conclusions, saving us all from the oppression of the Church. The 'New-Man' could now be free to re-invent the cosmos around himself. It would only be a matter of time before the Church would beg to be included among their ranks.

No story could be further from the truth. Facing an Islamic embargo on papyrus and spices, Europe returned to an agrarian society with little means of documenting itself. This allowed room for the invention of the 'Dark Ages,' an invention of one who called himself *Petrarch*. He records that on April 26, 1336 he was the first to climb *Mount Ventoux* (no matter people had been climbing it all along), looked out, pulled out a plum, and said, 'what a good boy am I!'

Well, not really, but his claim was just as outrageous. He claimed to be the first person to have seen and appreciate beauty. It was this act that began the process of moving the Dark Ages to the Enlightenment. One would think that such an epiphany would have inspired him to embrace this new found 'outer' beauty—not exactly. Among his first words were this:

"I turned my inward eye upon myself, and from that time not a syllable fell from my lips until we reached the bottom again. ... [W]e look about us for what is to be found only within."

— PETRARCH

A fan of St. Augustine, Petrarch then turned to his writings. There he finds the words, 'Platonism is the next closest thing to Christianity.' Disregarding Augustine's warnings against Hermeticism, Petrarch plunges into establishing Iamblicus' Platonism as the true inspiration of Christian doctrine. This sets the stage for future Platonists like Marsilio Ficino who, sponsored by the wealthy Medicis, charted a path to integrate Hermeticism within Christian doctrine. Occult texts like the *Corpus Hermeticum,* and Plato's Academies once shut down by the Church, were once again allowed to flourish.

It is difficult for us today to appreciate the full absurdity of Petrarch's claim. We look around and see all the technology and conveniences of modern life and find it easy to accept the propaganda, that all people that came before us were ignorant. But if we look at the accomplishments of a Roger Bacon, a Theodoric of Freiberg, or a Robert Grosseteste we can realize how truly 'scientific' the later Dark Ages truly were. Already they were using the scientific method to discover, making theories that are still profound. We believe that clocks and computers were impossible before the industrial era, yet, what do we make of it when an analog computer with finely machined gears is found dating back to 200 BC (the Antikythera Device)? This prodded Dorothy Sayer to write in 1947 in her *Lost Tools of Learning*:

"...if we are to produce a society of educated people, fitted to preserve their intellectual freedom amid the complex pressures of our modern society, we must turn back the wheel of progress some four or five hundred years, to the point at which education began to lose sight of its true object, towards the end of the Middle Ages."[15]

— DOROTHY SAYER

And indeed, soon after Bacon and Grosseteste things did begin to erode. It was here that the Scholastics succumbed to the assaults of the Petrarchs and the Ficinos. It was Sayer's belief that while this method ceased to be taught hundreds of years before her, the rationale of it lingered on until *1947* when she wrote her piece (remember that date). It was the abandonment of the

Scholastic *Trivium* and *Quadrivium* in education that caused the decline of society. This wasn't by accident.

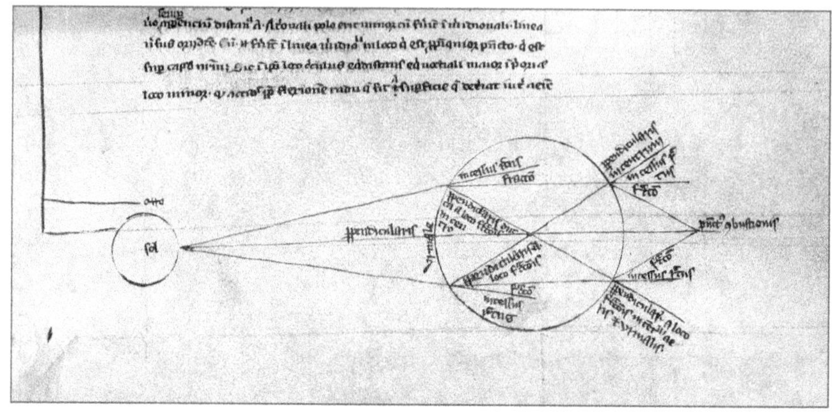

Roger Bacon's (1219–1292) analysis of light's refraction traveling through a spherical container of water - public domain

Not only were the Dark Ages not dark, the Scholastics built their system as a continuation of what came before such as St. Anselm and St. John Damascene. The New-Men of the Renaissance, however, were obsessed with finding the most ancient documents consistent with Plato to justify their schemes. Already we see the emerging scheme, that age trumps reason. They weren't objective observers. They were seeking a rationale for their preferred system of thought, something to make scholasticism obsolete. By appealing to the notion that real truth was within, they embarked on deconstructing history and education. With no reality to correct them, it implied that ALL could be known simply by excavating the mind for ideas. It is this notion of perfectibility that undergirds their system, that the quest for knowledge can be both completed and made obsolete.

SCIENCE AS GNOSTIC MYSTICISM

The term *science* had its first public usage in the British Royal Society, the 'invisible scientific college' modeled around the Rosicrucian ideal of a secret academy guarding eternal wisdom. The term is attributed to William Whewell who began using it in 1834. Before this, *science* merely meant 'knowledge consistent with observation.' It replaced the term 'natural philosophy.' Today the term is synonymous with 'advanced thinking' or 'higher thinking.'

They would have you believe that no one was 'scientific' before Newton, the inventor of the Scientific Method. But this is not true. Twelfth century with scholars like Grosseteste, Bacon, and Theodoric of Freiberg, and the like, were already engaged in the scientific method. Often these were built upon discoveries inherited from Eastern Christian refugees fleeing from Islam.

So what did the more modern 'great' scientists like Isaac Newton, René Descartes, and François Champollion bring to the table? How did they become the fathers of modern science? The answer is Hermeticism, the *pleroma*, through the writings of people like Athanasius Kircher. It was not that science didn't exist before then, it is that *NOW* all science had incorporated the Hermetic principle.

Like the marriage of Plato to Pythagoras, the cult of Hermes is essentially the marriage of a rather mundane Greek Bacchanalian lust cult to the mythical Egyptian God of writing and truth, Thoth. *Plato in his own writings admits Thoth is a made up tale!*

Rather than a declaration of *sinfulness* as in Christianity, it was expected that one would make a declaration of *innocence*. The basis of this confession was the ability of one to maintain a deniability of intent for one's sins before God (Anubis – Osiris); if one could prove wise enough to understand the two-fold, paradoxical nature of truth, one could claim truth was unknowable, thus unaccountable for one's actions.

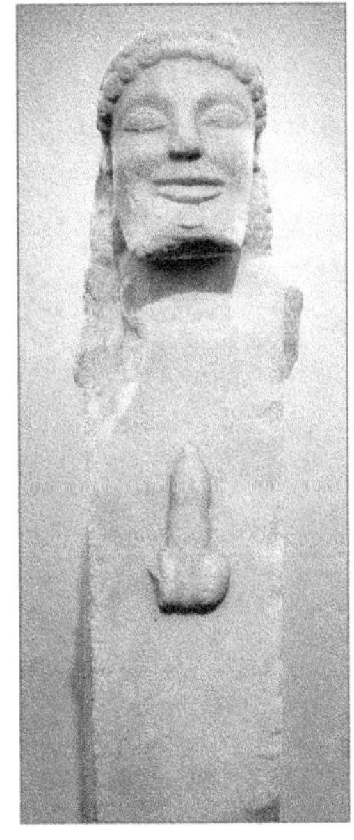

A Hermai *with erect phallus such as were destroyed in 415 BC by the youthful school of Socrates. Marble, ca. 520 BC. National Archaeological Museum of Athens. From Siphnos. Ricardo André Frantz (User:Tetraktys), 2006 Creative Commons, https:// en.wikipedia.org/wiki/File: 0007MAN-Herma.jpg*

This served as the basis for future Gnostic traditions to come. It is truth-as-paradox that is its distinguishing feature. Paradox has no mandate over what one should do, therefore, one is only accountable for their intentions.

To bolster this claim the Egyptian hieroglyphs were presented as if they were extremely ancient—to unlock their meaning was to unlock a lost profound wisdom passed down from the primordial language of Adam, to Plato. To unlock this language was to unlock mystical powers.

Modern scholarship has shown that most of these hieroglyphs were not mystical at all, just accounting records from when Egypt was an economic super power. Early Egyptologists like Jesuit *Athanasius Kircher* never actually tried to decipher them at all. Rather, believing they conveyed original primordial 'archetypes,' to read the hieroglyphs meant to prod these ancient reminisces in the mind. This opened the door to translating them in any such way as served your purpose. The mystic could claim he was 'God-like,' and who could prove him wrong?

Remember the Scholastic phrase, 'there is nothing in the Mind that is not first in the senses.' This meant that knowledge must be acquired. The mind was considered a *Tabla Rasa*, a blank sheet onto which everything one knew or experienced was written. This means the Word as '*Logos*' has a specific purpose—not only did it facilitate knowledge, it provided the logical structure for reason, a faculty available to each individual. *It was this that was offensive to the Platonist scheme and was confounded by the verse found at 1 John 5:7.*

---

1. Epiphanius, Saint, Frank Williams, and Karl Holl. *The Panarion of Epiphanius of Salamis: De fide. Books II and III.* Vol. 2. Brill, 2008.
2. Enfield, *The History of Philosophy,* p.325
3. Enfield, *The History of Philosophy,* p.547
4. Bruce, Frederick Fyvie. *The Canon of Scripture.* Intervarsity Press, Downers Grove, IL. 1988. p.156
5. Unger, D. J. 'Ancient Christian writers: Against the heresies.' Paulist Press, 1992. *Against Heresies*, St. Irenæus, 3.11.1
6. Hall, Manly P., and Knapp, J. Augustus. *The secret teachings of all ages: An Encyclopedic outline of Masonic, Hermetic, Qabbalistic and Rosicrucian Symbolical Philosophy.* 1978. Manly P. Hall, p.24. While claiming to be a unique work by the author, it is more than likely derived from the works of Athanasius Kircher.
7. Trismegistus, Hermes, and Salaman, Clement. *The Way of Hermes: New Translations of The Corpus Hermeticum and The Definitions of Hermes Trismegistus to Asclepius.* Inner Traditions, 1999. p. 9
8. Enfield, *The History of Philosophy,* p.228
9. Enfield, *The History of Philosophy,* p.325
10. Plotinus, MacKenna, Stephen, and Page, Bertram Samuel. *The Six Enneads.* Encyclopaedia Britannica, Chicago, 1952.
11. Plotinus, MacKenna, Stephen, and Page, Bertram Samuel. *The Six Enneads.* Encyclopaedia Britannica, Chicago, 1952.
12. Iamblichus, Bulmer-Thomas, Ivor. Robin Waterfield (tr.) *The Theology of Arithmetic: On the Mystical, Mathematical and Cosmological Symbolism of the First Ten Numbers.* Grand Rapids, Michigan: Phanes Press, 1988. 13.95.
13. Iamblichus, from the https://theosophytrust.org/282-iamblichus web site.
14. Enfield, *The History of Philosophy,* p.336
15. Sayers, Dorothy L. *The Lost Tools of Learning.* 1948.

THE SECRET APOCRYPHON (REVELATION) THROUGHOUT HISTORY

"This movement, while it may have roots in pre-Christian thought, became prominent in the second century AD, when it suddenly began to look dangerous. Irenæus, Bishop of Lyons, (who lived from about AD 130 to 200), Hippolytus (from about AD 170 to 236) and Tertullian (from about AD 160 to 225) all attacked Gnosticism, as Augustine was to do two hundred years later. Until 1945 our knowledge of Gnosticism was largely derived from these hostile accounts. In that year, however, an astonishing discovery was made near Nag Hammadi in Upper Egypt: a large collection of Coptic texts, comprising forty treatises of which only two had been known before. The copies found appear to be no earlier than the fourth century AD, but many of the works, including the amazing *Apocryphon of John* or *The Secret Book according to John* (which we had previously known only from a summary in Irenæus) were clearly composed centuries before."[1]

— A.D. NUTALL, OXFORD UNIVERSITY

It will be apparent from what follows, that Cerinthus *over-imagined* Christian theology in an attempt to make it more intriguing, more 'real.' In true gnostic fashion he dreams layers of subordinate divinities, an odd feature for someone who believe that all resolves in the One.

It will also be apparent that St. John's intent was to bring bring things back down to earth. Where Cerinthus imagines, John teaches. Where Cerinthus overwhelms with idols, John displays understanding.

Perhaps the greatest technological innovation of Man was when he figured out how to transcend pictograms and hieroglyphs and invent writing. Yet, this is precisely where Plato casts his warning. Not attributing this invention to the ingenuity of Man he imagines a demigod. He worries that writing opens the door for misinterpretation, that, in a sense, writing creates a vacuum into which the charlatan can pour ideas that were never there.

In a sense, pictures are 'dead images' when compared to the potential a sentence brings. Yet, Cerinthus imagines abstractions where the Apostles had none. This is a common feature shared by Hermeticists to come. What Cerinthus attempts Athanasius Kircher and François Champollion would later do, exploit the imprecision of idols opening the door for imaginations that were never intended. Like scientists to follow, their legitimate discoveries hide a troubling underside.

I believe the secret *Apocryphon of John* is perhaps one of, if not *the* most, corrupting influences of all time. It tries to legitimize the dead image.

Most of its life the *Apocryphon* existed in stealth. Perhaps had it been made public it would not have had its allure and would have been dealt with sooner. Curiously, what perplexed the Church for two thousand years still captivates and intrigues those who should know better.

Still, at times the *Apocryphon* did reveal itself in glimpses. I hope to show even more than glimpses once you know what to look for. The documents themselves remained secret to the general public until just after WWII. But once published they became suspiciously coincidental with the discovery of other Gnostic texts, but also curiously when Gnostic-inspired political movements, long in planning, were just hitting their stride. At that very time tried and true educational methods were being abandoned. Nazism, Socialism and Marxism were all contesting which would provide the best utopia. Traditional churches were being scrapped for new charismanias. Drug use was becoming an acceptable way of achieving enlightenment. All were portrayed as a new 'scientific' approach to life. It evokes the suspicion that much was coordinated.

This wasn't unique. The emergence of neoplatonic texts throughout history are coincidental with other similar societal 'disturbances.' The exposure to Arianism was clearly at the root of the Enlightenment. The writings of John Locke and John Milton, were inspired by Arian texts as were Newton's *Principia* and his *Two Corruptions of Scripture,* a public letter written by Newton to Locke attacking 1 John 5:7. The Renaissance began with the re-emergence of the *Corpus Hermeticum* at the Council of Florence, the very same text that again re-emerged at *Nag Hammadi*. Suspiciously, similar things were going on during the fourth century when neoplatonists were pressing the Empire to abandon Christianity. The same was clearly behind heresies like the Cathars and the Paulicians. In all we see a very ancient system of thought re-packaged as a higher wisdom only meant for a few.

THE SECRET *APOCRYPHON OF JOHN*

However, the mother text of all these, the *Apocryphon of John,* remained hidden. It represents not just one book, but a whole genre of literature and thought. The first recorded mention appears in the writings of St. Irenæus of Lyons in his *Against Heresies*, written around 170 AD:

AGAINST HERESIES, **St. Irenæus, excerpts Book 1, Chap. XX & XXIX**

1. Besides the above [misrepresentations], they adduce an unspeakable number of apocryphal and spurious writings, which they themselves have forged, to bewilder the minds of foolish men, and of such as are ignorant of the Scriptures of truth...

AGAINST HERESIES, **St. Irenæus, excerpts Chapter XXIX.**

Doctrines of Various Other Gnostic Sects, and Especially of the Barbe-liotes or Borborians. (Also known as *The Apocryphon of John*)

"1. Besides those, however, among these heretics who are Simonians, and of whom we have already spoken, a multitude of Gnostics have sprung up, and have been manifested like mushrooms growing out of the ground. I now proceed to describe the principal opinions held by them. Some of them, then, set forth a certain Aeon who never grows old, and exists in a virgin spirit: him they style Barbelos. They declare that somewhere or other there exists a certain father who cannot be named, and that he was desirous to reveal himself to this Barbelos. Then this Ennoea went forward, stood before his face, and demanded from him Prognosis (prescience). But when Prognosis had, [as was requested,] come forth, these two asked for Aphtharsia (incorruption), which also came forth, and after that Zoe Aionios (eternal life). Barbe-los, glorying in these, and contemplating their greatness, and in conception [thus formed], rejoicing in this greatness, generated light similar to it. They declare that this was the beginning both of light and of the generation of all things; and that the Father, beholding this light, anointed it with his own benignity, that it might be rendered perfect. Moreover, they maintain that this was Christ, who again, according to them, requested that Nous should be given him as an assistant; and Nous came forth accordingly. Besides these, the Father sent forth Logos. The conjunctions of Ennoea and Logos, and of Aphtharsia and Christ, will thus be formed; while Zoe Aionios was united to Thelema, and Nous to Prognosis. These, then, magnified the great light and Barbelos.

2. They also affirm that Autogenes [self-begotten] was afterwards sent forth from Ennoea and Logos, to be a representation of the great light, and that he was greatly honoured, all things being rendered subject unto him. Along with him was sent forth Aletheia, and a conjunction was formed between Autogenes and Aletheia. But they declare that from the Light, which is Christ, and from Aphtharsia, four luminaries were sent forth to surround Autogenes; and again from Thelema and Zoe Aionios four other emissions took place, to wait upon these four luminaries; and these they name Charis (grace), Thelesis (will), Synesis (understanding), and Phronesis (prudence) Of these, Chaffs is connected with the great and first luminary: him they represent as Sorer (Saviour), and style Armogenes. Thelesis, again, is united to the second luminary, whom they also name Raguel; Synesis to the third, whom they call David; and Phronesis to the fourth, whom they name Eleleth...”

As you can see, all this is rather cryptic. Irenæus specifically links this text to the beginnings of Gnosticism and their doctrine. It re-defines *Logos*. Yet, without some background it makes little sense.

There is a crucial link between the ancient world and the modern. It runs through Paul of Samosata who lived from 200 to 275 AD. He became bishop of Antioch in 260 and was condemned as a heretic in 272 for holding and teaching an anti-trinitarian, Monarchian doctrine. He regarded his office more as a way of making money than preaching the faith. Perhaps more important to this discussion is that a long string of heresies within the Church begins with him, in fact the sect is even named after him, the Paulicians. Eusebius of Caesarea records:

XXVIII. “In a treatise worked out by one of these against the heresy of Artemon, which Paul of Samosata has tried to renew in our time, there is extant an account which bears on the history which we are examining. For he criticizes the above mentioned heresy (which claims that the Saviour was a mere man) as a recent innovation, because those who introduced it wished to make it respectable as being ancient... For who is ignorant of the books of Irenaeus and Melito and the others who announced Christ as God and man? And all the

Psalms and hymns which were written by faithful Christians from the beginning sing of the Christ as the Logos of God and treat him as God."[2]

— EUSEBIUS OF CAESAREA, ECCLESIASTICAL HISTORY

Eusebius writes this as a contemporary so it is reliable. While there is no documented evidence of Paul of Samosata having the secret *Apocryphon*, there is much circumstantial evidence. He is commonly regarded as having acquired his heretical doctrine from Sabellius. The Paulicians are commonly regarded as the first in a line from Arius, through the Manichaeans, to the later Bogomils, through to the Cathars. And it IS known that these later sects DID base their doctrine on texts related to the secret *Apocryphon of John*. It is also documented that after the Albigensian Crusade the remnant Cathars fled to Calvinist churches becoming the influence behind the early English Reformation which led to John Milton, and later Newton.

Perhaps more telling is Paul of Samosata's early use of the term *'homoousios' (ὁμοούσιος)*. When Paul was condemned in 272 his use of the term was condemned also. His understanding was indistinguishable from the gnostic *Pleroma*, the spiritual abode out of which the Father and the Son were distinguished and emerged.[3] Historians have missed entirely the true importance of this term. Where they see a rather exotic debate over the existential nature of Christ, they miss a rather simple strategy, to install into the very defining Creed of Christianity a Gnostic loophole. *It was this very loophole that would need to be plugged before the Nicene Creed could reach its final form.* This fact forms the basis of the following argument. The term *'homoousios'* is the tell, it represents the debate behind the elimination of 1 John 5:7.

This secret *Apocryphon of John* represents not just one work, but a body of related works. The key text was sort of an abridged version of the *Apocryphon* called *The Secret Book of Bogomils,* also called the *Secret Supper* or *Interrogatio Joannis* (John's Questioning). It is in a sense a redacted version designed for liturgical use. Therefore, there is virtually no doubt that the *Apocryphon of John* was somehow behind all this. The pedigree proposed here is the same as on the official Unitarian church website: "Sabellius ⇒ Paul of Samosata ⇒ Arius ⇒ Bogomils (precursors of the heretical Cathars, Waldensians, and Anabaptists)"[4]

The confusion over 1 John 5:7 pivots on Lucian of Antioch who was the claimed bridge between Paul of Samosata and the Arians. A known disciple of the heretic Paul of Samosata, Lucian is the very person to which the New

Arians built their case against 1 John 5:7, to whom their fabricated *Recension* is attributed. The extreme importance of this fact will later be made apparent —the legitimacy of the verse rest upon this.

Lucian is commonly regarded as a publisher of sacred texts. Yet, he is also accused of being the teacher of the Arians including Arius. Somewhere before his death, Lucian had an epiphany, rejecting the Arian heresy and becoming the model of Christian thought.

It is documented that Lucian published a condemned gospel. The pivotal question is this, *was the condemned text written before or after Lucian's conversion?* Before WWII only a few knew of Cerinthus' gospel. Therefore, *nineteenth century scholars such as Westcott & Hort tagging Lucian seemed reasonable. This allowed them to claim that Bibles containing 1 John 5:7 were 'the heretical gospel Lucian wrote.' This provided the rationale for removing the verse and revising all the Bibles.* I will prove otherwise, that the condemned gospel was Cerinthus' secret *Apocryphon of John,* a text similar to Arius' own teachings. Paul of Samosata's use of the term *homoousios* and Lucian's later avoidance of the term is the clue.

Is this unbelievable? The fate of the entire Church rested upon guessing who wrote a text that supposedly didn't exist at the time!

If we accept the line of transmission from the modern Arians back to Paul of Samosata, and him back to the Sabellians (which it appears we must), can we establish a link from the Sabellians back to the *Apocryphon of John*? And would this not prove our point? First of all, let's establish Arius' link to the *Apocryphon.*

"Arius was not without adherents, even outside Alexandria. Those bishops who, like him, had **passed through the school of Lucian** were not inclined to let him fall without a struggle, as they recognized in the views of their fellow-student their own doctrine, only set forth in a somewhat radical fashion. In addressing to Eusebius of Nicomedia a request for his help, Arius ended with the words: **"Be mindful of our adversity, thou faithful comrade of Lucian's school ($\sigma\upsilon\lambda\lambda\upsilon\upsilon\kappa\iota\alpha\nu\iota\sigma\tau\dot{\eta}\varsigma$)"**; and Eusebius entered the lists energetically on his behalf. But Alexander too was active; by means of a circular letter he published abroad the excommunication of his presbyter, and the controversy excited more and more general interest."[5]

— *ENCYCLOPEDIA BRITANNICA* 1911, ARTICLE 'ARIUS'

This begins to establish that Arius had a secret doctrine and that it came from the school of Lucian. But, can we know precisely what this secret teaching was? I think we can.

Most of the writings of Arius have been lost, probably destroyed after Nicaea. However, one does exist called *Thalia*, it was copied and documented by St. Athanasius. We also now know for certain the actual *Apocryphon of John,* for it was published just after WWII. As we have begun to point out, the outcome of the Council of Nicaea spins over the use of the term '*homoousios*,' in the Nicene Creed. Yet, the term is unique and has a documentable pedigree. Also, the term was forced onto the delegates at the Council by Emperor Constantine in an attempt to resolve the Arian dispute. Clearly, Constantine, a new Christian, would have had no knowledge of the term had it not been 'suggested' to him from Arian sources. Yet, we also know the term had two paradoxical interpretations.

ARIUS' HIDDEN AGENDA

From where did the controversy at the Council of Nicaea arise? Below is a comparison of the use of the term in Arius' *Thalia* to similar texts in the *Apocryphon*:[6]

Proof of Borrowing from the Gnostic *Apocryphon of John* in Arius' *Thalia*

Use of the term 'ὁμοούσιος' in the text of Arius' *Thalia*

Greek	English	Issue
Ἀρχὴν τὸν Υἱὸν ἔθηκε τῶν γενητῶν ὁ ἄναρχος, καὶ ἤνεγκεν εἰς Υἱὸν ἑαυτῷ τόνδε τεκνοποιήσας, Ἴδιον οὐδὲν ἔχει τοῦ Θεοῦ καθ' ὑπόστασιν ἰδιότητος· οὐδὲ γάρ ἐστιν ἴσος, ἀλλ' οὐδὲ **ὁμοούσιος** αὐτῷ.	He who is without beginning made the Son a beginning of created things. He produced him as a son for himself by begetting him. He [the son] has none of the distinct characteristics of God's own being For he is not equal to, nor is he of the **same being** as him.	The term 'homoousios,' (ὁμοούσιος) a term with a Gnostic/ Hermetic past, has no precedent for use in a Christian context. It is not Biblical, and was ordered by Constantine to quell controversy. It seemingly has no route of transmission to the Council except from this.

Apocryphon of John	Arius' *Thalia*	*Similarity in Concepts*
He said to me, "[The Unit]y is a monarchy [with nothing] ruling over it. [It is] the Gold and Father of the All, the [h]oly, the invisible, [who ex]ists over the All, the one who [. . .] incorruption, [existing as] pure light, into which it is not possible for any light of the eye to gaze.	And so God Himself, as he really is, is inexpressible to all. He alone has no equal, no one similar, and no one of the same glory. We worship him as timeless, in contrast to him who in time has come to exist.	God, the inexpressible One, is pure light and has no similarity to the Son. There is a consistent avoidance of Logos as Truth.
(It is) the one whose name cannot be spoken because no one exists before It to name It. It is the immeasurable light, the pure one who is holy and unpolluted, the ineffable one who is incorruptibly perfect. It is neither perfection nor blessedness nor divinity, but It is a thing far superior to these. It is not boundless nor is It limited, but It is a thing far superior to these. For It is neither corporeal nor incorporeal. It is neither large nor small. It is not a quantity. It is not a creature. Neither is it possible for anyone to know It.	God is wise, for he himself is the teacher of Wisdom–Sufficient proof that God is invisible to all: He is is invisible both to things which were made through the Son, and also to the Son himself.	God is without name (contrary to the Bible) and is completely unknowable to even the Son.
She became a primal Human, which is the virginal Spirit, the triple male, the one belonging to the triple power, the triple na[med], the triple begotten one, the androgynous aeon which does not grow old…And I praise you and Autogenes and the three Aeons: the Father and the Mother and the Child, the perfect power.	So there is a Triad, not in equal glories. Their beings are not mixed together among themselves. As far as their glories, one infinitely more glorious than the other. The Father in his essence is foreign to the Son, because he exists without beginning.	Contrary to the conventional story, Arius did advocate a 'trinity' that 'does not grow old'

This Chart continues on the next page.

This is the Only-begotten who appeared from the Father, the divine Autogenes, the first-born son of the All of the Spirit of pure light.	We call him unbegotten, in contrast to him who by nature is begotten. We praise him as without beginning in contrast to him who has a beginning. He who is without beginning made the Son a beginning of created things. He produced him as a son for himself by begetting him. He [the son] has none of the distinct characteristics of God's own being For he is not equal to, nor is he of the same being (ὁμοούσιος) as him.	Use of the controversial term 'only/un-begotten' and 'homoousios' (ὁμοούσιος)
Now when the authorities appeared from the chief begetter, the chief ruler of the darkness, these were their names from the ignorance of he who had begotten them: The first is Yaoth. The second is Hermas, who is the eye of the fire.	Understand that the Monad [eternally] was; but the Dyad was not before it came into existence. It immediately follows that, although the Son did not exist, the Father was still God. Hence the Son, not being [eternal] came into existence by the Father's will, He is the Only-begotten God, and this one is alien from [all] others	Again, the use of the concept 'begotten'. God the Son is not eternal. Therefore, neither is *Logos*. Consequentially, Truth must also be created and not eternal, therefore it is potentially arbitrary.
And the Epinoia of the light was hidden within him so that the rulers might not know but our sister Sophia, who is like us, would set right her deficiencies through the Epinoia of the light.	Wisdom came to be Wisdom by the will of the Wise God. Hence he is conceived in innumerable aspects. He is Spirit, Power, Wisdom, God's glory, Truth, Image, and Word. Understand that he is also conceived of as Radiance and Light. The one who is superior is able to beget one equal to the Son, But not someone more important, or superior, or greater. At God's will the Son has the greatness and qualities that he has. His existence from when and from whom and from then — are all from God.	Wisdom (Sophia) is pre-existence 'light' from which "Spirit, Power, Wisdom, God's glory, Truth, Image, and Logos" evolve as secondary qualities. The implication is rather odd—God, while being 'unknowable' retains several esoteric 'knowables,' yet the Son (Logos) retains some of the ignorance. It was this very concept that Light *IS* God that was appealing to the New Arians, Isaac Newton, etc.

Thalia from William Bright's text of On the Councils 15, (The Historical Writings of St. Athanasius according to the Benedictine Text, Oxford: Clarendon, 1881, pp. 259-60). Apocryphon of John from Frederik Wisse

WHAT SHOULD JUMP out is not just the similarity of doctrines, but that *Arius uses the controversial term 'homoousios' in his Thalia*. Its usage is as we would expect, as recorded in the conventional story of the Council. Yet, historians typically explain the term away as a technical misunderstanding and leave it at that. Here we see the term opens the door for a lot of unconventional, gnostic theology, something we are seldom if ever told.

Considering all this, was *homoousios* a loaded term? Was there ulterior motives in forcing the term upon the Council of Nicaea? Did it intentionally leave a loophole for an Arian interpretation of the Doctrine? It should be pointed out that by the time of Julian the Apostate the Imperial family had become thoroughly heretical. Eusebius of Caesarea himself documents this forced use of the term in a letter to his church:

Eusebius' Letter to His Home Church at Caesarea
From *The Ecclesiastical History* of Socrates Scholasticus I:8.

"…even our most pious emperor himself was the first to admit that they were perfectly correct and that he himself had entertained the sentiments contained in them. He exhorted all present to give them their assent and subscribe to these very articles, thus agreeing in a unanimous profession of them—with the insertion, however, of that single word, **homoousios**, an expression which the emperor himself explained as not indicating corporeal affections or properties. Consequently the Son did not subsist from the Father either by division or by cutting off. For, said he, a nature which is immaterial and incorporeal cannot possibly be subject to any corporeal understanding; hence, our conception of such things can only be in divine and mysterious terms. Such was the philosophical view of the subject taken by our most wise and pious sovereign, and the bishops, because of the word **homoousios**, drew up this formula of faith [the Nicene Creed]:"

The term *homoousios,* so critical to the formulation of the most important Creed in all of Christianity was, according to Eusebius, foisted upon the Church. The letter does, in fact, portray the conventional story recorded by historians. But all this shows is Eusebius' innocence, and perhaps Constantine's. The dispute between the Orthodox and the semi-Arians did revolve around upon the acceptance of this term, yet, the term *does* have a demonstrable Gnostic history. Specifically, *homoousios, also* appears in the quintessential gnostic text, the *Corpus Hermeticum* often dated to around or just before the time of St. Irenæus.

This is not to say the term can't have a Christian understanding, but it does say that the term has a documentable history. The *Corpus Hermeticum* clearly is in a line beginning with the *Apocryphon of John.* The proof of this is not just what I present here, but the discoveries at Nag Hammadi proclaim this same fact. Indeed, as in the *Apocryphon,* it seemingly mimics John, using John's 'Light and Life' prolog to the actual Gospel as a model. While it seems to imitate it in style, its purpose moves in the complete opposite direction. *Poimandres* is the first dialogue in the *Corpus.*

"The *Poimandres* shows no dependence on Christian writings, but its thought has affinities with some aspects of early Christian thought. In particular, it has several points of contact with the Fourth Gospel, the date of which may be taken to be not very far from A.D. 100. Such points of contact are the conception of the divine as Life and Light, of the creative Logos, of the heavenly Man who descends and ascends again, of immortal life as a return to the Father, and of knowledge of God as the condition of attaining immortality. These points of contact, however, are not such as to suggest a literary dependence of *John* upon *Poimandres*, or *vice versa*.[7]

— CHARLES H. DODD, *THE BIBLE AND THE GREEKS*

PROOF OF THE GNOSTIC ORIGINS OF ARIANISM

The West was essentially ignorant of the *Corpus Hermeticum* also until the beginning of the Renaissance. In fact it was one of the critical ingredients that brought about the Renaissance. It was introduced at the Council of Florence in (1438-39) by an eastern mystic named Plethon (again, a play on 'Plato'). It was this text that secretly fueled the utopian theologies of Marsilio Ficino, Jakob Böhme, Giordano Bruno, and Cornelius Agrippa. Marsilio Ficino as a young boy was picked by the tremendously wealthy Medicis to lead the new 'platonic' school within Christianity. Ficino's books exist and are clearly in the same line of thought as the secret *Apocryphon*.

Hermes Trismegistus, considered the author of the text, came to be regarded as Enoch, a pre-Christian Christ, a pre-Hebraic Moses, the Greek version of Thoth, all rolled into one. Similar doctrines later appeared in the writings of the Jesuit Athanasius Kircher such as his *Oedipus Aegyptiacus* which fueled the later occult writings of Madame Blavatsky and Aleister Crowley (who considered himself Satan). These writings became the basis of the modern occult.

After the Council of Florence, the *Corpus Hermeticum* achieved near status as a third testament to the Bible. The book *the History of the Heavens* by Abbé Noël-Antoine Pluche (1688 – 1761) is a clear example of this. The fact that the *Corpus Hermeticum* was proved fraudulent by Isaac Casaubon in 1614 did not dissuade many theologians. While Casaubon proved the text from the wrong time period, advocates continued to insist that it represented a legitimate philosophy, even unto this day. Following the lead of the 17th century neoplatonist theologian Ralph Cudworth were modern gnostic scholars like Karen L. King, Bart Ehrman, and Elaine Pagels. These embarrassingly continue to claim that known fakes represent legitimate Christian theologies. By these scholars' own admission, these texts have had a subversive effect on Christianity from near the beginning. Even the ancient lore of the Knights Templar and Free Masons claim authenticity from such texts.

Most of this seems to hinge on Petrarch's claim that St. Augustine validates neoplatonism. Yet, Augustine himself condemned the Hermeticism, the basis of neoplatonism, as a heresy:

> **"Hermes presages these things as the devil's confederate, suppressing the evidence of the Christian name**, and yet foretelling with a sorrowful intimation, that from it should proceed the wreck of all their idolatrous superstitions: for **Hermes was one of those who (as the apostle says), 'Knowing God, glorified Him not as God**, nor were thankful, but became vain in their imaginations, and their foolish heart was full.'"
>
> — *THE CITY OF GOD*, VIII, XXIII, ST. AUGUSTINE

Without a doubt, the Orthodox side at Nicaea would have been resistant to using a non-Biblical term. However, without a doubt, they would have relished the opportunity for a resolution to the controversy dividing the Church. Therefore, as documented by Eusebius, they heard the term as invoking the concept of 'substance/essence.' In fact a similar use of *ousios* does appears in the Greek Lord's Prayer, "τον αρτον ημων τον **επιουσιος** δος ημιν σημερον" (Matthew 6:11), but this use only signifies that the Eucharistic bread has a 'higher being.' Oddly enough, since Milton, the term has taken on the more mundane meaning, 'daily bread.' But the attachment of the prefix '*homo*' to *ousios* has no Biblical foundation.

Without a doubt, the Arians would have heard the incorporation of the term as a concession to their doctrine… and it would have left a hidden backdoor to sneak in future philosophies. From "The Word 'Homoousios' from Hellenism to Christianity," by Pier Franco Beatrice:

> "… an anonymous alchemical text which mentions the "Orphic consubstantiality" (το 'Ορφαικον ὁμοοσιον) and the "Hermaic chain" (η 'Ερμαικη λυρα). This is the mystic doctrine of the **Egyptian *hierogrammateis* (scribe-priests)** relating to the universal harmony based on the divine kinship and sympathetic interlinking of natures consubstantial with one another."[8]

In other words the term forced into the Creed by Constantine was intentionally equivocal. It could be understood either as an orthodox term 'having the same being,' or as the very Egyptian concept they had hoped to eliminate, the *Pleroma*, the *One-Mind*!

At the heart of this 'shell game' was a complete re-definition of the term '*logos*' as locked in by the trinitarian verse found at 1 John 5:7 where the Son, Christ, is identified specifically as the eternal *Logos*. In Article 6 of the dialogue of Poimandres we see a reversal of the term *Logos*, it seemingly invokes a John-like light and life theology.

> "But I, Poimandres, do you understand this vision because it is also desired? And I know, I said. That light, O woman, I am the mind of your god, the liquid nature of the appearance from darkness; but the light from the mind is the word (*logos*), the son of God. What then? reputation. Thus know: what I see and hear in you is the word (*logos*) of the Lord, but the mind is Father God, *for they are not separated from each other, for the unity of these is life*. Thank you, I said. But the light does not waver, and he knew this, so he did."[9]
>
> — *CORPUS HERMETICUM*

But the case is completely revealed in Article 10, *Hermes to Tat* (Thoth) the term '*homoousios*' is referring to the *Pleroma*, the creator being 'of the same substance':

> "The Word (*logos*) of God leaped up from the lower elements to the pure creation of nature, and united with the creator Mind because he was of the same substance (ὁμοούσιος); and the lower elements of nature were finished, as they are reasonless word (a-logos) matter alone."[10]
>
> — *CORPUS HERMETICUM*

In other words we are seeing a very subtle but critical difference in the usage of the term. Whereas one sees 'substance' as the shared nature of the Trinity, the other sees it as sort of an umbrella substance above and beyond the Trinity of which the Trinity only participates. Make no mistake, this *IS* what the Arian party would have heard in the insertion of the term in the Creed. It was a well-familiar term within the Neoplatonists, and its savants Plotinus, Porphyry, and Iamblicus. It was the *Apocryphon of John* that developed the Pleroma concept, the *Corpus Hermeticum* following suit.

Now we can begin to envision a sequence of events. While scholars insist there is not to be found any debate surrounding 1 John 5:7, conceptually the debate is all over the place. The Orthodox and the Semi-Arians were really not all that far apart. But the true Arians, upon confronting *Logos* in the Bible, realize a compromise in doctrine is impossible, so they try to push the two sides in opposite directions. They remember the Hermetic term 'homoousios,' and realize a compromise could be built around the equivocal usage of the term. However, this puts the verse found at 1 John 5:7 in a precarious position. If it remained it would define the term they have just equivocated *making their equivocation obsolete!*

Sometime after the Council had disbanded, the order went out to publish the 50 Bibles sanctioned by the Council on the order of the Emperor Constantine. But by this time the victory of the Orthodox was waning, and the Neoplatonists were gaining ground. Constantine, under the pressure, acquiesced seeing the term as a compromise. Not wanting this to be put in jeopardy, and he being a new Christian, he was perhaps duped into believing 1 John 5:7 was not authentic. Subsequent emperors such as Julian the Apostate saw to it that all other Bibles within his reach be destroyed. The only ones that escaped are private ones held in remote areas. What the couldn't know was that the true writings of Lucian would one day again re-appear.

Thus, as Bishop Porphyrius proclaimed, the Codex *Sinaiticus* is indeed the product of Arianism. It is indeed one of the 50 'official' Bibles as Constantine as Tischendorf insisted and as Westcott and Hort later vindicate. The above presented scenario is the only one that accounts for all the evidence.

IS THIS ALL? CAN WE KNOW FOR SURE?

Yet, this all requires us to 'close the loop,' to provide reasonable evidence that the *Apocryphon of John* was indeed the same text passed from the Sabellians, through Paul of Samosata, and on to the heretical cults of the late Middle Ages and beyond.

Epiphanius of Salamis in the section referring to the Sabellians in his *Panarion* has this statement:

"But they have taken all of their error, and the sense of their error, from certain apocryphal works, especially the so-called **Egyptian Gospel**, as some have named it. There are many such passages in it, purporting to be delivered privately in the person of the Savior as mysteries, as though he is telling his disciples that the Father is the same, the Son is same, and the Holy Spirit is the same."[11]

— THE PANARION OF EPIPHANIUS OF SALAMIS

How do we know which *Egyptian Gospel* the Sabellians were referring to? The *Apocryphon of John* is one of just a few called *Egyptians Gospels*. As we have seen, the entire enterprise of these Gnostics was to marry Greek philosophy to Egyptian. Hippolytus quotes a passage about souls from a "Gospel according to the Egyptians" at *Haer.* 5.7.8–9.

"[The Naassenes] say that the soul is very hard to find and to perceive; for it does not continue in the same fashion or shape or in one emotion so that one can either describe it or comprehend its essence. And they have these various changes of the soul, set forth in the Gospel entitled *according to the Egyptians.*"[12]

— HIPPOLYTUS

Yet, there is a modern unwillingness to link the *Gospel of the Egyptians* to the *Apocryphon of John*, which itself is sometimes referred to as an 'Egyptian Gospel.' However, in the *Nag Hammadi* library 'discovered' in Egypt after WWII, in both codices NHC-III, and NHC-IV, the *Apocryphon* is literally bound back-to-back to the text *The Gospel of the Egyptians*. Both are of the same Gnostic philosophy, meaning both could be considered as one.

THE GOSPEL OF THE NEW ARIANS

So, we have established that the texts have a line of transmission through to the Renaissance. Can we carry that line through to the Enlightenment?

The poet/author John Milton's writings, particularly *Paradise Lost*, are considered foundational to the English Reformation and the Puritan movement. While America considers Puritan movements as nearly 'holy,' the English memory is not so pure. Cromwell's Civil War found Anglican clergy considered to be too Catholic running for their lives, cathedrals turned into horse barns, holy statues busted up with sledge hammers, and organs melted down to form bullets aimed at the very laity who once listened to their harmonies. The monarchy as well the clergy of the Church of England were banished, often killed. Much of the destruction they performed within churches is visible to this day. We've been told that this was all in the innocent pursuit of religious freedom.

John Milton's texts were critical in fueling the Puritan Movement. Milton himself was Secretary of Foreign Languages under Oliver Cromwell's renegade government. It was after the defeat of Cromwell's forces that Milton resigned and began writing texts like *Paradise Lost.* Cromwell used Freemasonry as an underground secret network to promote his freedom agenda.[13] The concept was later adopted by the French in similar *liberté* movements. I believe societies such as the Freemasons and the Royal Society were formed as concessions by the Realm to the non-conformists as part of the compromise for peace. It was into this milieu that steps Isaac Newton.

Two books addressing precisely this very issue (published by reputable publishers) were written by researchers Georgi Vasilev and A.D. Nutall. In Vasilev's book *Heresy and the English Reformation: Bogomil-Cathar Influence an Wycliffe, Langland, Tyndale, and Milton,*[14] he cites the following examples in John Milton's writings. Examples from that work:

PARADISE LOST, Book I; verses 34-49:

"… what time his Pride / Had cast him out from Heav'n, with all his Host / Of Rebel Angels, by whose aid aspiring / To set himself in Glory above his Peers, / He trusted to have equal'd the most High, / If he oppos'd; and with ambitious aim / Against the Throne and Monarchy of God? Rais'd impious Warr in Heav'n and Battel proud / With vain attempt. Him the Almighty Power / Hurld headlong flaming from th' Ethereal Skie / With hideous ruin and combustion down/To bottomless perdition…"

THE SECRET SUPPER AKA INTERROGATIO JOANNIS:

"… and with his tail he dragged away one-third of the angels of God, and he was banished from the throne of God and from the overlordship of the heavens. And Satan, descending to this firmament, was unable to find rest either for himself or for those who were with him."[15]

PARADISE LOST, Book I, verses 47-49

"…To bottomless perdition, there to dwell In Adamantine Chains and penal Fire, Who durst defie th' Omnipotent to Arms."

THE SECRET SUPPER AKA *INTERROGATIO JOANNIS*:

"And then Satan and all his army shall be chained and thrown in a lake of fire. And the Son and His elect shall walk on the firmament and shall imprison the Devil, locking him in chains indestructible and strong."

The questions becomes, If *Paradise Lost* is based upon the secret *Apocryphon of John*, how was Milton able to do this if the text did not exist? The fact that Milton and Newton were under the suspicion of heresy is found at the beginning of Milton's posthumously published work *A Treatise on Christian Doctrine compiled from the Holy Scriptures Alone*. It is essentially an apology for Arianism. It seems the king of England, not wanting to censor the text, thought it best to begin the publication with a warning. It begins with this 'assurance':

KING'S MOST EXCELLENT MAJESTY.

SIRE,

In obedience to Your Majesty's gracious command, I have executed a Translation of the recently discovered theological treatise of MILTON, which I have now the honour of laying most humbly at Your Majesty's feet.

With every sentiment of gratitude and attachment, I have the honour to be,

SIRE,

Your Majesty's

most humble servant, and dutiful subject,

CHARLES R. SUMNER.

Windsor, June 25, 1825

"... Doubts have always been entertained as to the real sentiments of Milton respecting the second person of the Trinity. Newton indeed is assiduous in praising his theological views, although he once so far qualifies his assertion, as to content himself with pronouncing that Milton is generally truly orthodox. Warton however has acknowledged the justice of Mr. Gallon's remark on a memorable passage in *Paradise Regained*, (I. 161 167,) that not a word is there said of the Son of God, but what a Socinian, or at least an Arian, would allow. The truth is, that who ever takes the trouble of comparing with each other the passages referred to in the note below, will find real and important contradictions in the language of Milton on this subject....This summary will be sufficient to show that the opinions of Milton were in reality nearly Arian, ascribing to the Son as high a share of divinity as was compatible with the denial of his self-existence and eternal generation, but not admitting his co-equality and co-essentiality with the Father. That he entertained different views at other periods of his life, is evident from several expressions scattered through his works…The pride of reason, though disclaimed by him with remarkable, and probably with sincere earnestness, formed a principal ingredient in his character, and would have presented, under any circumstances, a formidable obstacle to the reception of the true faith. But we may be permitted to regret that the mighty mind of Milton, in its conscientious, though mistaken search after truth, had not an opportunity of examining those masterly refutations of the Arian scheme, for which Christianity is indebted to the labours of those distinguished ornaments of the English Church."

Later, in the same book we find Milton's confession. We must remember the verse in question has yet to be eliminated from the Bible. Yet, he says 'it cannot be found it in any passage of Scripture.' The only way this is possible is if the growing 'New-Arian' movement now considers their writings and theology as normative:

Chapter V — On the Son of God

"I CANNOT enter upon subjects of so much difficulty as the Son of God and the Holy Spirit, without again premising a few introductory words. If indeed I were a member of the Church of Rome, which requires implicit obedience to its creed on all points of faith, I should have acquiesced from education or habit in its simple decree and authority, even though it denies that the doctrine of the Trinity, as now received, is capable of being proved from any passage of Scripture."[16]

— JOHN MILTON

This is a clear reference that the New Arians already considered 1 John 5:7 as inauthentic. ("The other passage, and which according to the general opinion affords the clearest foundation for the received doctrine of the essential unity of the three persons, is 1 John v. 7. *'there are three that bear record in heaven, the Father, the Word, and the Holy Ghost, and these three are one.'*"[17]) Then:

"This point appears certain, notwithstanding the arguments of some of the moderns to the contrary, that the Son existed in the beginning, under the name of the logos or word, and was the first of the whole creation, by whom afterwards all other things were made both in heaven and earth. *John* i. 1–3. 'in the beginning was the Word, and the Word was with God, and the Word was God,' &c. xvii. 5. 'and now, O Father, glorify me with thine own self with the glory which I had with thee before the world was.' *Col.* i. 15, 18. 'the first-born of every creature.' *Rev.* iii. 14. 'the beginning of the creation of God. 1 *Cor.* viii. 6. 'Jesus Christ, by whom are all things.' *Eph* iii. 9. 'who created all things by Jesus Christ.' *Col.* i. 16. 'all things were created by him and for him.' *Heb.* i. 2. 'by whom also he made the worlds, whence it is said, v. 10, 'thou, Lord, in the beginning hast laid the foundation of the earth;' on which point more will be said in the seventh Chapter, on the Creation. All these passages prove the existence of the Son before the world was made, but they conclude nothing respecting his generation from all eternity."[18]

— JOHN MILTON

The last line of the above is pure Arian doctrine direct from the dispute at Nicaea. The problem is not so much that dispute itself, but what lay hidden behind once that door is opened.

"Thee next they sang of all creation first,
Begotten Son, divine Similitude,
In whose conspicuous countenance, without cloud
Made visible, the Almighty Father shines,
Whom else no creature can behold; on thee
Impress'd, the effulgence of his glory abides,
Transfus'd on thee his ample Spirit rests."[19]

— JOHN MILTON, *PARADISE LOST*, III. 383

Clearly, Milton's theology is Arian, and it is a reasonable assumption that so was the Puritans. And, as has been said, Newton wrote an entire paper against the text. So, I ask again, from where did they attain their thoughts if they had no access to the works from which these thoughts were derived? Were not Milton and Newton part of a conspiracy?

From Nutall's book *The Alternate Trinity* we find:

"The tendency of my argument is to suggest that, long before William Blake, Gnosticism implies an alternative Trinity in which the Son opposes the Father. Those learned in Gnosticism will be eager to point out that Gnosticism has in fact a developed trinitarian conception of the divine nature which is directly opposed to the picture I have been drawing out... This divine triad is variously expounded. Nous, 'intelligence', is separated from the Father and identified as the Son. This Son, far from being morally superior to the Father figure, is seen, somewhat as Christ is seen in Arian theology, as a secondary entity: 'though coeval with the light that is before him .. . not equal to it in power'...Here, it might be said, is the real trinitarian doctrine of Gnosticism."[20]

— A.D. NUTALL

THE INSPIRATION BEHIND THE NAZIS?

When the *Apocryphon of John* finally did appear again it went from its discovery in Egypt, through French hands, finding its home in pre-Nazi Berlin. This is a *VERY* important detail. Called the *Berlin Codex,* officially named *Papyrus Berolinensis 8502,* it was discovered late in the nineteenth century, but was kept secret until after WWII and a coordinated release with the *Nag Hammadi library,* another very important detail. *Clearly, such a scheme needed planning, but by who? How did it seem to have schools of thought already in place at the time of its appearing?* No reasonable explanation has ever given, and as to why it was withheld from the public.

It is no secret the Nazis were obsessed with finding archaeological evidence proving the legitimacy of their cause. Already in the 1930s we find the Indiana Jones-like character, Otto Rahn (*Crusade Against the Grail*), scouring Europe. Considering the Cathars as representative of the authentic Church, he accused the Church of Rome calling it the true enemy of Christianity:

"Catharism was a heresy, and only theology provides us with the key to deciphering its mysticism and its secrets. Only a historian of civilizations is capable of describing the birth and decline of Occitan culture with dignity.... My desire was nothing more than to guide the men of my time to a hitherto unknown world that I had uncovered with a rope, my miner's lamp, and a lot of effort, and at the same time tell my contemporaries the story of the martyrdom of the Templar heretics."[21]

What the true religion of the Nazis was has been subject to much debate. Conventionally, the hypothetical religion of the Nazi Aryans, was called 'Armanen' by its founder Guido von List.[22] While there is no acknowledged connection between the Aryans and the Arians, there is more similarity than just the spelling of their names. Jörg Lanz, List's co-theorist, called the religion 'Ario-Christianity. It was he who founded the Nazi version of the Knights Templar in 1900. List himself was influenced by the theosophy of Madame Blavatsky, who we have shown was influenced by the writings of Fr. Athanasius Kircher and its Hermetic basis.

We must remember that at this point in time people did not have the same access to data that we now enjoy. Considering the limited availability of texts , is it that unlikely that people having parallel philosophies have the same source? Is it not more likely that similar philosophies had common roots?

The *Berlin Codex*, dated to the fifth century AD, was found in Akhmim, Egypt under unclear circumstances. It was sold in January 1896 to the German coptologist Carl Schmidt, a professor in theology and author of various Gnostic books, was a collector of ancient Gnostic manuscripts and translations including the *Pistis Sophia* and the *Acts of Peter*. Schmidt was also member of the German Oriental Society, an organization that in 1939 signed on to the Aryan Paragraph that allowed only people of Aryan pedigree (non-Jews) to be members. As Schmidt bought the *Codex* in 1896, it certainly must have been known before that date. What happened after that date is unclear also. The excuse for its secrecy is that the wars did not permit its release, but could it have been they believed the secret possession of the text endowed them with a certain power?

It is well documented that the Nazis were inspired by 'a Gnostic Myth.' This has been much researched by James. B. Whisker and published in his book *The Philosophy of Alfred Rosenberg: Origins of the National Socialist Myth*. Rosenberg is commonly credited with being the spiritual leader of the Nazis, and one of its most notorious and treacherous personalities. He held numerous leadership offices in the party. Rosenberg is considered one of the main authors of its ideological creeds, racial theory, persecution of the Jews, and the reformulation of Christianity along Nazi ideals. He was sentenced to death by hanging and executed on 16 October 1946. Whisker said this about Rosenberg's influence on the Nazis and the source:

"After the fall of the last Cathar stronghold, in October 1244 A.D. at Montsegur, a few of the group made it through the Roman Catholic lines and carried off the treasures. Among these was reputed to be a Holy Grail, and on it the initiate knowledge the Cathar gnosticism required for salvation. This is the great theme of both Ravenscroft's books, and of the Angebert's *The Occult and the Third Reich*. Otto Rahn's *Crusade Against the Grail*, published during the pre-war years, suggests that the location of the greatest of the Cathar treasures was known. **Possibly, too, the SS had located long lost books of Cathar theology, or books showing the esoteric Cathar interpretation of the New Testament books they accepted. The SS may have located the Cathar commentaries on books long used by Manichaean sects, including apocryphal books like *the Book of Enoch, the Book of Adam and Eve, The Gospel of Thomas*, or *the Childhood of Jesus*.**"[23]

— THE PHILOSOPHY OF ALFRED ROSENBERG: ORIGINS OF THE NATIONAL SOCIALIST MYTH, JAMES B. WHISKER

"In the 20th Century there have been two major developments which have changed what we know about the various "heresies." **One is the discovery of major documents and treatises either by leading gnostics or by their closest disciples and followers.** The other development is the interest shown by leaders of the Third Reich in these movements, and the subsequent study of the ideology in terms of such thought. Among the major works to appear reinterpreting the National Socialist movement in such terms are Pauwels and Bergiers' *The Morning of the Magician* (in French, and translated into many languages), Ravenscroft's *The Spear of Destiny and The Cup of Destiny* and Angebert's *The Occult and the Third Reich*."[24]

— THE PHILOSOPHY OF ALFRED ROSENBERG: ORIGINS OF THE NATIONAL SOCIALIST MYTH, JAMES B. WHISKER

It should be noted that Pauwels and Bergiers' *The Morning of the Magician* functioned precisely as a secret text amongst the emerging radicalized far left of the 70s. Curiously, many of these ideals were passed on into the New Age cults of the twentieth century. These were precisely texts revealed in the *Berlin Codex*.

IN CLOSING, the Church did attempt to fight back in the late 1800s. It is clear the great Cardinal Newman, author of the great *The Dream of Gerontius* which inspired both the Oxford Movement within the Church of England, and similar movements within the Roman Catholic Church was on to all this. Unfortunately he did not have the evidence confirming his suspicions as they were all published after his death. The similarity between the early pre-Nicaea heretics and the pre-modernists has been noticed by others:

"The religious philosophy of the Alexandrian Fathers recalls the Platonism of the men of Oxford. . . The school of the sophists are the noetics; Paul de Samosata is close to Whately. As for the Arians, they resemble the Protestants. By leaning over this distant past, Newman seizes there, as in a mirror, the ideal image of his entourage and he reassures himself in this reflection."[25]

— J. GUITTON, *LA PHILOSOPHIE DE NEWMAN*

Further:

"But in Newman's eyes it was not just a matter of chance resemblances across the gap that separated the fourth century from the nineteenth. As he saw it, there was a more organic link between the liberals of the nineteenth century and Arianism; to him they were the direct descendants of the anti-trinitarians of the eighteenth century, and Arians had been, of course, an important element within that broader group."[26]

— *ARCHETYPAL HERESY: ARIANISM THROUGH THE CENTURIES*, MAURICE WILES

---

1. Nuttall, Anthony David. *The Alternative Trinity: Gnostic heresy in Marlowe, Milton, and Blake*. Oxford University Press, 1998. p.8
2. Eusebius, Kirsopp Lake. *Eusebius: Ecclesiastical History*, Loeb Classical Library, p. 517. 1926.
3. The Catholic Encyclopedia, Chapman, J. Paul of Samosata. Robert Appleton Company. New York: (1911). http://www.newadvent.org/cathen/11589a.htm
4. Unitarian Universalist Association, website — https://www.uua.org/files/documents/tapestry/uu_history_timeline.pdf
5. Chisholm, Hugh, ed. *The Encyclopædia britannica: a dictionary of arts, sciences, literature and general information*. Vol. 29. At the University press, 1911. — article 'Arius'
6. Charinus, Leucius. "The Secret Book of John" and "Thalia," Academia.edu https://www.academia.edu/44862334/_The_Secret_Book_of_John_and_Thalia_ — The article only consists of a chart and apparently assumes the Apocryphon is derived from the Thalia. I contend otherwise.
7. Dodd, Charles H. *The Bible and the Greeks*, Hodder & Stoughton, London, 1954, p.204
8. Beatrice, Pier Franco. 'The word 'homoousios' from Hellenism to Christianity.' *Church History* 71, no. 2, 2002 : 243-272.
9. Ὁ δὲ Ποιμάνδρης ἐμοί , Ἐνόησας , φησί , τὴν θέαν ταύτην ὅτι καὶ βούλεται ; Καὶ γνώσομαι, ἔφην ἐγώ. Τὸ φῶς ἐκεῖνο , ἔφη , ἐγώ εἰμι νοῦς ὁ σὸς θεός, ὁ πρὸ φύ σεως ὑγρᾶς τῆς ἐκ σκότους φανείσης · ὁ δὲ ἐκ νοὸς φω τεινὸς λόγος , υἱὸς Θεοῦ. Τί οὖν ; φημί. Οὕτω γνῶθι · τὸ ἐν σοὶ βλέπον καὶ ἀκοῦον , λόγος κυρίου, ὁ δὲ νοῦς πατὴρ θεός· οὐ γὰρ διίστανται ἀπ' ἀλλήλων · ἕνωσις γὰρ τούτων ἐστὶν ἡ ζωή. Εὐχαριστῶ σοι , ἔφην ἐγώ. Ἀλλά δὴ νύει τὸ φῶς, καὶ γνώριζε τοῦτο, φησίν. — https://remacle.org/bloodwolf/erudits/hermestrismegiste/livre1.htm

Copenhaver, Brian P. *Hermetica: The Greek Corpus Hermeticum and the Latin Asclepius in a new English translation, with notes and introduction.* Cambridge University Press, 1995.

10. Ἐπήδησεν εὐθὺς ἐκ τῶν κατωφερῶν στοιχείων ὁ τοῦ Θεοῦ λόγος εἰς τὸ καθαρὸν τῆς φύσεως δημιούργημα, καὶ ἡνώθη τῷ δημιουργῷ νῷ · **ὁμοούσιος** γὰρ ἦν, καὶ κατελείφθη τὰ ἄλογα τὰ κατωφερῆ τῆς φύσεως στοιχεῖα, ὡς εἶναι ὕλην μόνην. — https://remacle.org/bloodwolf/erudits/hermestrismegiste/livre1.htm

Copenhaver, Brian P. *Hermetica: The Greek Corpus Hermeticum and the Latin Asclepius in a new English translation, with notes and introduction.* Cambridge University Press, 1995.

11. Williams, Frank, ed. *The Panarion of Epiphanius of Salamis, Books II and III. De Fide: Second.* Vol. 79. Brill, 2008.. Frank Williams trans.

12. Hippolytus, *Haer.* 5.7.8–9 by MacMahon, J.H. Trans. *Ante-Nicene Fathers*, Vol. 5. Edited by Alexander Roberts, James Donaldson, and A. Cleveland Coxe. Christian Literature Publishing Co., Buffalo, NY 1886. — Revised and edited for New Advent by Kevin Knight. http://www.newadvent.org/fathers/050105.htm.

13. Roberts, John M. *The Mythology of the Secret Societies.* Sribner, 1972.

14. Vasilev, Georgi. *Heresy and the English Reformation: Bogomil-Cathar Influence on Wycliffe, Langland, Tyndale and Milton.* McFarland, 2014.

15. Felt, Brian E. & Butler, Thomas. ed. *Monumenta Bulgarica: A bilingual anthology of Bulgarian texts from the 9th to the 19th Century.* Michigan Slavic Publications, Ann Arbor, 1996, p.193

16. Milton, John. *A Treatise on Christian Doctrine: Compiled from the Holy Scriptures Alone.* J. Smith, 1825. p.103

17. Milton, John. *A Treatise on Christian Doctrine: Compiled from the Holy Scriptures Alone.* J. Smith, 1825. p.124

18. Milton, John. *A Treatise on Christian Doctrine: Compiled from the Holy Scriptures Alone.* J. Smith, 1825. p.106

19. Milton, John. *Paradise lost,* 1667.

20. Nuttall, Anthony David. *The Alternative Trinity: Gnostic heresy in Marlowe, Milton, and Blake.* Oxford University Press, 1998. p.15

21. Rahn, Otto. *Crusade against the Grail: The Struggle between the Cathars, the Templars, and the Church of Rome.* Simon and Schuster, 2006 (1933). Prologue

22. Goodrick-Clarke, Nicholas. *The occult roots of Nazism: secret Aryan cults and their influence on Nazi ideology: the Ariosophists of Austria and Germany, 1890-1935.* Tauris Parke, 2005, p.56

23. Whisker, James B. *The philosophy of Alfred Rosenberg: origins of the national socialist myth.* Noontide, 1990. p.79

24. Whisker, James B. *The philosophy of Alfred Rosenberg: origins of the national socialist myth.* Noontide, 1990. p.41

25. J. Guitton, *La Philosophie de Newman,* Paris, 1933, from Wiles, Maurice. *Archetypal heresy: Arianism through the centuries.* OUP Oxford, 1996.

26. Wiles, Maurice. *Archetypal heresy: Arianism through the centuries.* OUP Oxford, 1996. p.168

NEWTON'S LETTER AGAINST 1 JOHN 5:7 AND A RESPONSE
EXCERPTS

While there was an initial controversy when Erasmus released his first translation of the Greek text which was missing the verse, it was quickly reinserted upon the examination of other texts. This was the condition of the dispute until a subversion began to emerge in England mid seventeenth century. It began with the first 'scientist' and later confirmed Arian, Isaac Newton. Here is a portion of the text near the end of the letter[1]:

TWO NOTABLE CORRUPTIONS OF SCRIPTURE:

In a Letter to a Friend, Isaac Newton (part 1: F. 1-36)

Sir;

XXXV. Having given you the history of the controversy, I shall now confirm all that I have said from the sense of the text it self. For without the testimony of "the Three in Heaven" the sense is good and easy, as you may see by the following paraphrase inserted into the text in a different character.

"WHO IS HE THAT OVERCOMETH THE WORLD BUT HE THAT BELEIVETH THAT JESUS IS THE SON OF GOD? that son spoken of in the Psalms where he saith, 'Thou art my son this day have I begotten thee.' **THIS IS HE THAT** after the Jews had long expected him, **CAME** first in a mortal body **BY** baptism of **WATER,**

AND then in an immortal one by shedding his **BLOOD** upon the crosse and rising again from the dead: **NOT BY WATER ONLY BUT BY WATER AND BLOOD**: being the son of God as well by his resurrection from the dead (Acts xiii, 33) as by his supernatural birth of the Virgin Luke I, 35): **AND IT IS THE SPIRIT** also **THAT** together with the water and blood **BEARETH WITNESS** of the truth of his coming, **BECAUSE THE SPIRIT IS TRUTH**, and so a fit and unexceptionable witness. **FOR THERE ARE THREE THAT BEAR RECORD** of his coming, **THE SPIRIT** which he promised to send, and which was since shed forth upon us in the form of cloven tongues and in various gifts, **THE** baptism of **WATER** wherein God testified this is my beloved son, **AND THE** shedding of his **BLOOD** accompanied with his resurrection whereby he became the most faithful martyr or witness of this truth. **AND THESE THREE**, the Spirit, the baptism and the passion of Christ **AGREE IN** witnessing **ONE** and the same thing (namely that the Son of God is come,) and therefore their evidence is strong. For the Law requires but two consenting witnesses, and here we have three. **AND IF WE RECEIVE THE WITNESS OF MEN THE** threefold **WITNESS OF GOD** which he bare of his Son, by declaring at his baptism This is my beloved Son, by raising him from the dead, and by pouring out his spirit on us, **IS GREATER** and therefore ought to be more readily received.

XXXVI. Thus is the sense plain and natural and the argument full and strong, but if you insert the testimony of "the Three in Heaven" you interrupt and spoil it. For the whole design of the Apostle being here to prove to men by witnesses the truth of Christs coming, I would ask how the testimony of "the Three in Heaven" makes to this purpose. If their testimony be not given to men how does it prove to them the truth of Christs coming? If it be, how is the testimony in heaven distinguished from that in earth? It is the same Spirit which witnesses in heaven and in earth. If in both cases it witnesses to us men, wherein lies the difference between its witnessing in heaven and its witnessing in earth? If in the first case it does not witness to men, to whom does it witness, and to what purpose? and how does its witnessing make to the design of St. John's discourse? Let them make good sense of it who are able: for my part I can make none."

— SIR ISAAC NEWTON

It met with this response (redacted) once it started to be made public[2]:

A LETTER TO SIR ISAAC NEWTON FROM GEORGE TRAVIS

By GEORGE TRAVIS, A.M.
PREBENDARY OF CHESTER, AND VICAR OF EASTHAM

Sir,

I NOW proceed to a consideration of the objections, which have been urged against the authenticity of the Verse, 1. John v. 7, by the late Sir Isaac Newton.

The learned Dr. Horsley has just given these objections to the public, in the fifth Volume of his Edition of the works of this illustrious man; to which he has prefixed the following advertisement. "

"A VERY imperfect copy of this tract, wanting both the beginning and the end, and erroneous in many places, was published at London in the year 1754, under the title of 'Two Letters from Sir Isaac Newton to Mr. Le Clerc,' But in the AUTHOR'S MS, the whole is one continued discourse; which, although it is conceived in the epistolary form, is not addressed to any particular person. It is now first published entire from a MS, in the Author's hand-writing, in the possession of the Rev, Dr, EKENS, DEAN OF CARLISLE."

[Conclusion]

But, Sir, I am contented to take the conclusion in its *strictest* terms, as to several parts of the evidence, herein before adduced to the originality of this verse. For I find myself, even in that situation, at liberty to affirm, that the $\alpha\pi o\sigma\tau o\lambda o\varsigma$,—the *Confession of Faith* of the *Greek* Church,—the Disputation, and the *Synopsis*, of *Athanasius*,—the *Greek* MSS of *Walafrid Strabo*, and of *Jerome*,—the quotation of *Euthymius Zygabenus*,—and the authority of the Council of *Ephesus* in A.D. 431, upon which the *Armenian* Version was framed, and adjusted,—form an accumulation of Greek testimonies, the authority of which cannot be denied, even upon the terms of the objection itself. For there is no color of reason, to asert that any of them have been '*corrected by the Latins*' And there is no ground, to suppose, that they are not, ALL, more ancient, in point of date, than the *Lateran* Council.

This most respectable objector, lastly, states his own paraphrase of this passage, in order to shew that the sense of St. *John*, without the testimony of the *Three in Heaven*, is (to use his own words) "*plain, and strong; but if you insert that testimony, you spoil it.*"

This *sense*, or *internal evidence*, of the passage, will be considered hereafter: in which consideration, I trust, the very opposite conclusion will appear. At the same time I most freely admit, in common with this illustrious objector, that I 'have that honor for St. John, as to believe that he wrote good sense' and, therefore do most implicitly 'take that sense to be his, which is [or which, at least, appears to me to be] the best.'

And here, Sir, I wish to take my leave of the objections, urged by this great ornament of human nature, this *first*, and chiefest, of the race of men:—from whom it will detract little, that he cherished an erroneous opinion as to this disputed passage; his errors being more than redeemed by his candor, his mistakes by his unaffected magnanimity. —His own declaration, stated in the outset of these observations, affords the fairest reason, the most available pretensions, to conclude, that, if Sir *Isaac Newton* had been apprised of all the positive evidence, which has been alledged, in the preceding pages, on behalf of the authenticity of this text (a great part of which was utterly unknown to him): he would not have cast the weight of his name into that scale, which (as it seems, he would then have confessed) ought not to preponderate in the present question.

— GEORGE TRAVIS

---

1. Newton, Isaac. *An historical account of two notable corruptions of scripture: In a letter to a friend.* R. Taylor, and sold by R. Hunter, 1830 Compiled from the Bishop Horsley's Edition 1785 taken from the authors own hand writing and a letter transcription from Oxford.
2. Travis, George. *Letter to Edward Gibbon author of Decline and Fall of the Roman Empire,* CF and J. Rivington at St. Paul's Churchyard, 1785, — Letter IV to Sir Isaac Newton

CHRISTIAN LOGOS REVEALED IN THE TRINITY
EXPLAINING THE INEXPLICABLE

"While these hereticks thus denied the Divinity, and rendered void the Incarnation and Redemption of Christ, they seemed not to have erred so grossly on the doctrine of the Trinity. As they were respectively descended from the Jews, though their notions were warped by the peculiar opinions of Simon Magus, they must have derived from both sources some knowledge of this mystick doctrine. Hence it is of importance to observe, that the Jews expressed their belief in this doctrine, in the identical terms, which occur in the suspected passage, "and the three are one."

[and from the footnote to the above] —That the term Λογος, adopted by St. John in the passage before us, had been previously used by the Jews in the determinate sense of ממדא, the Word of God, as distinct from the speech of God, is placed beyond a doubt by Rittangelius, *Lib. Jezir.* p. 81. sqq. ed Amst. 1642. In this work, which is ascribed to Abraham, by the Jews, and is confessedly the oldest of their Cabalistick works, we meet, Ibid, Sect. iii. p. 207. שלש אחד, "the three are one."[1]

— FREDERICK NOLAN

Athanasius' *Letter to Alexander of Alexandria* criticizes Arian doctrine, but it also proves they had their own 'trinity.' It was Alexander, bishop of Alexandria, who excommunicated Arius.

"Thus there are three subsistences. And God, being the cause of all things, is un-begun and altogether sole, but the Son being begotten apart from time by the Father and being created and founded before ages, was not [i.e., did not exist] before his generation. But being begotten apart from time before all things, he alone was made to subsist by the Father. For he is not eternal, co-eternal or co-unoriginate with the Father. Nor has he his being together with the Father, as some speak of relations, introducing two ingenerate beginnings, but God is before all things as being Monad and beginning of all."[2]

— ATHANASIUS, *ON THE COUNCILS OF ARIMINUM AND SELEUCIA*

Visit most any liturgical church on Trinity Sunday and you likely will hear a sermon on the Trinity. Yet, you will seldom hear it explained as it would risk heresy. The doctrine is considered both incomprehensible and a key to wisdom, doctrines seemingly at odds with each other. Therefore, some have wrongly interpreted this as a willed ignorance.

This leaves me in a similarly precarious situation of having to explain the inexplicable. I will try a different strategy. Whereas most explanations try to get as close as possible, I will go the other direction. I will try to show that inexplicability is essential, a necessary construct to protect the very basis of reason itself.

THE DESIGN OF THE INEXPLICABLE—IS SCIENCE *SCIENTIFIC*

The Christian Trinity is very much a stumbling block. Few know or care that its main testimony has been removed from their Bibles. Seldom will you hear anyone firmly advocating the Trinity, yet you will seldom hear anyone denying it either. The general sentiment seems to be, 'we are aware of this antiquated doctrine, please accept our apologies for we do not want to disturb anyone with an explanation.' The Doctrine is held as an abstract oddity, a counter-intuitive invention of the early Church, nothing more.

Curiously, the modern mind seems not too disturbed by greater absurdities like Schrödinger's Cat or Einstein's time paradoxes. Both are acceptable dissonances in a quest to find the one grand *unified* theory that explains everything. It just seems more, shall we say, 'scientific.'

However, even the Arians were never truly unitarian, as the quote above reveals. Even Aristotle, one of the most profound minds of all time, admitted to a trinity:

DE CAELO - On the Heavens - Book 1

"A magnitude if divisible one way is a line, if two ways a surface, and if three a body. Beyond these there is no other magnitude, because the three dimensions are all that there are, and that which is divisible in three directions is divisible in all. For, as the Pythagoreans say, the world and all that is in it is determined by the number three, since beginning and middle and end give the number of an 'all', and the number they give is the triad. And so, having taken these three from nature as (so to speak) laws of it, we make further use of the number three in the worship of the Gods."

— ARISTOTLE

Plato, seemingly, rejected the conventional trinitarian concept, yet allowed for devolving divinities similar to Cerinthus. Enfield explains:

"It is evident, from the preceding account of the doctrine of Plato concerning God and the soul of the world, that it differs materially from the doctrine of the Trinity afterwards received in the Christian church. Plato did not suppose three subsistences in one divine essence, separate from the visible world; but taught, that the $\Lambda o\gamma o\varsigma$ or *Reason of God*, is the seat of the intelligible world, or of Ideas, and that the Soul of the World is a third subordinate nature, compounded of intelligence and matter. In the language of Plato, the universe, being animated by a soul that proceeds from God, is the Son of God; and several parts of nature, particularly the heavenly bodies, are gods."[3]

— WILLIAM ENFIELD

For centuries there were those who debated the authenticity of 1 John 5:7. It was Newton's challenge to the verse combined with his universally accepted scientific method that led to the verse's removal. Why should a 'One' resolve into a 'Three'? Does not the One seem more elegant? Somehow more scientific? Did not Judaism make the concept obsolete?

The concept of the Trinity is, in fact, beyond explanation. But that is its virtue. *It is the abstract nature of the Trinity that makes it reasonable, and the Unitarian unreasonable. This is provable.* The alternative is impossible and is actually a principle of ignorance, what is philosophically called a 'monism.'

No matter how the gnostics tried to formulate or reformulate, their divinities were always secondary to the *pleroma*. Yet, their definition of it was always ambiguous and non-definitive. This is no accident, it is out of necessity. A pure monism is featureless, it has no 'notes' by which it can be known. Therefore it defies not only reason, but even analogy. This runs counter to the Christian Logos which promises a Divine whose features can be known at least analogously, features such as Truth, Beauty, and Being. *It is the very nature of the Arian 'One' (the Monad) that resolves into a darkness, an occult, because nothing of it can be known.* The Trinity, the Three in One, simply guarantees that the One has features, thus making it knowable.

However, this is the very thing that the scientist seeks in his pursuit of the *singularity*. It is also what the mathematician seeks in his one equation that explains everything. It is what the ancient Arians, Islamists, and Cerinthus all held in common. The concept is necessarily what is called 'complete,' for being 'all in one' it allows for nothing else. To understand this we must first understand the Liar's Paradox.

THE LIAR'S PARADOX

There is a well-known logical dictum, it is even found in the Bible:

'*ex falso quodlibet or ex contradictione sequitur quodlibet*'
'from a contradiction, anything follows.'

"One of Crete's own prophets has said it: '*Cretans are always liars, evil brutes, idle bellies.*' He has surely told the truth. For this reason correct them sternly, that they may be sound in faith instead of paying attention to Jewish fables and to commandments of people who turn their backs on the truth."

— EPISTLE OF PAUL TO TITUS, 1:12-13

The above verse is perhaps one of the strangest in the Bible. Like the Trinity, I doubt you will hear a sermon on it. The phrase is a peculiar paradox—it is self-referential, a logical tautology. The phrase is from *Epimenides* who himself is a *Cretan*, 'All Cretans are liars.' It can only be understood philosophically. Paul was making the reader aware that the corrupters of Faith frequently use irreconcilable paradoxes to confuse the faithful. The most simple version of the phrase is this:

This sentence is false.

Look at the phrase, is it true or isn't it? Is *Epimenides* lying or telling the truth? The fact is, if he is telling the truth he must necessarily be lying. If he is lying, he must be telling the truth. It's enough to make your brain hurt… but the Liar's Paradox is at the center of the proof why a theory that ends in *completeness* (unity) logically fails..

Historians hold that the Middle Ages ended when texts unheard of in the West began to infiltrate from the East. People like *Siger of Brabant* risked heresy when he tried to blend contradictory philosophy with religious doctrine. To stave off accusations he invoked the *Two-Fold Truth*, that *both sides of a contradiction could be regarded as 'true.'* It was just this sort of thinking that led to questions like 'how many angels can dance on the head of a pin?' That Siger was wrong became the much heralded *Principle of Non-Contradiction*. In a sense, like *Logos*, it is proof that there is certainty, something denied by the modern. The *Principle of Non-Contradiction* is basically this: *nothing can be both true and false at the same time.* Or, even more simply, *contradictories cannot both be true.* Yet, this is precisely what the unitarian must do, he's just not aware of it.

Frustrated with such corruptions, Protestants sought an alternative. They created many of their 'alone' theologies, Bible Alone, Faith Alone, God Alone… It was a flirt with this same monism. This frustration led to the modern re-invoking of the Greek sophist *Gorgias*, 'there is no truth, if there were you couldn't know it, if you could know it you couldn't teach it.'

When I took logic in college a very simple axiom was taught, 'get society to accept a logical tautology as truth and the framework of society will collapse.' In logic a tautological statement is one whose truth is determined entirely within itself', such as '*this statement is true.*' The Liar's Paradox takes this and turns is back onto itself. In other words, if we accept such a 'loop' as truth, it is a direct attack on the universality of Truth itself. It is a logical black hole from which there is no return.

Pondering the phrase creates a schizophrenia of sorts. Further, while the logic form is valid, its truth is not. Such statements reference nothing outside themselves. Their reasoning is entirely internal, therefore not verifiable. While it cannot be disproved, it cannot be proved either, it is its own 'complete' system.

Therefore, the phrase must be rejected at the outset as being irrelevant. If a logician finds such a phrase in a proof, he eliminates out of hand. It has the appearance of truth without ever being 'true.' However, Unitarianism, like science, believed that resolving into a One, a singularity, was the pinnacle of all truths. It was this concept that took hold following Isaac Newton and was popularized by the likes of the Royal Society of Science and the Freemasons. It seemed both profound and innocent enough—it wasn't.

THE *EUTHYPHRO DILEMMA* — THE IMPOSSIBILITY OF A PURE UNITY

By the first century before Christ, Judaism found itself in a philosophical box. Part of it expected the emergence of *Logos* (documented in the Targums). Part of it rejected such a notion out of hand. What began as a simple insight, that two Gods cannot exist side-by-side, evolved into a philosophical dilemma. Until then, the God they had envisioned was outwardly One, but *internally* both good and evil. You praised Him when he did you right, you cursed Him when He did you wrong. What was needed was a philosophical breakthrough, something to account for evil without blaming God.

This is where Christianity stepped in with a new insight. Rather than evil being an aspect of God, Christianity considered it an absence of the Good. It is what is called a 'privation'—evil doesn't have a natural 'created' existence. Like *cold* being the absence of *heat*, and *black* being the absence of *light,* evil doesn't exist *per se.* This might be hard to see, but is this that led to solving many paradoxes like Plato's *Euthyphro Dilemma*—things could have different aspects.

Failing to understand this, Gnosticism went wild. It began to construct realities out of everything the mind could conceive. In trying to incorporate All into the One, it began to envision them as imaginary. To the Idealist reality was made up of bogus 'things' that ought to be internal to the One. So, in a way you must mentally exterminate them, but where do you stop? Eventually this extermination leads to thoughts themselves. Thou shalt not kill? In the their system all matter is infused with life, so how do you work that out? Thou shalt not create a graven image? But aren't words sort of images? And don't they represent thought? Eventually, the only thing left is the equation, the geometric shape, some abstract that evades extermination. The mind freed from its anchoring in reality can only confuse it with the dream. Paradox becomes truths, the contradiction becomes reason.

Beginning with Newton's 'scientific' attack on the Trinity, science became infused with the 'all must resolve in the One,' what science now calls a 'singularity.' ***With the notion that all things could be eventually explained by science came the belief that everything must be reduced to an all inclusive 'one,' a closed intellectual formula that could explain everything.*** This became the subject of all their efforts.

Mathematicians *Bertrand Russell* and *Alfred North Whitehead*, spent years trying to prove the fundamental principle of math. Their *Principia Mathematica* spent hundreds of pages to prove $1 + 1 = 2$, something everyone knows intuitively. They were in this process when a young mathematician, *Kurt Gödel*, stepped in. What he proved shocked them…

Gödel's proof is very nearly *St. Anselm's* Ontological Proof of God, so let's try to understand that first. Anselm's proof has been simplified into this:

I can think of God, therefore God exists.

While this sounds preposterous, it is actually fully logical. Essentially, Anselm is saying this:

God is that which nothing greater can be thought. As the greatest possible being exists in the mind, even in the mind of the person who denies the existence of God, it therefore must also exist in reality.

The argument is essentially one of epistemology: how can we know that which exists beyond reason? Let's say I want to compare 'A' and 'B'. Which is better, A or B? I insist A is better, you insist B is better. Eventually, in our frustration, our little debate must ask, 'by what criteria?' To solve the problem we must appeal to a third element. *We need an outside, greater standard of comparison.* The fact that we can conceptualize something greater than A and B, means that thing must actually exist or our analogy would be impossible. Anselm's actual Ontological Argument runs something like this:

The comparative goodness of any two things cannot be determined solely by comparing them to each other, invariably a third 'ideal' is needed to set a standard of comparison. This not only holds true for any 'goodness', but also any goodness one can think of, such as 'greatness'. This applies when comparing any two commodities one can conceive, regardless how great. Therefore, for thought to be possible, a supreme 'Ideal,' or 'Greatness,' higher than any conceivable ideal, must exist or any comparison or description would be stymied. It is this supreme Ideal Greatness we call 'God'.

People have tried to criticize Anselm's logic for centuries, yet the proof still stands. Many disregarded it as sort of an oddity, then *Kurt Gödel* stepped in.

GÖDEL — THE MORE YOU KNOW, THE LESS YOU KNOW

Gödel thought about how he would solve the dilemma, can the pursuit of all science really be reduced to a singularity? Gödel turned to *the Liar's Paradox!* By turning 'I am a liar' into a mathematical formula, it gave him the tools to solve the dilemma. What Gödel realized is that the object of all science, of all mathematics, and, yes, even Arianism, the One, the singularity, is necessarily complete. It is this fact that destroys its reasonability. The proof is called *Gödel's Incompleteness Theory.* It is essentially this, 'nothing can prove itself':

1. Every 'strong enough' formal system is *incomplete,* in that at least one element can neither be proved or disproved
2. If that formal system admits as proof of its own *completeness,* it is necessarily inconsistent.

It basically is this: 1) a simple logically tight 'complete' system that tries to justify itself internally is necessarily paradoxical—it becomes the Liar's Paradox, it can be neither proved true or false. 2) A logically incomplete system is reasonable precisely because it references something external to the system, while it can be proved true, it has nothing to say about the thing external.

In some ways, because we can think it, it must exist. It can never be fully understood because once it is, it becomes complete and forces you back to a logically tight system. This is precisely what the Neoplatonic One-Mind is. A logically complete system that cannot prove its own consistency. Another version of the proof is this:

1. In any logical system, one can construct statements that are neither true nor false.
2. Therefore no consistent system can be used to prove its own consistency. No proof can be proof of itself.

Science has given us wonderful method, but it has brought us to the brink of absurdity. Therefore, it must deify some unexplainable enigma or some principle that practically functions as 'God' to them.

LOGOS IS THE KEY

"The study of the elements and compounds that form the sublunary world Proclus gives over to human reason; their nature we can know; we can construct a physics of bodies subject to generation and corruption. Of the heavenly substances, however, we can know only appearances; their nature is understandable only to the divine $\lambda o\gamma o\varsigma$."[4]

— PIERRE DUHEM, CATHOLIC PHYSICIST

After doing much research on our passage in 1 John, I came to an unavoidable questions. Is it possible that the verse was an early version of this very same insight? Was it designed to protect the incomprehensible nature of God, yet retained enough features so that it was knowable? Was it this that the Arians objected to? Was it this that replaced all of their devolving divinities?

As we've seen, to Plato *Logos* simply meant 'word'— speech, rhetoric, poetry, and the like. Christian *Logos* introduced an ethical component, something intended to go beyond a mere intellectual affirmation, but requiring a moral response.

While Plato regarded his system as a pursuit of truth, it was only filled with 'truisms.' Truth was as yet only a consistency in thought, a way of checking hypocrisy and emotional inspiration. This is where the extraordinary aspect of Christianity steps in. Truth is no longer an internal check and balance, it becomes <u>Truth</u>, an aspect of God himself, something external that insures the reasonability of the entire system. It is knowable because an element, Logos, is both internal and external.

Platonism regards the Divine as only 'the greatest good.' But what might be good for me might be bad for you, and vice versa. Ultimately, different 'goods' only insure an internal consistency. How can God be the greatest good if no one can agree what good is?

What is needed is a formula for ensuring a consistency, to the extent possible, of all there is. Truth becomes a conformity of mind to reality, and a willingness to act accordingly. While our 'goods' may differ, the path to Truth does not.

If everything that exists needs a sufficient cause for existing, at some point I must move beyond self and consider the Cosmic order. What is the sufficient cause for that? While I can envision Anselm's God, at some point God has to let me know if my pursuits are in vain. Surely, something, someone must come into the world, a Divine Logos to guide me.

> "It is impossible for the most true God, who is Truth Itself, the best, the wisest Provider, and the Rewarder of good men, to approve all sects who profess false teachings which are often inconsistent with one another and contradictory, and to confer eternal rewards on their members. For we have a surer word of the prophet, and in writing to you We speak wisdom among the perfect; not the wisdom of this world but the wisdom of God in a mystery. By it we are taught, and by divine faith we hold one Lord, one faith, one baptism, and that no other name under heaven is given to men except the name of Jesus Christ of Nazareth in which we must be saved. This is why we profess that there is no salvation outside the Church."

> — *UBI PRIMUM,* POPE LEO ON HIS ASSUMING THE
> PONTIFICATE, XII, 1824

The term 'Logos' first appeared around 500 BC, a term developed by Heraclitus the Philosopher. Today his philosophy is often mistakenly represented as 'the only thing certain is change.' This misrepresents his doctrine.

While Heraclitus did see reality as 'a being in constant change,' he also considered it a logical absurdity. He realized that a world without a permanence made the very concept of Truth impossible. Somewhere it needed an over-riding 'logical' permanence. *It was the Cosmic order that pointed to it.* Only in this could Truth have any meaning. Heraclitus named this self-sufficient, rational principle *Logos.* It is his term. He saw Logos as a reasonable, necessary condition of Truth.

> "All things are in flux; the flux is subject to a unifying measure or rational principle. This principle (*logos,* the hidden harmony behind all change) bound opposites together in a unified tension, which is like that of a lyre, where a stable harmonious sound emerges from the tension of the opposing forces that arise from the bow bound together by the string."[5]

> — HERACLITUS

To understand *Logos* we must understand St. John's use of the term. He was melding a Greek philosophical concept with an emerging Jewish tradition. Jews saw *Logos* as the great I AM emerging and becoming 'personified' over time. This is documented in their Targums.

Likewise, Greeks initially understood *Logos* as Heraclitus had proposed. But over time philosophers such as Plato began using the term re-defining it to suit their own novelties. Eventually Heraclitus Logos met with the Jewish Logos Personified forming the Trinity as St. John reveals it, verifying Universal Truth.

Let's say for argument's sake that the Unitarians are correct, our verse at 1 John 5:7 is a fabrication, a later invention. This implies that the concept of Christ the *Logos* was also a later invention, or at least a concept derived from Neoplatonism. The result of this is nothing remarkable at all. Christianity is simply a reiteration of something Plato has already revealed, merely a refined version of Socrates. Does this really explain all that happened at Nicaea?

The Arian version of *Logos* makes Truth arbitrary, a secondary creation, what they themselves call the Demiurge. How then are we to make sense of John's "in the beginning was the *Logos*" and "the *Logos* was the light (Truth) of men"? John's *Logos* is eternal, the same for everyone everywhere. That *Logos* became flesh is a principle unique to Christianity. Clearly, no other religion has held such a proposition.

Now, let's imagine we are a delegate at the Council of Nicaea. You are aware there is contention over the use of the word '*Logos*.' It's not that they want to banish the term, they want to re-define it making it a secondary novelty. You also see that another novel terms is being introduced. These are *equivocal* terms, something open to interpretation. What would you do? Might you not insist on incorporating a term of your own within the Creed to protect your interests? Particularly in the face of the Arians who were contesting all this?

Let's define *Logos* as we now know it, a "permanent, *always-eternal*, revealed *universal* Truth." This would be consistent with both the Greek and Jewish understanding of the term. Further, it would insure that novel terms such as *homoousios* had a limited application, that they could not be misunderstood as a Gnostic Pleroma. We would also expect this term to have a different source than the Bible precisely because it is these internal terms that need definition.

Franz Cumont was a researcher who initially believed that Christianity was actually Mithraism in disguise. Throughout Europe he found numerous Mithraic dens using a *pharmakon* based on absinthe/wormwood. Cumont popularized the notion that Mithraism was the basis the Christianity, something many still believe. Over time he realized that he was entirely mistaken, Mithraism did not show up until a hundred years or so after Christianity… the very time Gnosticism was starting to grow. Yet, I quote him here for he supplies critical evidence:

"What has been said brings out the importance attached by the adepts of star-worship to the idea of divine eternity,—an importance shown by the fact that some had actually made it the supreme principle of their religion. But there was another divine attribute correlative to the former. The stars are not only eternal gods, but also universal, their power is unlimited in space as in time. Already in Syria the Baals, who had become solar deities, bore the title of Mar'olam, which may be translated "Lord of the Universe" as well as 'Lord of Eternity,' and men undoubtedly liked to claim for them this double quality. With earthly genii or demons, who protected definite spots, were contrasted the celestial gods, who are **'catholic.'** This word, which was to have such a great destiny, was at first merely an astrological term: **it denoted activities which are not limited to individuals, nor to particular events, but apply to the whole human race and to the entire earth.**[6]

— FRANZ CUMONT

In other words, *catholic,* an astronomical term, originally meant '*universal, always-eternal truth.*' *St. Irenæus* was a disciple of St. John's disciple Polycarp, *the very person who documents the fraud of Cerinthus' gospel.* Writing in the second century in his book *Against Heresies* he specifically uses the very term *catholic,* later to used in the Nicene Creed. He specifically defines it: '*the tradition of truth [of the Church], one and the same through out the world*'. 'Catholic' derives from the Greek; *kath' holes tés oikoumenés* (throughout the whole world). Firmly believing that the basis of any knowledge must be an universal understanding of Truth. He defines the term 'Catholic':

"THE RULE OF TRUTH IS ONE IN THE CHURCH THROUGHOUT THE WORLD"

"… But just as the sun, God's creation, is one and the same throughout the world, so too the light, the preaching of the Truth, shines everywhere and enlightens all men who wish to come to the knowledge of the Truth."[7]

— ST. IRENÆUS, *AGAINST HERESIES*

Clearly, the **Creed is using a term that definitionally means precisely the same thing as *Logos, a term defined by 1 John 5:7.*** 'Catholic' does not simply mean 'universal Church,' or a mere franchise, it means universal Truth. Its intention is precisely to protect a concept that had come under assault by the Arian party. *The entire Church was declared 'catholic' at the Council because it was realized that the foundation of the Church was being threatened by the Arians. It was the philosophical Logos, united to the personhood of Logos, a concept that could have only been derived from 1 John 5.7 because only there is it specified <u>Christ is Logos</u>.*

1. Nolan, Frederick, *The Integrity of the Greek Vulgate, Received Text of the New Testament,* 1815, p.267
2. Athanasius, *On the Councils of Ariminum and Seleucia 16.*
3. Enfield, *The History of Philosophy*, p.133
4. Duhem, Pierre. *To save the phenomena: An essay on the idea of physical theory from Plato to Galileo.* University of Chicago Press, 2015, p.22
5. Jones, Robert (trans.), *Philosophic Fire: Unifying the Fragments of HERACLITUS*
6. Cumont, Franz. *Astrology and Religion among the Greeks and Romans.* GP Putnam's Sons, 1912. p.63
7. Unger, D. J. 'Ancient Christian writers: Against the heresies.' Paulist Press, 1992. *Against Heresies*, St. Irenæus, 3.11.1

CHAPTER TEN
THE COUNCIL OF NICAEA
PART ONE

"Before the Roman Catholic Church parted from the Orthodox Eastern Church, the united Church fought with and suppressed many so-called 'heresies,' some of which represented the views of primitive Christianity and the scene of many of these doctrinal fights was in Egypt. The one that interests us most is Arianism. Arius was an Alexandrian Presbyter early in the fourth century A.D. and fought hard for the doctrine of Unity, the simple conception of the Eternal God, as against all the hair splitting and irrational distinctions in the nature and persons of the Godhead, which finally crystallised in the doctrine of the Trinity, propounded and maintained with much personal acrimony by Athanasius. Athanasius himself was born in Alexandria and became Bishop of Alexandria. He may be counted as the father of Orthodoxy (as now understood in Christianity) and the real systematizer of the doctrine of the Trinity— "three in one and one in three." Up to the third century A.D. the Unitarians had been in the majority in the Christian Church, though subtle metaphysicians had started disputes as to the meaning of 'God becoming man,' the Logos or the Word, the Power of God, whether the Father and the Son were of the same substance or of similar substance, whether the Son could be said to have been created by the Father, and numerous questions of that kind."[1]

— *COMMENTARY ON THE QUR'ÁN*, ABDULLAH
YUSUF ALI

THE COUNCIL IS NOT EXPLAINED BY THE CONVENTIONAL STORY

In the Eastern Orthodox Church Constantine the Great is held as a saint. Legend holds that he is not entirely Roman, he is held by some to be half British, perhaps Welsh (Cambrian). At the time the Roman Empire had been split in two, and Constantine, stationed in what is now called York, was given dominion over the western half. From there he rescued Rome from barbarians, moving it to Byzantium, eventually naming the city after himself, Constantinople. He is partially a product of an early Christian Church some historians say never existed. It was he who convened the Council of Nicaea.

Everything that we have discussed so far is intended to clarify the real Council of Nicaea, the most pivotal affair in the Christian Church. Few today grasp the extent it defined the future of the Church.

The Council is seldom portrayed in its true context. The story is sloppy, it can't explain known facts. However, by not telling the true story the Church has done a disservice to itself. In its quest to be inspirational, it has set itself up for failure. By marginalizing the core doctrine of the Church, the party that should have failed, has now won.

In the conventional story the recently triumphant Emperor Constantine, having defeated the hoards threatening Rome, made an effort to promote peace throughout his Empire. He invited Christian bishops from all parts to a council at Nicaea. His intention is to unite the various factions and establish the Universal Christian Church. The delegates were encouraged to develop a Creed for the united Church to follow. However, along the way, a malcontent named Arius threatened the entire enterprise. Undaunted, Athanasius takes on Arius, and through holy wisdom saves the Church and its Orthodoxy. Defeated, Arius leaves and is stricken down by divine intervention, his intestines rupture, and dies right on the spot. Often the story is dramatized with legends such as St. Nicholas thrashing Arius in a fist fight. The Council ends. Good wins, bad loses. All this happens within a fairly short time-frame.

John Foxe's *Book of Martyrs* tells a much more sobering, less triumphant story:

> "The author of the Arian heresy was Arius, a native of Lybia, and a priest of Alexandria, who, in A.D. 318, began to publish his errors. He was condemned by a council of Lybian and Egyptian bishops, and that sentence was confirmed by the Council of Nice, A.D. 325. After the death of Constantine the Great, the Arians found means to ingratiate themselves into the favor of the emperor

Constantinus, his son and successor in the east; and hence a persecution was raised against the orthodox bishops and clergy. The celebrated Athanasius, and other bishops, were banished, and their sees filled with Arians.

In Egypt and Lybia, thirty bishops were martyred, and many other Christians cruelly tormented; and, A.D. 386, George, the Arian bishop of Alexandria, under the authority of the emperor, began a persecution in that city and its environs, and carried it on with the most infernal severity. He was assisted in his diabolical malice by Catophonius, governor of Egypt; Sebastian, general of the Egyptian forces; Faustinus, the treasurer; and Heraclius, a Roman officer.

The persecutions now raged in such a manner that the clergy were driven from Alexandria, their churches were shut, and the severities practiced by the Arian heretics were as great as those that had been practiced by the pagan idolaters. If a man, accused of being a Christian, made his escape, then his whole family were massacred, and his effects confiscated."[2]

— JOHN FOXE, *BOOK OF MARTYRS*

Now I am not so foolish as to believe that I'm the first to read Foxe. It is not uncommon for an organization to clean up a story to make it more palatable. But even Foxe moves from the Council of Nicaea to Julian the Apostate as if nothing else happened in between. This leaves us with the sobering questions: Which party actually was triumphant at the Council?

The story the modern Church tells says absolutely nothing about our verse 1 John 5:7. It vests its entire interest in the belief that story is of a much later date and had nothing to do with the Council. As we will find, to prove their case they point to Lucian of Antioch (240 312 AD) as publishing the book that later led the Church astray. This demands a question, how is it that a person publishes what results in a major version of the Bible containing the verse, dies thirteen years *before* the Council, and nobody knows of this text or verse until decades or so *after* the Council? The Council invites representatives from across the entire breadth of the Church, yet no one is familiar with the text and we can be assured it had absolutely no effect on the Council?

Tischendorf says he has proof the *Codex Sinaiticus* was one of the fifty Bibles published and sanctioned by the Council and approved by the Emperor. Because 1 John 5:7 is not found in the text it is proof that it doesn't belong in the Bible today. The implication is that the verse must now be considered something of misstep, while it may be OK to believe in the Trinity, it is now optional.

So, if the Trinitarians won, why not insert it into the Bible sanctioned by the Council and the Emperor? Why wait? Does it not depend upon *which party was the in charge at the time?* If the winning side can be shown was the Arians and they gained the sympathy of the Imperial Family, is this not a better explanation?

Early in my career I was taught that the entire fate of Christianity hung in the balance at the Council of Nicaea. The entire dispute centered around one word, in fact, one greek letter, the iota. It was this *iota* that changed the meaning of this *homoousios* from '*same* essence' to '*like* essence.' The first was represented by an Orthodox deacon named Athanasius, the second by a heretic named Arius. We can see the story begins to get more complex... and starts moving away from the facts. Will Durant in his book *Caesar and Christ* gives a summation:

"The Council met in the hall of an imperial palace. Constantine presided and opened the proceedings by a brief appeal to the bishops to restore the unity of the Church. He "listened patiently to the debates," reports Eusebius, "moderated the violence of the contending parties," and himself joined in the argument. *Arius reaffirmed his view that Christ was a created being*, not equal to the Father, but "divine only by participation." Clever questioners forced him to admit that *if Christ was a creature, and had had a beginning, he could change*; and that if he could change he might pass from virtue to vice. The answers were logical, honest, and suicidal. Athanasius, the eloquent and pugnacious archdeacon whom Alexander had brought with him as a theological sword, made it clear that if Christ and the Holy Spirit were not of one substance with the Father, polytheism would triumph. He conceded the difficulty of picturing three distinct persons in one God, but argued that reason must bow to the mystery of the Trinity. All but seventeen of the bishops agreed with him, and signed a statement expressing his view. The supporters of Arius agreed to sign if they might add one iota, changing *homoousion* to *homoiousion*. The Council refused, and issued with the Emperor's approval the following creed:

We believe in one God, the Father Almighty, maker of all things visible or invisible; and in one Lord Jesus Christ, the Son of God, begotten . . . not made, being of one essence (*homoousios*) with the Father . . . who for us men and our salvation came down and was made flesh, was made man, suffered, rose again the third day, ascended into heaven, and comes to judge the quick and the dead. . .

Only five bishops, finally only two, refused to sign this formula. These two, with the unrepentant Arius, were anathematized by the Council and exiled by the Emperor. An imperial edict ordered that all books by Arius should be burned, and made the concealment of such a book punishable with death."[3]

— WILL DURANT, *CAESAR AND CHRIST*

Notice that as yet the Creed has not the term 'Catholic.' The story also equivocates the term *homoousios* and all the baggage the term brings with it. The story has purposely left something out. Arius' beliefs were not that simple. The party represented here was actually the Semi-Arian. They argued exactly as above, *if Christ was a creature, and had had a beginning, he could change virtue to vice,* is exactly correct. But 'from virtue to vice' specifically means Truth could be arbitrary. Neither was Athanasius' triumph so easily had. His back story is missing. Worse still, it is the holes in this story that would be later filled by future Arian sympathetic historians setting the stage for future modernisms. Something more grand, more sinister was going on— something even the participants at the Council had trouble understanding.

Even to this day there is an interdenominational dispute over what really happened.

Typical beliefs on the 'Catholic' side are these.

- The Council brought the various factions together to unite and form the foundation of the Roman Catholic Church
- It affirmed Christianity as a sacramental, doctrinal religion due to the triumph of Athanasius
- It created the Nicene Creed critical to defining Orthodoxy
- It forced the followers of Arius to split from the Church forming non-orthodox factions including Islam
- It was called by Constantine the Great who either was already an orthodox Christian, or converted to it on his deathbed
- It ended the most critical controversy in the Church.
- ***It introduced a novel innovation that had been brewing, the Doctrine of the Trinity***

Typical beliefs on the 'non-denominational' side are:

- The Council corrupted early 'pure' Christianity and put it under the control of Rome
- It created a heretical 'Roman' church designed specifically to advance the power of the Empire

- It perverted the simplicity of original Christianity with introducing novel doctrines such as communion
- It created an unnecessary creed, a non-Biblical oath of allegiance to a corrupt Empire
- It legitimized a false belief system based upon eastern mythology

Little of this is precisely correct, yet, in a loose way, they are all *sort of true*. Constantine did create an Imperial Church, however, it did not last long for his nephew Julian the Apostate soon destroyed it. In fact, Constantine's church wasn't orthodox at all, he was under pressure from the Arians and Semi-Arians who were in the majority. The Council did not create the organization of the Church, the catholic 'novelties' were long accepted traditions. Neither the Doctrine of the Trinity, nor the Nicene Creed, nor the canon of scripture were determined at the Council. The cause of Athanasius was not confirmed at the Council, nor did he 'win' until much later. In fact the Arian factions regained power shortly thereafter, leaving Athanasius to flee for his life. From Edward Gibbon's *Decline and Fall of the Roman Empire* we find:

"But the triumph of Arianism had been preceded by the removal of the orthodox clergy, whom it was impossible either to intimidate or to corrupt; and the reign of Constantius was disgraced by the unjust and ineffectual persecution of the great Athanasius… The immortal name of Athanasius will never be separated from the catholic doctrine of the Trinity, to whose defence he consecrated every moment and every faculty of his being. Educated in the family of Alexander, he had vigorously opposed the early progress of the Arian heresy: he exercised the important functions of secretary under the aged prelate; and the fathers of the Nicene council beheld with surprise and respect the rising virtues of the young deacon. In a time of public danger the dull claims of age and of rank are sometimes superseded; and **within five months after his return from Nice the deacon Athanasius was seated on the archiepiscopal throne of Egypt. He filled that eminent station above forty-six years, and his long administration was spent in a perpetual combat against the powers of Arianism. Five times was Athanasius expelled from his throne; twenty years he passed as an exile or a fugitive; and almost every province of the Roman empire was successively witness to his merit, and his sufferings in the cause of the *Homoousion*, which he considered as the sole pleasure and business, as the duty and as the glory of his life.** Amidst the storms of persecution, the archbishop of Alexandria was patient of labour, jealous of fame, careless of safety; and although his mind was tainted by the contagion of fanaticism, Athanasius displayed a superiority of character and abilities which would have qualified him, far better than the degenerate sons of Constantine, for the government of a great monarchy."[4]

— EDWARD GIBBON, *DECLINE AND FALL OF THE ROMAN EMPIRE*

So, Athanasius fled for his life over a doctrine that had not been invented yet? What is more, the Arians too had their own version of the Trinity, so why would this be so controversial? Athanasius must have had his own version of *homoousios* or he wouldn't have found it acceptable.

It should be seen that Tischendorf's scenario cannot hold. Everything depends on which Bible was sanctioned and the Orthodox party being in power, which did not happen. What we do see, and better explains the evidence, is that wherever Athanasius flees, all remote areas away from the Empire, different Bibles are being used, most representative is the *Vetus Latina which did include the verse.*

I ask, does the plight of Athanasius sound like the dedication of someone to a doctrine that has yet to be formulated? This means a certain corruption did happen, but has seldom if ever been understood.

UNPACKING THE TEACHING OF AMMONIUS SACCAS

The school of thought that led to Arianism was founded by *Ammonius Saccas*. No less of an authority than Cardinal John Henry Newman attests as much, "It is thus, for instance, Platonism, or again, Origenism, has been assigned as the actual source from which Arianism was derived."[5] Origen, sometimes considered a Church Father, was a student of *Ammonius Saccas* and it speculated he taught a form of mystical Indian inspired Platonism.

Cardinal Newman also attests that the doctrine was secret, "Ammonius opened his school at the end of the second century, and continued to preside in it at least till A.D. 243; during which period, and probably for some years after his death, *the real character of his doctrines was carefully hidden from the world.*"[6]

Lucian of Antioch, Arius' teacher, died as an Orthodox priest. Yet, was lived a student of the heretic Paul of Samosata. In a letter from Arius to Eusebius of Nicomedia, the Arian influenced priest who baptized Constantine the Great on his deathbed, Arius states, "We are persecuted, because we say that the Son has a beginning, but that God is without beginning. This is the cause

of our persecution, and likewise, because we say that He is of the non-exis-
tent. And this we say, because He is neither part of God, nor of any essential
being. For this are we persecuted; the rest you know. I bid thee farewell in the
Lord, remembering our afflictions, my *fellow-Lucianist*, and true Eusebius."

This is an indication that an Arian inspired doctrine was taught by Lucian,
and that at least part of the dispute was based upon '*Logos* being a creation
and not eternal.' Again, Cardinal Newman agrees:

> "There is an historical, and not merely a doctrinal connexion between him
> [Lucian] and the Arian party. In his school are found, in matter of fact, the
> names of most of the original advocates of Arianism, and all those who were
> the most influential in their respective Churches throughout the East: — Arius
> himself, Eusebius of Nicomedia, Leontius, Eudoxius, Asterius, and others,
> who will be familiar to us in the sequel; and these men actually appealed to
> him as their authority…"[7]

> — CARDINAL NEWMAN

Yet, there was a later denial by this same party as to how deeply they were
influenced by Arius. What we are looking for is this: we know the Neoplatonist, and Arian schools are connected. We also know these later schools
referred to themselves as Unitarian (particularly as opposed to trinitarian).
Saccas is considered somewhat of an enigma, but it would help our cause if
we could trace Unitarianism back to him. Not only would it complete the
picture, it would provide a 'tell' in our later discussion.

That the modern Church has been by this issue is attested to by no less
than the Archbishop of Canterbury, Rowan Williams in his book *Arius:
Heresy and Tradition*. That academia is no longer sure is shown by Maurice
Wiles:

"Gone is the picture of the gradual flowering of a single, consistent vision of Christian truth, developing only in the sense of receiving an increasing precision of expression, something forced on the church by the need to combat perversions of that truth deliberately introduced by malevolent heretics. In its place has come a picture of the Christian church *seeking to discover what the truth might be* in the context of always-changing conditions and new problems. In that revised picture the roles of 'father' and 'heretic' are much less sharply contrasted."[8]

— MAURICE WILES, *ARCHETYPAL HERESY: ARIANISM THROUGH THE CENTURIES*

Therefore, I believe we have much reason to question the teachings of modern scholars. The 'modern' way of looking at the story can be displayed in the following graphic:

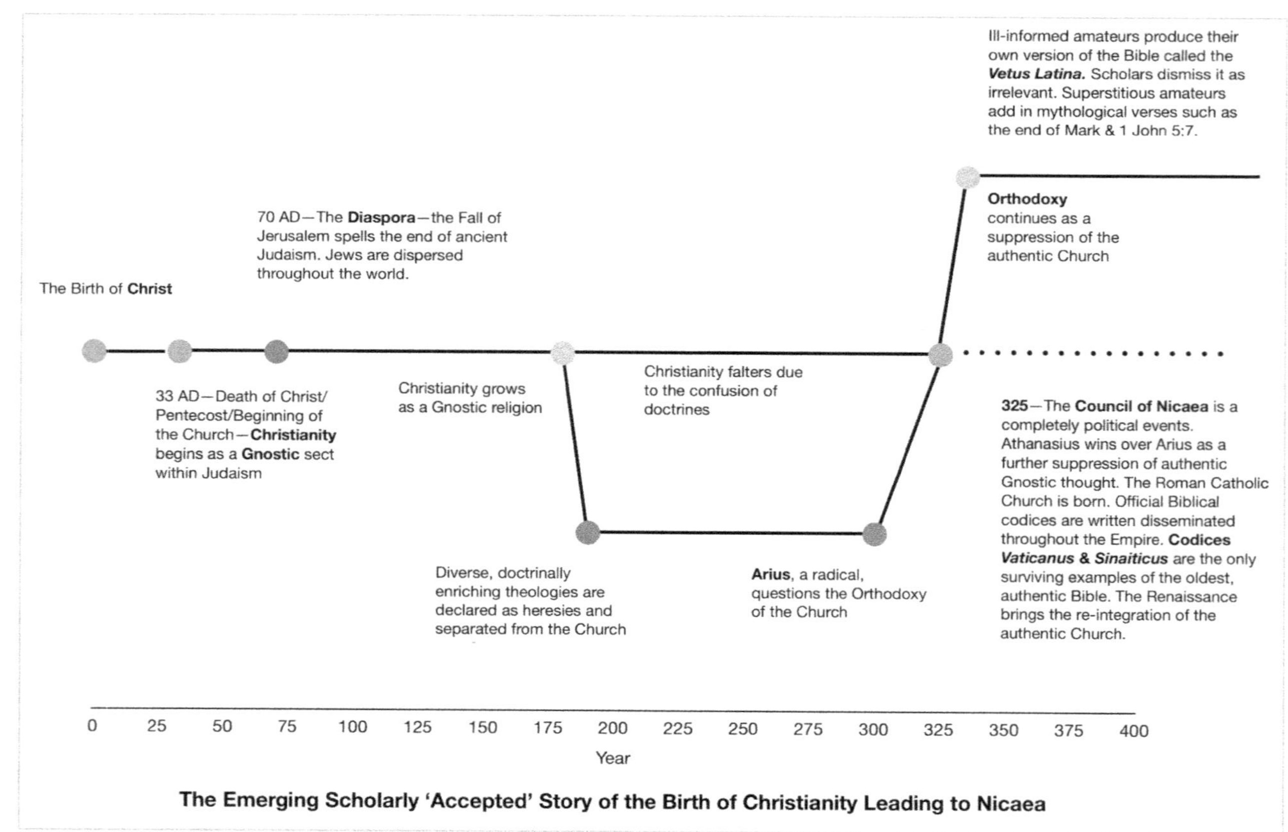

The Emerging Scholarly 'Accepted' Story of the Birth of Christianity Leading to Nicaea

This graphic shows the generally accepted timeline of early Christianity. Gnosticism is not a later arriving heresy, but is a *legitimate* branch of the early Church. They maintain it was the earliest, therefore the most authentic (a repeating Gnostic theme). This is the view of the early nineteenth century German Lutheran F.C. Baur and his Tübingen School of theology which is credited as giving birth to Modernism. In this version it is Orthodoxy that is the late-comer and doesn't take the upper hand until after the Council of Nicaea in 325. *They need this timeline to authenticate their faith.*

Oddly enough, and very telling, is that every step of the way this school of thought attacks and reinterprets St. John's Gospel. They re-date it to around 180 AD written by a Gnostic using John's name. They consider 1 John 5:7 inauthentic. They use the term Logos as proof of Gnostic doctrine.

In contrast is the scenario below:

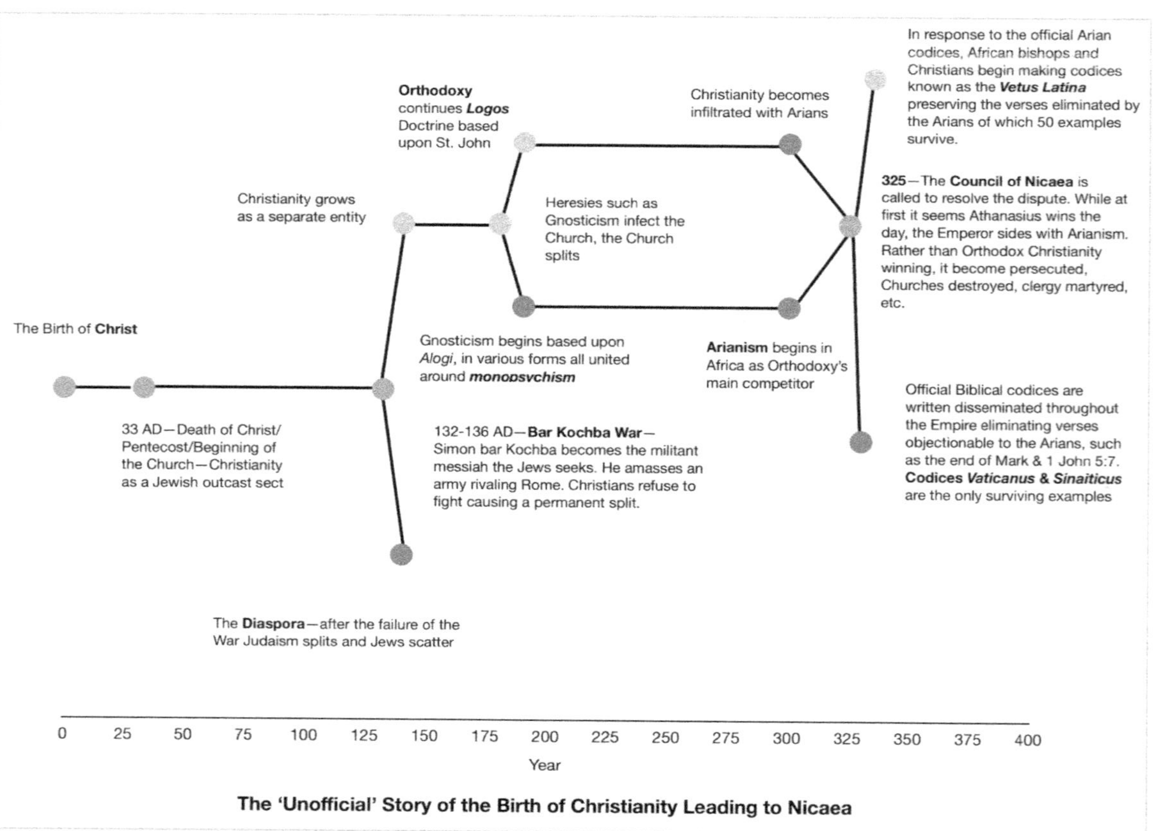

The 'Unofficial' Story of the Birth of Christianity Leading to Nicaea

Clearly, the first chart ignores a lot of evidence. The second chart shows something more realistic, that by even using their data, something is infiltrating the Church beginning around 170 AD, and gaining strength in the early to middle 200s. This makes sense if *Ammonius Saccas* formed the basis of the cult.

However, it demands a re-examination of the Arian heresy, and an understanding of why the 'Logos' of 1 John 5:7 was so dangerous.

The movement in question began as a cult within Christianity, often called the *Alogi,* that denied the doctrine of *Logos*. The Catholic Encyclopedia defines the *Alogi* as follows:

"*Alogi*— "Deniers of the Word". St. Irenæus (*Adv. Haer.*, III, ii, 9) makes a brief reference to persons who denied the manifestation of the Paraclete, and refused, in consequence, to admit the Gospel of St. John, wherein it is announced. He gives the party no name. St. Hippolytus combated such an error both in his Syntagma and in a special work entitled "In Defence of the Gospel of John and the Apocalypse." These works are lost, but a good share of their contents is believed to have been preserved by St. Epiphanius. St. Epiphanius (*Haer.* LI) gives a long account of the party of heretics who arose after the Cataphrygians, Quartodecimans, and others, and who received neither the Gospel of St. John nor his Apocalypse. He calls them Alogi (deniers of the Word) because, by rejecting the Gospel of St. John, they rejected the Logos which was revealed in that Gospel. Playing on the term, he observes, with a touch of sarcasm, that they are well named, "alogi," i.e. "without reason."[9]

Anglican Bishop Thomas Burgess writes at a time before the secret *Apocryphon* was known:

The first period (A. D. 101-300) contains no evidence against the verse, but much for it. There is no Greek Manuscript of the New Testament of this period. The oldest Greek copy extant is of much later date than the ancient Latin version of the Western Church, and: the writings of Tertullian and Cyprian, who made use of it; and posterior to the first of two Greek evidences, which I have to bring in defence of the verse; I mean the rejection of the writings of St. John by certain heretics of this period, whom Epiphanius calls ALOGI, on 'account of their denial of the Apostle's doctrine of the Divinity of the *Logos,* or the Word. This rejection of St. John's writings by the ALOGI applies to no part of his writings so strongly as to his first Epistle, and especially to the seventh verse of the fifth chapter of that Epistle, which must have been the most obnoxious to them of all the passages of St. John."[10]

— *A VINDICATION OF 1 JOHN 5:7*, BISHOP THOMAS
BURGESS

As we have already discussed, Enfield credited all early heresy to the rise and intrusion of *Orientalism* into western thought causing a marriage of incompatible principles. I quote Enfield here:

"The dreams of the Orientalists concerning the Divine nature were multiplied without end by the Christian Gnostics, particularly by Valentine, the founder of a sect which arose in the second century, and spread through Egypt, Syria, and Asia Minor. This fanatic conceived the divine nature to be a vast abyss, in the *pleroma* or fulness of which existed, as emanations from the first fountain of being, Æons of different orders and degrees. The source of Æons Valentine called *Bython*. To this he united a principle, which he called *Ennoia*, or *Sige*: from the union of these he supposed to be produced *Nous* and *Aletheia*, and from these, in succession. *Logos*, *Anthropos*, and *Ecclesia*; among the remote descendants of whom was Jesus Christ, and below him the *Demiurgus*, or Creator of the world, who held the middle place between God and the material world. This fanciful system (similar to that of the Jewish Cabbala, and doubtless derived from the same source, the Oriental doctrine of emanation) was highly displeasing to those Christian fathers who were disposed to think more soberly and reverently concerning the Divine nature. When they saw the doctrine of Christ corrupted by such absurd fictions, they were naturally led to inveigh against that false philosophy, from which they supposed them to have originated."[11]

— WILLIAM ENFIELD

Now I ask the reader to take particular notice to the above. It is alarmingly specific for a dispute that was supposed to revolve around the simple insertion of an iota. Keep in mind, Enfield's source is supposed to be the seventeenth century cleric, Athanasius Kircher. In fact, it looks awfully like the secret *Apocryphon of St. John, something that was not supposed to be known until after WWII.*

This is interesting. There is a consensus amongst some scholars that an anti-logos force was working within Christianity challenging the authenticity of St. John's Gospel. Why? Because they had a better one?

The verse in 1 John is often referred to as *The Testimony of the Heavenly Witnesses*. There are specific requirements under Jewish law as to how many witnesses are needed to convict—at least two, preferably three. The verse in question is the second Biblical reference to Logos as a doctrine. It is also the second to specifically mention the Trinity. Without the verse, two others are left without resolution. Removing the verse cripples both doctrines as now they don't have the required number of witnesses. What happened, I believe, is that Gnostics realized that they could get rid of two doctrines by simply removing one verse.

We know that *Ammonius Saccas* had an academy that taught a secret doctrine and that this gave birth to Neoplatonism. Numerous 'questionable' authorities, Christian and anti-Christian, attended his school such as Origen, Plotinus, Iamblicus, and Porphyry. No one doubts that Ammonius Saccas was the conduit, yet where is the documentation of his teaching? Cardinal Newman says this:

> He [Ammonius Saccas] committed nothing to writing, whether of his exoteric or esoteric philosophy, and when Origen, who was scarcely his junior, attended him in his first years, probably had not yet decidedly settled the form of his system. Plotinus, the first promulgator and chief luminary of Eclecticism, began his public lectures A.D. 244; and for some time held himself bound by the promise of secrecy made to his master. Moreover, he selected Rome as the seat of his labours, and there is even proof that Origen and he never met in Alexandria, on the contrary, the infant philosophy languished; no teacher of note succeeded to Ammonius; and even had it been otherwise, Origen had left the city for ever, ten years previous to that philosopher's death. It is clear, then, that he had no means of detecting the secret infidelity of the Eclectics; and the proof of this is still stronger, if, as [Johann Jakob] Brucker calculates Plotinus did not divulge his master's secret till A.D. 255, since Origen died A.D. 253. Yet, even in this ignorance of the purpose of the Eclectics, we find Origen, in his letter to Gregory expressing dissatisfaction at the actual effects which had resulted to the Church from that literature in which he himself was so eminently accomplished. "For my part," he says to Gregory, "taught by experience, I will own to you, that rare is the man, who, having accepted the precious things of Egypt, leaves the country, and uses them in decorating the worship of God."[12]

— CARDINAL JOHN HENRY NEWMAN

And again from NewAdvent:

"Neo-Platonism, the philosophy of the new pagan renaissance, had a prophet at Alexandria in the person of Ammonius Saccas. The Jews, too, who were there in very large numbers breathed its liberal atmosphere, and had assimilated secular culture. They there formed the most enlightened colony of the Dispersion. Having lost the use of Hebrew, they found it necessary to translate the Scriptures into the more familiar Greek. Philo, their foremost thinker, became a sort of Jewish Plato. Alexandria was, in addition, one of the chief seats of that peculiar mixed pagan and Christian speculation known as Gnosticism."[13]

WHAT WE NEED at this point is the trajectory of this teaching in early Christianity:

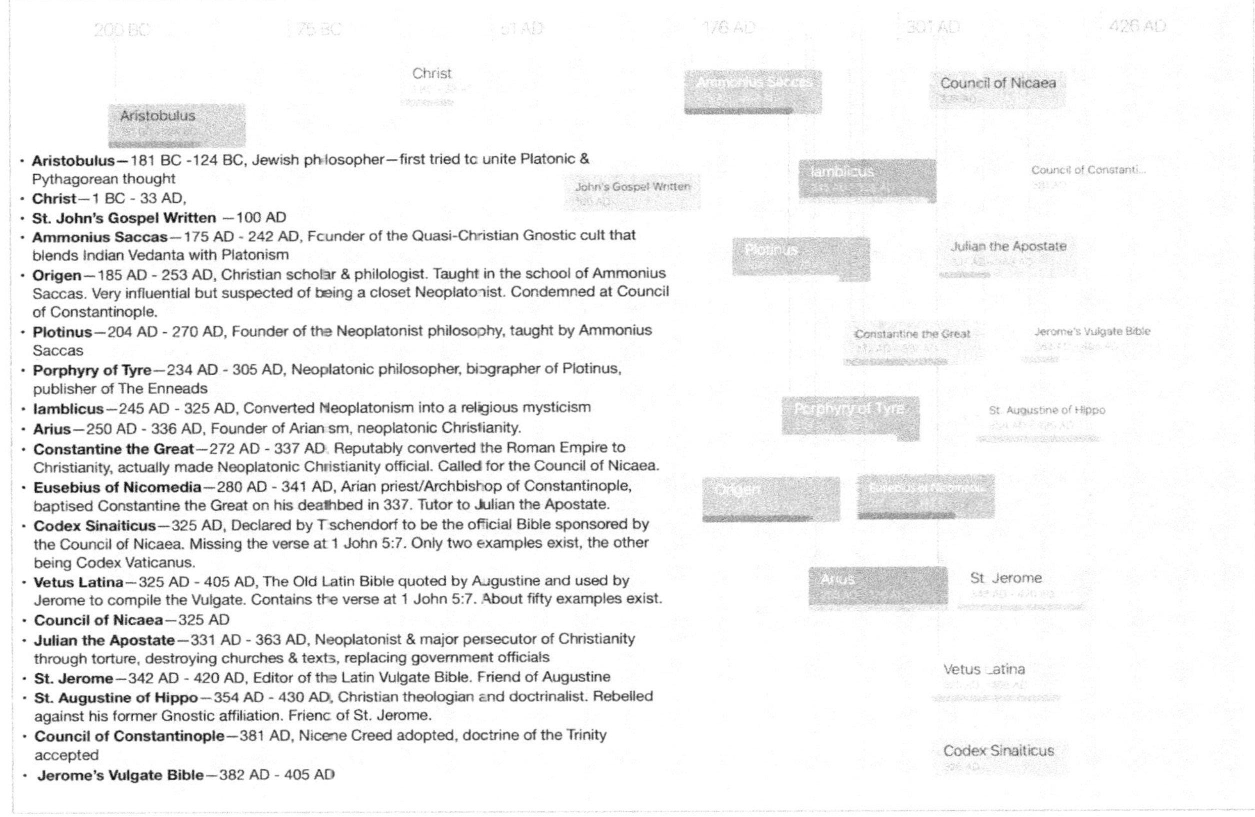

- **Aristobulus**—181 BC -124 BC, Jewish philosopher—first tried to unite Platonic & Pythagorean thought
- **Christ**—1 BC - 33 AD,
- **St. John's Gospel Written** —100 AD
- **Ammonius Saccas**—175 AD - 242 AD, Founder of the Quasi-Christian Gnostic cult that blends Indian Vedanta with Platonism
- **Origen**—185 AD - 253 AD, Christian scholar & philologist. Taught in the school of Ammonius Saccas. Very influential but suspected of being a closet Neoplatonist. Condemned at Council of Constantinople.
- **Plotinus**—204 AD - 270 AD, Founder of the Neoplatonist philosophy, taught by Ammonius Saccas
- **Porphyry of Tyre**—234 AD - 305 AD, Neoplatonic philosopher, biographer of Plotinus, publisher of The Enneads
- **Iamblicus**—245 AD - 325 AD, Converted Neoplatonism into a religious mysticism
- **Arius**—250 AD - 336 AD, Founder of Arianism, neoplatonic Christianity.
- **Constantine the Great**—272 AD - 337 AD. Reputably converted the Roman Empire to Christianity, actually made Neoplatonic Christianity official. Called for the Council of Nicaea.
- **Eusebius of Nicomedia**—280 AD - 341 AD, Arian priest/Archbishop of Constantinople, baptised Constantine the Great on his deathbed in 337. Tutor to Julian the Apostate.
- **Codex Sinaiticus**—325 AD, Declared by Tischendorf to be the official Bible sponsored by the Council of Nicaea. Missing the verse at 1 John 5:7. Only two examples exist, the other being Codex Vaticanus.
- **Vetus Latina**—325 AD - 405 AD, The Old Latin Bible quoted by Augustine and used by Jerome to compile the Vulgate. Contains the verse at 1 John 5:7. About fifty examples exist.
- **Council of Nicaea**—325 AD
- **Julian the Apostate**—331 AD - 363 AD, Neoplatonist & major persecutor of Christianity through torture, destroying churches & texts, replacing government officials
- **St. Jerome**—342 AD - 420 AD, Editor of the Latin Vulgate Bible. Friend of Augustine
- **St. Augustine of Hippo**—354 AD - 430 AD, Christian theologian and doctrinalist. Rebelled against his former Gnostic affiliation. Friend of St. Jerome.
- **Council of Constantinople**—381 AD, Nicene Creed adopted, doctrine of the Trinity accepted
- **Jerome's Vulgate Bible**—382 AD - 405 AD

In this chart we see many of the players who we have been speaking of, Plotinus, Iamblicus, Eusebius of Nicomedia, and Origen. It should also be noted that Enfield is using the same source as was Newman, Brucker:

> "The allegorical method of explaining the writings and traditions of the ancients, long practised in Egypt, having been adopted by the Jews who had been educated in the Alexandrian schools, and particularly by Philo, these examples were followed by Origen; and thus a fanciful method of interpreting the scriptures was encouraged, which opened a wide door to error and delusion. As the Alexandrian philosophers had, by this expedient, been able to accommodate the Pagan mythology to their respective systems; and as Ammonius had employed it to reconcile the supposed truths of Revelation with his new-modelled Platonism; so Origen hoped, by the same method, to establish a union between Heathen philosophy and Christian doctrine. His fundamental canon of criticism was, that wherever the literal sense of scripture was not obvious, or not clearly consistent with his tenets, the words were to be understood in a spiritual and mystical sense: a rule by which he could easily incorporate any fancies, either original or borrowed, with the Christian creed... These tenets, which approach nearer to the doctrine of Ammonius or Plotinus than to that of Christ, may be ultimately traced up to that emanative system, which gave rise to Gnosticism and to the Jewish Cabbala."[14]

> — WILLIAM ENFIELD

Origen's teaching were condemned at the Council of Constantinople, the very Council that completed and *actually* accepted the Nicene Creed. Origen, himself, was not condemned as a heretic because he was given no opportunity to repent.

So what was that doctrine? Did anybody ever write it down? Many would say, 'no,' yet, Porphyry, a student of Plotinus did write down his teaching in what is called the *Enneads*, something many occultists acknowledge. The *Enneads* are a work by Porphyry revealing the doctrines of Plotinus. The work is the best clue to their doctrine. The *Enneads* state something Enfield and Brucker have been making us familiar. It speaks, again, to this secret doctrine:

> "Erennius, Origen, and Plotinus had made a compact not to disclose any of the doctrines which Ammonius had revealed to them. Plotinus kept faith, and in all his intercourse with his associates divulged nothing of Ammonius' system. But the compact was broken, first by Erennius and then by Origen following

suit: Origen, it is true, put in writing nothing but the treatise *On the Spirit-Beings*, and in Gallienus' reign that entitled *The King the Sole Creator*. Plotinus himself remained a long time without writing, but he began to base his Conferences on what he had gathered from his studies under Ammonius. In this way, writing nothing but constantly conferring with a certain group of associates, he passed ten years."[15]

— PORPHYRY, *THE ENNEADS*

So we turn to the *Enneads* and they themselves reveal the core of their doctrine:

"Now are we to hold similarly that your soul and mine and all are one, and that the same thing is true of the universe, the soul in all the several forms of life being one soul, not parcelled out in separate items, but an omnipresent identity? If the soul in me is a unity, why need that in the universe be otherwise seeing that there is no longer any question of bulk or body? And if that, too, is one soul and yours, and mine, belongs to it, then yours and mine must also be one: and if, again, the soul of the universe and mine depend from one soul, once more all must be one. What then in itself is this one soul? First we must assure ourselves of the possibility of all souls being one as that of any given individual is. It must, no doubt, seem strange that my soul and that of any and everybody else should be one thing only: it might mean my feelings being felt by someone else, my goodness another's too, my desire, his desire, all our experience shared with each other and with the (one-souled) universe, so that the very universe itself would feel whatever I felt."[16]

— *PLOTINUS*

Now, this is nothing new. It is exactly what Enfield has been telling us, but it confirms that the core of the original Unitarian doctrine was *monopsychism*.

It is held by some scholars that Neoplatonism as found in the *Enneads* and taught by Ammonius Saccas has deep similarities to Indian thought of the *Vedanta*, often speculating that either he was an Indian mystic, or that he was at least schooled in the teachings. True or not should not matter to us, only that the teachings *are identical*. From *Neoplatonism and Indian Thought* R. Baine Harris:

"But does Plotinus depend on śruti? Apparently he seems to depend only on dialectic which is the process of going up from the sensible world to the One —though the principles of dialectic are given to a receptive man by Nous, yet Plotinus admits that someone is needed to show him the way. We know that Plotinus had a Guru or teacher called Ammonius Saccas and so in the case of Plotinus the Guru takes the place of śruti or scripture. The *Upanisads* very clearly tell us that he alone knows who has a teacher (*Ā cāryavān puruso veda*)."[17]

"Nemesius, ascribes the Neoplatonic view of the soul-body union to Plotinus's teacher Ammonius Saccas. While the hypothesis that Ammonius was himself an Indian missionary."[18]

As a matter of fact, I do happen to have a book, *Advaita Vedanta and Modern Science* by John Dobson. The very purpose of the book is to prove that the modern scientific idea of the singularity is identical to the teaching of the One-Mind taught by Vedanta. In fact, they credit themselves as inventors of the doctrine. Here is a quote from the book presumably from the Vedanta:

"When body-consciousness has melted away, and the Supreme Self has been realized, Where, where the mind is sent, there, there is gets Samādhi."[19]

Regardless of the pedigree, they both gave birth to the same child. To discriminate is precisely the act of reasoning, to be 'rational' which itself is an act of making distinctions, to logically divide such as dividing the idea 'man' into two constituent logical parts, 'rational' and 'animal.' To think that you can cease to discriminate and salvage identity is folly. What it is, however, IS an act of unification, for what else would be the result of ceasing to reason or to discriminate? Worse still, it is an act of subterfuge. As Gödel has taught us, it is a path to the impossible, a path to insanity, to a world where 'this sentence is false' is a truth. It is a Conscious-Unity, meditative absorption becoming one with reality, Unity, Singularity, Monopsychism, the very thing declared the basis of all heresy by the Catholic Church in the Condemnation of 1277.

---

1. Maulana, Helmi, and Hadis, Dan. *The Holy Qur'an: text, translation and commentary*, Karya Abdullah Yusuf Ali
2. Foxe, John. *Foxe's Book of Martyrs*. Morgan & Scott, 1899. Chp. 3—'Persecutions Under the Arian Heretics'

3. Durant, Will. *Caesar and Christ: The Story of Civilization, Volume III*. Vol. 3. Simon and Schuster, 2011. p.660

4. Gibbon, Edward *The Decline and Fall of the Roman Empire*. Strahan & Cadell, London. 1776, Chp. 21 - Council of Nicaea

5. Newman, John Henry. *The Arians of the Fourth Century*. Longmans, Green, and Company, 1901. p.6

6. Newman, John Henry. *The Arians of the Fourth Century*. Longmans, Green, and Company, 1901. p.107

7. Newman, John Henry. *The Arians of the Fourth Century*. Longmans, Green, and Company, 1901. p.6

8. Wiles, Maurice. *Archetypal Heresy: Arianism through the centuries*. OUP Oxford, 1996

9. The Catholic Encyclopedia, Havey, F., article 'Alogi' — In. New York: Robert Appleton Company, 1907 Retrieved February 25, 2023 from New Advent: http://www.newadvent.org/cathen/01331b.htm

10. Burgess, Thomas Anglican Bishop of St. David's, *A Vindication of 1 John 5:7, from the Objections of M. Griesbach*, 1756-1837, p.28

11. Enfield, *The History of Philosophy*, p.445

12. Newman, John Henry. *The Arians of the Fourth Century*. Longmans, Green, and Company, 1901. p.107

13. The Catholic Encyclopedia, Havey, F.. article, 'Clement of Alexandria,' Robert Appleton Company New York, 1908. — Retrieved March 9, 2023 from New Advent: http://www.newadvent.org/cathen/04045a.htm

14. Enfield, *The History of Philosophy*, p.461-4

15. Porphyry, MacKenna, Stephen (trans,) 'The Enneads,' *On the Life of Plotinus and the Arrangement of his Work from Plotinus*, https://sacred-texts.com/cla/plotenn/enn001.htm

16. Porphyry, MacKenna, Stephen (trans,) 'The Enneads,' *On the Life of Plotinus and the Arrangement of his Work from Plotinus*, https://sacred-texts.com/cla/plotenn/enn001.htm

17. Harris, R. Baine (ed.) 'Imagery in Plotinus and Indian Thought' in, *Neoplatonism and Indian Thought*, Norfolk, VA, 1982, p.241

18. Harris, R. Baine (ed.) 'Imagery in Plotinus and Indian Thought' in, *Neoplatonism and Indian Thought* (Norfolk, VA, 1982), 129.9 (*Dorrie*, op. cit., p. 54) The International Society for Neoplatonic Studies pp.119-120 n. 72.

19. Dobson, John Lowry. *Advaita Vedanta and Modern Science*. Vivekanada Vedanta Society, 1979. p.17

THE COUNCIL OF NICAEA
PART TWO

"In the most enlightened period of Arabian philosophy, the utmost that was attempted was, to apply the principles of philosophy to the correction of the absurdities of Mahometanism. The learned professors of their schools were, indeed, thoroughly convinced, that Islamism could not long subsist, unless it were corrected by philosophy. But in endeavouring to give a philosophical air to the crudities and absurdities of the *Koran*, the ingenuity of learned men, restrained by reverence for authority, framed a system of opinions, in which neither the true meaning and spirit of the Islamitic law were preserved, nor the freedom of philosophical speculation was indulged; whence numerous sects arose, in which an unnatural alliance was long maintained between philosophy and superstition."[1]

— WILLIAM ENFIELD

Defenders of the verse at 1 John 5:7 often concede too much to their opponents. Rather than denying that the Codices *Vaticanus* and *Sinaiticus* are spurious, let's concede that they are, in fact, the product of the Council of Nicaea.

1. That the verse may have been inserted at a later date does not necessarily invalidate the verse.

2. If the two codices *Vaticanus* and *Sinaiticus* <u>were</u> the official Bibles published by the Council does not hurt our case if they were published by the Arians/Neoplatonists then in the majority and in power.

3. The *Vetus Latina* Bible which did contain the verse may be both spurious *and* legitimate if they were written by people attempting to preserve the authentic doctrine of the Church in the face of Empire-wide persecution.

4. That *Sinaiticus* is the oldest *existing* text does not prove there weren't any older, particularly if there was a movement to destroy all non-Arian Bibles.

5. The fact that a phrase is missing from the text but noted in the margin does not necessarily mean it is inauthentic. It would not be uncommon for a cleric to retain an authentic tradition by noting it in the margin—it is done to this day.

While the Church was united momentarily at the Council of Nicaea, it was just prior to a rising coercive Arian/Neoplatonist movement. The Arian take over the Church was inevitable if it had not been for a documented 'miracle.' Hopefully it will be seen that the following scenario accounts for all the facts that the conventional scenario does not.

THE THALIA OF ARIUS & THE PERSECUTION OF ATHANASIUS

Arianism is a very subtle, abstract philosophy. Strictly speaking it is not so much 'anti-Trinity' as it is a conspiracy against how a trinity resolves. While the truly Christian doctrine places the Trinity at the very top, Arianism places it just below the top, the *pleroma*. The Trinity then becomes just another one of the imagined layers of demons and demigods. It is not just a rebellion against the number '3', but a slander against the Divine itself.

Few writings of Arius exist, so it is difficult to pin him with his own doctrine, but there are clues. The main writing of Arius is called *Thalia* meaning 'good cheer.' This is suspiciously like the word 'gospel,' which means 'good news.' The surviving version of his *Thalia* comes from Athanasius' oration against him.

The core of Arius' heresy is found in the following verse. As one can see, the heresy was not simply a dispute over the term *homoousios*. We must see it as setting up a logical paradox that once interjected confounded the honest debate. As has been said, the true Arian doctrine was kept secret, but this was largely a product of what I have called the *Unitarian Predicament*.

Conventionally, we do the Council an injustice. By seeing it as a debate between Orthodox vs. Arians, we miss the point. We have tended to see the counter side of the argument as Semi-Arians, but perhaps they would be better described as the *Devil's Advocates*.

It is customary within the Church that when someone is proposed for sainthood, or a vital doctrine proposed, that someone take the side of the Adversary. The purpose of this is not to promote the Devil, but to make absolutely sure that what is being proposed is free from error.

Arius, who truly represented the Adversary, and being that his doctrine was hidden, made it necessary that someone be his *Devil's Advocate* to insure that a free-from-error conclusion would be reached. This clearly was not something easily had—it took years and more than a few debates.

Not understanding the whole of his doctrine, the primary discussion was deposited on whether the *Logos had a beginning, a result of the predicament*. As John's text referred to the 'Son' and 'Logos' interchangeably, a dispute arose: how is a 'begotten' Son reconciled to the eternal Truth if they are essentially the same? This is displayed in Arius' writings:

> He who is without beginning made the Son/Logos a beginning of
>   created things.
> He produced him as a son for himself by begetting him.
> He [*Son/Logos*] has none of the distinct characteristics of God's own
>   being.
> For he is not equal to, nor is he of the same being as him.

— ARIUS, THALIA

Arius himself mentions his Trinitarian formula in his letter to Eusebius, Bishop of Nicomedia:

> "He has driven us out of the city as atheists, because we do not concur in what he publicly preaches: 'God always, the Son always; as the Father so the Son; the Son co-exists unbegotten with God; he is everlasting; neither by thought nor by any interval does God precede the Son; always God, always Son; he is begotten of the unbegotten; the Son is of God himself.'"

From where did this dispute arise if not from 1 John, the very verse that equates the two concepts? Yet, there were clearly those amongst the Arians who were willing to go further. The actions after the Council were recorded by the fifth century historian Sozomen in his ecclesiastical history under 'Chap. XXII — Machinations of the Arians and Meletians against St. Athanasius.' The Arian party, many of who pretended to be orthodox, "had altered the decrees of the Nicaean council":

> "The calumnies were substantiated by many bishops and clergy who were with John, and who sedulously obtained access to the emperor; **they pretended to great orthodoxy**, and imputed to Athanasius and the bishops of his party all the bloodshed, imprisonments, conflagrations of churches, and deeds of violence and lawlessness which had been perpetrated. But when Athanasius wrote to the emperor and proved the illegality of the ordination of John's adherents, **showing that they had altered the decrees of the Nicaean council,** that their faith was not sound, and that they persecuted and calumniated the orthodox, Constantine was at a loss to know whom to believe."

> — SOZOMEN, FIFTH CENTURY HISTORIAN

If they were willing to alter the decrees, why should we not believe they were willing to alter the authentic Biblical text? This means we should not expect the documentation of the dispute to exist. Is this not a problem for the revisionists? The Arians are altering documents, denying the decrees, yet Arius feigns orthodoxy as he pleads to the emperor to reinstall him. He also appeals to the concept 'catholic':

> "We have received this faith from the holy Gospels, in which the Lord says to his disciples, "Go forth and disciple all nations, baptizing them in the name of the Father, of the Son, and of the Holy Spirit." If we do not so believe this, and if we do not truly receive the <u>*doctrines concerning the Father, the Son, and the Holy Spirit*</u>, as they are taught by the whole catholic Church and by the sacred Scriptures, as we believe in every point, let God be our judge, both now and in the day which is to come."[2]

> — ARIUS, *RECANTATION TO THE EMPEROR CONSTANTINE*

Arius proceeds the above by an early version of the Nicene Creed, *a text known to be derived entirely from the Bible* aside from the term *homoousios*.

This fact Arius concedes as he feigns his orthodoxy. While the Creed, itself, appears to have as yet to become a trinitarian formula, Arius himself refers to "<u>*doctrines*</u> *concerning the Father, the Son, and the Holy Spirit*". He here admits to a *plurality* of Trinitarian 'doctrines'. I ask, where else is this other doctrine if not 1 John, *the only specifically Trinitarian formula in the Bible other than the formula for Baptism*?

So I ask, if this doctrine is not yet part of the Creed, from where is Arius quoting the text if not from Scripture? Is this not a lie? Is this why Tischendorf's Codex *Sinaiticus*, the 'official Bible of Nicaea,' is missing the verse? If one doubts me, Sozomen continues:

> "Many considered this declaration of faith as an artful compilation, and as **bearing an appearance of opposition to the Arian tenets, while, in reality, it supported them**; the terms in which it was couched being so vague that it was susceptible of diverse interpretations."

> — SOZOMEN

This is still a problem. How does one 'artfully' get around the tenets of faith if those same tenets of faith don't themselves exist? How does Arius know ahead of time what those tenets will be?

That the Arian party is wholesale making up both doctrines and evidence is shown in the sham trial he institutes against Athanasius:

> "Athanasius, having been urged to justify himself, presented himself repeatedly before the tribunal; successfully repelled some of the accusations, and requested permission to delay replying to the others. He was exceedingly perplexed when he reflected on the favour in which his accusers were held by his judges, on the number of witnesses belonging to the sects of Arius and Meletius who appeared against him, and on the indulgence that was manifested towards his accusers after their calumnies had been detected. As, for instance, when he was charged with having cut off the arm of Arsenius for purposes of sorcery, and with having seduced a certain female by bribery. Both these charges were proved to be false and absurd. When this female made the deposition before the bishops, Timothy, a presbyter of Alexandria, who stood by Athanasius, approached her according to a plan he had secretly concerted, and said to her, "Did I then, O woman, violate your chastity?" She replied, "But didst thou not?" and mentioned the place and attendant circumstances. He likewise led Arsenius into the midst of them, showed both his hands to the

judges, and requested them to make the accusers account for the arm which they had exhibited. For it happened that Arsenius, either acting under Divine inspiration, or grieved at hearing that Athanasius was accused of having slain him, escaped by night from the place of his concealment, and arrived at Tyre the day before trial. Both these accusations having been thus summarily dismissed, no mention of the first was made in the Acts of the Council; most probably, I think, because the whole affair was considered too indecorous and absurd for insertion."[3]

— SOZOMEN

This was not the end of things, for the Arian party then went straight to the emperor:

"But Eusebius, bishop of Nicomedia, and his partisans, went to the emperor, and represented that the synod of Tyre had enacted no decrees against Athanasius but what were founded on justice. They brought forward as witnesses, Theognis, Maris. Theodore, Valens, and Ursacius, and deposed that he had broken the sacred vase, and their calumnies were finally triumphant. The emperor, either believing their statements to be true, or imagining that unanimity would be restored among the bishops if Athanasius were removed, exiled him to Treves, a city of Gaul; and thither, therefore, he was conducted."
[4]

— LETTER FROM THE EMPEROR CONSTANTINE TO THE
SYNOD OF TYRE

So, why would the emperor accept Arius back into the Church if he was a heretic?:

"Being attacked with a disease which threatened to terminate in death, she [Constantia, the emperors sister] besought her brother, who went to visit her, to grant what she was about to ask, as her dying request: this request was, to receive the above-mentioned priest on terms of intimacy, and to rely upon him as a man of orthodox faith. "For my part," she added, "I am drawing nigh to death, and am no longer interested in the concerns of this life; the only apprehension I now feel arises from dread lest you should incur the wrath of God, and suffer any calamity, or the loss of your empire, since you have been induced to condemn good men to perpetual banishment." From that period, the emperor received the priest into favour…"[5]

— CONCERNING THE RECALL OF ARIUS

Clearly the Imperial family was perplexed by all this. Under these conditions if the Arians had omitted John's verse, under what authority had Athanasius to contest it? And would not the Arian party exploit the opportunity to quickly disseminate their version of the Bible? From Athanasius' account of Arius' death:

"It was Saturday, and he expected the next day to be readmitted into the church. The dispute ran high; the partisans of Eusebius were loud in their menaces, while Alexander had recourse to prayer. The Lord was the judge, and declared himself against the unjust. A little before sunset Arius was compelled by a want of nature to enter the place appointed for such emergencies, and here he lost at once both restoration to communion and his life. The most blessed Constantine was amazed when he heard of this occurrence, and regarded it as the punishment of perjury. It then became evident to every one that the menaces of Eusebius were absolutely futile, and that the expectations of Arius were vain and foolish. It also became manifest that the Arian heresy had met with condemnation from the Saviour as well as from the pristine church."

Yet, this was in 336 AD, *eleven years after the Council*. Further more, there is evidence that once the Emperor put his imprimatur on the documents of Nicaea that they were not to be tampered with. If he had fallen under the spell of the Arians, wouldn't it be likely he would censor the verse they found most repugnant? It would take until the end of the fourth century for an approved revision, for more treachery was yet to happen. That the verse in question was in fact censored should not be doubted. After the death of Constantine the Great, the Arians once again took power. This is backed up by the writings of the Apostolic Fathers showing how nuanced the debate had become:

"But it had no special interest for them. While the orthodox party clung to the ομοουσιος as enshrining the doctrine for which they fought, they had no liking for the terms αγεννητος and γενντος, as applied to the Father and the Son respectively, though unable to deny their propriety, because they were affected by the Arians and applied in their own way. To the orthodox mind the Arian formula ουκ ην πριν γεννηθηναι, or some Semi-Arian formula hardly less dangerous, seemed always to be lurking under the expression Θεος γεννητος as applied to the Son. "As you refuse to accept our ομοουσιος because though used by the fathers, it does not occur in the Scriptures, so will we decline on the same grounds to accept your αγεννητος"… This fully explains the reluctance of the orthodox party to handle terms which their adversaries used to endanger the ομοουσιος. But, when the stress of the Arian controversy was removed, it became convenient to express the Catholic doctrine by saying that the Son in His Divine nature was γεννητος, but not γενητος. And this distinction is staunchly maintained in later orthodox writers, e.g. John of Damascus."[6]

The debate was not merely over the spelling of *homoousios*, it had become a debate over *begotten* vs *only-begotten*. Again, where do they arrive at such a nuanced argument if not from difficulties posed by 1 John 5:7? The preface to John's Gospel only indicates that the *Logos* was eternal. When it states that *Logos* was 'made' flesh, it could be interpreted that *Logos* was later infused into Christ. Why then the debate over their co-eternality? It is well known that the Council of Nicaea was not trying to invent doctrine, but only discern it from Scripture and Tradition. Everywhere an insertion of a non-Biblical term resulted in a controversy. So, I ask again, from where did the doctrine arise that Christ WAS eternally identical to *Logos* <u>and</u> co-eternal with the Father if not from Scripture? If 1 John 5:7 was non-Biblical, where is the dispute that the Orthodox are introducing a non-Biblical doctrine? It is only by identifying Christ with the Son, with *Logos,* that a pre-born existence can be inferred, it is unique to this verse.

In his own way, Arius concedes this in his own writing. This heresy also extends to the concept of the Trinity, a doctrine the Arians are not supposed to have. Proof of this is the very words of Arius in a verse that seemingly is formulated to contest the Trinitarian unity expressed in 1 John 5:7:

So there is a Triad, not in equal glories.
Their beings are not mixed together among themselves.
As far as their glories, one infinitely more glorious than the other.
The Father in his essence is a foreigner to the Logos, because he exists
without beginning.

— ARIUS, *THALIA*

This is the problem posed in the *Euthyphro Dilemma*: Logos has a beginning, God does not. Are God's laws just because he created them, or because they pre-existed Him? When does *Truth* appear? Before or after God? If before, Truth pre-exists God, making him less than the 'Father of All,' a second class citizen. If after, God's laws become arbitrary, inconsistency is acceptable, Truths can be paradoxical undermining the very concept Logos. This is reflected in the very next verse of the *Thalia*:

> Understand that the Monad was; but the Dyad was not before it came
>   into existence.
> It immediately follows that, although the Logos did not exist, the
>   Father was still God.
> Hence the Logos, not being, came into existence by the Father's will,
> He is the Only-begotten God, and this one is alien from others.[7]

— ARIUS, THALIA

This means the Arians believed Truth was a creature secondary to God. Is this not Modernism, that Truth is arbitrary, that the Word could "pass from virtue to vice"?

These arguments make little sense if the verse did not exist. While we may protest 'there is no documentation,' is not the counter argument contained in the very words of Arius? Are they not written in obvious refutation of something? 'Not in equal glories.' 'Not mixed together.' 'Not being.' This is the full breadth of the heresy, God is not God if Truth is not co-eternal with Him.

Yet, 'though exiled, Athanasius continued his fight against the heresy:

> "From the depth of his inaccessible retreat the intrepid primate waged an incessant and offensive war against the protector of the Arians [Constantius]; and his seasonable writings, which were diligently circulated and eagerly perused, contributed to unite and animate the orthodox party.
>
> In his public apologies, which he addressed to the emperor himself, he sometimes affected the praise of moderation; whilst at the same time, in secret and vehement invectives, he exposed Constantius as a weak and wicked prince, the executioner of his family, the tyrant of the republic, and the Antichrist of the church."[8]

— EDWARD GIBBON

And as to what happened to Athanasius' party? This is a very important detail, ***they chanted a simple song.*** This means we should expect the proper rendition of the verse be in meter:

> "He says that Flavian of Antioch was the first who collected together a large band of monks, and uttered aloud the doxology, "**Glory be to the Father, and to the Son, and to the Holy Ghost.**" For among those who had gone before him, some had been accustomed to say, "**Glory be to the Father through the Son in the Holy Ghost,**" and that this latter form of doxology was the one more customarily received. He says that others again used a different form, saying, "**Glory be to the Father, in the Son, and in the Holy Ghost,**"[9]

> — PHILOSTORGIUS, SEMI-ARIAN HISTORIAN

THE COUNCIL OF ANTIOCH 341 AD

By 341 the Arian crisis was reaching critical mass. It was decided to call a Council to rectify that matter. While no Roman bishops attended nearly one hundred Eastern bishops did. Emperor Constantius II, by then irreligious, also attended. Their desire was to formulate a replacement for the Nicene Creed which had become encumbered with controversies such as the term "homoousios." It is from statements presented here that I believe the 'Semi-Arians' actually saw themselves as Devil's Advocates, and desired only an error-free resolution, for this is what this creed proposes:

> "The synod has for this reason always been known as the Synod of Antioch in Encaeniis, i.e., at the dedication, and was held in the summer of the year 341. Ninety-seven bishops assembled together and a large number of them were hostile to St. Athanasius, being professed Eusebians, all of them were Orientals and most of them belonged to the patriarchate of Antioch. Not a single Western or Latin bishop was present and the pope, Julius, was in no way represented. ...No one can deny that St. Hilary of Poitiers, who was a contemporary, styled it a Synod of Saints; that two of its canons were read at Chalcedon as the canons of the Holy Fathers; and that Popes John II, Zacharias, and Leo IV all approved these canons, and attributed them to Holy Fathers."[10]

> — PHILIP SCHAFF

Being self-declared 'Eusebians' in this context did not mean they were sympathetic to the Arians, in fact they desired to distance themselves from Arius, downplaying his influence. Yet, they also were not that impressed with Athanasius either. Shying away from controversy, they formulated a somewhat 'restrained' creed steeped in Biblical references, but prudently limited in its scope. They were 'testers' of Arius, not followers:

"When all the bishops had assembled in the presence of the emperor Constantius, the majority expressed great indignation, and vigorously accused Athanasius of having contemned the sacerdotal regulation which they had enacted, and taken possession of the bishopric of Alexandria without first obtaining the sanction of a council. They also deposed that he was the cause of the death of several persons, who fell in a sedition excited by his return; and that many others had on the same occasion been arrested and delivered up to the judicial tribunals. By these accusations they contrived to cast odium on Athanasius, and it was decreed that Gregory should be invested with the government of the Church of Alexandria. They then turned to the discussion of doctrinal questions, and found no fault with the decrees of the council of Nice. They dispatched letters to the bishops of every city, in which they declared that, as they were bishops themselves, they had not followed Arius. "For how," said they, "could we have been followers of him, when he was but a presbyter, and we were placed above him?" Since they were the testers of his faith, they had readily received him; and they believed in the faith which had from the beginning been handed down by tradition. This they further explained at the bottom of their letter, but without mentioning the substance of the Father or the Son, or the term consubstantial. They resorted, in fact, to such ambiguity of expression, that neither the Arians nor the followers of the decrees of the Nicœan Council could call the arrangement of their words into question, as though they were ignorant of the holy Scriptures. They purposely avoided all forms of expression which were rejected by either party, and only made use of those which were universally admitted. They confessed that the Son is with the Father, that He is the only begotten One, and that He is God, and existed before all things; and that He took flesh upon Him, and fulfilled the will of His Father. They confessed these and similar truths, but they did not describe the doctrine of the Son being co-eternal or consubstantial with the Father, or the opposite. They subsequently changed their minds, it appears, about this formulary, and issued another, which, I think, very nearly resembled that of the council of Nice, unless, indeed, some secret meaning be attached to the words which is not apparent to me. Although they refrained — I know not from what motive — from saying that the Son is consubstantial, they confessed that He is immutable, that His Divinity is not susceptible of change, that He is the perfect image of the substance, and counsel, and power, and glory of the Father, and that He is the first-born of every creature. They stated that they had found this formulary of faith, and that it was entirely written by Lucianus, who was martyred in Nicomedia, and who was a man highly approved and exceedingly accurate in the sacred Scriptures."[11]

— SOZOMEN

Lucian, martyred in 312, had by this time become St. Lucian and regarded as a high scholar. Because of this his writings formed the basis of the Antiochian Creed. It should be emphasized (as the above quote indicates), their desire was not to overturn the Nicene Creed, but to fix its discrepancies. One of these was the neglect to include a reference to the Heavenly Witnesses "these three are one" (ὡς εἶναι τῇ μὲν ὑποστάσει τρία, τῇ δὲ συμφωνίᾳ ἕν)—*something specifically mentioned in their Creed.*

JULIAN THE APOSTATE

Our discussion depends not only upon producing evidence of the authenticity of the verse, but on evidence of the suppression of the verse. We acknowledge that the oldest codices *Vaticanus* and *Sinaiticus* are missing the text, and that these codices do represent the official Bible of the Council. But we also acknowledge the evidence on the other side. That codices did use the verse as attested to by the *Complutensian Polyglot Bible* (Spain/'Gaul') and the *Vetus Latina* (north Africa). Both were from the most remote areas of the Empire. I believe the only solution that makes sense is an early censorship of the verse soon after the Council of Nicaea. A campaign to destroy and suppress Athanasius drove people to make their own private editions resulting in only remote areas having the authentic text. Perhaps it was even Athanasius himself in his exile that oversaw the production and dissemination of the text. Therefore, to prove our point there should be evidence of an empire-wide retaliation against the Orthodox by the Arian party.

First, I would argue that because some Bibles have 1 John 5:7 penciled in does not necessarily mean the verse is inauthentic. It could be the sign of the orthodox party trying to retain the verse in the face of censorship. We do have examples of just this, something the party of Tischendorf considers inauthentic.

Beginning with Constantine the Great, there was indeed a growing neoplatonic movement. Not only was Constantine pressured by Arian influence, he was baptised by a Semi-Arian bishop just before his death. As has been shown, whatever triumph the Orthodox had at the Council did not last long. With Constantine's death, the following emperors came to regard Christianity as a nuisance. What they preferred was a neoplatonic umbrella under which different religions would only be versions. This relative tolerance ended with Julian the Apostate:

> "Maximus [the neoplatonist] was one of those who had been saturated with the wisdom of Aedesius; moreover he received the honour of being the teacher of the Emperor Julian. After all his relatives had been put to death by Constantius, as I have recorded with more details in my account of Julian, and the whole family had been stripped bare, Julian alone was left alive, being despised on the score of his tender years and his mild disposition. Nevertheless, eunuchs from the palace took charge of him, and were assigned to keep watch so that he might not waver from the Christian faith. But even in the face of these difficulties he displayed the greatness of his genius. For he had their books so thoroughly by heart that they fretted at the scantiness of their erudition, since there was nothing that they could teach the boy. Now since they had nothing to teach him and Julian had nothing to learn from them, he begged his cousin's permission to attend the schools of the sophists and lectures on philosophy."[12]

> — EUNAPIUS, *LIVES OF THE PHILOSOPHERS AND SOPHISTS 'MAXIMUS'*

From the beginning of Julian the Apostate's reign until his death in 363 he brutally tormented Christians, particularly the orthodox. His intent was to stigmatize orthodoxy, driving it back into a religion of the lower class. He severely tortured St. Basil, the very saint who wrote the Doctrine of the Holy Spirit, what was to be the final completion of the Nicene Creed. In an attempt to force him to give up his faith, he was subjected to the tearing of his flesh until death.

Similar tortures were forced upon other Christians throughout the Empire. Julian prohibited Christian liturgies and Sacraments, prohibited the teaching of doctrine, burned churches, and perhaps more importantly, *banned the teachings of Athanasius*. Julian returned heretical, excommunicated Arian bishops to power. His intent was to return the Roman Empire to a neoplatonic Eclecticism.

At this point it is important to acknowledge a certain timeline. The Council of Nicaea, called for by Constantine the Great, was in 325. Julian's persecution and destruction of the Church was from 361 to 363. St. Augustine was born in 354 and died 430. Augustine's partner in re-establishing Christian doctrine was St. Jerome who was born in 347 and died 420. Jerome's primary task was to compile and edit what became the *Vulgate Latin Bible*, the Bible that became the cornerstone of Roman Catholicism until the revision of Bibles in the twentieth century. The history of Jerome and Augustine clearly indicates the trouble they were having finding texts to produce the Vulgate, Augustine primarily resorting to an early version of the *Vetus Latina* called the *Codex Veronenses.*[13]

About fifty examples of the *Vetus Latina* exist today. While it was considered more primitive than what became the Vulgate, Augustine believed it had a profundity that the others lacked. Perhaps more important to our discussion, the *Vetus Latina* was not compiled by scholars, *it was the Bible of the lower class*, the very people Julian was intentionally driving into exile. Also important is that Jerome and Augustine (a former heretic) came into prominence after the death of Julian. And one last thing, the *Vetus Latina* <u>had</u> the verse found at 1 John 5:7 "For there are three that bear record in heaven, the Father, the Word (*Logos*), and the Holy Ghost: and these three are one."

I believe what is happening is something few if any scholars accept—it is the fact that the Roman Empire, realizing that its days were numbered, was attempting to re-invent itself. Christianity is emerging as a dominant religion. Rather than fight it, the Empire decided to incorporate it. Yet, not everything Christian is of use to the Empire, so Christianity immediately became one consistent with the beliefs of the later Emperors who were closet Arians. When Christianity became inconvenient, it was re-defined or abolished. Do we not see this behavior even today?

"YOU HAVE WON, GALILEAN"

With Athanasius exiled to Gaul, Emperor Julian thought it prudent to allow the Jews to return to Jerusalem and reconstruct the Temple. At that time the Temple had only been left burnt from the previous destruction in 69-70 AD— there were still 'stones' left standing. Therefore the prophecy had not yet been fulfilled, "verily I say unto you, There shall not be left here one stone upon another, that shall not be thrown down" (Matthew 24:1-2 - KJV). Jews returning to reconstruct the Temple decided in a complete rebuild, and thus began the preparatory final demolition.

The design of Julian was to prove the core of Christian prophecy wrong by rebuilding the Temple. It would spell the end of the Church:

"Julian the apostate, wishing to falsify the predictions of Daniel and of Jesus Christ, attempted to rebuild the temple. For this purpose, he assembled the chief among the Jews, and asking them why they neglected the prescribed sacrifices, was answered, that they could not offer any where else but in the temple of Jerusalem. Upon this he ordered them to return to Jerusalem, to rebuild their temple, and restore their ancient worship, promising them his concurrence in carrying on the work."[14]

— HAYDOCK BIBLE COMMENTARY

In the midst of this reconstruction, on May 19, 363, a massive earthquake hit the Middle East causing massive fires to sweep through and destroy Jerusalem once again. It was upon this very event that the tide would turn in favor of Christianity. The historical accounts still exist:

"Emperor Julian the Apostate sought to permanently cripple Christianity by returning Jerusalem to the Jews in AD 363. The first goal was to rebuild the Temple. Evidently there were still enough Jews that had not dispersed to complete the demolition and begin re-construction. It all came to a halt when a massive earthquake was seen as a sign from God to stop.

The emperor [Julian the Apostate] in another attempt to molest the Christians exposed his superstition. Being fond of sacrificing, he not only himself delighted in the blood of victims, but considered it an indignity offered to him, if others did not do likewise. And as he found but few persons of this stamp, he sent for the Jews and enquired of them why they abstained from sacrificing, since the law of Moses enjoined it? On their replying that it was not permitted them to do this in any other place than Jerusalem, he immediately ordered them to rebuild Solomon's temple. Meanwhile he himself proceeded on his expedition against the Persians. The Jews who had been long desirous of obtaining a favorable opportunity for rearing their temple afresh in order that they might therein offer sacrifice, applied themselves very vigorously to the work. Moreover, they conducted themselves with great insolence toward the Christians, and threatened to do them as much mischief, as they had themselves suffered from the Romans. The emperor having ordered that the expenses of this structure should be defrayed out of the public treasury, all things were soon provided, such as timber and stone, burnt brick, clay, lime, and all other materials necessary for building. On this occasion Cyril bishop of Jerusalem, called to mind the prophecy of Daniel, which Christ also in the holy gospels has confirmed, and predicted in the presence of many persons, that the time had indeed come 'in which one stone should not be left upon another in that temple,' but that the Saviour's prophetic declaration should have its full accomplishment. Such were the bishop's words: and on the night following, a mighty earthquake tore up the stones of the old foundations of the temple and dispersed them all together with the adjacent edifices. Terror consequently possessed the Jews on account of the event; and the report of it brought many to the spot who resided at a great distance: when therefore a vast multitude was assembled, another prodigy took place. Fire came down from heaven and consumed all the builders' tools: so that the flames were seen preying upon mallets, irons to smooth and polish stones, saws, hatchets, adzes, in short all the various implements which the workmen had procured as necessary for the undertaking; and the fire continued burning among these for a whole day. The Jews indeed were in the greatest possible alarm, and unwillingly confessed Christ, calling him God: yet they did not do his will; but influenced by inveterate prepossessions they still clung to Judaism. Even a third miracle which afterwards happened failed to lead them to a belief of the truth. For the next night luminous impressions of a cross appeared imprinted on their garments, which at daybreak they in vain attempted to rub or wash out. They were therefore 'blinded' as the apostle says, and cast away the good which they had in their hands: and thus was the temple, instead of being rebuilt, at that time wholly overthrown."[15]

— SOCRATES SCHOLASTICUS, *ECCLESIASTICAL HISTORY*

I ask, look at photos of Roman pantheons from this period. Do you see many still intact? Do you not see toppled columns, slabs of stone that once functioned as roofs throne to the ground? Modern historians note that while contemporary Christians saw the earthquake in Jerusalem as a Divine Intervention, this alone does not represent the extent of mass destruction caused by the earthquake throughout the Empire. It was not just the Temple in Jerusalem that was destroyed, *it was temples to foreign gods everywhere.* It is this very event that modern historians admit gave the Church its practical opportunity to preach to all nations. It allowed for the Creed to be completed at the Council of Constantinople in 381 with the addition of Basil's Doctrine of the Holy Spirit.

At that very moment, while Julian was at war in Persia enforcing one of his many persecutions, he met his fatal blow. On his deathbed, hearing about the devastation, he would say days later, *νενίκηκάς με, Γαλιλαῖε* (*You have won, Galilean*). Julian's friend Libanius recounts:

> "…earthquakes were the harbingers of woe, destroying the cities of Palestine Syria either wholly or in part. We were sure by these actions that heaven had given us a sign of some great disaster, and, as we prayed that our guess should not be right, the bitter news reached our ears that our great Julian was being carried out in his coffin."[16]

— PHILOSTORGIUS, LETTER ATTRIBUTED TO CYRIL ON
THE REBUILDING OF THE JERUSALEM TEMPLE

It is here that we must take stock of all our now revealed facts. The religion that was triumphing at the time of the Council of Nicaea was not Christianity, it was Neoplatonism in its many guises, Arianism was one. It was this that was in the majority at the time of the Council. So how do we explain the change in fate? The inescapable conclusion is this: Christianity was allowed to survive so that it could be subverted. Athanasius was allowed to triumph so that he could be made a renegade. What we see emerging in the Roman Empire is the rise of a heresy.

Look back at our chart. What you will see is a string of 'prophets' whose memory Neoplatonism calls 'the Golden Chain." Our chart reveals this chain in its latter stages. This apostolic 'Chain' is still acclaimed by Occultists and New Agers: 1) Seven Sages, 2) Pythagoras, 3) Heraclitus, 4) Parmenides, 5) Empedocles, 6) Philolaus, 7) Plato, 8) Aristotle, 9) **Ammonius Saccas**, 10) **Plotinus**, 11) **Porphyry**, 12) **Iamblicus**, 13) **Emperor Julian**, 14) Hypatia, 15) Proclus, 16) Damacius. Notice the distance in time between Aristotle and Ammonius Saccas for the chain breaks there. The time span is impossible for an apostolic chain. It is made up history, Aristotle had no such doctrine.

We must abandon our notion that the Church was given us whole and finished on the day of Pentecost. Yes, the seed was planted, but our mettle was still to be tested, then as it is now. If we are to look for a pure, ancient, pristine early Church to aspire to, we will not find one. What we will find is a Church of mixed theologies, of impure saints, of questionable doctrine. What we will find is a Church that needed to struggle, that needed to be purified, that needed to tempered like a fine sword. It needed to see the Adversary for what he was. And it was through this that the Divine plan could be fulfilled, the plan of the Adversary could be thwarted.

Yes, it was the Neoplatonists that triumphed at Nicaea… but their victory would only last for just over thirty-eight years, until May 19, 363. It was here that the fully tempered Church was born, prophecies fulfilled, doctrines solidified. Hear the people of that time, 'it was Divine Intervention.' It was here that the aims of Athanasius would begin to be fulfilled. It was here that the Trinitarian God could finally show itself and be fully professed. It was here that the passage, 1 John 5:7, **"For there are three that bear record in heaven, the Father, the *Logos/Son*, and the Holy Ghost: and these three are one,"** was safe to be returned to its proper place.

Again, look around. Once you see this the evidence is everywhere. The ruins of the Jewish Temple are still there as are the ruins of the pantheons of Rome. The Church today is still being undermined by these same Arian factions, yet it still survives. Realize this, 'You, you Galilean, you have been victorious.'

---

1. Enfield, *The History of Philosophy,* p.435
2. Sozomen, *Ecclesiastical History,* 2, 27. LPNF, ser. 2, vol. 2, 277. Arius, *Recantation to the Emperor Constantine* (*Socrates, Historia Ecclesiastica, 1. 26*) http://legalhistorysources. com/ChurchHistory220/LectureTwo/AriusLetter3.htm
3. Sozomen, 'Athanasius and the Council of Tyre, 335' *Historia Ecclesiastica,* Chap. XXV. Illegal Deposition of St. Athanasius https://www.earlychurchtexts.com/public/ sozomen_on_athanasius_and_the_council_of_tyre.htm
4. Sozomen, 'Athanasius and the Council of Tyre, 335' *Historia Ecclesiastica,* Chap. XXV. Illegal Deposition of St. Athanasius https://www.earlychurchtexts.com/public/ sozomen_on_athanasius_and_the_council_of_tyre.htm Chap. XXVIII. Exile of St. Athanasius through the machinations of the Arian faction.
5. Sozomen, 'Athanasius and the Council of Tyre, 335' *Historia Ecclesiastica,* Chap. XXVII. Concerning the Presbyter by whom Constantine was persuaded to recall Arius
6. Ignatius, Saint, and Polycarp, Saint. *The Apostolic Fathers.* Vol. II. MacMillan, 1890. J.B. Lightfoot, p.94
7. derived from Williams, Rowan. *Arius: Heresy and Tradition.* Wm. B. Eerdmans Publishing, 2002.
8. Gibbon, Edward *The Decline and Fall of the Roman Empire.* Strahan & Cadell, London. 1776 - Chp. 21 Council of Nicaea
9. Recorded from the Arius sympathetic historian Philostorgius, l. iii. c. 13. CHAP. 13. Photius, Patriarch of Constantinople, *Epitome of the Ecclesiastical History of Philostorgius.* Edward Walford trans https://www.tertullian.org/fathers/philostorgius.htm
10. (Synod of Antioch in Encaeniis A.D. 341; NPNF02, vol 14, <www.newadvent.org/fathers/3805.htm>)
11. Sozomen. Bishops assembled at Antioch. Book 3.5; NPNF02, vol 2
12. Eunapius, *Lives of the Philosophers and Sophists* 'Maximus' (English translation)". www.tertullian.org. 1921. pp. 343–565 https://www.tertullian.org/fathers/eunapius_02_text.htm

13. H.A.G. Houghton. *Augustine's Text of John. Patristic Citations and Latin Gospel Manuscripts*. Oxford: OUP, 2008. ISBN 978-0-19-954592-6
14. Haydock, George Leo. *Commentary on The Holy Bible*. E. Dunigan and Brother, 1852. on St Matthew Chap 24, verse 2
15. Socrates Scholasticus, *Ecclesiastical History*, Book III, Chap. XX, ca. A.D. 379-450
16. Levenson, David B. "The Palestinian Earthquake of May 363 in Philostorgius, the Syriac Chronicon Miscellaneum, and the Letter Attributed to Cyril on the Rebuilding of the Jerusalem Temple." Journal of Late Antiquity 6, no. 1 (June 24, 2013): 60–83. https://doi.org/10.1353/jla.2013.0010. p.62

THE ANTIOCHIAN CREED OF 341 AD

THE 'SYMBOLUM ANTIOCHENUM' DERIVED FROM ST. LUCIAN

Agreeably to the Evangelical and Apostolical tradition, we believe in one God the Father Almighty, the Creator, Maker, and Governor of the Universe, of whom are all things; and in one Lord Jesus Christ, his Son, the only begotten of God, by whom are all things, begotten of the Father before the worlds, God of God, all from all, the only one from the only one, the perfect from the perfect, King from King, Lord from Lord, the living Word (*Logos*), the living wisdom, the true light , the way, the truth, the resurrection, the shepherd, the door, the unchangeable and invariable image of the Father's God head, essence, and will, and power, and glory; born before all creation; who was declared in the Gospel "and the Word was God"; by whom all things were made; and by whom all things consist; who, in these last days, came down from above, and was born of a Virgin, according to the Scriptures; and was made man; the Mediator between God and Men; the Apostle of our faith, the Prince of Life, as he says "I came down from heaven, not to do my own will, but the will of Him who sent me"; who suffered for us, and rose again on the third day, and ascended into heaven, and sitteth on the right hand of the Father, and shall come again with glory and power, to judge the living and the dead. And [we believe] in the Holy Ghost, who is given to believers for consolation, and sanctification, and perfection, according to our Lord Jesus Christ's direction to his disciples, saying, "Go ye unto all nations, baptizing them in the name of the Father, and of the Son, and of the Holy Ghost," the Father being truly a Father, and the Son truly a Son, and the Holy Ghost truly a Holy Ghost — the names being given not vainly and unmeaningly, but accurately expressing the respective subsistence, order, and glory of each of the Persons named; SO THAT THEY ARE THREE IN SUBSTANCE AND ONE IN CONSENT. Having therefore this faith, and holding it before God and Christ from the beginning to the end, we anathematize all heretical heterodoxy. And if anyone, contrary to the sound and right faith of the Scripture, shall teach that there ever was a time, or period, or age, before the Son was begotten, let him be anathema; and if anyone shall say that the Son is a creature, or one of the creation, or a production as one of the productions [of nature], or a work as one of the works [of nature]; and [shall teach] otherwise than as the Holy Scriptures have delivered each of the aforesaid [doctrines] from each [of its respective Scriptures], or shall teach any other thing than what we have received, let him be anathema. For all things out of the Holy Scriptures, which have been delivered to us by the Prophets and Apostles, we believe and follow.[1]

Πιστεύομεν ἀκολούθως τῇ εὐαγγελικῇ καὶ ἀποστολικῇ παραδόσει εἰς ἕνα θεὸν πατέρα παντοκράτορα, τὸν τῶν ὅλων δημιουργόν τε καὶ ποιητὴν καὶ προνοητήν, ἐξ οὗ τὰ πάντα· καὶ εἰς ἕνα κύριον Ἰησοῦν Χριστόν, τὸν υἱὸν αὐτοῦ, τὸν μονογενῆ θεόν, δι' οὗ τὰ πάντα, τὸν γεννηθέντα πρὸ τῶν αἰώνων ἐκ τοῦ πατρός, θεὸν ἐκ θεοῦ, ὅλον ἐξ ὅλου, μόνον ἐκ μόνου, τέλειον ἐκ τελείου, βασιλέα ἐκ βασιλέως, κύριον ἀπὸ κυρίου, λόγον ζῶντα, σοφίαν ζῶσαν, φῶς ἀληθινόν, ὁδόν, ἀλήθειαν, ἀνάστασιν, ποιμένα, θύραν, ἄτρεπτόν τε καὶ ἀναλλοίωτον, τῆς θεότητος οὐσίας τε καὶ βουλῆς καὶ δυνάμεως καὶ δόξης τοῦ πατρὸς ἀπαράλλακτον εἰκόνα, τὸν πρωτότοκον πάσης κτίσεως, τὸν ὄντα ἐν ἀρχῇ πρὸς τὸν θεόν, λόγον θεὸν κατὰ τὸ εἰρημένον ἐν τῷ εὐαγγελίῳ· «καὶ θεὸς ἦν ὁ λόγος», δι' οὗ τὰ πάντα ἐγένετο, καὶ ἐν ᾧ τὰ πάντα συνέστηκε, τὸν ἐπ' ἐσχάτων τῶν ἡμερῶν κατελθόντα ἄνωθεν καὶ γεννηθέντα ἐκ παρθένου κατὰ τὰς γραφὰς καὶ ἄνθρωπον γενόμενον, μεσίτην θεοῦ καὶ ἀνθρώπων ἀπόστολόν τε τῆς πίστεως ἡμῶν καὶ ἀρχηγὸν τῆς ζωῆς, ὥς φησιν ὅτι «καταβέβηκα ἐκ τοῦ οὐρανοῦ, οὐχ ἵνα ποιῶ τὸ θέλημα τὸ ἐμόν, ἀλλὰ τὸ θέλημα τοῦ πέμψαντός με», τὸν παθόντα ὑπὲρ ἡμῶν καὶ ἀναστάντα τῇ τρίτῃ ἡμέρᾳ καὶ ἀνελθόντα εἰς οὐρανούς, καὶ καθεσθέντα ἐν δεξιᾷ τοῦ πατρὸς καὶ πάλιν ἐρχόμενον μετὰ δόξης καὶ δυνάμεως κρῖναι ζῶντας καὶ νεκρούς. καὶ εἰς τὸ πνεῦμα τὸ ἅγιον, τὸ εἰς παράκλησιν καὶ ἁγιασμὸν καὶ τελείωσιν τοῖς πιστεύουσι διδόμενον, καθὼς καὶ ὁ κύριος ἡμῶν Ἰησοῦς Χριστὸς διετάξατο τοῖς μαθηταῖς λέγων «πορευθέντες μαθητεύσατε πάντα τὰ ἔθνη βαπτίζοντες

αὐτοὺς εἰς τὸ ὄνομα τοῦ πατρὸς καὶ τοῦ υἱοῦ καὶ τοῦ ἁγίου πνεύματος»,
δηλονότι πατρός, ἀληθῶς πατρὸς ὄντος, υἱοῦ δὲ ἀληθῶς υἱοῦ ὄντος, τοῦ δὲ
ἁγίου πνεύματος ἀληθῶς ἁγίου πνεύματος ὄντος, τῶν ὀνομάτων οὐχ ἁπλῶς
οὐδὲ ἀργῶς κειμένων, ἀλλὰ σημαινόν των ἀκριβῶς τὴν οἰκείαν ἑκάστου τῶν
ὀνομαζομένων ὑπόστασίν τε καὶ τάξιν καὶ δόξαν, **ὡς εἶναι τῇ μὲν ὑποστάσει
τρία, τῇ δὲ συμφωνίᾳ ἕν.** ταύτην οὖν ἔχοντες τὴν πίστιν καὶ ἐξ ἀρχῆς καὶ
μέχρι τέλους ἔχοντες ἐνώπιον τοῦ θεοῦ καὶ τοῦ Χριστοῦ πᾶσαν αἱρετικὴν
κακοδοξίαν ἀναθεματίζομεν. καὶ εἴ τις παρὰ τὴν ὑγιῆ τῶν γραφῶν ὀρθὴν
πίστιν διδάσκει λέγων ἢ χρόνον ἢ καιρὸν ἢ αἰῶνα ἢ εἶναι ἢ γεγονέναι πρὸ τοῦ
γεννηθῆναι τὸν υἱόν, ἀνάθεμα ἔστω. καὶ εἴ τις λέγει τὸν υἱὸν κτίσμα ὡς ἓν τῶν
κτισμάτων ἢ γέννημα ὡς ἓν τῶν γεννημάτων ἢ ποίημα ὡς ἓν τῶν ποιημάτων
καὶ μὴ ὡς αἱ θεῖαι γραφαὶ παραδέ δωκαν τῶν προειρημένων ἕκαστον ἀφ'
ἑκάστυυ, ἢ εἴ τι ἄλλο διδάσκει ἢ εὐαγγελίζεται, παρ' ὃ παρελάβομεν, ἀνάθεμα
ἔστω. ἡμεῖς γὰρ πᾶσι τοῖς ἐκ τῶν θείων γραφῶν παραδεδομένοις ὑπό τε
προφητῶν καὶ ἀποστόλων ἀληθινῶς τε καὶ ἐμφόβως καὶ πιστεύομεν καὶ
ἀκολουθοῦμεν. (Creed of Antioch 341; Migne Graeca, PG 26.723-724)

---

1. Ferrando, Mike. *The Comma Calmly Considered, Symbolum of Antioch 341 AD*, July 10,
    2022 — Found and translated in, 'The Christian Examiner, and Church of Ireland Magazine,'
    vol 2, 1826, p. 57-58)

THE AUTHENTICITY OF THE VETUS LATINA

"However, ten or fifteen years before his [Lucian's] martyrdom, he was reconciled to the Church; and we may suppose that he then recanted whatever was heretical in his creed"[1]

— CARDINAL JOHN HENRY NEWMAN

IT TAKES ONE TO KNOW ONE

There is clearly a discussion immediately following the Council of Nicaea as to what is the 'authentic' Bible. Many scholars insist that the absence of a documented debate over the verse at 1 John, means that the verse was already missing and not part of that Bible.

Yet, is this reasonable? It seems reasonable if the debate at the Council were actually Trinitarians vs. Unitarians, but, it wasn't. Records show both 'visible' sides accepted the Trinity in one form or another. The true controversy was whether *Logos* was co-eternal with the *Father*. Demoting the Son makes him the Demiurge, something found in Cerinthus' falsified version of John's Gospel. My question is, under these *new* terms is it likely the verse was missing? Is it not 1 John 5:7 that implies such a co-eternality? If not, from where else in the Bible?

Nonetheless, it was the desire of the Council under orders of Emperor Constantine to disseminate 50 'official' Bibles, a number coincidentally the same as the number of *Vetus Latina* Bibles. However about 98% of the 8000 Latin Vulgate editions contain the verse. Only 480 of the Greek text contain the verse, almost all of which are of the early second millennium. This is perhaps explained by the fact that Greek texts made it to Europe by refugees from Islam who were also destroying Bibles. It could also be explained that this may have been an early point of controversy between the Western Roman and Eastern Orthodox churches, the latter being more sympathetic heterodoxy very early on. These numbers are debatable as different sources list different numbers.

So, if the official Bible has been authorized by the Empire, why wasn't the case closed at that point? Why are people like St. Jerome and St. Augustine still trying to find the most legitimate text?

St. Augustine of Hippo represents a very interesting predicament. He lays right at the center of the very problem we are trying to solve. While he is considered a saint in the western Church, he is suspect in the East for his flirtation with heresy. Yet, in some ways this puts Augustine at an advantage. Not only does he know the Adversary, he is relentless in defining him. Augustine becomes a cornerstone of western Christianity. St. Jerome said of him, he "established anew the ancient Faith."

Before his conversion to Christianity in 386, Augustine was first a Manichaean, and then a Neoplatonist. In other words he was well-familiar with everything at issue here. Therefore, if our theory is correct, we would expect that Augustine would be very critical not of just Neoplatonism, but the form of Neoplatonism he knew, Hermeticism. Augustine's academic standards were high, he often prodded Jerome to higher standards in compiling what became the *Latin Vulgate*. Yet, Augustine preferred the more crude version of the Bible, the *Vetus Latina*. Why? Cardinal Nicholas Patrick Wiseman (1802-1865), first Archbishop of Westminster in his essay on our disputed verse points out:

"He [Augustine] informs us, that when at Carthage, before his conversion, he utterly despised and neglected the Scriptures, on account of the rudeness of their style. He went to Milan, without the slightest religious object, and there at length began to view them in a totally different light. From listening to St. Ambrose, he discovered that many things in them which had appeared to him absurd and ignoble, were full of meaning and dignity. He remained for some time in a state of doubt and wavering; and strong obstacles presented themselves to his complete search after truth. One of these I must give in his own words: 'Behold, there are no longer absurdities in ecclesiastical books which seemed absurd, and they can be understood in a different and honest way. I will set my feet on the level on which I was placed as a child by my parents, until the clear Truth is found. But where should it be sought? when will it be sought? Ambrose is not free, *he is not free to read. Where do we get the codices themselves? whence or when do we compare? from whom do we take them?*"[2]

— CARDINAL PATRICK WISEMAN

The problem is Augustine never specifically quotes 1 John 5:7 in any of his writings. In one case he comes close to it in his examination of 1 John, but the work is never completed. And then there is Augustine's mystical interpretation of the Trinity which seems to be based on the verse.

Part of the dilemma is this: Augustine states specifically that the next closest philosophy to Christianity is Platonism. It was upon this phrase, found by Petrarch in the early Renaissance, that seemingly gave legitimacy to the emerging Neoplatonist movement. It gave Augustine's stamp of approval to a doctrine he was clearly against as revealed in his long critique of Hermeticism.

Therefore, we are fighting two issues, 1) the fact that the two most authoritative writers of that era somewhat seem to ignore the verse, and; 2) is Augustine sanctioning Neoplatonism?

So, why is this important? What seems to be missed by almost all scholars is that Arianism is really a *Christian version* of Neoplatonism. It is the verse at 1 John 5:7 that they would find most repugnant. So, I ask this, why are Jerome and Augustine using Bibles that include the verse?

St. John Damascene, someone considered a bonafide saint in both the East and West, specifically states that Platonism is a heresy. It was the Aristotelian school that confronted the errors of Plato, and corrected them. However, one could still say, 'the next closest philosophy to Plato is Aristotle.' Damascene refers to Aristotelian doctrine often in his *Fount of Knowledge* to explain the basis of the faith. Thomas Aquinas does the same.

The article on Augustine found at the Catholic *New Advent's* website refers to Philip Schaff's commentary on him:

"The same learned critic thus wisely concludes his study: "So long, therefore, as his philosophy agrees with his religious doctrines, St. Augustine is frankly neo-Platonist; as soon as a contradiction arises, he never hesitates to subordinate is philosophy to religion, reason to faith. He was, first of all, a Christian;

the philosophical questions that occupied his mind constantly found themselves more and more relegated to the background" (op. cit., 155). But the
method was a dangerous one; in thus seeking harmony between the two
doctrines he thought too easily to find Christianity in Plato, or Platonism in the
Gospel. More than once, in his "Retractions" and elsewhere, he acknowledges
that he has not always shunned this danger. Thus he had imagined that in
Platonism he discovered the entire doctrine of the Word and the whole
prologue of St. John. He likewise disavowed a good number of neo-Platonic
theories which had at first misled him—the cosmological thesis of the
universal soul, which makes the world one immense animal—the Platonic
doubts upon that grave question: Is there a single soul for all or a distinct soul
for each?"[3]

— PHILIP SCHAFF

Clearly, there is some hangover from Augustine's prior faith. Some criticism of Augustine is justified. Yet, no one has ever accused Augustine of
Arianism. And, as we shall see, Neoplatonism and Arianism are practically
the same thing. As Schaff says, Augustine rejected the core doctrine of
Neoplatonism, the Universal Soul. Therefore, the proof they seek is not there.

If we accept the notion that Augustine was an expert on heresies for
having been one, and if we accept that ancient Gnosticism is essentially the
same as Neoplatonism, and in turn these both share the same essential errors
as Hermeticism, then Augustine has actually quite a lot to say. Augustine
devotes at least five chapters of his famous *City of God*:

"Hermes then follows out at great length the statements of this passage, in
which he seems to predict the present time, in which the Christian religion is
overthrowing all lying figments with a vehemence and liberty proportioned to
its superior truth and holiness, in order that the grace of the true Saviour may
deliver men from those gods which man has made, and subject them to that
God by whom man was made. But when Hermes predicts these things, he
speaks as one who is a friend to these same mockeries of demons, and does not
clearly express the name of Christ. On the contrary, he deplores, as if it had
already taken place, the future abolition of those things by the observance of
which there was maintained in Egypt a resemblance of heaven,—he bears
witness to Christianity by a kind of mournful prophecy. Now it was with reference to such that the apostle said, that "knowing God, they glorified Him not
as God, neither were thankful, but became vain in their imaginations, and their

foolish heart was darkened; professing themselves to be wise, they became fools, and changed the glory of the incorruptible God into the likeness of the image of corruptible man," and so on, for the whole passage is too long to quote. For Hermes makes many such statements agreeable to the truth concerning the one true God who fashioned this world."[4]

— ST. AUGUSTINE

The final words, "one true God who fashioned this world," are specifically against the Neoplatonic model and that of Cerinthus, both hold that the world was a mistake and fashioned by the Demiurge.

We find that neither Augustine nor Plato are simple characters. Which Plato was Plutarch invoking? The old Plato who at the time was seen as merely a collector of ancient wisdoms? Or the Middle Platonist modern scholars have created at the time of Christ? Or, the later 'new' Neoplatonist invented by Iamblicus? And how do we reconcile this with Plato's denouncement of Hermes Trismegistus, the God of the Occult who Socrates himself denounced? Augustine is clear for those who would look. He's drawn a line, and on the major issue at hand Hermes is on the other side—Hermes represents the very same religion Augustine has rejected.

ST. AUGUSTINE'S PREFERRED BIBLE

Having thus dispensed with the issue of Augustine's orthodoxy we are now ready to address the bigger issue. As has been mentioned, St. Jerome and Augustine were friends, and Augustine was very influential on Jerome's great work, the *Latin Vulgate Bible. Neither had a standardized Bible from which to appeal to!* While we have accepted that *Sinaiticus* and *Vaticanus* are indeed the 'official Bible' produced by the Council, *why isn't Augustine using it as his standard? Why isn't the case closed? Why did it take until the 20th century to switch Bibles?* What did this great thinker of western Christianity use as his source?

This is exactly Cardinal Wiseman's question, and his reasoning—if it can be shown which Bible Augustine used, and that the Bible had the verse, then a lot of the argument against the verse falls away. Similarly, the same would happen if there were a text of Augustine's that contained the verse. In fact Wiseman goes one step further, he believes that he has found that very text in the '*Basilica of the Holy Cross (Santa Crose) in Jerusalem,*' in Rome. While the text does have a title later affixed to the end referring to Augustine, *De*

Testimonm Scripturarum Augustini contra Donatistas et Ydola, Wiseman believes this is the wrong title. He believes the text isn't just referring to Augustine, it was written by Augustine and is his *Speculum.* Wiseman states:

> "...this work quotes the text of the Heavenly Witnesses, as a dogmatical proof of the Trinity. In the second chapter, which is entitled, *De Distinctione Personarum,* fol.19, *ver.* We have the following passage:— *Item Johannis in aepistula ...Item illic Tres sunt qui testimonium dicunt in caelo Pater, Verbum et Spiritus. et hii tres unum sunt.* [Again, in the epistle of John ...Also there are three who bear witness in heaven, the Father, the Word, and the Spirit and these three are one.] I need hardly point out to my readers the coincidence between this manuscript and the one above quoted, in the use of the word *dicunt* instead of *dant* [they *say* instead of *give*]. It is the reading of Idatius Clarus, the oldest ecclesiastical writer who quotes this portion of the text."[5]

> — CARDINAL WISEMAN

Wiseman's argument is simply this. The work found at the Basilica seems to be what Augustine describes as his *Speculum*:

> "And wishing to benefit all, and for those who were able to read many books and for those who were not able, he selected from both the divine Testament, the Old and the New, with a preliminary preface, the divine precepts or prohibitions pertaining to the rule of life, and of these he made one codex; so that anyone who wanted to read it could recognize in it how obedient or disobedient he was to God, and he wanted this work to be called the *Speculum.*"[6]

> — CARDINAL WISEMAN

Wiseman finds that when Augustine quotes the Bible in the document, the quotes are from the *Vetus Latina,* Augustine's preferred version. The work also has titles seemingly derived from Augustine's known mystical interpretation of the Three Witnesses text. As further proof Wiseman cites "St. Augustine, in his ordinary works, used the Italian recension from which the verse had been lost at an early period. His *Speculum,* as we learn from Posidius, was written for the unlearned, and hence he made use in it of the *African* recension, which universally contained the verse."

1. Io. V. 7.

nel M.S. di Santa Croce

Cardinal Wiseman's tracing of the very verse in question from the codex found at the Basilica.

Wiseman does not have all the resources we have today. In his book *Augustine's Text of John: Patristic Citations and Latin Gospel Manuscripts*, H.A.G. Houghton uses several examples of Augustine including sermons to determine which Bible he quoted most often. Augustine's following quote confirms that there were some corrupted Scripture circulating and they are being corrected by comparison to ancient manuscripts *in many languages.* Augustine says:

"However, since you bring these proofs [concerning Mani] from manuscripts which you say have been falsified… tell me, what do you do but claim that you could not have falsified the manuscripts in any way as they are already in the hands of all Christians? Because if you had begun to do this, you would soon be shown up by the truth of the oldest exemplars. Therefore, for the same reason that they cannot be corrupted by you, they cannot be corrupted by anyone. For whoever first dared to do this would be refuted by comparison with many ancient manuscripts, especially because the same text is transmitted not in one language but in many. Even now, indeed, several faults in manuscripts are corrected against older ones or those in the source language."[7]

— ST. AUGUSTINE

But this is not the scenario the school of Tischendorf wants us to believe. To them there is only one text, sanctioned by the Empire, and that alone is to be trusted. Remember, Augustine's conversion is in 386, after both the

Council of Nicaea and Constantinople, the very time period of the majority text that Tischendorf's school regards as corrupted. Houghton also quotes this:

> "As for the translations themselves, the *Itala* is preferable to the rest; for it keeps more closely to the words and gives the sense with clarity."[8]

> — ST. AUGUSTINE

Houghton explains that while there is some dispute over the word '*Itala*,' that this generally refers to the *Vetus Latina*. And even going so far as to narrow it down:

> "Augustine reads *credentibus* in fifteen citations of John 1:12, a literal rendering of τοις πιστευουσιω paralleled only in **Codex Veronensis.**" [a version of the *Vetus Latina*][9]

> — H.A.G. HOUGHTON

Now whether Augustine used other codices matters not. He must consider the *Codex Veronensis* as authentic, and it is an example of the *Vetus Latina*, which did have the verse:

5:7 — Quoniam tres sunt, qui testimonium dant in cælo: Pater, Verbum, et Spiritus Sanctus: et hi tres unum sunt.

5:7 — *And there are three who give testimony in heaven, the Father, the Word, and the Holy Ghost. And these three are one.*

Further, Jerome has this to say about out missing verse:

The Prologue to the Canonical Epistles of Jerome

"The order of the seven Epistles which are called canonical is not the same among the Greeks who follow the correct faith and the one found in the Latin codices, where Peter, being the first among the apostles, also has his two epistles first. But just as we have corrected the evangelists into their proper order, so with God's help have we done with these. The first is one of James, then two of Peter, three of John and one of Jude.

Just as these are properly understood and so translated faithfully by interpreters into Latin without leaving ambiguity for the readers nor [allowing] the variety of genres to conflict, especially in that text where we read the unity of the trinity is placed in the first letter of John, where much error has occurred at the hands of unfaithful translators contrary to the truth of faith, who have kept just the three words water, blood and spirit in this edition omitting mention of Father, Word and Spirit in which especially the catholic faith is strengthened and the unity of substance of Father, Son and Holy Spirit is attested."[10]

— ST. JEROME

I ask the reader to take note here. The quote above includes the phrase, "without leaving ambiguity for the readers nor [allowing] the variety of genres to conflict." It is precisely this argument recognized by Jerome at this early date, that later becomes the Internal Argument.

Not to quote only a Roman Catholic source, I now quote the Protestant David Martin (1638-1721) who early on wrote against the Catholic priest, Richard Simon. Simon (1638-1712) was one of the first Catholic priests to condemn the verse, only to find that his own writings themselves would be later condemned as heretical. I here offer this hard to find text in a much redacted version of Martin's, *A Critical Dissertation Upon the Seventh verse Fifth Chapter of St. John's First Epistle,* referring to the section on the *Vetus Latina*:

"Th'o the Greek Tongue had spread it self thro' all the *West,* and become as it were an universal language in those Countries, upon first preaching the Gospel there, the *Latin* was yet more generally known, and admitted as the common language not only in *Italy,* but in many other nations withal. For this cause, in order to make the New Testament more easy to be read and understood by all sorts of people, it was translated into Latin in the first or second Century. The persons concern'd in so important an affair are unknown to us; this barely is come to our knowledge, that their Version was much approv'd of, and immediately receiv'd in all the *Western* Churches, and soon after in the *African.* As this Translation was the first that appear'd, and in all probability was compil'd in *Italy,* it has been distinguish'd from others since made, by the title of *antiqua,* and *Italica,* and sometimes by the word *Vulgata,* or *Common,* because as I have above observ'd, it was the vulgar and ordinary Version us'd in all the *Latin* Churches.

S. *Fulgentius,* Bishop of Ruspe in *Africk,* liv'd in the beginning of the 6th Century, at a time the Italick Version was only read in the Churches. This pious Bishop, with the other Africans of his Age, suffer'd much from the *Arian* Kings. *Thrasimone* caus'd him to appear at *Carthage* to answer the

Objections those Hereticks had drawn up against the Eternity of the Son of God, and his equality with the Father. We all see, the utmost exactness and precaution in chusing Texts of Scripture was requisite in S. *Fulgentius*, and above all the application of none whose genuineness might be suspected. We have extant among his works the answers to these Questions, and we there find alledg'd in proof of the Son's Consubstantiality with the Father this Passage of S. *John, There are three, that bare record in heaven, the Father, the Word, and the Holy Ghost, and these three are one.* This verse is withal quoted in a tract of the same *Fulgentius* concerning the Trinity, which he dedicates to *Felix.*

Of all these passages thus inserted into the Confession of Faith St. *John's* verse was more particularly insisted on than the rest; so decisive was it thought by the African Churches in proving the doctrine of the Trinity. *But, say they, that it may yet appear more clear than day light, that the Godhead of the Holy Ghost is one with the Godhead of the Father and the Son, see it prov'd by the testimony of the Evangelist St. John, who writes thus, There are three, which bear record in heaven, the Father, the Word, and the Holy Ghost; and these three are one. Do's the Apostle say, these three are not distinct from each other, except in the case of equality, or some other great difference, that distinguishes 'em? In no wise; but he says, these three are one only and the same thing.* Hi tres unum sunt.

These Bishops would truly have wanted, shall I say, discretion or honesty, had they made use in this affair of a Text not generally receiv'd as Holy Scripture. Could they have invented a more ready means to draw upon 'em the insults of the *Arians*, who taking advantage from this error would not have fail'd to cry out against the Orthodox to Hunerick as Men who had urg'd false records instead of the genuine Texts of Scripture the King's Edict had requir'd? Men were the same then they are now, and have we at this day, I say not, hundreds of Bishops, who by concert would employ a forg'd Text in the Faith's defence; but is there one single Bishop, only one Man of Letters, who has the least Honour or Conscience, who would thus risque his reputation, and prostitute his religion? Can we imagine the *Arians* were less diligent then to examine the arguments of the Orthodox, than the most zealous opposers of our Holy Mysteries are now? No surely; and the forgery of the Passage in question had been too palpable to have escap'd the Eyes of the *Arians*, who, had they been able to read only, would have wanted nothing farther to discover the cheat.

Nor would it have been enough to justify the Orthodox for inserting it into their Confession of Faith, to say, they had found it in some of their own Copies. At that time, as before and since, particular MSS. might easily be incorrect, but the Faith of the Church was not to be built on faulty and inauthoritative MSS; this was to be grounded Copies on receiv'd in the Publick service, and to which most others were generally conform'd.[11]

— DAVID MARTIN

The great Anglican Theologian Frederick Nolan in his book *An Inquiry into the Integrity of the Greek Vulgate, Received Text of the New Testament* said the following:

"In the single instance of the text of the heavenly witnesses a difficulty arises, as it cannot be denied that this verse has been wholly lost in the Greek Vulgate. But I cannot admit that the integrity of the sacred text is at all affected by this consideration. Were the Greek Church the only witness of its integrity, or guardian of its purity, the objection would be of vital importance. But in deciding the present question, the African Church is entitled to a voice not less than the Byzantine, and on its testimony we receive the disputed passage. In fact, as the proper witnesses of the inspired Word are the Greek and Latin Churches, they are adequate witnesses of its integrity. The general corruption of the text received in these Churches in the vast tract of country which extends from Armenia to Africa was utterly impossible. A comparative view of their testimony enables us to determine the genuine text in every point of the smallest importance. And after the progressive labor of ages, in which every thing that could invalidate their evidence from the testimony of dissenting witnesses has been accumulated, nothing has been advanced by which it is materially affected. To the mind which is not operated on by these considerations, nothing further need be advanced in the shape of the argument."[12]

"2. As the African Church possessed this competency to deliver a pure unsophisticated testimony on the subject before us; that which it has borne is as explicit as it is plenary, since it is delivered in a Confession prepared by the whole church assembled in council. After the African provinces had been overrun by the Vandals, Hunneric, their king, summoned the bishops of this church and of the adjacent isles to deliberate on the doctrine inculcated in the disputed passage. Between three and four hundred prelates attended the Council which met at Carthage; and Eugenius, as bishop of that see, drew up the Confession of the orthodox, in which the contested verse is expressly quoted. That a whole church should thus concur in quoting a verse which was not contained in the received text is wholly inconceivable; and admitting that 1 John v 7 was thus generally received, its universal prevalence in that text is only to be accounted for by supposing it to have existed in it from the beginning.

3. The testimony which the African church has borne on the subject before us is not more strongly recommended by the universal consent, than the immemorial tradition of the evidence which attests the authenticity of the contested passage. Victor Vitensis and Fulgentius, Marcus Celedensis, St. Cyprian, and Tertullian, were Africans, and have referred to the verse before us. Of these witnesses, which follow each other at almost equal intervals, the first is referred to the age of Eugenius, the last to that nearly of the Apostles. They thus form a traditionary chain, carrying up the testimony of the African Church until it loses itself in time immemorial."[13]

— FREDERICK NOLAN, ANGLICAN THEOLOGIAN

---

1. Newman, John Henry. *The Arians of the Fourth Century.* Longmans, Green, and Company, 1901. p.6

2. Wiseman, Cardinal Nicholas Patrick Stephen. *Essays On Various Subjects,* 'Two Letters on some parts of the Controversy concerning the Genuineness of 1 John v. 7,' Charles Dolman, London, 1853 —*"Ecce jam non sunt absurda in libris ecclesiasticis quae absurda videbantur, et possunt aliter atque honeste intelligi. Figam pedes meos in eo gradu, in quo puer a parentibus positus eram, donee inveniatur perspicua Veritas. Sed ubi quaeretur? quando quaeretur? Non vacat Ambrosio, non vacat legere. Ubi ipsos codices qucerimus? unde aut quando comparamus? a quibus sumimus?"*

3. The Catholic Encyclopedia. Saint Augustine, New York, 1886, Portalié, E. 1907. *Life of St. Augustine of Hippo.* Robert Appleton Company, New York p. 51— Retrieved March 9, 2023 from New Advent: http://www.newadvent.org/cathen/02084a.htm]

4. Augustine, 'Chapter 23.—What Hermes Trismegistus Thought Concerning Idolatry, and from What Source He Knew that the Superstitions of Egypt Were to Be Abolished,' *The City of God,* Philip Schaff,

5. Wiseman, Cardinal Nicholas Patrick Stephen. *Essays On Various Subjects,* 'Two Letters on some parts of the Controversy concerning the Genuineness of 1 John v. 7,' Charles Dolman, London, 1853.

6. *"Quique prodesse omnibus volens, et valentibus multa librorum legere et non valentibus, ex utroque divino Testamento, Vetere et Novo, praemissa praefatione, praecepta divina seu vetita ad vitae regulam pertinentia excerpsit, atque ex his unum codicem fecit; ut qui vellet legeret, et in eo vel quam obediens Deo inobediensve esset agnosceret, et hoc opus voluit Speculum appellari."*— Wiseman

7. H.A.G. Houghton. *Augustine's Text of John. Patristic Citations and Latin Gospel Manuscripts.* Oxford: OUP, 2008. ISBN 978-0-19-954592-6. p.19 (*Contra Faustum 32.16*)

8. H.A.G. Houghton. *Augustine's Text of John. Patristic Citations and Latin Gospel Manuscripts.* Oxford: OUP, 2008. ISBN 978-0-19-954592-6. p.7—*in ipsis autem interpretationibus, Itala ceteris praeferatur; nam est uerborum tenacior cum perspicuitate sententiae. (De doctrina christiana 2.15.22)*

9. Comment on John 1:12, H.A.G. Houghton. *Augustine's Text of John. Patristic Citations and Latin Gospel Manuscripts.* Oxford: OUP, 2008. ISBN 978-0-19-954592-6.

10. Caldwell, Thomas S. J. (trans.) Marquette University in Milwaukee, WI. The translation comes from the *Codex Fuldensis* (c. A. D. 541-546), one of the earliest copies of the Vulgate. This Latin codex is available at http://books.google.com, and the Latin text above is found on pg. 399. The preface claims to be by Jerome, the translator of the Latin Vulgate. The prologue has textual critical value because it bears on the question of the authenticity of the Johannine Comma, 1 John 5:7

11. Martin, David. [pastor of the French congregation at Utrecht] *A Critical Dissertation Upon the Seventh verse Fifth Chapter of St. John's First Epistle, wherein the authentickness of this text is fully prov'd against the Objections of the modern Arians*, referring to the section on the *Vetus Latina*, William and John Innys, 1719

12. Nolan, Frederick. *An Inquiry Into The Integrity of the Greek Vulgate, Received Text of the New Testament*, 1815, p.572

13. Nolan, Frederick. *Testimony of the African Church Bible*

THE ARGUMENT IN FAVOR OF LEGITIMACY

"That the expressions are all in the style of St. John, and have a perfect connexion with what goes before 'em, and follows after 'em. The preceding verses relate to the Person of Jesus Christ, and his dignity as the Messiah and Son of God; and the words of the 7th confirm those great truths by the deposition of three witnesses, the *Father, the Word, and the Holy Ghost.* To these three witnesses from heaven are joyn'd in the following verse three witnesies upon earth, *the Spirit, the Water, and the Blood.* No words can be more justly connected; one verse answers to the other; there is the same testimony throughout, the same number of witnesses, a distinction and opposition of the places where they are; the witnesses of the 8th verse are in earth, of the 7th in heaven. The 8th Verse by a distinction so notify'd throws us back upon the 7th, and like the Seraphim in Isaiah's Vision, they correspond together. This is all plain, and strikes at first sight."[1]

— DAVID MARTIN

The fifth century Church historian Socrates of Constantinople (also known as Socrates Scholasticus), acknowledging the corruption of 1 John, says the following:

"But they did not know that in the Catholic Church of John it is written in the old copies that "there is no spirit that separates Jesus from God." **Because they**

removed this wisdom [passage] from the ancient copies, they sought their own divinity through the economy of man. For these ancient interpreters also pointed this out, as if they were the ones who created this epistle, willingly liberating man from God. But humanity is reconciled to the divinity; and there are not two [divinities], but one."[2]

— SOCRATES OF CONSTANTINOPLE

This all poses a peculiar problem for those who base their faith on *Sola Scriptura*. Here we have early evidence of a corruption. Which version of Scripture is the correct one? The oldest? The most prevalent? The most scholarly? Are some correct in some parts and deficient in others? In some ways it was *Sola Scriptura* that made Tischendorf's task all the easier—once he proclaimed his Scripture the oldest, the product of the Council of Nicaea, the debate was over. They win, we lose. Codex *Sinaiticus* becomes the 'only' Scripture. How do you challenge this if not through Tradition and Doctrine?

To say the verse is inauthentic and added later one has to surmise that a lot of people conspired to add it. While it may seem plausible for the Catholic Church to pull off such a conspiracy, either the Church was willing to undermine one of its own fundamental doctrines by removing the verse, or willing to undermine the Council approved Bible by adding the verse. Dodging this, they ask us to believe that the verse was conspiratorially added by working-class, semi-illiterate people because it was something akin to a fad. Is it really conceivable that people who feared for their lives added the most controversial of verses on a whim? And, how would these working-class people conspire with the most learned of ancient authorities? Tell me that line of transmission in a society where having even one book was a luxury. They argue that the Trinity, the highest of Christian doctrines, first appeared as a fad among peasants.

Two Anglican theologians, Westcott & Hort, took on the debate around 1853. Their conclusion was published in 1881, a date curiously aligning with the appearance of new found Gnostic texts. Their finding was that Bibles long regarded as faithful had been corrupted early on. By who? By the saint, martyr, and scholar Lucian, the very person on whose writings the Antiochian Creed was based. Why did they pick him? Westcott & Hort's research curiously begins soon after Bishop Thomas Burgess rediscovers the Antiochian Creed, based upon St. Lucian's writings and which referenced the Three Heavenly Witnesses, a verse that is not supposed to exist. St. Lucian would have to be 'taken down.'

Westcott & Hort's theory is now regarded as accepted fact, the simplest explanation to the problem. But is it really? Their theory demands something of a 4th century conspiracy. It is constructed out of few facts and unproven speculations. What they do have are an increasing number of Greek texts that do not include the verse combined with a theory explaining why Bibles that do are irrelevant.

We, on the other hand, propose a theory that is entirely consistent with not only well-known facts, but even lesser known facts. Why their text is legitimate and ours is not is largely determined by what fits *their* theory best. Aside from their theory there is not much to tell which text is older, even they admit they are only decades apart.

Let's set aside this history for a moment. Even if the history as I have presented it is in error, should we not at least expect the Bible to be consistent with itself? What if there were internal evidence that the text had been tampered with? What if the verse completes a pattern that its removal neglects?

THE FIRST PROBLEM

- Trinitarian concepts inferred by the verse are documented long before the Council of Nicaea.
- Much of this dispute at Nicaea centered around concepts inferred by the verse such as *Logos,* and whether implied doctrines are relevant.
- The rule that two 'witnesses' at minimum are needed to validate a testimony (three being preferred), is actually based on Jewish jurisprudence. Therefore, *Logos*, to be considered legitimate, requires at least two references in the Bible.
- There are only two references in the Bible to the Son as Logos, the prolog to John's Gospel and at 1 John 5:7 where this very term is associated with the Trinity, and calling them the Holy Witnesses. The Baptismal formula would be a second witness to the Trinity, but it says nothing of Logos.
- This creates a dilemma: with the elimination of the verse the Bible does not meet the witness requirements of Jewish Law. It breaks the minimum standard of the law, cancelling not only the Doctrine of the Trinity, but the Doctrine of *Logos*.

THE SECOND PROBLEM

- The internal evidence does seem to show that something is missing. The structure of the texts surrounding the phrase doesn't make complete sense, particularly when 5:6 is linked to 5:8. This is difficult for the average person not familiar with Greek grammar to see.
- There is actually plenty of external evidence that the verse is authentic, but most has been regarded as circumstantial. The one that wouldn't be circumstantial, that of Lucian as used in 341, would be left to Westcott & Hort to discredit.
- Their argument against the verse has never actually been proven. The following objections would have to be surmounted: 1) discrediting the testimony of common people is not the same as proving them false, something merely counting examples cannot do; 2) the Trinitarian doctrine in itself is not and has never been heretical, they have made no attempt to prove otherwise; and, 3) the doctrine that identifies Christ as Logos and is consubstantial with God the Father has never been proved theologically defective, which they have also failed to do.

These above criteria have not been met. Therefore, all they have shown is that certain Bibles do not include the verse and that they prefer the others. What they lack is a *modus operandi,* you cannot accuse somebody of murder simply by point ing to dead people in a cemetery. Nor can you make one up out of conjectures.

INTERNAL EVIDENCE OF TAMPERING

"John looked back at Christ's speech, John v. 31–39. coll. John viii. 12, 18. And the same thing that Jesus had taught there, he wanted to prove to his readers by the same arguments in which case, comma 7 can hardly be missing." The expression is peculiar to St. John. No other Evangelist or Apostle calls the Son of God THE WORD. The *scope* of the passage leads to the addition of greater testimony than had been alleged. St. John had hitherto testified of Christ from his own and the other Apostles' personal knowledge. But greater testimony than human testimony was necessary, as our Savior said of himself (John v. 33, 34.) "Ye sent unto John, and he bare witness unto the truth; but I receive not testimony from man."[3]

— BISHOP THOMAS BURGESS

The Internal Argument is based upon Greek grammar and whether there are markers within the text that would indicate something is missing. At first glance this can appear confusing because Greek has grammatical rules English does not. I will try to make it simple. The argument has been represented by Bishop Thomas Burgess. I present it here and hope to explain it after.

THE INTERNAL ARGUMENT

A Vindication of 1 John, v.7. From the Objections of M. Griesbach,
Thomas Burgess, Bishop of St. David's 1756-1837

"The subject of this passage being the evidences of Christ's incarnation, and the testimony, which was borne to it by the Spirit, St. John asserts that this testimony is of the strongest and most indisputable kind, first by its union with two other testimonies, and then by the superiority of divine testimony over human. By the Levitical Law, the testimony of one witness was not held to be true. (John viii. 13. 17.) For "in the mouth of two or three witnesses shall every word be established." (2 Cor. xiii. 1.) To the testimony of the Spirit the Apostle adds the testimony of the Father and the Son. If then the Spirit is declared to be truth, because it was not alone; (John viii.16.) "for there are three that bear record" it could not be said to " bear record" because it is truth. The bearing of record depended on the will of God; belief in the record depended on its truth; its truth (humanly speaking) on the union of two or three witnesses. The Spirit, therefore, did not bear witness because it was' truth; but it is here declared to be truth, or a true witness, because it was one of three witnesses. Instead, therefore, of a causal particle to connect the two clauses, it should be a conjunctive; instead of OTI [*that*] it should be KAI [*and*]. And so (if I mistake not) it is read in the Neapolitan Manuscript. Whitby and others endeavour to remove the difficulty of the common reading by a large arbitrary ellipsis. "And it is the Spirit that beareth witness, (and on his testimony we may rely;) because the Spirit is truth." The reading of the Neapolitan Manuscript requires no ellipsis; is a natural introduction to the next verse; and gives simplicity and perspicuity to the passage. *Και το Πνευμα εστιν το μαρτυρουν* **Και** *το πνευμα εστιν η αληθεια.* " And it is the Spirit that beareth witness; avd the Spirit is truth, for there are three that bear record." The frequent repetition of KAI is familiar to St. John, as in the fourth chapter of the Epistle, ver. 22, 33, 24. But be this as it may; the question of the authenticity of the seventh verse does not depend on the reading of the sixth, though the connection of the two verses appears to be improved by what I conceive to be the Neapolitan reading.

"There are three that bear record,"—τρεις μαρτυρουντες—three persons—distinguished as persons by the masculine participle; of which the Spirit is declared to be one. But who are the three? If we admit the reading of all Greek Manuscripts but one, we must admit the following reading in defiance of grammar and the context: *Τρεις εισιν οι μαρτυρουντες* **ΤΟ** *Πνευμα, και* **ΤΟ** *υδωρ και* **ΤΟ** *αιμα.* And thus *Πνευμα,* which in ver. 6 has, itself, a neuter participle, is, in the next verse, when accompanied with *two other neuter* nouns, most unexpectedly, and solecistically [A nonstandard usage] connected with a masculine participle; a violation of grammar, which is a stronger evidence of the *loss* of some intervening sentence, than the existence of a verse in only one manuscript is, of *interpolation.* But in the seventh verse we have the three witnesses, already recorded by St. John in his Gospel, and, at the same time, language of a legitimate construction. For *Πνευμα* being by signification masculine, though by form neuter; and being one of the three μαρτυρουντες in verse 7, retains its construction in the eighth, and associates with it the other neuter nouns, which follow its construction.

Without the seventh verse, the solecisms of the eighth will be unaccountable and indefensible: Without the *έν* of the seventh verse, the article with *έν* in the eighth verse is equally unaccountable, as Wolfius and the Bishop of Calcutta have observed. For it is not said: *έν εισι,* nor *εις έν εισι,* but *εις το έν εισι.* Therefore, that article TO [*neuter article translated as 'the' – Τρεις εισιν οι μαρτυρουντες* **ΤΟ** *Πνευμα, και* **ΤΟ** *υδωρ και* **ΤΟ** *αιμα.*] is an indication that something has preceded it, to which it is referred, in this sense that those earthly witnesses and the heavenly witnesses are three, but at the same time one, they vote in this business.

With the: seventh verse, the witness (*μαρτυρια*) which God bare of his: Son in the ninth verse, has an obvious reference to the *πατηρ,* one of the μαρτυρουντες in the seventh. But without it there is no expressed reference; for though *Πνευμα,* which occurs in the sixth verse may, in a general sense, be understood, of God, yet, as one of the witnesses to the Son, recorded in the Gospel, it is always mentioned, not as the Father, but the Holy Spirit."[4]

In essence the argument is this: In English we often use the definitive article 'the' to proceed a noun, however, our usage has no implication of gender, 'the' is neuter. This is not so in Greek. It usually requires a definitive articles proceeding all nouns, that agrees with the gender of the noun. This seems foreign to many English speakers where nouns are usually genderless. English usually only indicates gender in references to humans or animals, but in many other languages this is common. For example, in French 'the' is represented — *le* (male-singular), *la* (female-singular), *les* (plural), etc. In Greek these articles are: *o* (masculine), *η* (feminine), and *το* (neuter), and their plural counterparts. There are other factors but they are not important to this discussion. If there is a gender mismatch it indicates either something is missing, or very poor grammar. Below are these articles:

<u>Masculine Definitive Article</u>:
Nominative Singular: *ό*
Nominative Plural: *οι*

<u>Feminine Definitive Article</u>:
Nominative: *ή*
Nominative Plural: *αι*

<u>Neuter Definitive Article</u>:
Nominative: *το*
Nominative Plural: *τά*

Here is the original Greek text, the English has been adjusted to match:

Complete Greek Textus Receptus

1Jn 5:6 — *ουτος εστιν ο ελθων δι υδατος και αιματος ιησους ο χριστος ουκ εν τω υδατι μονον αλλ εν τω υδατι και τω αιματι και το πνευμα εστιν το μαρτυρουν οτι το πνευμα εστιν η αληθεια*

1Jn 5:7 — *οτι τρεις εισιν οι μαρτυρουντες εν τω ουρανω ο πατηρ ο λογος και το αγιον πνευμα και ουτοι οι τρεις εν εισιν*

1Jn 5:8 — *και τρεις εισιν οι μαρτυρουντες εν τη γη το πνευμα και το υδωρ και το αιμα και οι τρεις εις το εν εισιν*

IN ENGLISH

1Jn 5:6 — This is he that came by water and blood, even Jesus Christ; not by water only, but by water and blood. And it is the Spirit that beareth witness, because the Spirit is truth.

1Jn 5:7 — For there are three witnesses in heaven, the Father, the Word, and the Holy Ghost: and these three are one.

1Jn 5:8 — And there are three that bear witness in earth, the Spirit, and the water, and the blood: and these three agree in one.

ORIGINAL GREEK BYZANTINE VERSION

1Jn 5:6 — ουτος εστιν ο ελθων δι υδατος και αιματος ιησους χριστος ουκ εν τω υδατι μονον αλλ εν τω υδατι και τω αιματι και το πνευμα εστιν το μαρτυρουν οτι το πνευμα εστιν η αληθεια

1Jn 5:7 — οτι τρεις εισιν οι μαρτυρουντες

1Jn 5:8 — το πνευμα και το υδωρ και το αιμα και οι τρεις εις το εν εισιν

NOW I WILL TRANSLATE this into English with the genders represented in superscripts *m*, *n*, and *f*, (*m*ale, *n*euter, and *f*emale). It must be noted (such as in French), these cases must be consistent throughout or it is a sign something has been either tampered with, or the writer did not understand the language. — articles marked masculine[m], neuter[n], feminine[f] — (Articles such as 'the' and 'these' must match the gender of their target noun). The Byzantine Greek text is an example where the full verse is missing:

LITERAL ENGLISH FROM THE BYZANTINE GREEK

1Jn 5:6 — This is he that came by water and blood, even Jesus Christ; not by the water only, but by the water and the blood. And the Spirit is the One witnessing, because the[n] Spirit[n] is the[f] truth[f].

1Jn 5:7 — And there are[m] three witnesses[m]

1Jn 5:8 — the[n] Spirit[n], and the[n] water[n], and the[n] blood[n]; and the[n] three are to the[n] one.

The three male witnesses of verse 7 do not match the target counterparts which are all neuter. This implies that the male target nouns have been removed. **The masculine remnant of the original verse 5:7 now does not match the truncated neutral remnant of verse 5:8. Also, 'In heaven' in verse 7 and 'on earth' in verse 8 have been eliminated, this leaves the 'in' undefined (in what?).** Bishop Burgess:

"Without the seventh verse, the solecisms [grammatical mistakes] of the eighth will be unaccountable and indefensible: Without the ἐν (in/on) of the seventh verse, the article with ἐν (in/on) in the eighth verse is equally unaccountable,"

"The words *in terra* [on earth] in those Latin copies, which omit the 7th verse, indicate the absence of the verse, which contained their correspondent terms. The article of the eighth verse refers to a *previous union* of testimony; and the testimony of God the Father, in the ninth verse, implies a previous mention of the Father. When Christ speaks of himself in the Gospel, (John v.31.) he confirms his own testimony: by that of the Father. He does not, on that occasion, mention the Spirit, but he there twice appeals to the testimony of the Father. The witness, therefore, in the ninth: verse, is that of the Father; and its reference is to the Father in the seventh verse."[5]

— BISHOP BURGESS

To hide this, versions such as the American Standard clip off verse 6 to form verse 7, and the former verse 7 is added to verse 8.

1Jn 5:6 — This is he that came by water and blood, *even* Jesus Christ; not with the water only, but with the water and with the blood.

1Jn 5:7 — And it is the Spirit that beareth witness, because the Spirit is the truth.

1Jn 5:8 — For there are three who bear witness, the Spirit, and the water, and the blood: and the three agree in one.

EARLY CHANT?

Some scholars consider the above inconclusive. What Burgess is alluding to was a Greek poetical form called the 'strophe.' Many are not aware, and many Bibles don't indicate it, that when texts have a certain meter to them it means they were once poetry, *like the verses of a song.* Often they loose this in translation because rhythms change with the number of syllables, etc. used. When a sort of parallelism is apparent, as in our verses, it means the verses were meant to form mirror images of each other. Removing a verse demands the question, why then the singular poetic meter? If one verse has a certain pacing and rhythm, and the next does not, it could indicate something is missing.

Georgios Babiniotis is a Greek linguist, philologist, and former Minister of Education and Religious Affairs of Greece. He was approached with this very question by a 'Mr Sayers' who has a blog on Burgess' Gender Agreement Theory:

> "So for Modern Linguistic analysis what is important is not the mere grammatical "gender agreement rule" (which would lead to the usage of neuter gender : «καὶ τρία εἰσὶ τὰ μαρτυροῦντα ἐν τῇ γῇ...»), but the overruling schema of "syntactic parallelism" which is much more stronger than a simple gender agreement rule. Conclusion. The issue we refer to has more to do with the linguistic style of the passage; it is the result of a stylistic selection which is far beyond the usage of a grammatical/syntactic rule that would lead to neuter gender and which furthermore would eliminate verse 5.7."[6]

— GEORGIOS BABINIOTIS

I hope to make sense of this by illustrating it in English using a seldom referred to lectionary reading from the ancient Sarum Rite of England. The Sarum Rite is one of the most ancient of all Christian liturgies where documentation still exists. Here is the epistle for the Octave of Easter, beginning with chapter 5, verse 4, of the first epistle of St. John.

> "WHATSOEVER is born of GOD overcometh the world: and this is the victory that overcometh the world, even our faith. Who is He that overcometh the world, but he that believeth that JESUS is the SON of GOD? This is He that came by water and blood, even JESUS CHRIST; not by water only, but by water and blood. And it is the SPIRIT that beareth witness, because the SPIRIT is Truth. For there are three that bear record in heaven, the FATHER, the WORD, and the HOLY GHOST: and these three are one. If we receive the witness of men, the witness of GOD is greater: for this is the witness of GOD which He hath testified of his SON. He that believeth on the SON of GOD hath the witness in himself: he that believeth not GOD hath made Him a liar, because he believeth not the record that GOD gave of His SON. And this is the record, that GOD hath given to us eternal life; and this life is in His SON. He that hath the SON hath life; and he that hath not the SON of GOD hath not life."

The Greek version of our verses would read like this according to Babiniotis:

The use of masculine gender and not neuter on 5.8...

...*καὶ τρεῖς εἰσιν οἱ μαρτυροῦντες ἐν τῇ γῇ,* [and there are three who bear witness on earth,]

...*τὸ Πνεῦμα καὶ τὸ ὕδωρ καὶ τὸ αἷμα* [the Spirit and the water and the blood]

...*καὶ οἱ τρεῖς εἰς τὸ ἕν εἰσιν* [and these three are one]

...IS LINGUISTICALLY JUSTIFIED on the pattern of "syntactic parallelism", i.e. on the ground that it makes a pattern completely the same ("parallel") in structure with that of 5.7.

...*ὅτι τρεῖς εἰσιν οἱ μαρτυροῦντες ἐν τῷ οὐρανῷ,* [for there are three who bear witness in heaven,]

...*ὁ Πατήρ, ὁ Λόγος καὶ τὸ Ἅγιον Πνεῦμα* [the Father, the Word and the Holy Spirit]

...*καὶ οὗτοι οἱ τρεῖς ἕν εἰσι* [and these are the three in one]

...therefore, the corrected English reading for the Epistle for the Sarum Octave of Easter should read like this:

WHATSOEVER is born of GOD overcometh the world: and this is the victory that overcometh the world, even our belief. It is He that overcometh the world, even he that believeth not that JESUS is the SON of GOD. This is he who came by the water and blood, Jesus the Christ, not in the water only, but in the water and the blood; And it is the SPIRIT that beareth witness, because the SPIRIT is Truth.

For there are three that bear witness in heaven,
the FATHER, the LOGOS, and the HOLY GHOST:
and these are the three in one.

And there are three who bear witness on earth,
the Spirit and the water and the blood:
and these three are one.

If we receive the witness of men, the witness of GOD is greater: for this is the witness of GOD which He hath testified of his SON. He that believeth on the SON of GOD hath the witness in himself: he that believeth not GOD hath made Him a liar, because he believeth not the record that GOD gave of His

SON. And this is the record, that GOD hath given to us eternal life; and this life is in His SON. He that hath the SON hath life; and he that hath not the SON of GOD hath not life.

This fulfils the requirements of a Greek strophe. Could this be the hymn the followers of Athanasius sang when they sensed victory to their cause?

BISHOP BURGESS FINDS ANOTHER CREED

As has been pointed out previously, there is a legitimate question, why if 1 John 5:7 was the subject of a dispute, where is the contemporary documentation? Bishop Thomas Burgess, who proposed the grammatical resolution above, discovered just such a document in 1825 and published his research that very same year. It was a creed written during the Council of Antioch held in 341 called the *Symbolum Antiochenum.*[7]

As has been shown by the prior quote from Sozomen, the purpose of the Council was to mitigate the controversies generated at Nicaea. "They resorted, in fact, to such ambiguity of expression, that neither the Arians nor the followers of the decrees of the Nicene Council could call the arrangement of their words into question, as though they were ignorant of the holy Scriptures. They purposely avoided all forms of expression which were rejected by either party, and only made use of those which were universally admitted."[8] In their effort they purposely tried to resolve the controversy through direct quotes from scripture, the avoidance of controversial terms, and by acknowledging truths as both sides saw it. The record shows that many attendants referred to themselves as 'Eusebians,' rejected outright that they had been influenced by Arius, and were to a man from the Eastern Church. This can only mean that they were Semi-Arians and that the creed they penned reflects their true thoughts and convictions.

The quote proves few things. First, that Arius had not as much influence as most think, his doctrine was not that persuasive or remained secret. Secondly, that the two actual sides of the debate were not as far apart as commonly reported. While the Imperial family was slipping away from fold (Constantius II was considered irreligious at this point), Christianity was not at the doctrinal brink of collapse.

Perhaps most importantly, whatever credal statements that appeared in the *Symbolum Antiochenum* were designed precisely to be moderate, level-headed, and *an acknowledgment of issues assumed to be well-known and agreeable to both parties*. The Creed was specifically formulated to resolve known issues in a way acceptable to both parties. It is precisely a reference to our disputed verse that appears near the end of the document. It must be considered either a proposed resolution to a disputed point, or a statement of an acceptable fact:

> "...the Father being truly a Father, and the Son truly a Son, and the Holy Ghost truly a Holy Ghost — the names being given not vainly and unmeaningly, but accurately expressing the respective subsistence, order, and glory of each of the Persons named; SO THAT THEY ARE THREE IN SUBSTANCE AND ONE IN CONSENT."

— SYMBOLUM ANTIOCHENUM

This fact proves that the *Codex Sinaiticus*, while being an authorized Imperial version, was spurious and running afoul of the wishes of the Nicene Council for there is no evidence that the Semi-Arians held such beliefs.

I turn your focus towards St. Lucian. The very fact that this council deferred to his writings, and that it referenced the verse in dispute speaks volumes. It is his writings and scholarship that were the model for the Antiochian Creed. We have seen his history and the controversies surrounding it, *he came from heresy, converted, and died a martyr.* Like St. Augustine, he directly knew the Adversary. Despite being proclaimed experts on all this, Westcott & Hort still went ahead accusing Lucian of publishing a heretical gospel and shifted that accusation to any Bible that didn't agree with *Sinaiticus.* This shift in what they called the *Lucian Recension* means that Westcott & Hort either weren't aware of the above (meaning they weren't experts), or they were aware and committed a deliberate act of deception. *To do so would mean that they are personally declaring heretical not only a major Council of the Church, but also its attendees and the entire Eastern Church that sponsored it.*

Yet, this is precisely what they have done. Westcott & Hort had to have known of Bishop Burgess' discovery. Published in an 1825 edition of 'the Quarterly Review' was an article proclaiming Burgess' discovery, "In letters from which we are favoured with extracts, the Bishops of Winchester, Durham and Hereford, together with other prelates, whose names are not mentioned, have expressed themselves either as almost, or as entirely, persuaded that the verse is genuine."[9] Burgess' discovery in 1825 proceeds Westcott & Hort's research. This means their selecting of Lucian as the scapegoat for their cause was intentional, that they had to have known precisely what they were doing.

Rather than trying to understand why two 'official' versions of the Bible had emerged, they chose to slander one and promote the other. Why?

THE ELLIPSIS OF VATICANUS

The fact the verse might be authentic also appears in the *Codex Vaticanus*. Where the verse in question ought to be is signified by ellipsis (…), a common acknowledgment that text has been left out. Critics have said this doesn't indicate anything.

Citing the paper 'The Originality of Text-Critical Symbols in *Codex Vaticanus*' by Philip B. Payne and Paul Canart:

> "Throughout the margins of the Vaticanus NT are approximately 765 pairs of dots resembling a dieresis or umlaut. Examination of various categories of these "umlauts" reveals a prevailing pattern. Almost all umlauts occur next to lines of text which differ significantly from some other NT manuscripts. The frequency of textual variants in these lines is far greater than in lines that have no umlaut. This strongly supports the conclusion that umlauts in the margins of *Vaticanus* mark textual variants."[10]

— PHILIP B. PAYNE AND PAUL CANART

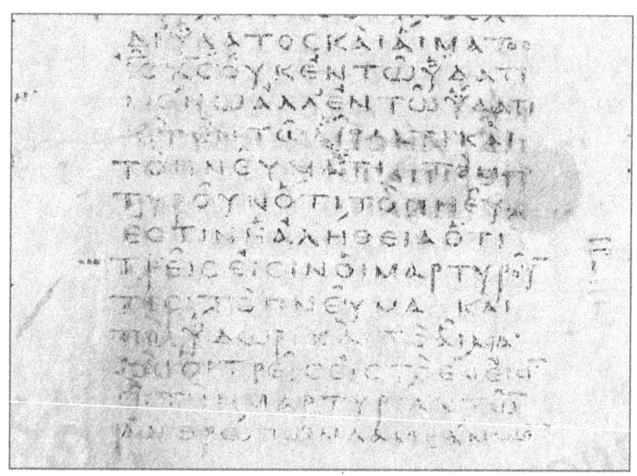

*The three dot ellipsis in Codex Vaticanus at 1 John representing an omission. **Folio 1441**, 2nd/Middle Column, Bottom seven lines = 1st John 5:7-8 (public domain)*

"The discovery that eleven umlauts unambiguously match the original ink of Codex *Vaticanus* has four significant implications for textual criticism. 1. It demonstrates that its scribe was aware of textual variants and believed them to be sufficiently important to note. 2. It supports the view that its scribe desired to preserve the most original form of the text possible. 3. The third implication follows from the evidence for the originality of the *Vaticanus* umlauts in general and from two correlations between umlauts and documented textual variants. First, in the vast majority of lines where *Vaticanus* has umlauts, other manuscripts preserve significant variants. Second, the frequency of significant variants in these lines is far higher than in lines without umlauts. These two correlations provide a statistical basis for the first time for concluding that the majority of variants that were available to the scribe of *Vaticanus* have survived in other manuscripts. 4. These umlauts are windows that give insights into the history of the text before *Vaticanus* even for passages for which no early papyri have survived."[11]

— PHILIP B. PAYNE AND PAUL CANART

I would add, could not the marks also signify pressure from authorities to leave the said verse out?

---

1. Martin, David. *A Critical Dissertation Upon the Seventh verse Fifth Chapter of St. John's First Epistle, wherein the authentickness of this text is fully prov'd against the Objections of the modern Arians*, referring to the section on the *Vetus Latina*, William and John Innys, 1719

2. Socrates of Constantinople. *Historia ecclesiastica*, VII:32 — *Αὐτίκα γοῦν ἠγνόησεν, ὅτι ἐν τῇ καθολικῇ Ἰωάννου γέγραπτο ἐν τοῖς παλαιοῖς ἀντιγράφοις, ὅτι «πᾶν πνεῦμα ὃ λύει τὸν Ἰησοῦν ἀπὸ τοῦ Θεοῦ οὐκ ἔστι.» Ταύτην γὰρ τὴν διάνοιαν ἐκ τῶν παλαιῶν ἀντιγράφων περιεῖλον οἱ χωρίζειν ἀπὸ τοῦ τῆς οἰκονομίας ἀνθρώπου βουλόμενοι τὴν θεότητα. Διὸ καὶ οἱ παλαιοὶ ἑρμηνεῖς αὐτὸ τοῦτο ἐπεσημήναντο, ὥς τινες εἶεν ῥᾳδιουργήσαντες τὴν ἐπιστολήν, λύειν ἀπὸ τοῦ Θεοῦ τὸν ἄνθρωπον θέλοντες· συνανείληπται δὲ ἡ ἀνθρωπότης τῇ θεότητι· καὶ οὐκέτι εἰσὶ δύο, ἀλλὰ ἕν.*

3. Burgess, Thomas, Bishop of St. David's *A Vindication of 1 John,v.7, From the Objections of M. Griesbach*, 1756-1837, p.26

4. Burgess, Thomas, Bishop of St. David's *A Vindication of 1 John,v.7, From the Objections of M. Griesbach*, 1756-1837. p.22

5. Burgess, Thomas, Bishop of St. David's *A Vindication of 1 John, v.7, From the Objections of M. Griesbach*, 1756-1837. p.27

6. Babiniotis, Georgios, quoted at Johannine Comma Blogspot. https://johanninecomma.blogspot.com/2020/09/voulgaris-vindicated-by-leading-greek.html

7. Ferrando, Mike. *The Comma Calmly Considered, Symbolum of Antioch 341 AD*, July 10, 2022 — Found and translated in, 'The Christian Examiner, and Church of Ireland Magazine,' vol 2, 1826, p. 57-58)

8. Sozomen. Bishops assembled at Antioch. Book 3.5; NPNF02, vol 2

9. Review of'A letter to the clergy of the diocese of St. David's on a passage of the second *Symbolum Antiochenum* of the fourth century as an evidence of the authenticity of 1 John v. 7 by Thomas Burgess, 1825"in The Quarterly Review, vol 33, no. 65, 1826, p. 101-102)

10. Payne, Philip B.and Canart, Paul. 'The Originality of Text-Critical Symbols in *Codex Vaticanus*', p.106 https://pbpayne.com/wp-admin/Payne2000NovT-Vaticanus_umlauts_1Cor14_34-35.pdf

11. Payne, Philip B.and Canart, Paul. 'The Originality of Text-Critical Symbols in *Codex Vaticanus*'. p.113 https://pbpayne.com/wp-admin/Payne2000NovT-Vaticanus_umlauts_1Cor14_34-35.pdf

HISTORICAL TESTIMONIES

"I am utterly disinclined to believe—so grossly improbable does it seem—that at the end of 1800 years 995 copies out of every thousand, suppose, will prove untrustworthy; and that the one, two, three, four or five which remain, whose contents were till yesterday as good as unknown, will be found to have retained the secret of what the Holy Spirit originally inspired. I am utterly unable to believe, in short, that God's promise has so entirely failed, that at the end of 1800 years much of the text of the Gospel had in point of fact to be picked by a German critic out of a waste-paper basket in the convent of St. Catherine;"[1]

— DEAN JOHN WILLIAM BURGON

THE PROBLEM

The very fact that there was confusion over the specific text of the Bible, proves that conflicting versions existed. Before 325 different branches of Christianity only had the version of the Gospel promoted by that evangelizing Apostle. The first New Testament to try to include all four Gospels was that of Tatian called the *Diatessaron*. His attempt was a harmony of the Gospels written in a more-or-less chronological order. This very concept means that major portions would be left out. It would be no wonder that Councils like Nicaea be called to sort things out. This is not necessarily a warlike dispute, but just as likely merely an honest effort to find resolution. Further, the fact that the Empire published an Authorized Bible for dissemination does not by itself mean that the matter had been sorted out and that it represented the final 'Holy Inspired' Bible. This should be common sense from the evidence.

Also, the fact that there are conflicting versions during that time period should not be alarming either. This is easily explained by the Diocletian persecution and the terror campaign of Julian the Apostate, different groups were isolated and generating their own versions. It is also reasonable to think that the 'official' Imperial Bible be one that reflects the beliefs of the ruling class, and that the genuine Bible not be prevalent until after the Arian-leaning rulers are overthrown. Several other key points:

- Tischendorf insisted the discovery of *Sinaiticus* proved the verse was inauthentic being both the oldest Biblical text AND the one certified by the Council of Nicaea. But, common sense demands there must have been earlier versions.
- Modern theologians teach that the Council of Nicaea was the beginning of the certification of Trinitarian Doctrine, yet the representative text, according to them, is already missing—one cannot certify a text that doesn't exist.
- Yet, it does make sense that the Arians may have had influence on the Imperial family forcing them to publish a spurious Bible more conducive to civil harmony or a number of other reasons.
- It would also make sense that if the Trinitarians actually triumphed at the Council that they would insert the verse yet, there is no evidence of this—if they conspired to insert it later, why not now?
- However, if the Trinitarians DID NOT triumph (as we contend) AND the precise wording of the Creed was unsettled due to Arian influence (which is also a fact of history) then it makes senses that they publish their Bible without the verse.
- It would also make sense that that Trinitarian dissidents who included the verse and whose lives were in jeopardy, produce their own more crude unofficial Bible (the *Vetus Latina*) for their own use and that it proliferate 'logarithmically' through cultures influenced by them (Africa, Gaul)

The question is, if the Trinitarians were yet to triumph and Athanasius had been exiled for years, why would we expect the verse be included in *Vaticanus* and *Sinaiticus*? Why should we expect it to be the final 'inspired' version? Might we not also expect that if 1 John was originally the Introduction to his Gospel, that the Arians relegate it to an epistle? The *Muratorian Canon* only lists two Letters of John, leaving a doubt over which two of the three were considered 'epistles.' 1 John does not read like a letter, it reads like an introduction.

However, it would make complete sense that in a climate of controversy debates be delayed until a later Council when more evidence was gathered and the specific text be sussed out.

Therefore, what we should expects is just this sort of 'sussing things out,' people not aware of a controversy, those who are aware, those who take their heritage for granted and those who don't, all leading up to a crisis, a bit of a dispute. After this it would be reasonable to expect a coming together of those who agree, and a departure of those who don't. To expect one 'Holy' definitive Bible at Nicaea is unreasonable, just as is pointing to the middle of the debate and declaring it the final resolution. The notion that God directly handed to his people a completed, pristine inerrant Bible is folly. It is this expectation that is at least partially responsible for the problem.

Below is the testimony of many in chronological order. It should reveal as we have said:

FIRST CENTURY EVIDENCE

MATTHEW 28:19-20 — "Go therefore and make disciples of all nations, baptizing them in the name of the Father and of the Son and of the Holy Spirit, teaching them to observe all that I have commanded you. And behold, I am with you always, to the end of the age."

THE DIDACHE (AD 35–60) — "But concerning baptism, thus shall ye baptize. Having first recited all these things, baptize in the name of the Father and of the Son and of the Holy Spirit in living (running) water. . . . But if thou hast neither, then pour water on the head thrice in the name of the Father and of the Son and of the Holy Spirit."

SECOND TO FOURTH CENTURY EVIDENCE

"The first period (A.D. 101—300) contains no evidence against the verse, but much for it. There is no Greek Manuscript of the New Testament of this period. The oldest Greek copy extant is of much later date than the ancient Latin version of the Western Church, and: the writings of Tertullian and Cyprian, who made use of it; and posterior to the first of two Greek evidences, which I have to bring in defence of the verse; I mean the rejection of the writings of St. John by certain heretics of this period, whom Epiphanius calls ALOGI, on 'account of their denial of the Apostle's doctrine of the Divinity of the Logos, or the Word. This rejection of St. John's writings by the ALOGI applies to no part of his writings so strongly as to his first Epistle, and especially to the seventh verse of the fifth chapter of that Epistle, which must have been the most obnoxious to them of all the passages of St. John, which: record THE WORD. He is twice mentioned in the first Epistle, once in the Gospel, and once in the Apocalypse. In the Apocalypse, he is called theWord of God; in the Gospel, and in the first chapter of St. John's Epistle, the Word of life; and in the fifth chapter of the first Epistle, THE WORD; and in this last passage, especially, he is mentioned, as the second person of the Trinity: "There are three that bear record in Heaven, the Father, the Word, and the Holy Spirit."[2]

— BISHOP THOMAS BURGESS

"To an early part of the second period belong the following passages: Basil. (adv. Ennom. L. V.) says, *Οι απεριερως πιστευοντες εις Θεον και Λογον και Πνευμα, μιαν ουσαν Θεοτητα, και μονην προσκυνητικην.* (Those who believe exclusively in God and Reason and Spirit, one Godhead, and one pilgrim.) The Nomocanon published by Cotelerius, has, *Αυτα τα τρια Πατηρ και Υιος και αγιον Πνευμα, εν ταυτα τρια.* (These three Father and Son and Holy Spirit, in the same three.) Among its principal indirect evidences may be placed those Latin manuscripts and Latin citations, which omit the seventh verse, but retain in terra in the eighth; such as the manuscripts, which Griesbach says are mentioned by Stephens, Hentenius, Lucas Brugensis, and others; and the passages of Facundus, in his Defensio trium Capitulorum"[3]

— BISHOP BURGESS

Justin Martyr (100–165 AD)

"In the name of God, the Father and Lord of the universe, and of our Savior Jesus Christ, and of the Holy Spirit, [new converts] then receive the washing with water" (First Apology, 61)[4]

I**RENÆUS OF LYONS** (c.130–c. 202 AD) —Irenaeus was a disciple of Polycarp, who had been a disciples of the apostle John. He presented a thorough defense of the economic Trinity, that is, how the members of the Godhead relate to one another and the history of salvation. The cooperating of the three is expressed as…

"the Father planning everything well and giving his commands, the Son carrying these into execution and performing the work of creating, and the Spirit nourishing and increasing [what is made]" (*Against Heresies* 4.38.3)[5]

In his Against Heresies X.1, Irenæus wrote:

"The Church, though dispersed throughout the whole world, even to the ends of the earth, has received from the apostles and their disciples this faith: [She believes] in one God, the Father Almighty, Maker of heaven and earth, and the sea, and all things that are in them, and in one Christ Jesus, the Son of God, who became incarnate for our salvation; and in the Holy Spirit, who proclaimed through the prophets the dispensations of God, and the advents, and the birth from a virgin, and the passion and the resurrection from the dead…"

He also wrote:

"This, then, is the order of the rule of our faith. . . God the Father, not made, not material, invisible, one God, the creator of all things: this is the first point of our faith. The second point is this: the Word of God, Son of God, Christ Jesus our Lord, Who was manifested to the prophets according to the form of their prophesying and according to the method of the Father's dispensation, through Whom (i.e. the Word) all things were made; Who also, at the end of the age, to complete and gather up all things, was made man among men, visible and tangible, in order to abolish death and show forth life and produce perfect reconciliation between God and man. And the third point is: the Holy Spirit, through Whom the prophets prophesied, and the Fathers learned the things of God, and the righteous were led into the way of righteousness; Who at the end of the age was poured out in a new way upon mankind in all the earth, renewing man to God."

ATHENAGORAS OF ATHENS (c.133–190 AD)

"Who…would not be astonished to hear men who speak of God the Father, and of God the Son, and of the Holy Spirit, and who declare both their power in union and their distinction in order, called atheists?" (*A Plea for the Christians*, 10).

HIPPOLYTUS OF ROME (c. 170—c. 235 AD)

"The economy of harmony is led back to one God; for God is one. It is the Father who commands, and the Son who obeys, and the Holy Spirit who gives understanding. The Father who is above all, and the Son who is through all, and the Holy Spirit who is in all" (Against the Heresy of the One Noetus, 8; ANF 5:226)[6]

ORIGEN (c.184–c. 253 AD) in his reference on Psalm 122 (123 in the KJV Bible)

"Behold, the eyes of bondservants in the hands of their lord, as the eyes of a bondwoman in the hands of their lady, so are our eyes towards the Lord our God, until he may pity us; spirit and body are the bondservants of the Lord **Father and Son**; but the soul is the bondwoman of the lady **Holy Spirit**. **And the Lord our God is three, for the three are one.**"[7]

IGNATIUS OF ANTIOCH (c.108–140 AD)

"I have confidence of you in the Lord, that ye will be of no other mind. Wherefore I write boldly to your love, which is worthy of God, and exhort you to have but one faith, and one [kind of] preaching, and one Eucharist. For there is one flesh of the Lord Jesus Christ; and His blood which was shed for us is one; one loaf also is broken to all [the communicants], and one cup is distributed among them all: there is but one altar for the whole Church, and one bishop, with the presbytery and deacons, my fellow-servants. Since, also, **there is but one unbegotten Being, God, even the Father; and one only-begotten Son, God, the Word and man; and one Comforter, the Spirit of truth;** and also one preaching, and one faith, and one baptism; and one Church which the holy apostles established from one end of the earth to the other by the blood of Christ, and by their own sweat and toil; it behoves you also, therefore, as "a peculiar people, and a holy nation," to perform all things with harmony in Christ."

St. Cyprian of Carthage (c.210–258 AD)

"The Lord says, "I and the Father are one;" and again it is written of the Father, and of the Son, and of the Holy Spirit, "And these three are one." And does any one believe that this unity which thus comes from the divine strength and coheres in celestial sacraments, can be divided in the Church, and can be separated by the parting asunder of opposing wills? He who does not hold this unity does not hold God's law, does not hold the faith of the Father and the Son, does not hold life and salvation. This sacrament of unity, this bond of a concord inseparably cohering, is set forth where in the Gospel the coat of the Lord Jesus Christ is not at all divided nor cut, but is received as an entire garment, and is possessed as an uninjured and undivided robe by those who cast lots concerning Christ's garment, who should rather put on Christ."[8]

[In reference to the above] "The Lord saith, "I and the Father are One:" and again of the Father and the Son and the Holy Ghost it is written, "and these three are One." And does any one believe that this unity, proceeding from the divine immutability, cohering by heavenly mysteries (*sacramentis coelestibus cohserentem*), can be rent in the Church, and separated by the divorce of contending wills? He who does not hold this unity does not hold the law of God, does not hold the faith of the Father and the Son, does not hold life and salvation. This mystery of unity, this bond of concord inseparably cohering, is shown, when in the Gospel the coat of our Lord Jesus Christ is not divided in any wise nor rent, but is received as a whole vesture, an incorrupt and undivided coat, by those who cast lots for the vesture of Christ, who should put on Christ. The divine Scripture speaketh and saith."[9]

— REV. H. T. ARMFIELD

Tertullian (c. 160 AD–c. 220 AD)

"Tertullian, taking up the same idea of the three heavenly, witnesses to the Baptismal Covenant, draws a conclusion still closer to the language and reasoning of the seventh and ninth verses. *Si in tribus testibus [humanis] omni stabit verbum, quanto magis sufficit ad fiduciam spei nostra etiam numerus nominum divinorum.* [If in three [human] witnesses the word can stand, how much more is the number of divine names sufficient for the confidence of our hope.] "If we receive the witness of man, the witness of God is greater."[10]

"the mystery of the economy. . .which distributes the Unity into a Trinity, placing in their order the three Persons--the Father, the Son, and the Holy Ghost: three however, not in condition, but in degree; not in substance, but in form; not in power, but in aspect; yet of one substance, and of one condition, and of one power, inasmuch as He is one God, from whom these degrees and forms and aspects are reckoned, under the name of the Father, and of the Son, and of the Holy Ghost."[11]

"He put to flight the Paraclete and crucified the Father". Like other early Christian theologians, the crux of the issue was a twisting of Scripture. He asserted, "[A]ll the scriptures display both the demonstration and the distinctness of the Trinity: and from them derived also our standing rule, that speaker and person spoken of and person spoken to cannot be regarded as one and the same.[12]

St. Clement of Alexandria (Titus Flavius Clemens) — (d. ~215 AD)

"I will close this period with two remarkable passages of Clemens Alexandrinus, and Tertullian; which, though not quotations from 1 John v. 7. appear to be founded upon it. "Clemens Alexandrinus (or some writer certainly the oldest, as Bengelius calls him) says, *Παν ρημα ισταται δυο και* ΤΡΙΩΝ ΜΑΡΤΥΡΩΝ, *επι* ΠΑΤΡΟΣ *και* ΥΙΟΥ *και* ΑΓΙΟΥ ΠΝΕΥΜΑΤΟΣ, *εφ ων* ΜΑΡΤΥΡΩΝ *και βοηξων αι ενιται λεγομεωαι φυλασσεξαι οφειλουσιν* [*There are two and* THREE WITNESSES, *on the* FATHER and the SON *and the* HOLY GHOST, *because of the* WITNESSES *and cries, those who say, they say, they keep, they owe*] Clemens, considers, the presence of the, Father, the, Son, and, the, Holy Spirit, witnesses, our promises at our baptism, as obligatory, on our obedience, Tertullian, taking up the same idea of the three heavenly, witnesses to the Baptismal Covenant, draws a conclusion still closer to the language and reasoning of the seventh and ninth verses. Si in *tribus testibus* [humanis] omni stabit verbum, quanto magis sufficit ad fiduciam spei nostra etiam *numerus nominum divinorum*. [If in *three* [human] *witnesses* the word can stand, how much more is the *number of divine names* sufficient for the confidence of our hope.] "If we receive the witness of man, the witness of God is greater."[13]

EVIDENCE FROM GNOSTIC SOURCES

GNOSTIC 2ND CENTURY — quotes mimicking the Trinity

Even before the spread of Arianism, Gnosticism had infected the early Church. Most scholars believe that John in his Epistles attempted to expose and refute the early Gnostic proclivities in the Church. The First Epistle would have attracted the relentless hostility of Gnostics. Valentinian Gnostics did not believe in the simple Trinity of the Father, Son, and Holy Ghost. They identified Sophia (Divine Wisdom). The Logos (or "Word" – one of the three witnesses in the Comma) was believed to be just one of the many Aeons (emanations of God).

CORPUS HERMETICUM—"From the beginning of the beginning. And the beginning of the one and the only one, and the beginning is moving, the beginning is born, and the only one is moving. And three these, God and Father and the Good, and the World, and the Human. And the Human and the World the God have, and the Human the World, and the World of the Son, and the Human of the World, the Human."[14]

THE SECRET APOCRYPHON OF JOHN, The "Trinity" and "there are three" in—"There was not a plurality before me, but there was a likeness with multiple forms in the light, and the likenesses appeared through each other, and the likeness had three forms. He said to me, "John, John, why do you doubt, or why are you afraid? You are not unfamiliar with this image, are you? – that is, do not be timid! – I am the one who is with you (pl.) always. I am the Father, I am the Mother, I am the Son.[15]

NAG HAMMADI LIBRARY—"For from the light, which is the Christ, and the indestructibility, through the gift of the Spirit the four lights (appeared) from the divine Autogenes. He expected that they might attend him. **And the three (are) will**, thought, and life. And the four powers (are) understanding, grace, perception, and prudence. And grace belongs to the light-aeon Armozel, which is the en placed over the second aeon. **And there are three** other aeons with him: conception, perception, and memory. And the third light is Daveithai, who has been placed over the third aeon. **And there are three** other aeons with him: understanding, love, and idea. And the fourth aeon was placed over the fourth light Eleleth. **And there are three** other aeons with him: perfection, peace, and wisdom. These are the four lights which attend the divine Autogenes, (and) these are the twelve aeons which attend the son of the mighty one, the Autogenes, the Christ, through the will and the gift of the invisible Spirit. And the twelve aeons belong to the son of the Autogenes. And all things were established by the will of the holy Spirit through the Autogenes."[16]

LATE EARLY CHURCH INTO THE MIDDLE AGES EVIDENCE

St. Athanasius (c.296–373) — Bishop of Alexandria; Confessor and Doctor of the Church. Athanasius was the center of the cause against Arianism.

> "The authority of the "Coptic Fragment" (published by Dr. O. von Lemm among the *Mémoires de l'académie impériale des sciences* de S. Péterbourg, 1888) and corroborated by the undoubted maturity of judgement revealed in the two treatises "Contra Gentes" and "De Incarnatione", which were admittedly written about the year 318 before Arianism as a movement had begun to make itself felt" — NewAdvent

> "But also, is not that sin-remitting, life-giving and sanctifying washing [baptism], without which, no one shall see the kingdom of heaven, given to the faithful in the Thrice-Blessed Name? In addition to all these, John affirms, 'and these three are one.'"[17]

> "Even as my soul is one, but a triune soul, reason (logos), and breath; so also God is one, but is also triune, Father, Word (*Logos*), and Holy Ghost.... For as soul, reason and breath are three features, and in substance one soul, and not three souls; so Father, Word (*Logos*), and Holy Ghost, [are] three persons, and one God in substance, and not three gods"[18]

St. Jerome (c.341–420) — Jerome's Prologue to the Canonical Epistles:

> "The order of the seven Epistles which are called canonical is not the same among the Greeks who follow the correct faith and the one found in the Latin codices, where Peter, being the first among the apostles, also has his two epistles first. But just as we have corrected the evangelists into their proper order, so with God's help have we done with these. The first is one of James, then two of Peter, three of John and one of Jude. Just as these are properly understood and so translated faithfully by interpreters into Latin without leaving ambiguity for the readers nor [allowing] the variety of genres to conflict, especially in that text where we read the unity of the Trinity is placed in the first Letter of John, where much error has occurred at the hands of unfaithful trans-

lators contrary to the truth of faith, who have kept just the three words water, blood and spirit in this edition omitting mention of Father, Word and Spirit in which especially the catholic faith is strengthened and the unity of substance of Father, Son and Holy Spirit is attested."

"In this Preface St. Jerom complains of certain Latin Translators, who in their Versions of the New Testament had omitted the seventh verse of the fifth Chapter of St. John's Epistle; and for this cause he blames 'em as *unfaithful Interpreters*, who turning aside from the true Religion had attempted to throw out of their Translation this Text, which is (saith he) *one chief Support of the Catholick Faith.*

This Preface had pass'd without contradiction for St. *Jerom's* to our own time, with the other Prefaces he had compos'd upon Holy Scripture. The Writers, who in the sixteenth Century made the first attacks upon the genuineness of St. *John's* Text, objected nothing against it: but in the following Ages men grew more daring, and this Preface has stood the charge of divers Cricks in the last, who have treat edit as supposititious. Mr. *Simon* is one of the most zealous in opposing its authentickness, and is carried so far by his heat, as oft to entangle himself in greater difficulties, than he would throw upon the Preface.

Yet when all's done, 'tis of little importance , whether we ascribe it to St. *Jerom*, or some other Person; for should we not be able to prove it his, 'twould yet be no less true, that the passage has been always in his Bible; I have given of this full proof already."— *A Critical Dissertation Upon The Seventh Verse of the Fifth Chapter of St. John's First Epistle, There are Three, that bear record Heaven, &c.*[19]

— PASTOR DAVID MARTIN

St. Augustine of Hippo (354–430) — Augustine was a former member of the Manichaean heresy. He is considered one of the premier doctors of the Church. Augustine refers to the Trinity in *City of God*, Book 5, Chapter 11. He writes:

"Therefore God supreme and true, with His Word and Holy Spirit (**which three are one**), one God omnipotent, creator and maker of every soul and of every body;"[20]

Augustine was in the process of writing a series of homilies on the First

Epistle of John, but for unknown reasons it was not completed, ending with 1 John 5:1-3. However, he did begin to address 1 Jn 5:7-8 in *Contra Maximinum*, who was a bishop in the heretical sect of the Arians. This exposition is sometimes considered Augustine's *mystical interpretation*.

"I would not have thee mistake that place in the epistle of John the apostle where he saith, "There are three witnesses: the Spirit, and the water, and the blood: and the three are one." Lest haply thou say that the Spirit and the water and the blood are diverse substances, and yet it is said, "the three are one:" for this cause I have admonished thee, that thou mistake not the matter. For these are mystical expressions, in which the point always to be considered is, not what the actual things are, but what they denote as signs: since they are signs of things, and what they are in their essence is one thing, what they are in their signification another. If then we understand the things signified, we do find these things to be of one substance. Thus, if we should say, the rock and the water are one, meaning by the Rock, Christ; by the water, the Holy Ghost: who doubts that rock and water are two different substances? yet because Christ and the Holy Spirit are of one and the same nature, therefore when one says, the rock and the water are one, this can be rightly taken in this behalf, that these two things of which the nature is diverse, are signs of other things of which the nature is one. Three things then we know to have issued from the Body of the Lord when He hung upon the tree: first, the spirit: of which it is written, "And He bowed the head and gave up the spirit:" then, as His side was pierced by the spear, "blood and water." Which three things if we look at as they are in themselves, they are in substance several land distinct, and therefore they are not one. But if we will inquire into the things signified I by these, there not unreasonably comes into our thoughts the Trinity itself, which is the One, Only, True, Supreme God, Father and Son and Holy Ghost, of whom it could most truly be said, "There are Three Witnesses, and the Three are One:" so that by the term Spirit we should understand God the Father to be signified; as indeed it was concerning the worshipping of Him that the Lord was speaking, when He said, "God is a Spirit:" (John 4:24) by the term, blood, the Son; because "the Word was made flesh"(John 1:14): and by the term water, the Holy Ghost; as, when Jesus spake of the water which He would give to them that thirst, the evangelist saith, "But this said He of the Spirit which they that believed on Him were to receive" (John 7:39) Moreover, that the Father, Son, and Holy Ghost are "Witnesses," who that believes the Gospel can doubt, when the Son saith, "I am one that bear witness of myself, and the Father that sent me, He beareth witness of me" (John 8:18) Where, though the Holy Ghost is not mentioned, yet He is not to be thought separated from them. Howbeit neither concerning the Spirit hath He kept silence elsewhere, and that He too is a witness hath been sufficiently and openly shown. For in promising Him He said, "He shall bear witness of me" (John 15:26. These are the "Three Witnesses, and the Three are One, because of one substance. But whereas, the signs by which they were signified came forth from the Body of the Lord, herein they figured the Church preaching the Trinity, that it hath one and the same nature: since these Three in threefold manner signified are One, and the Church that preacheth them is the Body of Christ. In this manner then the three things by which they are signified came out from the Body: of the Lord: like as from the Body of the Lord sounded forth the command to "baptize the nations in the Name of the Father and of the Son and of the Holy Ghost" (Matt 28:19). "In the name:" not, In the names: for "these Three are One," and One God is these Three. And if in any other way this depth of mystery which we read in John's epistle can be expounded and understood agreeably with the Catholic faith, which neither confounds nor divides the Trinity, neither believes the substances diverse nor denies that the persons are three, it is on no account to be rejected. For whenever in Holy Scriptures in order to exercise the minds of the faithful any thing is put darkly, it is to be joyfully welcomed if it can be in many ways but not unwisely expounded."'

"Augustine was the first of the African Fathers who interpreted the eighth verse mystically. But it does not follow from such an interpretation, that he had not the seventh verse in his copy; because it was impossible for him to interpret it literally, consistently with the meaning, which he ascribed to unum (one), namely, unity of essence. There are passages in the works of Augustine, (such as the Father and the Son and the Holy Spirit are one; and for there are three persons, the Father, and the Son, and the Holy Spirit; and these three, because they are of one substance, are one – (*Pater et Filius, et Spiritus Sanctus unum sunt; and Tres enim personæ sunt, Pater, et Filius, et Spiricas Sanctus; et hi tres, quia unius substantiæ sunt, unum sunt*,) which appears evidently taken from the seventh verse. Yet his allegorical interpretation of the eighth verse, according to Mr. Porson's argument, implies that he had not the seventh verse in his copy. "The argument from Augustine's allegory is so full and strong, that Beza fairly says, "*Non legit Augustinus.*" ("Augustine does not read.") This argument would have more strength, than it has, if Augustine had not understood by "*unum,*" unity of essence. It could not be said that the spirit, the water, and the blood, are one in essence. He, therefore, applied it, not absurdly, not absurdly, as he says, to the only three that are one in essence, the

Father, the Son, and the Holy Spirit." The literal meaning being, in his sense of it impossible, he necessarily had recourse to allegory, and applied the passage to the Trinity. *Non potuit non ad allegoricam confugere* (He could not but take refuge in the allegorical), says Bengelius, who did not "avoid the argument," as Mr. Porson thought, but met it with a full conviction, that Augustine read the seventh verse in his copy. (Augustine) was not so ignorant of the holy saying that he inserted his whole sentence, and a eloquent paraphrase of the sentence, even using the name of the VERB. He gives the following reason, why Augustine could not have been ignorant of the seventh verse: Augustine flourished in that climate, in which both his predecessors and successors used books, were those exhibiting the Dictum, and indeed the codices of Cassiodorus and Fulgentius, where the Dictum was read, had, as is evident from the Proleg. §841, 844."[21]

— BISHOP BURGESS

St. Gregory of Nazianzen (c.329–390 AD), is considered a doctor of the Church. He was probably taught in the same school as St. John Chrysostom. Another of Gregory's classmates was Julian, later known as Julian the Apostate. At this early stage Gregory was already suspicious of him. He was functioning as Bishop of Constantinople, forbidding Arians to hold public office, when the Council of 381 was called. Semi-Arians refused to acknowledge him, a new Bishop was installed.

Oration 31, Fifth Theological Oration, On the Holy Spirit — XIX. "But to my mind, he says, those things are said to be connumerated and of the same essence of which the names also correspond, as Three Men, or Three gods, but not Three this and that. What does this concession amount to? It is suitable to one laying down the law as to names, not to one who is asserting the truth. For I also will assert that Peter and James and John are not three or consubstantial, so long as I cannot say Three Peters, or Three Jameses, or Three Johns; for what you have reserved for common names we demand also for proper names, in accordance with your arrangement; or else you will be unfair in not conceding to others what you assume for yourself. What about John then, when in his Catholic Epistle he says that there are Three that bear witness, the Spirit and the Water and the Blood? Do you think he is talking nonsense? First, because he has ventured to reckon under one numeral things which are not consubstantial, though you say this ought to be done only in the case of things which are consubstantial. For who would assert that these are consubstantial? Secondly, because he has not been consistent in the way he has happened upon his terms; for after using Three in the masculine gender he adds three words which are neuter, contrary to the definitions and laws which you and your grammarians have laid down. For what is the difference between putting a masculine Three first, and then adding One and One and One in the neuter, or after a masculine One and One and One to use the Three not in the masculine but in the neuter, which you yourself disclaim in the case of Deity? What have you to say about the Crab, which may mean either an animal, or an instrument, or a constellation? And what about the Dog, now terrestrial, now aquatic, now celestial? Do you not see that three crabs or dogs are spoken of? Why of course it is so. Well then, are they therefore of one substance? None but a fool would say that. So you see how completely your argument from connumeration has broken down, and is refuted by all these instances. For if things that are of one substance are not always counted under one numeral, and things not of one substance are thus counted, and the pronunciation of the name once for all is used in both cases, what advantage do you gain towards your doctrine?"[22]

ORATION 45, IV. — "And when Infinity is considered from two points of view, beginning and end (for that which is beyond these and not limited by them is Infinity), when the mind looks into the depths above, not having where to stand, and leans upon phænomena to form an idea of God it calls the Infinite and Unapproachable which it finds there by the name of Unoriginate. And when it looks into the depth below and at the future, it calls Him Undying and Imperishable. And when it draws a conclusion from the whole, it calls Him Eternal. For Eternity is neither time nor part of time; for it cannot be measured. But what time measured by the course of the sun is to us, that Eternity is to the Everlasting; namely a sort of timelike movement and interval, coextensive with Their Existence. **This however is all that I must now say of God; for the present is not a suitable time, as my present subject is not the doctrine of God, but that of the Incarnation. And when I say God, I mean Father, Son, and Holy Ghost; for Godhead is neither diffused beyond These**, so as to introduce a mob of gods, nor yet bounded by a smaller compass than These, so as to condemn us for a poverty stricken conception of Deity, either Judaizing to save the Monarchia, or falling into heathenism by the multitude of our gods. For the evil on either side is the same, though found in contrary directions. Thus then is the Holy of Holies, Which is hidden even from the Seraphim, and is glorified with a thrice-repeated Holy meeting in one ascription of the title Lord and God, as one of our predecessors has most beautifully and loftily reasoned out." *and…*

XXX. — "But, O Pascha, great and holy and purifier of all the world — for I will speak to you as to a living person — O Word of God and Light and Life and Wisdom and Might — for I rejoice in all Your names — O Offspring and Expression and Signet of the Great Mind; O Word conceived and Man contemplated, Who bearest all things, binding them by the Word of Your power; receive this discourse, not now as first-fruits, but perhaps as the completion of my offerings, a thanksgiving, and at the same time a supplication, that we may suffer no evil beyond those necessary and sacred cares in which our life has been passed; and stay the tyranny of the body over us; (You see, O Lord, how great it is and how it bows me down) or Your own sentence, if we are to be condemned by You. **But if we are to be released, in accordance with our desire, and be received into the Heavenly Tabernacle, there too it may be we shall offer You acceptable Sacrifices upon Your Altar, to Father and Word and Holy Ghost; for to You belongs all glory and honour and might, world without end. Amen."**[23]

St. John Chrysostom (c.349–407), also a Doctor of the Church, highly regarded by the Eastern Orthodox.

Adversus Judaeos (Homily 1:3) — "Three witnesses below, three witnesses above, showing the inaccessibility of God's glory."[24]

Pseudo-Chrysostom, *De Cognitione Dei et in Sancta Theophania* —

"But, O Father, and Word, and Spirit, the triune being and might and will and power, deem us, who confess you as the unconfused and indivisible substance, also worthy to be the ones standing at your right hand when you come from heaven to judge the world in righteousness, for rightly yours is the glory, honor, and worship, to the Father and to the Son and to the Holy Spirit, now and for always, and for eternity."[25]

Cyril of Alexandria (c. 376–444)

"the two natures being brought together in a true union, there is of both one Christ and one Son."[26]

St. Eucherius (c. 380–c. 449), served as Archbishop of Lyon

"QUESTION Also in his epistle John states: There are three things that bear witness, water, blood, and the spirit. What is indicated in this? Resp. It also seems to me similar to this passage, that in his Gospel he speaks of the passion of Christ, saying: One of the soldiers the spear pierced his side; and immediately, blood and water came out; and he who saw it bore witness. In the same place he had said of Jesus above: He gave up the ghost with his head bowed. Some, therefore, argue from this passage as follows: Water baptism, blood seems to indicate martyrdom, but it is the spirit itself that passes martyrdom to the Lord. Many, however, understand the Trinity here by the very mystical interpretation, by the fact that it is perfect [f. perfect] she herself bears witness to Christ: the water indicating [indicating] the Father because he himself said of himself, They have forsaken me the fountain and the living water: showing Christ in the blood [demonstrating] certainly through the blood of passion; but with the spirit manifesting the Holy Spirit [manifesting.] Now these three things testify about Christ in this way, speaking in the Gospel himself: I am the one who gives testimony about myself; and he that sent me, the Father, beareth witness of me. And again: when the Paraclete comes, whom I will send to you, the Spirit of truth, who proceeds from the Father, he will bear witness about me. Therefore the Father bears witness when he says: This is my beloved son. When the Son says: I and the Father are one. The Holy Spirit is said of him: And he saw the Spirit of God descending like a dove coming upon him."

"The words of Eucherius are thus incorrectly quoted by Griesbach: "To the question, what is signified by the words of John: There are three things that bear witness, water, blood, and spirit? It will be answered: John is seen looking back to the place of the Gospel, ch. 19. 34: of the water and blood flowing from the side of Christ, in the following words: bowing his head he delivered: But to explain certain water from baptism, blood from martyrdom; the spirit of him who passes to the Lord through martyrdom. However, there are many here: to understand the Trinity with a mystical interpretation: the water the Father, the blood Christ, and the spirit manifesting the Holy Spirit."
[27] The chief defect of this quotation is in the omission of the important word MIHI at the beginning of the passage, which distinguishes Eucherius's own opinion from the two other opinions, which are afterwards mentioned. Griesbach does not appear to have taken his quotation immediately from the original, but from some other source, which seems to have misled him and the other opponents of the verse into the opinion, that Eucherius applied the eighth

verse allegorically to the Trinity. The words, with which Griesbach's quotation begins, stand thus in the original: It seems to me similar to this passage, that he speaks in his Gospel of the passion of Christ, saying, one of the soldiers opened his side with a lance, &c. Eucherius states three opinions respecting the interpretation of the eighth verse, his own, referring to the crucifixion, (which was also the opinion of Cassiodorus;) that of certain others, who understood it of baptism, &c.; and lastly, the opinion of the majority, who interpreted it mystically of the Trinity. "It seems to me—FEW therefore—MANY however." (MIHI videtur—QUIDAN ergo—PLURES tamen.) Whoever these few and many were, it is clear that Eucherius was not "one of the many who embraced the mystical interpretation."[28]

— BISHOP BURGESS

VIGILIUS OF THAPSUS (Vigilius Tapsensis) (5th century), Bishop of Thapsus in what is now Tunisia, theologian, banished by the Arian King Huneric. He wrote one treatise, *Adversus Nestorium et Eutychem Libri quinque pro defesione Synodi Chalcedonensis*, often shortened to simply *Contra Eutychetem*.

"...none has had more influence than the assertion that the seventh verse rests chiefly, if not solely, on the authority of Vigilius Tapsensis, "a base forger," as Dr. Carpenter calls him, of the fifth century. This assertion is the final result of his elaborate inquiry. *Therefore, the controversial seventh paragraph especially, not to say only, IS BASED ON THE TESTIMONY, FAITH AND EVEN THE AUTHORITY of VIGILII TAPSENSIS, and of the books attributed to this author, before whom no one clearly raised it (Igitur comma controversum septimum precipue, ne dicam unice, NITITUR TESTIMONIO, FIDE, ATQUE AUCTORITATE VIGILII TAPSENSIS, et librorum huic attributorum auctori, ante quem nemo clare id excitavit).* This final result of his investigation is very erroneous and inadmissible.[29]

— BISHOP BURGESS

"It cannot be admitted that Vigilius Tapsensis was the first who clearly quoted the verse, since it was not only expressly appealed to, by his contemporaries the African Bishops, but, nearly fifty years before them, was distinctly cited by Eucherius, Bishop of Lyons. ***Eucherius, Episcopus Lugdunensis, (says Griesbach) he is thought to be the first who, about the year 440, openly called into question the words in the book of formulae, ch. II. in these words: III. (this*** *is the triple number) refers to the Trinity in the epistle of John. There are three who bear witness in heaven, the Father, the Word, and the Holy Spirit, and there are three who bear witness on earth, the Spirit, water, and blood.*[30] This is clearly the passage of St. John, though not the whole passage. Griesbach indeed denies it to be a quotation of the Apostle; but Bengelius, who was quite as conversant with the enquiry, says that Eucherius quotes the verse not only *aperte* but *apertissime*.[31]

— BISHOP BURGESS

St. Fulgentius (late 5th–early 6th century), Bishop of Ecija, Spain.

"For the blessed John the Apostle testifies that there are three who bear witness in heaven, the Father, the Word, and the Holy Spirit; and the three are one. Even the most blessed Martyr Cyprian in his epistle on the unity of Eccl. he confesses, saying: He who breaks the peace and concord of Christ, works against Christ. He who gathers elsewhere besides the Church scatters the Church of Christ. And in order to show that there is one Church of one God, he immediately inserted these testimonies from the scriptures: The Lord says, I and the Father are one; and again of the Father and the Son and the Holy Spirit it is written: And the three are one."[32]

"The African Church from Tertullian to Fulgentius, that is, for somewhat more than 400 years, is the chief witness to the authenticity of 1 John v. 7, as the depository of the ancient Latin version [*Vetus Latina*], which contained the verse, and by the testimony, which the African Bishops bore to it in the fifth century. The Latin translation was their Bible for ordinary use; but it cannot be supposed that this learned Church was without the Greek text of the New Testament: Greek was spoken and written at Carthage in its Pagan state,"when they had no such motive for its use, as the Christian Church had in the study of the Scriptures."[33]

— BISHOP BURGESS

St. John Damascene (676–754/787), often considered the Thomas Aquinas of the Eastern Orthodox Church. His *Fount of Knowledge* is a classic 'Summa Theologica' of Christian doctrine. He served the Church under Muslim rule publishing the whole of Christian theology so as it might be preserved for future generations.

THE FOUNT OF KNOWLEDGE, *Chapter VII from* **The Arbiter** —
"Whence it is that the followers of Nestorius' teaching refuse to affirm either
one nature in Christ or one hypostasis, since they hold there to be no union of
the hypostases in themselves but suppose Him who was of Mary to be a mere
man who contained within Himself the entire divine illumination. And it is by
this that He differs from the rest of men, since in each one of these the divine
illumination is only partially realized. Nevertheless, they confidently assert
that the person of Christ is one, explaining that the relation of God the Word to
the man born of Mary is one person, because He worked the entire divine
dispensation in the person of the divinity of God the Word. In this sense the
bad treatment accorded the man is rightly referred back to God, because both
the honour and the ill treatment accorded the prefect by the subjects of the
emperor is referred back to the emperor himself. In any event they declare that
the appellation of *Christ* is indicative of this relation. Thus, they do not hesi-
tate to call Christ one, because, as has been said, the relation is one, even
though there may be several participating in it. So, I think that it should be
clear to them that revere the Incarnation of the Saviour that we say that the
Person of Christ is one, although not in the sense employed by the friends of
Nestorius, that is, not in the mere relation of God to man. And it should be
clear that we use the term *person* in such a Sense as to declare the Person of
Christ to be one hypostasis of a man like, let us say, that of Peter or of Paul."

"…instructed by the Holy Trinity, it teaches rightly and religiously and cries
out: We believe in Father and Son and Holy Ghost; one Godhead in three
hypostases; one will, one operation, alike in three persons; wisdom incorporeal, uncreated, immortal, incomprehensible, without beginning, unmoved,
unaffected, without quantity, without quality, ineffable, immutable, unchangeable, uncontained, equal in glory, equal in power, equal in majesty, equal in
might, equal in nature, exceedingly substantial, exceedingly good, thrice radi-
ant, thrice bright, thrice brilliant. Light is the Father, Light the Son, Light the
Holy Ghost; Wisdom the Father, Wisdom the Son, Wisdom the Holy Ghost;
one God and not three Gods; one Lord the Holy Trinity discovered in three
hypostases. Father is the Father, and unbegotten; Son is the Son, begotten and
not unbegotten, for He is from the Father; Holy Ghost, not begotten but
proceeding, for He is from the Father. There is nothing created, nothing of the
first and second order, nothing of lord and servant; but there is unity and trinity
—there was, there is, and there shall be forever—which is perceived and
adored by faith—by faith, not by inquiry, nor by searching out, nor by visible
manifestation: for the more He is sought out, the more He is unknown, and the

more He is investigated, the more He is hidden. And so, let the faithful adore God with a mind that is not overcurious. And believe that He is God in three hypostases, although the manner in which He is so is beyond manner, for God is incomprehensible…Think of the Father as a root, and of the Son as a branch, and of the Spirit as a fruit, for the substance in these three is one. The Father is a sun with the Son as rays and the, Holy Ghost as heat. The Holy Trinity transcends by far every similitude and figure. So, when you hear of an offspring of the Father, do not think of a corporeal offspring. And when you hear that there is a Word, do not suppose Him to be a corporeal word. And when you hear of the Spirit of God, do not think of wind and breath. Rather, hold your persuasion with a simple faith alone. For the concept of the Creator is arrived at by analogy from His creatures. Be persuaded, moreover, that the incarnate dispensation of the Son of God was begotten ineffably and without seed of the blessed Virgin, believing Him to be without confusion and without change both God and man, who for your sake worked all the dispensation. And to Him by good works give worship and adoration, and venerate and revere the most holy Mother of God and ever-virgin Mary as true Mother of God, and all the saints as His attendants. Doing thus, you will be a light worshiper of the holy and undivided Trinity, Father and Son and Holy Ghost, of the one Godhead, to whom be glory and honour and adoration forever and ever. Amen."

FACUNDUS, Bishop of Hermiane (6th century), his most important work is *Defensio trium capitulorum* sent to Emperor Justinian. He was attempting to returning the heretical monophysites back to the broader Church. Yet, they in turn, accused the Church of Nestorianism (what became the basis of Islam). This came to a head at the Council of Chalcedon. The Council ultimately rejected both the Nestorian and Monophysite heresies, supporting the Trinitarian formulation of Christ's nature. Facundus' letter diffused the Origenists who were trying to influence Justinian, making it pivotal to the results.

In Defense of the Three Chapters of the Council of Chalcedon, Book XII to the Emperor Justinian Paris MDXXX — "For even John the Apostle in his epistle concerning the Father and the Son and the Holy Spirit says thus: There are three that bear witness on earth, spirit, water, and blood; and these three are one: in the spirit signifying the Father, as the Lord speaks to the Samaritan woman according to the Gospel of John himself, saying: Believe me, for the hour will come, &c. (John. iv. 21.) but in the water signifying the Holy Spirit, as in the same Gospel he explains the words: of the Lord saying: Whoever sows, &c. John.vii.37 whereupon he added: And this he said of the Spirit, &c. but in the blood signifying the Son, since he himself partook of the holy Trinity in flesh and blood. John therefore said not. The Apostle, speaking of the Father and the Son and the Holy Spirit, There are three persons who bear witness in the earth, the spirit, and the water; and blood, and these three are one. What then do they answer the Apostle for John? Who are these three who are witnessed on earth, and who are said to be one? Did God? Are the Fathers? are the Sons and the Holy Spirit? Of course not. But these three are the Father, the Son, and the Holy Spirit, yet even if there is not one name that is commonly predicated of all of them in the masculine gender, just as persons are commonly predicated of them in the feminine gender. Or if perhaps they who dispute about the word in what he said: There are three that bear witness on earth, the spirit, the water, and the blood, and these three are one: they do not want to understand the Trinity, which is one God, should answer according to the very words that he set forth for the Apostle John. Can these three, who are witnessed on earth, and who are said to be one, be called spirits, waters, and blood? However, the testimony of John the Apostle, B. Cyprian of Cathage, ancient and martyr, in his Epistle, or book, which he wrote on the Trinity, understands that it was said about the Father and the Son and the Holy Spirit. For he said: The Lord says, I and the Father are one; and again it is written of the Father and the Son and the Holy Spirit: And these three are one."

"For in this way the Church of Christ, even when she did not yet use the name of person to distinguish the Father and the Son and the Holy Spirit, believed and preached three, the Father and the Son and the Spirit. Holy; as we have taught in the testimony of John above, where it was said: There are three that bear witness ON EARTH, spirit, water, and blood; and these three are one: and the name of the personas, not except when Sabellius attacked the church, was necessarily taken up for the use of preaching; so that those who have always been believed and called three, the Father, the Son, and the Holy Spirit, may also be called by the same and common name of persons."[34]

— BISHOP BURGESS

WALAFRID STRABO (c. 808–849), an Alemannic Benedictine monk and theological writer. His *De exordiis et incrementis quarundam in observationibus ecclesiasticis rerum* deals with customary ecclesiastical usages.

"... and let not the variety of discourses challenge themselves, in that particular place, where we read of the unity of the Trinity in the first epistle of John: in which we also find that by unfaithful translators much erred from the truth of the faith, the terms of only three, that is, water, blood, and spirit in their own edition they put; and to those who omit the Father, the Word, and the Spirit; in which the Catholic faith is especially strengthened, and the one substance of the Godhead of the Father, the Son, and the Holy Spirit is confirmed."[35]

END OF THE MIDDLE AGES TO THE RENAISSANCE EVIDENCE

Peter Lombard (ca. 1095–1160), is famous for his seminal text *the Book of Sentences* used for centuries as the basis of the Western Education. Originally called *Quatuor libri Sententiarum* it was largely derived from the writings of St. John Damascene. It was the primary source of the reaching of the early Church Fathers in the Middle Ages.

"But to go higher. I come now to Lombard, Bishop of Paris, and sirnam'd for his extensive knowledge *Master of the Sentences*; he flourish'd in the 12th Century let us hear how he speaks in the first Book of his sentences, at the close of his second Distinction: *That the Father and the Son are one, says he, not by confusion of Persons, but by Unity of Nature, St. John hath taught us in his Canonical Epistle, saying, There are three which bear record in heaven, the Father, the Word, and the Holy Ghost, and these three are one.* If this celebrated Preacher's Bible was now extant in any Library, what esteem shou'd we not have for it? what deference would not be paid to its Authority? But as to this passage, we have it, for we see it copied from this Bible in Lombards citation."[36]

— PASTOR DAVID MARTIN

St. Thomas Aquinas (c.1225–74), philosopher, theologian, doctor of the Church. He is noted for many writings, but primarily for his *Summa Theologica*, a continuation of the tradition began by St. John Damascene, and continued by Peter Lombard.

"...It is said: "There are three who bear witness in heaven, the father, the Word, and the Holy Ghost" (1 Jn. 5:7). To those who ask, "Three what?" we answer, with Augustine, "Three persons." Therefore there are but three persons in God."

"I answer that, As was explained above, there can be only three persons in God. For it was shown above that the several persons are the several subsisting relations really distinct from each other. But a real distinction between the divine relations can come only from relative opposition. Therefore two opposite relations must needs refer to two persons: and if any relations are not opposite they must needs belong to the same person. Since then paternity and filiation are opposite relations, they belong necessarily to two persons. Therefore the subsisting paternity is the person of the Father; and the subsisting filiation is the person of the Son. The other two relations are not opposed to each other; therefore these two cannot belong to one person: hence either one of them must belong to both of the aforesaid persons; or one must belong to one person, and the other to the other. Now, procession cannot belong to the Father and the Son, or to either of them; for thus it would follows that the procession of the intellect, which in God is generation, wherefrom paternity and filiation are derived, would issue from the procession of love, whence spiration and procession are derived, if the person generating and the person generated proceeded from the person spirating; and this is against what was laid down above. We must frequently admit that spiration belongs to the person of the Father, and to the person of the Son, forasmuch as it has no relative opposition either to paternity or to filiation; and consequently that procession belongs to the other person who is called the person of the Holy Ghost, who proceeds by way of love, as above explained. Therefore only three persons exist in God, the Father, the Son, and the Holy Ghost."

St. Robert Bellarmine (1542–1621), one of the thirty-three doctors of the Church. As a Jesuit scholar he was the judge during the trial of Galileo. Bellarmine's most famous work was *Disputations about Controversies of the Christian Faith against the Heretics of this Age*.

Chapter Six: the Third Class: from the New Testament — "The eleventh place is from I John ch.5, *"There are three who give testimony in heaven, the Father, the Word, and the Holy Spirit, and these three are one; and there are three who give testimony on earth, the spirit, the water, and the blood."* By which place St. John means to show that Christ is true God and true man; and for that reason he adduces divine and human testimonies; for neither when he says 'there are three who give testimony in heaven' does he mean by 'in heaven' a heavenly place but the quality of the testimony; otherwise even the angels are in heaven and have not seldom given testimony to Christ, and yet

John posits that there are only three witnesses in heaven, the Father, the Word, and the Holy Spirit.

Therefore by the witnesses who are in heaven are understood divine witnesses as distinct from human and created witnesses; and therefore too a little later he says, "If we accept the testimony of men, the testimony of God is greater." Just as, therefore, spirit, water, and blood are three earthly testimonies and proved the true humanity of Christ, namely when on the death of Christ the spirit flowed from his mouth and blood and water from his side; so too the Father, the Word, and the Holy Spirit are three divine persons, and have given divine testimony of the true divinity of Christ, both often elsewhere and also in his baptism and transfiguration.

But Gregory Blandrata objects, first, that the words 'there are three who give testimony in heaven' are read by no author save Jerome, who had too little shame. Second, the spirit, water, and blood are not otherwise said to be one than the Father, Word, and Holy Spirit are; and therefore, as the spirit, water, and blood are not one in number, nay and not in species either, so neither are the Father, Word, and Holy Spirit one in number, or in species, but only by agreement of will.

I reply that Blandrata not only has too little shame but too much impudence when, imitating Erasmus, he says Jerome has too little shame; not only does Blandrata have too little shame, I say, but he is lacking in skill or is a liar when he says that only Jerome so read the passage. For it was so read by Hyginus, Cyprian, Idacius, Athanasius, Theophilus, the author of the dispute of the same Athanasius with Arius at the Council of Nicea, Fulgentius, Eugenius of Carthage.

But as to what concerns the words 'and these three are one', one must know that the words are not contained in many Latin codices where the discussion is about the spirit, water, and blood. For in the Louvain Bible there are noted in the margin fifteen manuscripts that do not have the words. Now the Greek codices do indeed have them but in different ways. For of the Father, Son, and Holy Spirit they say *and these three are one*, but of the spirit, water, and blood they say 'and these three are in one', where you openly see that the spirit, water, and blood are not one, but only conspire in one testimony."

Chapter Five: On the Other Terms — "Trinity, in Greek *trias*, is also not expressly contained in Scripture, yet it is deduced evidently from Matthew last chapter, "Baptize all nations in the name of the Father, the Son, and the Holy Spirit." And I John ch.5, "There are three that give testimony in heaven, Father, Word, and Holy Spirit." And this name is used by all the Fathers, even the most ancient, as Dionysius the Areopagite; also by Justin, Gregory Thaumaturgus, Tertullian, Cyprian, and all later ones.

But it is to be observed that Trinity does not signify the unity of three, as Valentinus Gentilis has thought, but simply a triple of persons, as is plain both from the Greek trias and from the sentence of the Athanasian Creed, "We venerate Trinity in Unity." For how absurd it would be to say, "We venerate a Unity of Three in Unity."

Next, if the term Trinity expressly signified Unity, how would the Fathers not be blamed who oppose Unity to Trinity, and say a Unity in essence is considered a Trinity in persons, and again that in Trinity a number is discerned, in the essence something numbered is not found? Fulgentius says, "Trinity is referred to the persons, Unity to the nature." The eleventh Council of Toledo, "In the relations of persons number is seen; in the substance of divinity something numbered is not seen." Which is explained at length by Isidore.

St. Thomas Aquinas, although he says that Trinity seems said as if it were a unity of three if one considers the sound of the term, yet he affirms that this is not properly signified by this term, but only the number of three persons.

It is also to be observed that Genebrard does not rightly attribute to Calvin that he said the essence is not comprehended in the persons. For it is clear that Valentinus Gentilis had said the Trinity is a unity of three and he had declared the three to be Essence, Son and Holy Spirit; by which words he had put the essence in place of the first person and numbered it along with the other two. For these are the words of Gentilis, "Three run together in the Trinity, Essence, which is called the Father, Son, and Holy Spirit. And this is the true Trinity, which is a unity of Three, not of four; whatever Lord Calvin says about the word."

But this madness is refuted by Calvin who says that essence is not comprehended in the Trinity, as if it were one of the number of the three, but it is included in all three, which indeed is very true, and would that Calvin had always erred thus."[37]

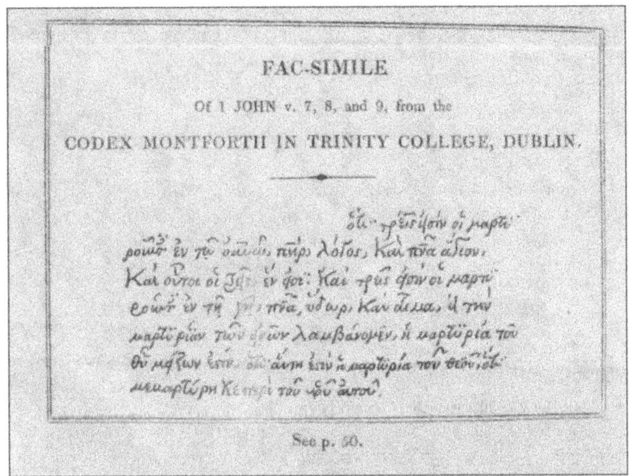

*Codex Montfortianus — Erasmus, who was one of the first to introduce a Greek version of the Bible to Europe, left out 1 John 5:7 until he saw this codex. Erasmus called it **Codex Britannicus**. It is dated to about the late 15th century. (public domain)*

Edmund Calamy (1671–1732), was an English Nonconformist churchman and historian.[38]

SERMON 1, I JOHN. v. 7, For there are Three that hear Record in Heaven, the FATHER, the WORD, and the HOLY GHOST; and these Three are One.

"I know not a Passage in all the New Testament so contested as this. Tho' it has of a long Time been own'd and used both in the Greek and Latin Church, and is in all our Modern Versions, (a very few only being excepted) yet have we some that reject it as spurious, and won't allow it to be a Part of the Sacred Scripture, but represent it as brought in out of Design, and added by those that had a Turn to serve. This is so heavy a Charge, that it had need be well prov'd, considering how severe a Denunciation St. John has in the very Close of the Canon of Scripture…"

---

1. Burgon, Dean John William and Miller, Edward. *The Traditional Text of the Holy Gospels*, p.12
2. Burgess, *A Vindication of 1 John, v.7. From the Objections of M. Griesbach*, p.28
3. Burgess, *A Vindication of 1 John, v.7. From the Objections of M. Griesbach*
4. The Gospel Coalition — https://www.thegospelcoalition.org/essay/trinitarianism-in-the-early-church/

5. The Gospel Coalition — https://www.thegospelcoalition.org/essay/trinitarianism-in-the-early-church/

6. The Gospel Coalition — https://www.thegospelcoalition.org/essay/trinitarianism-in-the-early-church/

7. Translation by KJV Today *"Ἰδοὺ ὡς ὀφθαλμοὶ δούλων εἰς χεῖρας τῶν κυρίων αὐτῶν, ὡς ὀφθαλμοὶ παιδίσκης εἰς χεῖρας τῆς κυρίας αὐτῆς, οὕτως οἱ ὀφθαλμοὶ ἡμῶν πρὸς Κύριον Θεὸν ἡμῶν, ἕως οὗ οἰκτειρήσαι ἡμᾶς, κ. τ. ἑ. Δοῦλοι κυρίων* **Πατρὸς καὶ Υἱοῦ** *πνεῦμα καὶ σῶμα· παιδίσκη δὲ κυρίας τοῦ* **ἁγίου Πνεύματος** *ἡ ψυχή. Τὰ δὲ τρία Κύριος ὁ Θεὸς ἡμῶν ἐστιν·* **οἱ γὰρ τρεῖς τὸ ἕν εἰσιν.**" http://textus-receptus.com/wiki/Main_Page

8. "The Early Church Fathers and Other Works", Wm. B. Eerdmans Pub. Co. 1867 Edinburgh, Scotland

9. Armfield, Rev. H. T. *The Three Witnesses: the Disputed Text in St. John Considerations New and Old.* p.153

10. Burgon, Dean John William and Miller, Edward. *The Traditional Text of the Holy Gospels*, P.32

11. Tertullian, *Against Praxeas*, II—Ante-Nicene Fathers (Grand Rapids, MI: Eerdmans, 1971),3: 598. https://www.reasonablefaith.org/writings/scholarly-writings/christian-doctrines/a-formulation-and-defense-of-the-doctrine-of-the-trinity

12. Tertullian, *Against Praxeas*, I & II. — https://www.thegospelcoalition.org/essay/trinitarianism-in-the-early-church/

13. Burgon, Dean John William and Miller, Edward. *The Traditional Text of the Holy Gospels*, p.32

14. Festugière, André-Jean — *Εκ μιου δε αρχης τα παντα ηρτηται, η δε αρχη εκ του ενος και μονου, και η μεν αρχη κινειται, ινα παλιν αρχη γενηται, το δε εν μονον εστηκεν, ου κινειται. και τρια τοινυν ταυτα, ο θεος και πατηρ και το αγαθον, και ο κοσμος, και ο ανθρωπος και τον μεν κοσμον ο θεος εχει, τον δε ανθρωπον ο κοσμος· και γινεται ο μεν κοσμος του θεου υιος, ο δε ανθρωπος του κοσμου, ωσπερ εγγονος.—*, (Google translate) Festugière was a French Dominican friar. His expertice was Neoplatonism, and Hermeticism.

15. Wisse, Frederik. "The Nag Hammadi Library and the Heresiologists." *Vigiliae Christianae.* 1971

16. Wisse, Frederik. "The Nag Hammadi Library and the Heresiologists." *Vigiliae Christianae.* 1971

17. Translation by 'KJV Today'—*"Τί δὲ καὶ τὸ τῆς ἀφέσεως τῶν ἁμαρτιῶν παρεκτικὸν, καὶ ζωοποιὸν, καὶ ἁγιαστικὸν λουτρὸν, οὗ χωρὶς οὐδεὶς ὄψεται τὴν βασιλείαν τῶν οὐρανῶν, οὐκ ἐν τῇ τρισμακαρίᾳ ὀνομασίᾳ δίδοται τοῖς πιστοῖς; Πρὸς δὲ τούτοις πᾶσιν Ἰωάννης φάσκει· «Καὶ οἱ τρεῖς τὸ ἕν εἰσιν.»"*

18. *"Ὥσπερ ἡ ψυχή μου μία ἐστὶν, ἀλλὰ καὶ τρισυπόστατος, ψυχή, λόγος, καὶ πνοή· οὕτω καὶ ὁ Θεὸς εἷς ἐστιν, ἀλλ᾽ ἔστι καὶ τρισ υπόστατος, Πατὴρ, Λόγος, καὶ Πνεῦμα ἅγιον.... Ὡς γὰρ ψυχὴ, λόγος καὶ πνοὴ τρία πρόσωπα, καὶ μία φύσις ψυχῆς, καὶ οὐ τρεῖς ψυχαί· οὕτω Πατὴρ, Λόγος καὶ Πνεῦμα ἅγιον, τρία πρόσωπα, καὶ εἷς τῇ φύσει Θεὸς, καὶ οὐ τρεῖς θεοί."* – *Quaestiones Aliae*, – https://www.pentecostaltheology.com/johannine-comma-1-john-57-trinity-vs-oneness-debate/ – http://khazarzar.skeptik.net/pgm/PG_Migne/Athanasius%20the%20Great%20of%20Alexandria_%20PG%2025-28/Disputatio%20contra%20Arium.pdf

19. Martin, David. *A Critical Dissertation Upon the Seventh verse Fifth Chapter of St. John's First Epistle, wherein the authentickness of this text is fully prov'd against the Objections of the modern Arians*, referring to the section on the *Vetus Latina*, William and John Innys, 1719

20. *"Deus itaque summus et verus cum Verbo suo et Spiritu sancto, quae tria unum sunt, Deus unus omnipotens, creator et factor omnis animae atque omnis corporis,"*English translation by New Advent, http://www.newadvent.org/fathers/120105.htm

21. Burgess, Thomas. Bishop of St. David's. *A Vindication of 1 John, v.7. from the Objections of M. Griesbach*, p.46

22. Browne, Charles Gordon and Swallow, James Edward. *Nicene and Post-Nicene Fathers, Second Series*, Vol. 7. Philip Schaff and Henry Wace ed., Christian Literature Publishing Co., Buffalo, NY, 1894. Revised and edited for New Advent by Kevin Knight. http://www.newad vent.org/fathers/310231.htm.

23. Nazianzen, Gregory. *Orations*, Oration 45-Second Oration on Easter from New Advent, – https://www.newadvent.org/fathers/310245.htm

24. *"Κάτω τρεῖς μάρτυρες, ἄνω τρεῖς μάρτυρες, τὸ ἀπρόσιτον τῆς τοῦ Θεοῦ δόξης δηλοῦντες."* — Translation by KJV Today

25. *"Ἀλλ', ὦ Πάτερ, καὶ Λόγε, καὶ Πνεῦμα, ἡ τρισυπόστατος οὐσία, καὶ δύναμις, καὶ θέλησις, καὶ ἐνέργεια, ἡμᾶς τοὺς ὁμολογοῦντάς σου τὰς ἀσυγχύτους καὶ ἀδιαιρέτους ὑποστάσεις, ἀξίωσον καὶ τῆς ἐκ δεξιῶν σου στάσεως, ἡνίκα ἔρχῃ ἐξ οὐρανῶν κρῖναι τὴν οἰκουμένην ἐν δικαιοσύνῃ· ὅτι πρέπει σοι δόξα, τιμὴ καὶ προσκύνησις, τῷ*—Translation by KJV Today, https://www.pente costaltheology.com/johannine-comma-1-john-57-trinity-vs-oneness-debate/

26. *Fourth Letter of Cyril to Nestorius*, NPNF2 14:198) — https://www.thegospelcoalition.org/ essay/trinitarianism-in-the-early-church/

27. *"Ad Quæstionem quid significetur Joannis verbis: Tria sunt, quæ testimonium perhibent aqua, sanguis, et spiritus? Respendetur: Videri Joanhem respicere ad locum Evangelii, cap. 19. 34: de aqua et sanguine e latere Christi profluente, collatis verbis: inclinato capite tradidit: spititum. Quosdam vero aquam explicare de baptismo, sanguinem de martyrio; spiritum de eo ipso, qui per martyrium transit ad Dominum. Plures tamen hic ipsam: mystica interpretatione intelligere Trinitatem: aqua Patrem, sanguine 'Christum, spiritu autem spir- itum sanctum manifestante."*

28. Burgess, Thomas, Bishop of St. David's. *A Vindication of 1 John, v.7. - from the Objections of M. Griesbach*, 1756-1837, p.44

29. Burgess, Thomas, Bishop of St. David's. *A Vindication of 1 John, v.7. from the Objections of M. Griesbach*, 1756-1837, p.5

30. Eucherius, Episcopus Lugdunensis, (says Griesbach) *primus esse putatur qui circa annum 440 aperte verba in dubium vocata excitavit in libro formularum cap. II. his verbis: III. (h. e. numerus ternarius) ad Trinitatem (sc.refertur) in Joannis epistola. Tres sunt qui testimonium dant in cælo, Pater, Verbum et Spiritus S. et Tres sunt qui testimonium dant in terra, Spiritus, aqua et sanguis.*

31. Burgess, Thomas, Bishop of St. David's. *A Vindication of 1 John, v.7. - from the Objections of M. Griesbach -*, 1756-1837

32. *"In Patre ergo et Filio et Spiritu Sancto unitatem substantiæ accipimus, personas confundere non audemus. Beatus enim Joannes Apostolus testatur Tres sunt, qui testimonium perhibent in cælo, Pater, Verbum, et Spiritus Sanctus; et tres unum sunt. Quod etiam beatissimus Martyr Cyprianus in epist de unitate Eccl. confitetur dicens: Qui pacem Christi et concor- diam rumpit, adversus Christum facit. Qui alibi præter Ecclesiam colligit, Christi Ecclesiam spargit. Atque ut unam Ecclesiam unius Dei esse monstraret hæc confestim testimonia de scripturis inseruit: Dicit Dominus, Ego et Pater umun sumus; et iterum de Patre et Filio, et Spiritu Sancto scriptum est: Et tres unum sunt."*

33. Burgess, Thomas, Bishop of St. David's. *A Vindication of 1 John, v.7. - from the Objections of M. Griesbach -*, 1756-1837 p.39

34. Burgess, Thomas, Bishop of St. David's. *A Vindication of 1 John, v.7. from the Objections of M. Griesbach*, 1756-1837, p. 14, 19

35. *"Quæ (epistolæ,) si sicut ab eis (Græcis) digestæ sunt, ita quoque ab interpretibus fideliter in Latinum verterentur eloguium; nec ambiguitatem legentibus facerent, nec sermonum sese varietas impugnaret, illo præcipue loco, ubi de unitate Trinitatis in prima Johannis epistola positum legimus: in qua etiam ab injfidelibus translatoribus multum erratum esse a fidei veritate comperimus, trium tantummodo vocabula, hoc est, aquæ, sanguinis et spiritus in ipsa sua editione ponentibus; et Patris, Verbique, ac Spiritus omittentibus; in quo maxime et fides Catholica roboratur, et Patris et Filii et Spiritus Sancti una Divinitatis substantia comprobatur."*

36. Martin, David. *A Critical Dissertation on 1 John v. 7*, pastor of the French congregation at Utrecht (1717), p.14

37. Bellarmine, Robert. *Disputationum De controuersiis christianae fidei* (*Disputations about Controversies of the Christian Faith*). Peter L P Simpson August 2013. 1615. *http://books. google.com/books?id=vqJaa8h_teQC&pg=PP22&dq=bellarmini+controversiae&hl=en& sa=X&ei=5ZGvUcO9HtS44APBqoHgAg&ved=0CDkQ6AEwAjgU —*

38. Calamy, Edmund. SERMON 1

ARIANISM BECOMES FREEMASONRY
ISAAC NEWTON, THE SECOND ARIUS

"And I rejoiced to think that I had found in Anaxagoras a teacher of the causes of existence such as I desired, and I imagined that he would tell me first whether the earth is flat or round; and whichever was true, he would proceed to explain the cause and the necessity of this being so, and then he would teach me the nature of the best and show that this was best; and if he said that the earth was in the centre, he would further explain that this position was the best, and I should be satisfied with the explanation given, and not want any other sort of cause."[1]

— PLATO (SOCRATES), *PHÆDO*

The formation of the American Experiment, the formation of "a government of the people, by the people, and for the people" still lay far off in the future. Yet, the seeds of its viability were planted in Plato's distant past, and begin blooming in the era we now examine. Democracy, what the Greeks regarded as 'mob rule,' was the question… how to achieve a balance between *freedom* and *rules*, and what would determine these rules, questions that even to this day have not yet been resolved. It is still a question of *pharmakon* vs. *Logos—would the freedoms of this new society be based upon internal whims and fantasies, or an allegiance to simple, firm eternal truths?* Up to this point, eternal truths were determined by religion, but now this would change. What was once regarded as reasonable enforcement, soon became regarded as abuses. While the questions of this era are justified, their resolutions were often Arian derived and cloaked in a new term, 'science.'

ORDER FOR ORDER'S SAKE

This is the conventional history of science: Aristotle discovered the logical system of deduction, then considered a near revolution from the superstitions of before. While this system served mankind well, by the 1600s it was failing. Philosophers, people like Descartes, Hegel, Kant, *et al,* began formulating a replacement. It was they who determined that the root cause was Aristotle's deductive logic. Without something to check its reasonings it was leading to all sorts of misconceptions, flat earths, superstitions, cosmic crystalline spheres, witch trials, inquisitions, lions, tigers and bears, Oh My! Thankfully, along came Isaac Newton. It was he who saved us from such treacheries with his Scientific Method. Thankfully, the Men of Reason could now step in, the Dark Ages could end, the Enlightenment begin.

One of their first inventions was inductive logic. Where Aristotle saw eternal truths, the enlightened saw hypotheticals, speculations that would all require testing. The solution was called the Scientific Method. Yet, search as you might, you will not find a clear explanation of what the Scientific Method actually is. Scour Newton's writings you will not find it. Yet, it does exist. It is found near the end of his *Principia* in versions only intended for the Royal Society. It is Arian.

But is it really likely no one thought of Induction before Newton? Really? Are we to believe ancient Man knew that sex led to birth, but he could not figure out that births were the result of sex? That a pregnant woman only hypothetically gives birth to children?

Understand, I am a big fan of Aristotle, but I believe we've given him too much credit. We've confused the *cataloguer* of knowledge with the *discoverer* of knowledge. In this we've missed a key point. Aristotle's 'truths' never represented the thoughts and inspirations of one single person. They represent the collective wisdom of an entire era, a search for *Logos*. To the modern, Aristotle has become a scapegoat, a way of denigrating an entire tradition by exploiting a single person.

This is an odd quirk of the modern. Rather than seeing saints and prophets as seekers and defenders of wisdom, they prefer to see them as misguided revolutionaries. Therefore, they should be replaced by well-guided 'scientific' revolutionaries. In this way they have deified the men of science as saints, people who owe no allegiance to prior wisdom. They've created the martyrs of science not so much to give them honor, but to advance an agenda. And this they've done with St. Newton.

Yet, these scientists *did* discover something. It was the methods of proposing hypotheses, of testing assumptions, and then through trial and error coming up with a solution. Seldom did the bonafide scientist fall asleep and wake up with a swoon and say 'voila'! Most often they were taking the thoughts collected by uncredited people like Athanasius Kircher, testing them, and promoting them as discoveries of their own. To do otherwise would reveal their real agenda, to undermine the *Logos* of the past and replace it with 'a new way of thinking.'

What is seldom admitted is this: Cloaked in an anti-religious veneer they portray themselves as the product of pure rational thought, when in fact they worship another God. This God has been stripped of all person-ness, of all individuality, and appears as a de-personified scientific principle. It is not that Gods don't exist, it is that to them these principles function as gods. They have adopted the god of Arianism, the philosophy is Hermeticism, and cloaked it with formulas and algorithms.

Therefore, modernism was largely a means of advancing occult philosophy by dressing it up with scientific terms. Carl Jung took the occult pleroma and re-labelled it the collective unconscious. Freud took Talmudic mysticism and Greek mythology, and created the struggle of the ego and the Oedipal Complex. Hegel took Hermeticism and invented the dialectic process that eventually exploited by Marx and F.C. Baur. What has escaped scrutiny is that Isaac Newton took Arianism and gave us Modern Science. From its inception it was designed to undermine traditional Christian dogma.

The real scientific method was discovered long before Newton. It was simply this: 'Truth is conformity of Mind to Reality.' Before *Logos*, reason could only move in one direction, it could speculate, but it could not verify. It didn't have the tools. In other words, science was originally a flight away from Idealism, not a dive into it. These tools, like the prism, microscope, telescope, and astrolabe were in use long before Newton. They were tools of observing reality. But with the moderns came a new use, to dissect reality, take it apart, and convey the idea that what we observed with our eyes was only an illusion. The advancements of modern science inevitably led to contradictions of time and space, imagined realities, fictions that have no basis in testable observations. This is by design. Is this not Idealism?

As the Middle Ages drew to a close, and advanced thinking came to Europe, a huge debate developed. Would it be Plato's or Aristotle's system that best represented truth. At this point in time neither had a clear advantage, neither was without flaws. Aristotle seemed to have the edge, but his world seemed to not have a beginning. Plato's did, but explained less. Overtime, it was Aristotle that won the day, but not without adjustments. It was his method that was fixed and adopted by the Church, becoming Scholasticism.

Scholasticism was a huge benefit to theology, it gave it structure but most importantly it allowed for a marriage between science and faith. It was for this reason both Islam and Judaism had their versions of Scholasticism. However, the more the scientific method advanced thought, the more its investigations became troublesome.

Scientific method became obsessed with reduction. Seeking the One, it resorted to taking things more and more apart hoping to find a 'god particle' or something equivalent. The quest was never meant to find anything solid, it was a quest to prove that there was never anything solid about reality, that all was pleroma. The more the method advanced knowledge, the less certain its revelations became—was there a limit to how far something could be taken apart? What was that limit?

Scholasticism taught that there was a limit. It called it the *hylomorph*. It was content to resolve into two imponderables, the *hyle*, representing imponderable 'matter', and *morph* representing a knowable outer 'form.' In doing this it escaped the paradoxes of Heisenberg, Einstein, and Schödinger. Everything that existed was the combination of uniformed, less than real 'prime matter,' and an informing 'idea.' This solution gave science a confined territory and sealed it off from destroying the obvious.

While Aristotle's method had to contend with both mind and reality, Platonists only had to contend with mind alone. Everything could be solved by idea—*a complete reversion to the method of old.*

Reality is a grand instructor to Mind, but if the habit isn't practiced early on, Mind never learns the habit… it becomes spoiled by experience. Experience gradually becomes the new *pharmakon* as it becomes obsessed with thinking unrealities. This is the modern Mind, it is no longer capable of being instructed by Reality. Mind begins to regard all of reality as a servant. It can do no other, it has never been taught what to do with the *phenomena*.

While the foundation of this over-analysis was laid by Newton, he refrained. They credited him with discovering gravity, when in fact he only described its mathematics. Over time scientists began to believe that to describe something mathematically was to discover it. This allowed historians of science to go back and claim that mathematical describers had newly discovered things nobody before had known.

Pierre Duhem was a late nineteenth century physicist. He asked precisely

the same question, 'how does phenomena relate to understanding?' Specifically, did Galileo actually discover something new, or have we been misled?
Duhem, invoking the axiom of early philosophy 'to save the phenomena,'
looked to the second century BC Greek astronomer Hipparchus:

> "Adrastus of Aphrodisias, whose teachings have been preserved by us by
> Theon of Smyrna, records how Hipparchus felt about his own discovery: 'Hip-
> parchus singled out as deserving the mathematicians attention the fact that one
> may try to **account for phenomena by means of two hypotheses as different
> as that of eccentric and that which uses concentric circles bearing
> epicycles.**"[2]

— PIERRE DUHEM, PHYSICIST

The consequence of this is remarkable. Galileo had not discovered something entirely new. Hipparchus had already discovered what those after had
claimed, the planetary cycles. That Galileo had single-handedly brought the
world out of ignorance was a fabrication. Further, Hipparchus understood the
scientific method, *that the hypotheses must match the phenomena, he just
didn't have the mathematical tools.*

The very act of interpreting the phenomena is an act of taking something
complicated and finding a way to make it simple. Thoughts are confirmed by
observation, and observation is confirmed by reasonable thoughts. But hidden
within this theory is something else: all scientific method is a version of
Occam's Razor, that the simplest explanation that accounts for *all* the facts is
to be preferred, *but not so simple that it cannot.* This acknowledged a stopping
point where over simplification explained less and less. In not knowing where
to stop, modern science has become more and more abstract and less and less
real. *Every scientific theory, therefore, is rigged to end in ultimate simplicity,
the Arian Unified One.* It is the very Monopsychism condemned in the 1270s
by the Catholic Church at the height of this very debate.

> "The Condemnations of 1270 threw down the gauntlet to Siger de Brabant and
> his radical colleagues in the faculty of liberal arts. Tempier listed thirteen
> propositions that he condemned as false and heretical, declaring that anyone
> who taught them "knowingly" or "asserted" them as true was *ipso facto*
> excommunicated. It went without saying that anyone who persisted in advo-
> cating the forbidden propositions would be subject to the processes and
> punishments of the Inquisition. The banned propositions reveal the major

doctrines most offensive to the conservative theologians. Some were associated with Averroës' theory of the soul and the doctrine of *monopsychism* for example, "That there is numerically one and the same intellect for all humans.""[3]

Duhem has judged correctly, as did the series of Condemnations of 1270. It was at this very time Christianity began to be overwhelmed with something it has yet to understand, the Occult. The modern scientific method, founded in Hermeticism, necessarily leads back to it as reductionism gradually destroys the conceptual understanding of reality. It is a revisitation of Ammonius Saccas, a parallel system to Arianism. Christians were not trying to hide under the cover of ignorance, as science has taught us. They were trying to insulate the West from the corrupting influence of the East, a system that perhaps began with Socrates. It is was here we find the emergence of the Freemasons, the Arian/Hermetic social club whose allegiance was to secret writings, and the Gnostic principle of reality.

THE SCIENCE OF ISAAC NEWTON

"Some have supposed, that by Love, Hesiod, and the other theogonists, meant the soul or animating principle in the universe. But it is a sufficient refutation of this opinion to remark, that they suppose this divinity derived from Chaos, in common with others. By Love, they probably understood that attractive principle in nature by which homogeneous bodies are united. To this principle they poetically ascribed the attributes of reason and wisdom, to intimate, that in the formation of the world all things were constituted by harmonious laws." [4]

— WILLIAM ENFIELD

It is commonly believed that Newton founded modern science while isolating himself in the countryside from the plague. His two main advancements were 1) his Theory of Light, and; 2) his Laws of Motion. As he was in isolation, it is taught that he did this through his own ingenuity alone. For this he is regarded as a somewhat of a scientific mystic.

Yet, Newton himself said that his knowledge was built on the shoulders of giants. Many today think he was just being glib. But most of his theories existed long before Newton, and his explanations are still a long way from being the final word. His theory of light is merely a revision of the late medieval theory derived from Christian scholars like Robert Grosseteste (c.1168—1253). Indeed, it even needed to be substantially later cleaned up Thomas Young (we will run into him again). The medievalists themselves had inherited it from Christian refugees fleeing Islam. They believed that the color spectrum was produced by the weakening of light through a medium:

"... a hypothesis, supposing that both refraction and reflection by a dense medium weakened white light so that it absorbed different degrees of darkness from the medium and thereby became differentiated into different colours of the spectrum: 'colours produced by the weakening of white light'[5]

Now granted, Newton's theory made the medieval obsolete, but only temporarily. Newton's explained things the medievalists could not. However, it was only a matter of time before it was realized the medievalists explained what Newton could not. Shining a light through a prism, the light goes through various thickening of the glass, thus resulting in different colors, dark to light. To Grosseteste, this theory of light was founded upon Biblical principles, and it was through this that the universe was generated— 'Let there be Light!'

"He [Grosseteste] held that the characteristic property of light was its ability to propagate itself instantaneously in straight lines in all directions without loss of substance, and that in this way light had generated the universe. In the beginning of time God had created out of nothing unformed matter (*materia prima*) and light (*lux*) which, by auto-diffusion, had produced the dimensions of space and then all subsequent beings. For this reason Grosseteste believed that the study of optics was the key to the understanding of the physical world; and it was impossible to study optics without geometry, for light behaved according to geometrical laws."[6]

The German Dominican Theodoric of Freiberg (d. *c.*1311) elaborated on the theory:

"If radiation from the sun enters obliquely into any body of the kind discussed, such oblique incidence is necessary in this way for the production of these colours: the radiation after its emergence from the opposite side of the [transparent] body is differentiated into the four usual colours; and a solid [opaque] body on which it falls is coloured with the same colours in the same order, namely, so that the brighter colours, red and yellow, keep to the side of the original line of incidence and consequently on the side of the passage of such radiation near the angles and angular sides, then the other less bright colours, green and blue, follow in their place and always, as has been said above, in the same inviolable order by which yellow follows red, and after that comes green, and finally blue."[7]

— THEODORIC OF FREIBERG, *DE MAGIS ET MINUS*

It should be noted here is that what they called 'green' is now called cyan. This older light theory was documented by Jesuit priest Athanasius Kircher (1602 — 1680) who for better or worse, was a major influence in the 1600s. His *Oedipus Aegyptiacus* is still influential to this day, most of which would have run afoul of Rome for its advocacy of Hermeticism. Many emerging 'scientists' of the modern era based their early research on proving Kircher right or wrong.

The difference between the two theories is that while Grosseteste believed that light had to follow eternal laws formulated by God, Newton believed light *was* God. Whereas the older theory accounts for colors through 'darkening,' Newton's accounts for colors through refraction angles. Newton's theory made the old obsolete for centuries, and became part of our common high school science instruction. However, not long after Newton people like Goethe began to try to replicate Newton's experiments—often they didn't work. What had Newton done differently? Did he leave something out of his instructions?

Johann Wolfgang von Goethe (1749–1832), normally considered a poet, spent forty years of his life trying to replicate Newton's experiment. His conclusion was that the older theory had not been disproved. Newton had done something not obvious. He projected his light through a pinhole. This led Goethe to ask, 'was it the prism that produced the color spectrum, or the edges of the pinhole?' He came to the conclusion that without the edge the colors would not be produced. The phenomena are still left unexplained. Goethe's theory is just now gaining followers.

Below is one of Kircher's diagrams. It shows that Newton's prism effects were known centuries earlier[8]:

roscidæ nubes, & omnia crystallina, in qua radius sola refractionis virtute dissipatur: nam radios solares rectâ, atque normalit er vitrum permeantes, nulla ratione fœdari intuemur. At si per inæquale densioris aëris diaphanum ferantur, quantò intimius pene- | trarint, tantò obscuriore colore inficiuntur; quantò verò minus, tantò clariori. Lux ergo per crystallinum prisma permeans minus densum diaphanum passâ, dilucidior rubet, meraciore verò colore languet. Verum ut hæc oculari demonstratione proponantur;

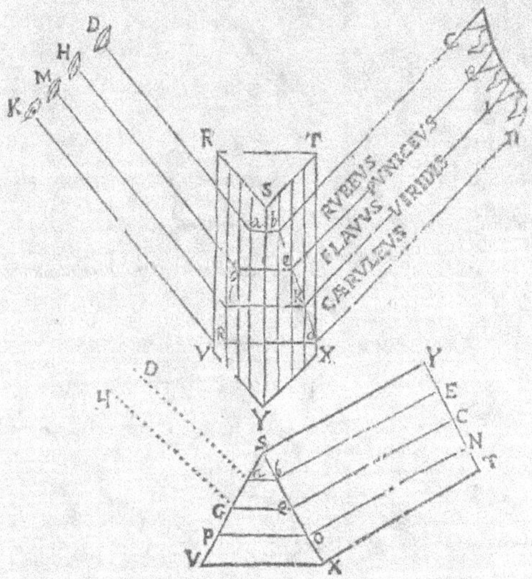

Sit prisma R T S V X Y: sitque Sol Ce. l. n. oculus D H M K. In hoc duplex situs rerum videtur, unus per radium reflexum qui res nec mutat nec in figura nec colore; sed inversas exhibet, sitque, quando res normaliter vitrum penetrant. Alter per radium refractum, & hic res quidem, nec naturali situ, nec colore exhibet, sed nunc curvas, nunc circulares, omni colorum genere adornatas. Refractio igitur sola causat in hoc varia ista colorum discrimina, non autem reflexio, quia reflexio vitrum normaliter transiens non aliter res exhibet ac sunt, sed uti domus, ædificia, arbores in ripa fluminum inversas. At radius Solis, ubi oblique in latus aliquod prismatis inciderit, bis refractus ad oculum revertitur, atque hac refractione multum à pristino vigore recedit; cum medium quoque inæqualis sit densitatis. Hinc lumen refractum, & in varia profunditate diaphani varia refractione debilitatum, fœdatumque, colores reddit nunc magis, ac minus ad album, & nigrum accedentes. Notantur autem in prismate tres præcipui colores, ruber, flavus, cœruleus; flavus ut plurimum mediat inter utrumque rubrum, & cœruleum terminantes; viridis autem, cro- | ceus, & puniceus è vicinis coloribus componuntur. Ita autem in vitro per refractionem oriuntur. Sit primò radius C, qui in vitrum in puncto b incidit, & quoniam per medium densius transeundum est, ex brefringitur in a; atque ex a in D: quoniam verò in a b brevis transitus est, hoc loco quidem colorem produceret omnium minimè fœdatum, alboque sive luci simillimum; quoniam tamen S Y angulus solidus umbra sua radium transcantem non parum obfuscat, hinc non albus, seu flavus, sed rubore intensissimo rubet. Iterum quoniam radius Solis n in vitrum incidit in O, refrangetur is in medio profundissimo O R, ubi videlicet vitrum maximè latum est, ex O in R, & hinc in K. Inde fit, ut per medium diaphani profundissimi, radius tum vi refractionis bis factæ, tum multiplicationis superficierum, à genuina sua puritate multum degenerans, in colorem abeat umbrosum nigro vicinum, videlicet cœruleum confinem luci & tenebris. Iterum quoniam e radius in vitrum incidit, in e refringitur, is ex e in g, & hinc in visum H incurrit, media videlicet vitri profunditate, ubi refractio nec à vicinis utrinque umbris angulorum solidorum

Caufæ colorum in vitro triangonis.

T X V R.

Athanasius Kircher's Diagram of color separation caused by light shining through a prism (*Ars magna lucis et umbrae, 1671*). The translation is in the notes. Notice the difficulty in explaining the color 'peacock'. (public domain)

THERE WAS another contention with Newton that exists to this day. Newton's gravitational equation was formulated before electro-magnetism was understood. This equation is still used to understand the movements of planets. Yet, the equation ignores electromagnetism altogether, a force an order of magnitude millions times stronger than gravity.

The 'white-washing' of the history of science is not unique to Newton. At the very height of Galileo's dispute with the Church, two Jesuit astronomers, Christoph Scheiner and his student, Johann Georg Locher, developed the mechanics of how the Earth could orbit the Sun. They published the hypothesis in a book, *Disquisitiones Mathematicae de Controversiis et Novitatibus Astronomicis.*[9] Scheiner was actually the priest who Galileo debated at his famous trial. It should be noted that Galileo had only one real claim, 'that it (the earth) moves.' It was based on his observations through a telescope and his theory based upon *a diagram from Copernicus in homage to Hermes Trismegistus*! Galileo had no real scientific mechanics to explain his theory. Yet, the Church, the side that was supposed to be ignorant, did. Scheiner and Locher explained how a small body (such as the earth) could perpetually stay in orbit by 'falling' around a larger body (such as the Sun). The very mechanics claimed 'discovered' nearly a half century later by Newton were already known by the Church. Kircher himself later poked fun at the two Jesuit astronomers calling their hypothesis a "vain fabrication."[10]

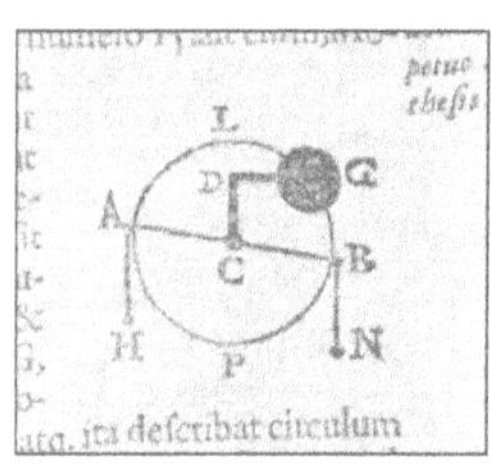

Jesuit astronomers, Christoph Scheiner and Johann Georg Locher, celestial mechanics predating Newton by half a century. Disquisitiones Mathematicae de Controversiis et Novitatibus Astronomicis.

In 1987, Pietri Redondi, after a long search in the Vatican Archives, published Galileo's actual Trial Documents.[11] The main subject was not 'did the earth move' as commonly reported. It was whose philosophy best accounted for truth and was most compatible with Church doctrine, Aristotle's or Plato's. Galileo was an ardent follower of Plato, particularly the Hermetical variety. Clearly, there were serious problems with what both philosophy's teaching had become, but what seems to be missed is that the main issue between the two was considered settled back in the 1270s.

But didn't most people at that time believe the Earth was flat? Well, that was actually a done-deal in 1230 when astronomer Johannes de Sacro-Bosco (John of Holywood) published *On the Sphere of the World*, (*De sphaera mundi*).[12] Most every university student would have been required to read it. Sacro-Bosco is also famous for contesting the accuracy of the Julian Calendar 400 years before Galileo.

At the very time Westcott & Hort were re-writing the Bible, a propaganda campaign was mounted against Christianity. Two entirely fictionalized histories of science were developed and promoted in two books, *History of the Conflict between Religion and Science* (John William Draper), and *A History of the Warfare of Science with Theology in Christendom* (Andrew Dickson White). The books promoted a conflict that never happened, that the Catholic Church had purposely promoted the Flat Earth Theory in an effort to keep people ignorant so they would not doubt the Bible. Part of this Flat Earth Theory was the story that Christopher Columbus had to fight off the panic of his crew because they believed they would fall off the edge of the earth and be eaten by monsters. All this was to hide the fact that Columbus' discovery of the Caribbean Islands (1492) had actually found man-eating cannibals, something the word 'caribbean' actually means.

So, what is the point? The point is this: While we all purport that we now live in a more civil technologically advanced society, do we really? The twentieth century brought more loss of human life than any other point in time. We treat the earth as if it were a biological being and we its mere parasites. Modern solutions to pending disasters often result in more loss of life than had we done nothing. Modern life styles seldom are in pursuit of knowledge, but social relevancy. Perhaps most importantly, there has been little if any attempt to tell the real story perpetuating a blind faith in something that has often led to disaster.

THE THEOLOGY OF ISAAC NEWTON

John Salza in *Why Catholics Cannot Be Masons* says, "Masonry not only unites men of different faiths into one spiritual brotherhood, but also unites the deities of different religions into one spiritual godhead. The *Masonic Bible* calls this monstrous syncretism the "unity of the Godhead." He also quotes, "there is no absolute to be known; all truths, including the mathematical, are relative."[13] The grounding principle sounds innocent enough, who wouldn't want a universal brotherhood? Salza spends much time explaining why masonry runs afoul of dogma, but no where do you get the idea he has a conceptual understanding of the problem. Yet, he does realize the target is the Trinity.

Many assume the heart of Masonry is naturalism, as it is in science. Yet, this is not consistent with its belief that all is symbol only. This seems confusing until one realizes that the true pursuit is the Monopsyche, natural reality is only used as a method of scientific reductionism that convinces the mind of its unreality.

There are numerous references in Salza's book that have obvious parallels to the *Apocryphon*, perhaps the most is the 'all seeing eye.' These principles are guarded by the utmost secrecy under the penalty of a symbolic death. So, how do we account for these parallelisms?

It has been shown that the text of the Secret *Apocryphon of John* survived and was used well into the eighth or ninth century. In a text on the Anthropomorphite Controversy of 399 AD, translated from the Romanian *Mistagogia: Experienta lui Dumnezeu in Orthodoxie* we find this summation of the theology of the *Audians*:

"... we make God himself corporeal who is instead **"all eye, all glory [light]."**...Here we find a number of things: the echo of Nicea-Constantinople in "light of light" and the procession of the Spirit; the mingling language so prominent in the Macarian Homilies and Syriac Christianity generally; and a new element, **the identification of the Spirit with light, such that the Father is the Glory, the Son its "ray", and the Holy Spirit its light.**"[14]

This is the heritage of the real religion of Newton. Whereas before Christians only saw 'light' as a metaphor for 'Wisdom' or a vehicle by which God formed the cosmos, the Newton's religion would take the phrase literally, God *was* light. It was on this that sects like the Audians built their religion. It was a concept derived from the secret writings falsely attributed to St. John. From an article published called, **'Newton's Arian Epistemology and the Cosmogony of *Paradise Lost'*** [John Rogers], we find this:

"Heretics both, John Milton and Isaac Newton were, as most scholars now agree, Arians. In reasoned opinions that during their lifetimes they voiced safely outside the public space of the printed theological treatise, both Milton and Newton asserted a version of the fourth-century theology of Arius and his followers..."[15]

"The image of God Newton shares in the "General Scholium," the deity who is **all eye and all ear**, has its origin in the description of God with which the early church father Irenaeus attempted to refute the Gnostics. In his characterization of the abstract mechanics of Gnosticism's divine psychomachia, Irenaeus accuses the Gnostics, in their ascription to God of the affections and passions of men, of a mistaken understanding of the nature of divinity. He allows for the possibility that the faculties of perception, understanding, and will might interact within any given man in the highly differentiated manner described by the Gnostics. But God, Irenaeus insists, is not a "compound": he is "not as man, nor are his thoughts like ours".[16]

In other words, following Gnostic metaphysics, Newton believes God is more-or-less light itself. He perhaps gets the idea from Milton:

for Spirits that live throughout
Vital in every part, not as frail man
In Entrails, Heart or Head, Liver or Reins Cannot but by annihilating
    die;
Nor in thir liquid texture mortal wound
Receive, no more that can the fluid Air:
All Heart they live, **all Head, all Eye, all Ear**,
All Intellect, all Sense, and as they please,
They Limb themselves, and colour, shape or size Assume,
as likes them best, condense or rare.[17]

Newton's *Principia* went on to become the bedrock of modern science and scientific theory. It is primarily a book of mathematical formulas, and says little about what gravity actually is, or scientific method. This is a major problem confronting us even now—while order can give the appearance of an intelligence behind that order, it is not necessarily so. Today, Artificial Intelligence can give the appearance of intelligence, when in fact it can only produce order. Unlike Aristotle's *quiditty*, a machine can never know *whatness*, it can only mimic it. A machine has no ability to think abstractly—unfortunately, neither does the modern human.

Newton's *Principia* went through several editions before an essay was added near the end called the 'General Scholium.' It was here where Newton reveals his true self. It is here that Newton's book on celestial mechanics becomes his *Summa Theologica*. It was here God ceased to be Father, *Logos*, and Holy Ghost and became the impersonal, Masonic *Architect of the Universe*.

THE FORMATION OF THE NON-CONFORMISTS AND THE PURITANS

We now enter a very difficult but critical point in our discussion. We may find we have to re-adjust some long-held, heart-felt loyalties. My intent in the following is not to denigrate or paint Puritans in a savage light. It is, however, to show that pure, outwardly civil intentions can be fueled by an ill-conceived ideological foundation.

We tend to hold in our hearts a lofty idea of the Pilgrims, the Mayflower, and that of Thanksgiving. We see the Pilgrims as a simple, grateful, sincere group of Christians fleeing the oppression of the Church of England. We revere them as bravely laying the foundation of America. Weren't they who boldly struggled to finish what the Church was hesitant to do?

Yet, we ignore some facts. While we may mentally liken the Pilgrim's to the landing on the moon, in reality, they were not the first in America. The founding of Plymouth Rock was proceeded by St. Augustine, Jamestown, Santa Fe, and was only thirteen years ahead of the founding of Green Bay Wisconsin. Their early city of Salem found itself embroiled in witch trials, dubious cultish behavior, and questionable medical experimentation.[18] The Pilgrims were 'Puritans,' a name with a gnostic past. The Cathars also referred to themselves as 'the pure ones.' Both were Reformationists and would have been thrilled with King Henry VIII separation of the English Church from the Roman, yet the Puritans believed this didn't go far enough. The Puritans were not necessarily commoners either, Brewster, held prominent positions, even within the English government. Later, they founded Harvard University.

Clearly, their conventional 'humble' story does not explain all the facts, it doesn't explain their underlying idealogical motivation. Aristotle said, "the first in intention, is the last in execution." The intention began with Cerinthus' false gospel, the last in execution is revealed by Karen King of Harvard.

Several 'non-conforming' sects were plaguing the English Church, many resurrecting heresies long thought past. (public domain)

Not many are familiar with Scrooby, Nottinghamshire, England. It is a very small village, very out of the way, and has little to see…except for one thing, the birthplace of the Puritans.

Scrooby is on the fork of a road, one leg running to York, the other to Scotland. The Post Office was significant as it separated the mail destined for the two, its clerk was William Brewster (1566-1644).

While in Scrooby, I noticed a poster displayed in the local parish church displaying Brewster's genealogy. One could immediately notice a distinct change in Brewster's naming convention after his first child. From Jonathan he went thereafter to Patience, Fear, Love, and Wrestling. I believe this reveals Brewster's state of mind at the point of his conversion.

Brewster, as postmaster (who also served as the Archbishop's bailiff), gave him the opportunity to intercept mail intended for various bishops and other dignitaries throughout the Kingdom. He could then disseminate secret information to the rising non-conformists. Needless to say this got him into trouble once found out.

Brewster eventually had to flee to Calvinist Holland. There, being exposed to the Anabaptists, he became a convert, eventually a leader in a new movement called the Pilgrims. On his return to England, he began publishing books condemning the English Church. Of these were authors like David Calderwood, author of the most notorious *The Altar of Damascus,* a book condemning the English Church and the Realm.

On one hand you might see this as the Puritan's objection to certain doctrines of the Church of England, and that might be a fair point. However, it was Calderwood's objection to the Queen's re-defining of ecclesiastical power within the Realm that was the true point of contention. He saw this as a power grab to control non-conforming, 'baptist' parties.

Originally, baptist churches were started by clergy within the English Church. Contentions were rising within the government as to how many clergy (particularly bishops) the Church could have. As an effort to continue to serve all the people, non-conforming churches were started. Over time, non-conforming churches began to create doctrines of their own influenced by emerging trends such as the works of John Milton.

This resulted in a dispute over the Sovereign's mandate, as head of the Church, to control heresies. It is marked by Calderwood's words: "For howsoever for removing of offence taken at the metaphorical title of *Head,* it was changed in more proper termes of *supreme governour* under the reigne of Queene Elizabeth, yet the sense remaineth still."

It should be remembered, the first call against Hermeticism came from within Calvinist ranks, Casaubon's declaration that the *Corpus* was fake. Yet, the new theology calling itself 'reformed' was infiltrating all denominations. A new alliance was forming on both sides which is revealed in those for and against 1 John 5:7. Unclear about the ideological underpinnings of this new movement would find not only catholics cooperating with protestants, but just as likely blaming each other. Unnoticed was that scientific advancements of Copernicus, Columbus, Galileo, Kircher, and Newton, were all leveraged to advance Hermeticism and Arianism.

The Puritans were threatening to start a war, overturning the Realm which was sworn by oath to protect the Gospel of Christ from the various heresies springing up. The Pilgrim's concept of 'freedom' had heretical roots—the debate posed here is still unresolved—*is a truly free society obligated to grant freedom to those bent on that society's destruction? And further, who decides?*:

"The title then of Supreme Governour in the oath is explained by the preceeding words of the statute, to which, and for observation of the which, the oath is subjoyned, viz. that the Prince hath all manner of spirituall or Ecclesiastical jurisdiction, and all manner of privileges and preeminences any way touching or belonging to the same, which was before, or may be lawfully exercised for visitation of the Ecclesiasticall state, reformation, order, and correction of the same, and of **all manner of errors, heresies, schismes, abuses, offences, contempts and enormities**, and that he may commit the exercise of the same to any of his naturall born subjects, whom it shall please his highness to constitute commissioners in causes Ecclesiastical, to judge, discern, and correct in **matters of Idolatry, simonie, errour and heresie,** and all other causes Ecclesiasticall whatsoever. This oath of supremacie is different from the oath of fidelity or allegeance devised of late."

— DAVID CALDERWOOD, *THE ALTAR OF DAMASCUS*

Now granted, what one church might find wholesome, the other might find dangerous, and freedom might find some solution. But this was not that. The Puritans were no small threat, they resulted in the execution of Charles the I, king of England, the overturning of the Realm being replaced by the Commonwealth headed by Oliver Cromwell, the banishment and execution of Anglican clergy, compliant churches becoming 'congregationalist,' others were turned into horse barns and the like. Under the republic a standing army was established to keep the rule, organ pipes were melted down becoming the bullets aimed at the very people that once heard them singing the glory to God.

This Commonwealth lasted from 1649 to 1660 when the people retaliated, compromises made, and the Monarchy was re-installed. But even this was short-lived. By 1688 the *Glorious Revolution* (aka *Bloodless Revolution*), inspired by Puritans, successfully had a coup replacing James II with the Dutch William & Mary. Brewster, a conspirator, had escaped with his life to America, Plymouth Rock to be precise. Oliver Cromwell before being executed founded the Freemasons as a means of secretly continuing the movement Brewster had begun. Over time, it became the conduit for proliferating secret 'ideas' throughout Europe, particularly Napoleon's France. As a compromise to the Puritans, the Presbyterian Church was given legitimacy, the British Royal Society of Science was established legitimizing the new theology of 'science.' On December 25, 1642 Isaac Newton was born—he was raised in this milieux.

RE-WRITING TRADITION

The British Commonwealth ended in 1660. The Glorious 'Bloodless' Revolution of 1688 replaced the British monarchy with one of German 'saxon' descent. This meant there would be allowed less than eight years to re-establish the legitimate Monarchy before being undermined.

In an attempt to document legitimate British tradition, Percy Enderbie published a history book in 1661, *Cambria Triumphans: Brittain in its Perfect Lustre*. It claimed to be "The Origen and Antiquity of that Illustrious Nation, the succession of their kings and princes, from the first, to King Charles." However, the Bloodless Revolutionaries would see that this story not last. It would be replaced by one legitimizing their Germanic takeover. English Puritans appealed to distant Dutch/German relatives of the monarchy to participate in a bloodless coup. Anciently, the German church was founded by bishop Wulfilas, a refugee from Nicaea having been ordained Arian bishop by Eusebius of Nicomedia.

Long before Augustine of Canterbury 'converted' Britain to Christianity in 597, it was held that Britain had been a Christian nation. Enderbie's book included several accounts emphasizing this. British tradition had held that civilization was first brought to the Islands by the Greek Trojan warrior, Brutus, who fled there from the Battle of Troy. Constantine the Great had a British heritage long before Nicaea. Even some evidence not in Enderbie's book seemed to support this. Bede's history of the English Church includes an episode where at the Synod of Whitby in 664, long-held Christian customs were debated against the newer Roman ones. Some have dated the Christian *Stowe Missal* before Augustine's arrival where, again, the liturgy clearly has a different source than the Roman. Even Augustine's arrival was held to have found locals 'angelically' singing Christian hymns.

The founding and naming of Britain (after Brutus) went back into antiquity. Enderbie's work began with this tradition:

"In the time of *King Edward I.* at *Lincolne*, where held a Parliament, after much diligent search of Antiquities and due examination, as the greatest matter of right of a Kingdom required: Apological letters were sent to the Pope of *Rome*, sealed with an hundred seals and witnesses thus, The King of England, from a deliberate council convened at Lincoln, declaring his right, wrote back a letter of this tenor, sealed with a hundred seals:[19] wherein is declared and justified that in the time of *Hely* and *Samuel* the Prophet, *Brutus* a *Trojan* landed here, and by his own name called the Country *Britannia*, before named Albion: From his name he called Britain and his allies the Britons:[20] and having three Sons, *Locrinus*, *Albanactus*, and *Camber*, at his death devided the Island into three parts or provinces. *Loegria*, now *England*, (though *Welsh* keep the old name) was given to *Locrinus* the eldest Son; *Albania*, Scotland, to

Albanact the second Son. *Cambria*, now mis-called *Wales*, to *Camber* his third
Son. To his firstborn Locrino he gave that part which was once called Loegria,
but now called England; To his second son Albanatus he gave Albany, which
is now called Scotland; On the third day he gave Cambria, which is called
Wales, to the Cambrians, reserving the royal dignity of Locrino;[21] this conjecture may suffice for this business, it being testified by so many Domestic all
and forrain, private and publick witnesses, that this his tripartite division was
here from the beginning, and the first name of *Brittain* given by *Brutus*."[22]

— CAMBRIA TRIUMPHANS, PERCY ENDERBIE (1661)

But Enderbic's book also included a more speculative variety. Particularly
important is the traditional memories of two important British sites, *Salisbury*
(Stonehenge) and *Glastonbury*, Both at one time were considered essential
testaments to Britain's early Christian past, but today they have been taken
over by illegitimate New Age cults. *Stonehenge*, rather than being a pre-
historic burial site converted to a pagan astronomical clock, was at one time a
memorial to fallen British Christians having died in battle with the saxons:

"Geffry of Mon tells us that this *Ambrosius* caused Churches to be repaired,
which had been spoyled by the *Saxons*. He caused also the great stones to be
set on the plain of *Salisbury*, which is called *Stone-hedge*, in remembrance of
the Brittains that were slain and buryed there in the raign of *Vortiger*. This
ancient monument is yet to be seen, and is a number of stones rough and of a
grey colour, twenty-five foot in length and about ten foot in breadth, they are
conjoyned by two and two together, and every couple sustained a third stone
lying overthwart gatewise, which is fastened by the means of tenons that enter
into mortases of those stones not closed by any cement. It appeareth that there
hath been three rancks going round as circles one within another, whereof the
utmost and largest containeth in Compasse 300 foot, but the other rancks are
decayed, and therefore hard to reckon how many stones there be...

The Chronicles of the *Brittains* do testifie, that whereas the Saxons about
the year of our Lord 450 had slain 48 of the *Brittains* Nobility by treason, and
under colour of treaty, *Aurelius Ambrosius* now King of the *Brittains*, desirous
to continue their memory with some worthy monument, caused these stones to
be set up in the place of their murther and burial, the which stones had been
first brought from *Affrick* into *Ireland*, and had been placed on Mount *Killare*,
and from thence by the industrious means of *Merlin* were; conveyed to this
place, to the foresaid end."[23]

— CAMBRIA TRIUMPHANS, ENDERBIE (1661)

Today, *Geoffrey of Monmouth's (Geffry of Mon's)* history is considered discredited, perhaps because of its association with Merlin the Magician. Yet, Enderbie only lists him as a prophet. The question is, have we really proved that at one time prior ruins of Stonehenge *weren't* a Christian memorial as Enderbie claimed?

Perhaps more important was the traditions of *Glastonbury*. It claimed that the first Christian church anywhere was planted there, "Thus he writeth. *At what time Christian Religion was first publickly received in this Island, there were established in the same...*" And, how would you prove it wasn't? Enderbie documents this tradition now considered too fantastic:

"... Joseph of Arimathea, a noble Man of *Jury* specially remembred of Posterity for his charitable Act in burying the Body of our Saviour; This Man was appointed by St. *Philip* the Apostle then preaching the Christian Faith in *Gallia*, to instruct the ancient *Brittains*, among whom he began first, as some write, to institute an Eremitical life in a place then called *Duellonia*, and afterwards *Glastenbury*, where himself and his Companions imitating the austerity and zeal of solitude, which they had observed in Mary Magdalen, (with whom they travelled out of *Jury* unto *Marsilia* in *France*) sequestred themselves from all worldly Affairs, that they might freely attend to the exercise of piety which they professed; yea some Writers of former Ages have writ, that the Apostles St. *Peter* and St. *Paul*, in their own persons at several times, came into *Brittain*; and that afterwards one *Sucton* a noble Mans Son of that Country, being converted by such Christians as first planted the Faith there, and called (after his Baptisme) *Beatus*, was sent by them to *Rome* unto St. *Peter*, to be better instructed and confirmed in Christianity, and that in his return homewards through *Switzerland*, he found in the Inhabitants there such a desire and readinesse to receive the Christian Faith, as he resolved to continue in that place, where he erected an Oratory to exercise a Monastical life, and departed the world about the year of Grace 110. but who were the very first Teachers, and at that time the Christian Faith was first of all received there, it is not certainly known (saith this Author.) Howbeit it is likely that in the Expedition of *Claudius* the Emperor, which was about the third year of his Reign, and twelve years after the Ascension of our Saviour, some Christians of Rome and Scholars of the Apostles themselves became first known unto the *Brittains*; who in processe of time were drawn by the Exhortations and Examples of their Teachers to embrace the Truth."[24]

— *CAMBRIA TRIUMPHANS*, ENDERBIE

I present the above stories not merely to present a quirk in English history. It to put you purposely in a predicament.

In the late 18th century Sonnini de Manoncourt in his travels to Constantinople was presented with a Greek manuscript by the Sultan Abdoul Achmet. It was claimed to be the lost last chapter of the book of Acts. It included the following verses:

Acts 29:1 — And Paul, full of the blessings of Christ, and abounding
   in the spirit, departed out of Rome, determining to go into Spain,
   for he had a long time proposed to journey thitherward, and was
   minded also to go from thence to Britain.
2 — For he had heard in Phoenicia that certain of the children of
   Israel, about the time of the Assyrian captivity, had escaped by sea
   to "the Isles afar off" as spoken by the Prophet, and called by the
   Romans Britain.
3 — And the Lord commanded the gospel to be preached far hence to
   the Gentiles, and to the lost sheep of the House of Israel.

So, is it authentic or not? Would Tischendorf consider it authentic or not, particularly remembering he only had one example, ultimately two, to confirm his theory?

Whether these traditions are fantasies or have some grounding in fact is a bit beside the point. Who has the right to re-write a nation's tradition or declare its documents valid? After the Glorious Revolution, British history and tradition were revised to create sympathy for its conquerors, a way of de-legitimizing its former inhabitants. The Cambrian 'Welsh' were now to be considered a primitive race, even denied the use of their traditional language.

Is this not what the Arian invaders to Christianity are doing? Rather than being satisfied with their own beliefs, are they not cleverly trying to corrupt another's tradition from within, introducing foreign documents, forcing people to prove which are more authentic? Do they not expect Christian traditions to fade into the past, yet when theirs are proved false promote their's anyway? Do they not abuse the term 'scientific' when it suits their needs?

Everywhere I look I find a long history of Arianism re-writing history. At the Enlightenment emerging scientific elite took on themselves the privilege of judge and jury to discredit what they considered the unscientific. To this end, they justified creating societies both public and secret designed to psychologically manipulate history so as to make it more conducive to their doctrines. In a sense they had discovered a new *pharmakon*, the power to orchestrate opinion. This paved the way for the Arian take-over of society.

THE OCCULT FOUNDATION OF THE BRITISH ROYAL SOCIETY

"Despite his secrecy about his theological views, the heretical tendency of Newton's beliefs was not unknown to some of his contemporaries. William Whiston, his successor as Lucasian Professor at Cambridge, described him as one whose study led him to recognize that 'what has long been called Arianism is no other than old uncorrupt Christianity'".[25]

— MAURICE WILES

We tend to see the Pilgrims as simple, courageous Christians who, braving the perils of the ocean and wilderness, came by way of the Mayflower to Plymouth Rock to plant the ideal utopian community. We honor them as early frontiersmen who, thankful for surviving these perils, began the custom of Thanksgiving. Just as Conservatives see this as an act of supreme piety, Liberals see it as an act of supreme colonialism. Neither side is exactly true. Their main goal was to rid Christianity of its unnecessary encumbrances, it is a religious version of scientific reductionism.

The Royal Society, formally called 'The Royal Society of London for Improving Natural Knowledge,' was established on November 28, 1660. Harvard University was establish in Cambridge, Massachusetts in 1636 by the Puritan clergyman John Harvard. They were intended to be parallel institutions promoting the new scientific Christianity, "dreading to leave an illiterate ministry to the churches" per Harvard's charter.

In many ways we can understand the spirituality of the Royal Society by looking at the theology promoted by Harvard University. While we must grant that both institutions advanced the cause of education, they both smuggled in monopsychism, that the One-Mind was more scientific than the Three-Divinities. Inspired by the Cambridge Platonists, the Puritan theological model is a spin-off from the Dutch Reformed. It is based on Arminianism, itself a spin-off from the Waldensians who themselves were a spin-off from the heretical

Cathars.[26] Overtime, Harvard evolved into Transcendental Unitarianism, itself a spin-off of early Hermeticists such as Jakob Böhme, and Hinduism. Numerous Puritan clergymen were trained early on at Harvard before the institution became secularized. All of these have an undeniable basis in Arianism.

The Newtonian 'unitarian' model was very profitable... at first. Keeping God at arm's length, it looked for intermediary unified scientific causes and effects. The tendency over time is to dismiss the first cause and to regard the intermediary as first causes in themselves... light becomes divine as does gravity.

With the non-conformists gaining strength, the Church of England began to be embroiled in controversy. This presented an opportunity for Newton to rehabilitate the Church along more scientific lines, making it more acceptable to emerging public opinion. To this end, the British Royal Society was set up to award and grant accolades upon those willing to dissent from tradition and come over to the new faith.

The spiritual inspiration behind the British Royal Society was actually Elias Ashmole. He was one of its principal founders. Numerous members of the Society were closet Arians as well as were many early Freemasons. Along with Newton, those inspired by Milton and Ashmole were John Locke, William Stukeley, William Whiston, and later Joseph Priestley. Inspired by the utopian Francis Bacon, Locke was considered the Father of Liberalism. It was to him that Newton's 'Two Notable Corruptions of Scripture' was written as an open letter, a letter purposely intended to discredit the Church and force a new Arian perspective among scholars.

Copernicus' Diagram of the Solar-Centric Cosmos with its usually removed tribute to Hermes Trismegistus. "As a matter of fact, not unhappily do some call it the lantern; others, the pilot of the world. [Hermes] Trismegistus calls it a 'visible god'... (public domain)

- **Elias Ashmole**—Hermeticist, inspired by Francis Bacon. As a founding Fellows of the Royal Society, he was an antiquarian, mystic. He represents the intersection of science and magic, something science was supposed to be making obsolete. As a collector of Hermetically inspired artefacts (probably inspired by Kircher's *Kircherian Museum*), it formed the basis of what became the Ashmolean Museum.

- **William Stukeley**— Fellow of the Royal Society. He became a Freemason (eventually Master) in 1721, as the "remains of the mysterys of the antients". He appears to have believed in the monopsychic god, explaining his adherence to Pythagorean and Neoplatonic doctrine.
- **William Whiston**—was an English clergyman. He was an open proponent of Arianism (openly rejecting the Nicene Creed), debating archbishops Thomas Tenison and John Sharp on the Trinity. As a staunch Unitarian, he wrote An Historical Account of Two Notable Corruptions of Scripture, a commentary on Newton's treatise.
- **Joseph Priestley**—chemist and fellow of the Royal Society. He was staunchly anti-Logos as defined by the Church, supporting the Alogi Unitarians as representative of true early Christianity. In 1838 he published *A History of the Corruptions of Christianity*.

All this was habilitated by Newton's attack on the Trinity. A Bible free of 1 John 5:7 allowed the New Arians to define, or un-define theology in any way they wished. In Newton's first law of reasoning we find his method—"*We are to admit no more causes of natural things than such as are both true and sufficient to explain their appearances.*" This allowed them to deify anything they regarded as a First Cause, whether it was mathematical or physical. Much more than a doctrinal religion, Freemasonry, the former pipeline for political rebellion, became not only a protected conduit for disseminating the new secret theology, but eventually a feed-line back for savants such as Napoleon's back from Egyptian archaeological sites.

A FINAL WORD AS TO NEWTON'S THEORY OF LIGHT

Poet and scientist Wolfgang von Goethe spent forty years of his life examining Newton's theory and came to the conclusion it was ill-conceived. Spending years replicating Newton's experiments producing rainbows with prisms, he came to the conclusion the experiments did not work. Newton had rigged the experiment.

"Along with the rest of the world I was convinced that all the colours are contained in the light; no one had ever told me anything different, and I had never found the least cause to doubt it, because I had no further interest in the subject... But how I was astonished, as I looked at a white wall through the prism, that it stayed white! That only where it came upon some darkened area, it showed some colour, then at last, around the window sill all the colours shone... It didn't take long before I knew here was something significant about colour to be brought forth, and I spoke as through an instinct out loud, that the Newtonian teachings were false."

— JOHANN WOLFGANG VON GOETHE

Jesuit Louis-Bertrand Castel displayed the problem in his *Optique des couleurs* (1740), a treatise on the melody of colours. A French mathematician, he entered the order of the Jesuits in 1703.

The chart shows the very same colors Goethe noticed when looking at lighted boundaries through a prism. If one looks at a black strip on a white sheet of paper through a prism, you will notice a two color red/yellow band on one side, and a deep blue/cyan band emanating from the other side. These are Goethe's boundary colors which account for the color spectrum in a completely different way. Most notable is that green becomes an artificial color, a mixture of the boundary colors yellow and blue.

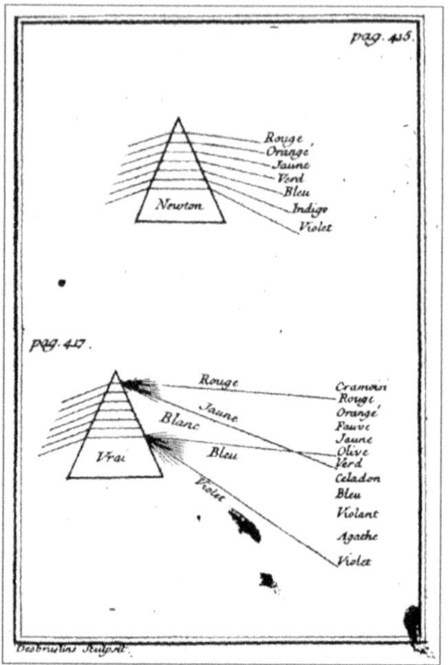

This diagram shows Newton's theory as opposed to 'Truth' (Vrai). Notice particularly that olive and verd (green) are not the result of the refraction of light through the prism, but the result of the crossing and mixture of jaune (yellow) and bleu (blue). (public domain)

A similar color transformation happens when looking through haze. If light *backlights* the haze (such as the Sun at sunset) you see bands of yellowed turning to orange/red the thicker the haze gets. When light reflects off the haze (such as when looking up at the sky catching light reflected from the Earth) you see cyan, turning to deep blue, then black as the haze thins. When you allow for the fact that what the ancients called 'green' we now call 'cyan,' it is apparent this is the very light theory maintained from ancient times.

Newton's light theory can't account for this phenomena. Nor can it account for magenta, a color that does not exist in Newton's spectrum. Yet, today it is considered a primary color along with cyan. The eye itself cannot 'see' magenta, it is a color artificially produced by the eye's inability to make sense out of blue/red disturbance. Mixing magenta and cyan will give you deep blue, a primary color that under Newton's theory should not be mixable.

Neither Newton's nor Goethe's theory can explain all these phenomena. However, it was Newton's theory alone that we were taught. Beethoven said of Goethe, "Can you lend me the *Theory of Colours* for a few weeks? It is an important work." While there are many today who have yet to accept Goethe's theories, it has had some notable adherents, Hermann von Helmholtz, Rudolf Steiner, Ludwig Wittgenstein, Werner Heisenberg, and Kurt Gödel.

It was Newton's prestige that swayed the Enlightenment, and this very same prestige that caused people to question whether their Bibles were the Word of God, or a fabrication from an earlier time—that Newton's Arianism would be a suitable replacement.

---

1. *Dialogues of Plato: Containing The Apology of Socrates, Crito, Phaedo, and Protagoras.* Colonial Press, 1899. translation Benjamin Jowett

2. Duhem, Pierre. *To save the phenomena: An essay on the idea of physical theory from Plato to Galileo.* University of Chicago Press, 2015. p.8

3. Rubenstein, Richard E. *Aristotle's Children: How Christians, Muslims, and Jews Rediscovered Ancient Wisdom and Illuminated the Middle Ages.* Houghton Mifflin Harcourt; 2004 — p.216

4. Enfield, *The History of Philosophy,* 1839 – p.69

5. Crombie, Alistair Cameron. *Robert Grosseteste and the origins of experimental science.* Clarendon Press, 1953. p. 65

6. Crombie, Alistair Cameron. *Robert Grosseteste and the origins of experimental science.* Clarendon Press, 1953. p.104

7. Crombie, Alistair Cameron. *Robert Grosseteste and the origins of experimental science.* Clarendon Press, 1953. p.247

8. From Kircheri, Athanasii, *Ars magna lucis et umbrae,* 1671 (translation) — "Let the prism RTS VXY: circle Sol Ce. 1.n. eye DHMK In this a double position of things is seen, one by a reflected ray which changes things neither in shape nor in color; Fed exhibits inversions, and occurs when objects normally penetrate the glass. The other is refracted by a ray, and here indeed the object, neither in its natural position nor in color, is now curved, now circular, adorned with every kind of color. Refraction therefore alone causes in this these various differences of color, but not the reflection, because the reflection passing through the glass does not present things differently as they are, fed as houses, buildings, trees on the banks of rivers turned upside down. But the sun's ray, when it has fallen obliquely on some side of the prism, is refracted twice and returns to the eye, and by this refraction it recedes much from its former vigor; when the medium also becomes unequal in density. Hence the light refracted, and weakened by the various refractions of the diaphanous at various depths, and given to foes, renders now more and less colors approaching white and black. Now the three principal colors are noted in the prism, red, yellow, and blue; the yellow, for the most part, mediates between the two reds, and the blue ends; and green, crocus, and pink are composed of neighboring colors. And so they arise in glass by refraction. The cause of the colors in the triangular glass Let the ray C, which falls on the glass at the point b, and since it must pass through the denser middle, be refracted from b to a; and from a to D: [side note —*cause of colors in a prism*] indeed, since there is a short transition from a to b, at this point it would indeed produce a color least foul of all, and most similar to white or light; since, however, the solid angle SY not a little obscures the passing ray by its shadow, hence it is not white or yellow, but reddens with a very intense blush. Again, since the sun's ray n falls on the glass at O, it will be refracted in the deepest middle OR, where the glass is obviously the widest, from O to R, and from here to K. Let it be from there. so that through the middle of the deepest diaphanous, the rays of both the surfaces, degenerating much from their true purity, turn into a shadowy black neighboring color, that is to say, the blue border of light and darkness. Again, since the ray from e falls into the glass, it is refracted at e, it is from e ing, and from here it enters the view H, namely at the middle depth of the glass,

where the refraction is neither overshadowed by the neighboring shadows of the solid angles TX, VR, SY, nor too much it has depth; hence he clothed himself with a crimson garment, which, like the rest, is purer, so he is also clothed in a white color, or something nearer to light; the other two colors, the green and the peacock [color], are not the first, fed from the borders of the hair; green, indeed, from yellow and blue; and the *pavonaceus* [peacock species], which here and there is the most splendid in the hills of the Peacocks, has its origin from a mixture of green and blue. Ge. Po. Y X. And all these differences of colors vary according to the nature of the light, as the experimenter will notice. Therefore, the cause of the colors in a prism, as in every other angular crystalline body, is no other, that the first solid angle of the snow casts shadows, by which the light of the Sun is refracted in different ways through a medium that is dense in different ways, and is variously modified by the shadows, and is colored by the various things that we look at with wonder. It shows the difference in colors."

9. Scheiner, Christoph and Locher, Johann Georg. *Disquisitiones Mathematicae de Controversiis et Novitatibus Astronomicis.* 1614

10. Graney, Christopher. 'How a Jesuit Astronomer and His Student beat Isaac Newton to a Key Idea by more than 50 Years,' May 2019 — https://www.vaticanobservatory.org/sacred-space-astronomy/how-a-jesuit-astronomer-and-his-student-beat-isaac-newton-to-a-key-idea-by-more-than-50-years/

11. Redondi, Pietro. *Galileo Heretic*, Princeton University Press. 1987

12. Johannes de Sacro-Bosco (John of Holywood) *On the Sphere of the World* (*De sphaera mundi*), 1230

13. Salza, John, *Why Catholics Cannot Be Masons,* TAN Books, 2008. Chp. 7 The Masonic Bible and The Short Talk Bulletin, "Masonic Geometry," Vol. 12, No. 5, 1934.

14. Ica, I. Jr. *Mistagogia: Experienta lui Dumnezeu in Orthodoxie* (Sibiu: Deisis, 1998) 184-267. (The Form of God and Vision of the Glory: Some Thoughts on the Anthropomorphite Controversy of 399 AD) https://www.marquette.edu/maqom/morphe.html

15. Rogers, John. *Newton's Arian Epistemology and the Cosmogony of Paradise Lost,* ELH, Volume 86, Number 1, Spring 2019, pp. 77-106 (Article) Published by Johns Hopkins University Press

16. Rogers, John. *Newton's Arian Epistemology and the Cosmogony of Paradise Lost,* ELH, Volume 86, Number 1, Spring 2019, pp. 77-106 (Article) Published by Johns Hopkins University Press

17. Milton, John. *The Complete Poetry of John Milton,* ed. John T. Shawcross, Anchor, New York. 1971, book 6, lines 344–53.

18. Jan Irvin

19. *Rex Angløe ex deliberato concilio apud Lincolniam convocato pro jure suo declarando, literam hujus tenoris rescripsit centum sigillis signatam*

20. *De nomine suo Britanniam sociosque suos Britones appellavit*

21. *Locrino primogenito dedit illam partem qua quondam Loegria, nunc vero Anglia nominatur ; Albanacto filio Secundo dedit Albaniam, qua nunc Scotia vocitatur; Cambrio vero tertio jilio dedit Cambriam, qua Wallia appellatur, reservata Locrino regia dignitate*

22. Enderbie, Percy. *Cambria Triumphans: Brittain in its Perfect Lustre* 1661

23. Enderbie, Percy. *Cambria Triumphans: Brittain in its Perfect Lustre* 1661, p.184

24. Enderbie, Percy. *Cambria Triumphans: Brittain in its Perfect Lustre* 1661 p.131

25. Wiles, Maurice. *Archetypal Heresy: Arianism Through the Centuries*, The Secret Arianism of Isaac Newton, Oxford, p.77

26. https://www.britannica.com/topic/Unitarianism, https://www.britannica.com/topic/Arminianism

NEWTON'S SCHOLIUM, ALCHEMICAL WRITINGS & RELATED TEXTS

EXCERPTS

EXCERPT 'ON LIGHT' FROM THE SECRET APOCRYPHON OF JOHN [LONG VERSION]

And I asked to know it, and he said to me, "The Monad is a monarchy with nothing above it. It is he who exists as God and Father of everything, the invisible One who is above everything, who exists as incorruption, which is in the pure light into which no eye can look.

"He is eternal, since he does not need anything. For he is total perfection. He did not lack anything, that he might be completed by it; rather he is always completely perfect in light. He is illimitable, since there is no one prior to him to set limits to him. He is unsearchable, since there exists no one prior to him to examine him. He is immeasurable, since there was no one prior to him to measure him. He is invisible, since no one saw him. He is eternal, since he exists eternally. He is ineffable, since no one was able to comprehend him to speak about him. He is unnameable, since there is no one prior to him to give him a name.

"He is immeasurable light, which is pure, holy (and) immaculate. He is ineffable, being perfect in incorruptibility. (He is) not in perfection, nor in blessedness, nor in divinity, but he is far superior. He is not corporeal nor is he incorporeal. He is neither large nor is he small. There is no way to say, 'What is his quantity?' or, 'What is his quality?', for no one can know him. He is not someone among (other) beings, rather he is far superior. Not that he is (simply) superior, but his essence does not partake in the aeons nor in time. For he who partakes in an aeon was prepared beforehand. Time was not apportioned to him, since he does not receive anything from another, for it would be received on loan. For he who precedes someone does not lack, that he may receive from him. For rather, it is the latter that looks expectantly at him in his light.

———

—EXCERPTS[1]—

NEWTONS PRINCIPIA.

THE

MATHEMATICAL PRINCIPLES

OF

NATURAL PHILOSOPHY,

BY SIR ISAAC NEWTON;

TRANSLATED INTO ENGLISH BY ANDREW MOTTE.

TO WHICH IS ADDED

NEWTON'S SYSTEM OF THE WORLD;

BOOK III.

IN the preceding Books I have laid down the principles of philosophy, principles not philosophical, but mathematical: such, to wit, as we may build our reasonings upon in philosophical inquiries. These principles are the laws and conditions of certain motions, and powers or forces, which chiefly have respect to philosophy: but, lest they should have appeared of themselves dry and barren, I have illustrated them here and there with some philosophical scholiums, giving an account of such things as are of more general nature, and which philosophy seems chiefly to be founded on; such as the density and the resistance of bodies, spaces void of all bodies, and the motion of light and sounds. It remains that, from the same principles, I now demonstrate the frame of the System of the World. Upon this subject I had, indeed, composed the third Book in a popular method, that it might be read by many; but afterward, considering that such as had not sufficiently entered into the principles could not easily discern the strength of the consequences, nor lay aside the preju-dices to which they had been many years accustomed, therefore, to prevent the disputes which might be raised upon such accounts, I chose to reduce the substance of this Book into the form of Propositions (in the mathematical way), which should be read by those only who had first made themselves masters of the principles established in the preceding Books: not that I would advise any one to the previous study of every Proposition of those Books; for they abound with such as might cost too much time, even to readers of good mathematical learning. It is enough if one carefully reads the Definitions, the Laws of Motion, and the first three Sections of the first Book. He may then pass on to this Book, and consult such of the remaining Propositions of the first two Books, as the references in this, and his occasions, shall require.

RULES OF REASONING IN PHILOSOPHY & GENERAL SCHOLIUM

RULE I.

We are to admit no more causes of natural things than such as are both true and sufficient to explain their appearances.

To this purpose the philosophers say that Nature does nothing in vain, and more is in vain when less will serve; for Nature is pleased with simplicity, and affects not the pomp of superfluous causes.

RULE II.

Therefore to the same natural effects we must, as far as possible, assign the same causes.

As to respiration in a man and in a beast; the descent of stones in Europe and in America; the light of our culinary fire and of the sun; the reflection of light in the earth, and in the planets.

RULE III.

The qualities of bodies, which admit neither intension nor remission of degrees, and which are found to belong to all bodies within the reach of our experiments, are to be esteemed the universal qualities of all bodies whatsoever.

For since the qualities of bodies are only known to us by experiments, we are to hold for universal all such as universally agree with experiments ; and such as are not liable to diminution can never be quite taken away. We are certainly not to relinquish the evidence of experiments for the sake of dreams and vain fictions of our own devising; nor are we to recede from the analogy of Nature, which uses to be simple, and always consonant to itself. We no other way know the extension of bodies than by our senses, nor do these reach it in all bodies; but because we perceive extension in all that are sensible, therefore we ascribe it universally to all others also. That abundance of bodies are hard, we learn by experience ; and because the hardness of the whole arises from the hardness of the parts, we therefore justly infer the hardness of the undivided particles not only of the bodies we feel but of all others. That all bodies are impenetrable, we gather not from reason, but from sensation. The bodies which we handle we find impenetrable, and thence conclude impenetrability to be an universal property of all bodies whatsoever. That all bodies are moveable, and endowed with certain powers (which we call the *vires inertiæ*) of persevering in their motion, or in their rest, we only infer from the like properties observed in the bodies which we have seen. The extension, hardness, impenetrability, mobility, and *vis inertiæ* of the whole, result from the extension, hardness, impenetrability, mobility, and vires inertia of the parts; and thence we conclude the least particles of all bodies to be also all extended, and hard and impenetrable, and moveable, and endowed with their proper *vires inertia.* And this is the foundation of all philosophy. Moreover, that the divided but contiguous particles of bodies may be separated from one another, is matter of observation; and, in the particles that remain undivided, our minds are able to distinguish yet lesser parts, as is mathematically demonstrated. But whether the parts so distinguished, and not yet divided, may, by the powers of Nature, be actually divided and separated from one an other, we cannot certainly determine. Yet, had we the proof of but one experiment that any undivided particle, in breaking a hard and solid body, suffered a division, we might by virtue of this rule conclude that the undivided as well as the divided particles may be divided and actually separated to infinity.

Lastly, if it universally appears, by experiments and astronomical observations, that all bodies about the earth gravitate towards the earth, and that in proportion to the quantity of matter which they severally contain; that the moon likewise, according to the quantity of its matter, gravitates towards the earth; that, on the other hand, our sea gravitates towards the moon; and all the planets mutually one towards another; and the comets in like manner towards the sun; we must, in consequence of this rule, universally allow that all bodies whatsoever are endowed with a principle of mutual gravitation. For the argument from the appearances concludes with more force for the universal gravitation of all bodies than for their impenetrability; of which, among those in the celestial regions, we have no experiments, nor any manner of observation. Not that I affirm gravity to be essential to bodies: by their *vis insita* I mean nothing but their *vis inertiæ*. This is immutable. Their gravity is diminished as they recede from the earth.

RULE IV.

In experimental philosophy we are to look upon propositions collected by general induction from, phenomena as accurately or very nearly true, notwithstanding any contrary hypotheses that may be imagined, till such time as other phenomena occur, by which they may either be made more accurate, or liable to exceptions.

This rule we must follow, that the argument of induction may not be evaded by hypotheses.

GENERAL SCHOLIUM[2]

The hypothesis of vortices is pressed with many difficulties. That every planet by a radius drawn to the sun may describe areas proportional to the times of description, the periodic times of the several parts of the vortices should observe the duplicate proportion of their distances from the sun; but that the periodic times of the planets may obtain the sesquiplicate proportion of their distances from the sun; the periodic times of the parts of the vortex ought to be in the sesquiplicate proportion of their distances. That the smaller vortices may maintain their lesser revolutions about *Saturn, Jupiter,* and other planets, and swim quietly and undisturbed in the greater vortex of the sun, the periodic times of the parts of the sun's vortex should be equal; but the rotation of the sun and planets about their axes, which ought to correspond with the motions of their vortices, recede far from all these proportions. The motions of the comets are exceedingly regular, are governed by the same laws with the motions of the planets, and can by no means be accounted for by the hypothesis of vortices ; for comets are carried with very eccentric motions through all parts of the heavens indifferently, with a freedom that is incompatible with the notion of a vortex.

Bodies projected in our air suffer no resistance but from the air. With draw the air, as is done in Mr. *Boyle's* vacuum, and the resistance ceases; for in this void a bit of tine down and a piece of solid gold descend with equal velocity. And the parity of reason must take place in the celestial spaces above the earth's atmosphere; in which spaces, where there is no air to resist their motions, all bodies will move with the greatest freedom; and the planets and comets will constantly pursue their revolutions in or bits given in kind and position, according to the laws above explained; but though these bodies may, indeed, persevere in their orbits by the mere laws of gravity, yet they could by no means have at first derived the regular position of the orbits themselves from those laws.

The six primary planets are revolved about the sun in circles concentric with the sun, and with motions directed towards the same parts, and al most in the same plane. Ten moons are revolved about the earth, Jupiter and Saturn, in circles concentric with them, with the same direction of motion, and nearly in the planes of the orbits of those planets; but it is not to be conceived that mere mechanical causes could give birth to so many regular motions, since the comets range over all parts of the heavens in very eccentric orbits; for by that kind of motion they pass easily through the orbs of the planets, and with great rapidity; and in their aphelions, where they move the slowest, and are detained the longest, they recede to the greatest distances from each other, and thence suffer the least disturbance from their mutual attractions. This most beautiful system of the sun, planets, and comets, could only proceed from the counsel and dominion of an intelligent and powerful Being. And if the fixed stars are the centres of other like systems, these, being formed by the like wise counsel, must be all subject to the dominion of One; especially since the light of the fixed stars is of the same nature with the light of the sun, and from every system light passes into all the other systems: and lest the systems of the fixed stars should, by their gravity, fall on each other mutually, he hath placed those systems at immense distances one from another.

This Being governs all things, not as the soul of the world, but as Lord over all; and on account of his dominion he is wont to be called *Lord God*, παντοκρατορ, or *Universal Ruler*; for *God* is a relative word, and has a respect to servants; and *Deity* is the dominion of God not over his own body, as those imagine who fancy God to be the soul of the world, but over servants. The Supreme God is a Being eternal, infinite, absolutely perfect; but a being, however perfect, without dominion, cannot be said to be Lord God; for we say, my God, your God, the God of *Israel*, the God of Gods, and Lord of Lords ; but we do not say, my Eternal, your Eternal, the Eternal of *Israel*, the Eternal of Gods; we do not say, my Infinite, or my Perfect : these are titles which have no respect to servants. The word *God* [*Dr. *Pocock* derives the Latin word *Deus* from the *Arabic du* (in the oblique case *di*). which signifies *Lord*. And in this sense princes are called *gods*, *Psal.* lxxxii. ver. 6; and *John* x. ver. 35. And *Moses* is called a *god* to his brother *Aaron*, and a *god* to *Pharaoh*, (*Exod.* iv. ver. 16; and vii. ver. 1). And in the same sense the souls of dead princes were formerly, by the Heathens, culled *gods*, but falsely, because of their want of dominion.] usually signifies *Lord*; but every lord is not a God. It is the dominion of a spiritual being which constitutes a God: a true, supreme, or imaginary dominion makes a true, supreme, or imaginary God. And from his true dominion it follows that the true God is a living, intelligent, and powerful Being; and, from his other perfections, that he is supreme, or most perfect. He is eternal and infinite, omnipotent and omniscient; that is, his duration reaches from eternity to eternity; his presence from infinity to infinity; he governs all things, and knows all things that are or can be done. He is not eternity or infinity, but eternal and infinite; he is not duration or space, but he endures and is present. He endures for ever, and is every where present; and by existing always and every where, he constitutes duration and space. Since every particle of space is *always*, and every indivisible moment of duration is *every where,* certainly the Maker and Lord of all things cannot be *never* and *no where*. Every soul that has perception is, though in different times and in different organs of sense and motion, still the same indivisible person. There are given successive parts in duration, co-existent parts in space, but neither the one nor the other in the person of a man, or his thinking principle; and much less can they be found in the thinking substance of God. Every man, so far as he is a thing that has perception, is one and the same man during his whole life, in all and each of his organs of sense. God is the same God, always and every where. He is omnipresent not *virtually* only, but also *substantially*; for virtue cannot subsist without substance. In him [**This was the opinion of the Ancients. So *Pythagoras*, in *Cicer. de Nat. Deor.* lib. i *Thales, Anaxagoras, Virgil*, Georg. lib. iv. ver. 220; and Æneid, lib. vi. ver. 721. *Philo Allegor*, at the beginning of lib. i. Aratus, in his Phaenom. at the beginning. So also the sacred writers; as St. *Paul*, Acts, xvii. ver 27, 28. St. *John's* Gosp. chap. xiv. ver. 2. *Moses*, in *Deut.* iv. ver. 39; and x ver. 14. *David, Psal.* cxxxix. ver. 7, 8, 9. *Solomon*, 1 *Kings*, viii. ver. 27. *Job*, xxii. ver. 12, 13, 14. *Jeremiah*, xxiii. ver. 23, 24. The Idolaters supposed the sun, moon, and stars, the souls of men, and other parts of the world, to be parts of the Supreme God, and therefore to be worshipped; but erroneously] are all things contained and moved; yet neither affects the other: God suffers nothing from the motion of bodies; bodies find no resistance from the omnipresence of God. It is allowed by all that the Supreme God exists necessarily; and by the same necessity he exists *always* and *every where*. Whence also he is all similar, all eye, all ear, all brain, all arm, all power to perceive, to understand, and to act; but in a manner not at all human, in a manner not at all corporeal, in a manner utterly unknown to us. As a blind mail has no idea of colours, so have we no idea of the manner by which the all-wise God perceives and understands all things. He is utterly void of all body and bodily figure, and can therefore neither be seen, nor heard, nor touched; nor ought he to be worshipped under the representation of any corporeal thing. We have ideas of his attributes, but what the real substance of any thing is we know not. In bodies, we see only their figures and colours, we hear only the sounds, we touch only their outward surfaces, we smell only the smells, and taste the savours; but their inward substances are not to be known either by our senses, or by any reflex act of our minds: much less, then, have we any idea of the sub stance of God. We know him only by his most wise and excellent contrivances of things, and final causes; we admire him for his perfections; but we reverence and adore him on account of his dominion: for we adore him as his servants; and a god without dominion, providence, and final causes, is nothing else but Fate and Nature. Blind metaphysical necessity, which is certainly the same always and every where, could produce no variety of things. All that diversity of natural things which we find suited to different times and places could arise from nothing but the ideas and will of a Being necessarily existing. But, by way of allegory, God is said to see, to speak, to laugh, to love, to hate, to desire, to give, to receive, to rejoice, to be angry, to fight, to frame, to work, to build ; for all our notions of God are taken from the ways of mankind by a certain similitude, which, though not perfect, has some likeness, however. And thus much concerning God; to discourse of whom from the appearances of things, does certainly belong to Natural Philosophy.

Hitherto we have explained the phenomena of the heavens and of our sea by the power of gravity, but have not yet assigned the cause of this power. This is certain, that it must proceed from a cause that penetrates 'to the very centres of the sun and planets, without suffering the least diminution of its force; that operates not according to the quantity of the surfaces of the particles upon which it acts (as mechanical causes use to do), but according to the quantity of the solid matter which they contain, and propagates its virtue on all sides to immense distances, decreasing always in the duplicate proportion of the distances. Gravitation towards the sun is made up out of the gravitations towards the several particles of which the body of the sun is composed; and in receding from the sun decreases accurately in the duplicate proportion of the distances as far as the orb of Saturn, as evidently appears from the quiescence of the aphelions of the planets; nay, and even to the remotest aphelions of the comets, if those aphelions are also quiescent. But hitherto I have not been able to discover the cause of those properties of gravity from phenomena, and I frame no hypotheses; for whatever is not deduced from the phenomena is to be called an hypothesis; and hypotheses, whether metaphysical or physical, whether of occult qualities or mechanical, have no place in experimental philosophy. In this philosophy particular propositions are inferred from the phenomena, and afterwards rendered general by induction. Thus it was that the impenetrability, the mobility, and the impulsive force of bodies, and the laws of motion and of gravitation, were discovered. And to us it is enough that gravity does really exist, and act according to the laws which we have explained, and abundantly serves to account for all the motions of the celestial bodies, and of our sea.

And now we might add something concerning a certain most subtle Spirit which pervades and lies hid in all gross bodies; by the force and action of which Spirit the particles of bodies mutually attract one another at near distances, and cohere, if contiguous; and electric bodies operate to greater distances, as well repelling as attracting the neighbouring corpuscles; and light is emitted, reflected, refracted, inflected, and heats bodies; and all sensation is excited, and the members of animal bodies move at the command of the will, namely, by the vibrations of this Spirit, mutually propagated along the solid filaments of the nerves, from the outward organs of sense to the brain, and from the brain into the muscles. But these are things that cannot be explained in few words, nor are we furnished with that sufficiency of experiments which is required to an accurate determination and demonstration of the laws by which this electric and elastic Spirit operates.

END OF THE MATHEMATICAL PRINCIPLES.

EXCERPTS FROM NEWTON'S SECRET HERMETICAL TEXT

[3]OF NATURES OBVIOUS LAWS & PROCESSES IN VEGETATION.

Note that it is more probable the æther is but a vehicle to some more active spirit & the bodies may be concreted of both together, they may imbibe æther as well as air in generation & in it æther the spirit is entangled. This spirit perhaps is the body of light because both have a prodigious active principle, both are perpetual workers because all things may be made to emit light by heat, the same heat cause (heat) banishes also the vital principle. It is suitable with infinite wisdom to derive effects from this not to multiply causes without necessity Noe heat is so pleasant & benign as part sun's. light & heat have a mutual dependance on each other & no generation without heat. Heat is a necessary condition to light & vegetation.* No substance so indifferently, subtly & swiftly pervades all things as light & no spirit searches bodies so subtly piercingly & quickly as part vegetable spirit. [*heat excites light & light & light excites heat, heat excites the vegetable principle & that excites increases heat.]

Of heat. agitates æther & that agitated stirs up light & heat, æther is agitated by rushing inbetween this or by sudden extrusion.

Of light.

Of fire is either or flame a gross body or vapor. the first whose parts are in a vehement motion among themselves & excite it to emit light or flame. the first either wants a principle of preserving that state as hot iron or borrows it from an external agent as coal or hath it within it self as the sun. &c. The last is nothing but the parts of fumes turned to coals.

Cold & freezing have diverse principles because a thing will freeze without growing colder & grow colder without freezing also because things freeze not proportionably to their fluidity as in water oil ☿ spirit V. Cold is only rest, freezing is by an agent as fumes of lead coagulate ☿. Congelation is made when any agent enters settles on the parts & makes them porous & rough or rather adheres to their out side & acquiesces by cold.

fluidity is preserved by the æthers agitation & smoothness of parts. ☿ composed of hard metalline globules Hardness & union of parts by æthers extrusion & their roughness.

Volatility & fixity.

Action of salts dissolving, promoting fusion, fighting, precipitating. Diverse liquors coagulated & liquefied by diverse causes as whites of eggs by heat & lime, coral &c.

Propension & aversion to mix.

Pellucidity opaqueness. Elasticity. Expansiveness

Of the contrivance of vegetables & animals of sensible qualities. Of the souls union Of God. whatever I can conceive without a contradiction, either is or may effected be made by something that is: I can conceive all my own powers (knowledge, activating matter &c) without assigning them any limits Therefore such powers either are or may be made to be.

Example. All the dimensions imaginable are possible. A body by accelerated motion may become infinitely long or transcend all space distance in any finite time assigned also it may become infinitely long. This if thou deniest this because you apprehends a contradiction in the notion & if thou apprehends none thou wilt grant it to the power of things.

Arg 2. The world might have been otherwise then it is (because there may be worlds otherwise framed then this) Twas therefore no necessary but a voluntary & free determination if it should be thus. And such a

voluntary [cause must be a God.] determination implies a God. If it be said the world could be not otherwise than it is because it is determined by an eternal series of causes, it is to pervert not to answer the 1st prop: for I mean not that the ⊕ [world] might have been otherwise notwithstanding the precedent series of causes, but that the whole series of causes might from eternity have been otherwise here, because they as well as because they may be otherwise in other places

Nothing can be changed from what it is without putrefaction. Of ☿. violent separations & coalitions no putrefaction can be without changing alienating the thing putrefied from what it was Nothing can bee generated or nourished (but of putrified matter) without precedent putrefaction.[4]

---

1. Translated from the Latin
2. Newton, Isaac *Principia* (*Philosophiae naturalis principia mathematica*), Last Edition 'General Scholium.' Apud Guil. & Joh. Innys, Regiæ Societatis typographos, Londini, 1713 & 1726 [the General Scholium only appears in some of the very last editions]
3. Translated from the Latin
4. Isaac Newton from his hidden alchemical writings. Translated from The Newton Project, Oxford University — https://www.newtonproject.ox.ac.uk/

CHRISTIANITY AT THE CROSSROADS

THE REEMERGENCE OF THE SCHOOL OF IAMBLICUS

"That there was anciently, amongst the Egyptians such a man as Thoth, Theuth, or Taut, who, together with letters, was the first inventor of arts and sciences, as arithmetic, geometry, astronomy, and of the hieroglyphic learning, (therefore called by the Greeks Hermes, and by the Latins Mercurius) cannot reasonably be denied; it being a thing confirmed by general fame in all ages, and by the testimonies not only of Sanchoniathon a Phenician historiographer, who lived about the times of the Trojan war, and wrote a book concerning the theology of the Egyptians, and Manetho's Sebennyta, an Egyptian priest, contemporary with Ptolemy Philadelphus; but also of that grave philosopher Plato, who is said to have sojourned thirteen years in Egypt, that in his Philebus speaks of him as the first inventor of letters, (who distinguished betwixt vowels and consonants determining their several numbers) there calling him either a god or divine man"[1]

— RALPH CUDWORTH, *THE TRUE INTELLECTUAL SYSTEM OF THE UNIVERSE*

ENGLAND'S SCHOOL OF KIRCHER — THE CAMBRIDGE PLATONISTS

L et's recap. Within the Church of Rome a seventeenth century scholar, Jesuit Fr. Athanasius Kircher rose to preeminence with his brotherhood. Sending emissaries throughout the world, he collected perhaps one of the great catalogues of history and thought. But, his main allegiance wasn't to his scholastic training, it was to Egyptian mysticism. Therefore, Kircher had no true filter by which to judge his findings.

His most influential book was *Oedipus Aegyptiacus*. Believing he could read heiroglyphs, it helped to re-legitimize the very Hermeticism proved fraudulent by Isaac Casaubon. Kircher's lack of judgment allowed him to read into his evidence whatever he needed to support his theory.

Kircher's exaggerated view of Egyptian Pyamids, a place he had never been.

Perhaps a point should be made. Traditionally it has been taught that science is a process of thought following the evidence. Philosophy is supposed to be the corrective, its job is to reason backwards through the evidence making sure all the while that the concepts align with the facts. The weak spot in this scheme is when the evidence itself is fraudulent or improperly understood. It can appear to justify thoughts that have no foundation, give confidence in philosophies that don't deserve it.

The Jesuit school at its best was this very corrective—at its worst it compromised the evidence allowing it to claim authority it didn't have. A case in point is Kircher's magnum opus, *Oedipus Aegyptiacus*. The two most notorious high priests of the Occult, Aleister Crowley and Madame Blavatsky, both were students of the text. They can both claim to be students of the Catholic Church. While I doubt many within the Church would take the text entirely serious today (or even know about it), the modern Church is blind to the fact that such heresy came from within its midst, further complicating the matter.

. . .

But Kircher was not the only *enfant terrible* the Jesuits produced. In 1606 a young boy, René Descartes, set off for the Jesuit college of La Flèche, France. At that point the college was only two years old. Its purpose was to instruct Catholics in the high religious science of Scholasticism. The college lasted until 1800 when it was turned into a military college by Napoleon.

This was long enough for the college to produce two 'notorious' figures. The other was English arch-atheist David Hume. In some ways Descartes was the prototype for Rousseau's Savoyard Priest, a person considering himself loyal to the Church, yet holding to little of its doctrines. "I found myself beset by so many doubts and errors that I came to think I had gained nothing from my attempts to become educated but increasing recognition of my ignorance. And yet I was at one of the most famous schools in Europe, where I thought there must be learned men if they existed anywhere on earth."[2]

It should be understood, Scholasticism once considered itself the only 'perennial philosophy,' the *philosophia perennis*. However, with the imprimatur of the Jesuits, texts like Kircher's could give rise to an opposing *philosophia perennis*. The designs of these *new* (neo) platonists was to procure that very title and take it for its own. Whereas one sought to conform thought to reality, the other sought to create an entirely new philosophy based upon the self-evidency alone. So, in fact this *philosophia perennis* is the antithesis to the other.

While Descartes considered Kircher an idiot, both were at the center of an alliance against the Church-sanctioned *philosophia perennis*. It was in this philosophical climate Ralph Cudworth was born.

RALPH CUDWORTH — RELAUNCHING HERMES

Phaedrus: "Yes, Socrates, you can easily invent tales of Egypt, or of any other country."

— EXCERPT FROM PLATO'S *PHAEDRUS* CONCERNING
THE LEGEND OF THOTH

In some ways Ralph Cudworth (1617 – 1688) was a clone of Kircher. Both were Hermeticists. Both were sympathetic to Neoplatonism. Both were preeminent thinkers in their own Churches, Cudworth being in the Church of England. Cudworth, however, was a follower of Descartes. Perhaps most importantly, both Cudworth and Kircher were fascinated with all things

Egyptian. Not only did they see the completion of Greek mythology in Egyptian mysticism, they also believed that Christianity was an extension of ancient Egyptian philosophy, the key was locked away in its hieroglyphs.

The fact is they had no systematic way of deciphering hieroglyphs, only the eruditions of Kircher who believed that the meanings could be had through mystical divination. The only sources they had were works like *The Hieroglyphs of Horapollo*, completely fabricated out of Gnostic thought. The system was like a circular argument, beginning with Gnosticism and then confirmed by Gnosticism.

"Many writers pretended to have found the key to the hieroglyphics, and many more professed, with a shameless impudence which is hard to understand in these days, to translate the contents of the texts into a modern tongue. Foremost among such pretenders must be mentioned Athanasius Kircher, who, in the 17th century, declared that he had found the key to the hieroglyphic inscriptions; the translations which he prints in his *Oedipus Aegyptiacus* are utter nonsense, but as they were put forth in a learned tongue many people at the time believed they were correct."[3]

— SIR WALLIS BUDGE, EGYPTOLOGIST

Since the Council of Florence in 1439 the Church had struggled with the legitimacy of the Gnostic *Corpus Hermeticum* introduced at that time by 'the second Plato,' Plethon. An eastern mystic, he became a 'rock star' at the Council seducing the Medicis to sponsor the then child Marsilio Ficino to become a Catholic priest, an emissary for their cause. Ficino was the first in a long string of occultists within the Church dedicated to promoting the Neoplatonic arts including Agrippa, Giordano Bruno, and later Kircher. The infection became so accepted that even Copernicus' diagram of Solar Centricity had a caption in honor of Hermes Trismegistus.[4]

For a short time, Hermeticism was entertained as a potential lost branch of Christianity, that is until the philologist Isaac Casaubon proved in 1614 that the text was a fabrication of the second century. He did this by proving that certain texts within the *Corpus* were clearly from the wrong century. Ralph Cudworth, undaunted, merely eliminated the fraudulent bits and claimed the rest authentic. This allowed him to retain the philosophy of Hermeticism and found a new school of thought, later called the *Cambridge Platonists*. Originally sympathetic to Puritanism, Cudworth later rejected it and focused on making the Church of England more 'scientific.' His writings reflect this:

"... in that first *Hermetick* book, entitled, *Poemander*; some also in the fourth book, inscribed Crater, and some in the thirteenth called the sermon in the mount, concerning regeneration; which may justly render those three whole books, or at least the first and last of them, to be suspected. We shall here repeat none of Casaubon's condemned passages, but add one more to them out of the thirteenth book, or sermon in the mount, which, however omitted by him, seems to be more rankly Christian than any other... *Tell me this also, who is the cause or worker of regeneration? The son of God, one man by the will of God.* Wherefore, though Athanasius Kircherus contend with such zeal for the sincerity of all these *Trismegistick* books; yet we must needs pronounce of the three forementioned, at least the *Poemander* properly so called, and the sermon in the mount, that they were either wholly forged and counterfeited by some pretended Christians, or else had many spurious passages inserted into them. Wherefore it cannot be solidly proved from the *Trismegistick* books after this manner, as supposed to be all alike genuine and sincere, that the Egyptian Pagans acknowledged one universal Numen [Mind]."[5]

— RALPH CUDWORTH, THE ROYAL SOCIETY (1662)

Apparently, never considered at all was that perhaps the underlying philosophy was a continuation of the School of Cerinthus, a heresy. Cudworth could not leave the hieroglyph question alone. In them he saw not only the resolution to old philosophical dilemmas, but the new anti-scholastic future of the Church.

Cudworth's philosophy is very nuanced. He recognizes the problems with *monopsychism*, but its simple solution to the problem of thought and communication appeals to him. Therefore, on one hand his doctrine seems worthy, but on the other opens the door for the Church sanctioning foundational occult theosophies. Cudworth seeks a balance between contradicting theories, freewill and the One Universal Mind, while at the same time never fully escaping from knowledge being merely recollection. Like Kircher, his system was put forth in a "learned tongue."

What is now apparent is that Cudworth invokes the very party that led to the Arian school condemned at Nicaea, Neoplatonism. Many of the people Cudworth quotes were Neoplatonists, such as Iamblicus. But he also quotes Manetho, the very person Champollion would later invoke to rescue his theory:

"Again, besides this Thoth, or Theuth, who was called the first Hermes, the Egyptians had also another eminent advancer or restorer of learning, who was called δευτερος ῾Ερμης, the second Hermes—they perhaps supposing the soul of Thoth, or the first Hermes, to have come into him by transmigration; but his proper Egyptian name was Siphoas, as Syncellus out of Manetho informs us: Σιφωας, ο και ῾Ερμης, υιος ῾Ηφαιστου — *Siphoas , (who is also Hermes) the son of Vulcan.*—That is he, who is said to have been the father of Tat, and to have been surnamed Τρισμεγιστος, Ter Maximus, (he being so styled by Manetho, Jamblichus, and others.) And he is placed by Eusebius in the fiftieth year after the Israelitish Exitus, though probably somewhat too early. The former of these two Hermes was the inventor of arts and sciences; the latter, the restorer and advancer of them: the first wrote in hieroglyphics upon pillars, εν τη συρριγικη γη, (as the learned Valesius conjectures it should be read, instead of Σηριαδεκη) which Syringes what they were, Am. Marcellinus will instruct us. The second interpreted and translated those hieroglyphics, composing many books in several arts and sciences; the number whereof set down by Jamblichus must needs be fabulous, unless it be understood of paragraphs or verses. Which Trismegistic or Hermetic books were said to be carefully preserved by the priests in the interior recesses of their temples."[6]

— RALPH CUDWORTH

Perhaps even more telling, Cudworth quotes the very passage we began this book with. True to form, he misses the warning of the *pharmakon*, the warning that worshipping Hermes would lead to ignorance. Yet, he is convinced that it is upon Hermes theological foundation that all religions are built:

"...but in his [Socrates/Plato] Phedrus attributeth to him [Thoth] also the invention of arithmetic, geometry and astronomy, together with some ludicrous recreations, making him either a god or demon: ηκουσα περι Ναυκρστιν τνν Αιγθπτου, γενεσθαι των εκει παλσιων τινα θεων, ου και το υρεον το ιρον ο και καλουσιν Ιβιω, αυτω δε ονομα τω δαιλμοωι ειναι Θευς — *I have heard (saith he) that about Naucratis, in Egypt, there was one of the ancient Egyptian gods, to whom the bird Ibis was sacred, as his symbol or hieroglyphic the name of which demon was Theuth.* — In which place the philosopher subjoins also an ingenious dispute betwixt this Theth and Thamus, then king of Egypt, concerning the convenience and the inconvenience of letters; the former boasting of that invention ως μνημης και σοφιας **φαρμακον** [phar-

makon], *as a remedy for memory, and great help to wisdom*—but the latter contending, that it would rather beget oblivion, by the neglect of memory, and therefore was not so properly μνημης as υπομνησεως **φαρμακον**, *a remedy for memory, as reminiscence, or the recovery of things forgotten — adding, that it would also weaken and enervate men's natural faculties by slugging them, and rather beget* δοζαν σοφιας, *than* αληθειαν, *a puffy conceit and opinion of knowledge* —by a multifarious rabble of indigested notions, than the truth thereof. Moreover, since it is certain, that the Egyptians were famous for literature before the Greeks, they must of necessity have some one or more founders of learning amongst them, as the Greeks had: and Thoth is the only or first person celebrated amongst them on this account, in remembrance of whom the first month of the year was called by that name. Which Thoth is..."
7

— RALPH CUDWORTH

He misinterprets entirely Plato's warning, that the price of such a mnemonic system is that the student would cease to *conceptually* understand, thus creating a legion of sophists. It was just this that led to what Plato termed *sophistry*, people who could quote, but never comprehend. Cudworth sets something in motion, the idea that despite evidence to the contrary, something could be true none-the-less. He also ignores the following line in the text, *that the story of Theuth is an invented tale!*

I believe it is here that a certain dance with the Devil emerges—the notion that facts are irrelevant so long as the result is 'right thinking.' Cudworth is clearly contriving the evidence so as to produce the results he prefers, that Hermeticism can be salvaged by linking the philosophy to Thoth. He helped initiate the movement that something could be true regardless of the evidence. It was just this that led to the condemning of 1 John 5:7.

MAINSTREAMING ARIUS

We assume scholars to be dispassionate observers, that they weigh the evidence and give a fair, impartial solution. But the conclusion historians came to concerning Nicaea was not that. They were not so committed to the Truth, they were following the whims of the majority. The 'official' sanctioned Bible of Nicaea was not that of the Orthodox. How could it be? Constantine died in 337, baptized by someone suspected of Arianism. That Constantine had to submit to Arian authority proves who was in charge of the

Church. It is perhaps for this reason he would have to wait to the last moment hoping for a better course.

There is a very clever shell game going on. The codices *Vaticanus* and *Sinaiticus* are missing 1 John 5:7, the very verse that for nearly two thousand years was considered authentic. Under normal conditions, these codices would have been considered spurious. But that does not fit the moderns' intention—they have to make what most regarded as the inspired text, the one that is corrupted. They would leverage the word '*inerrant.*' In their quest to find the perfect 'infallible' Bible, of which few if any examples exist, they decided to disregard tradition and put their entire faith in the belief that the average of all Bibles represented the inspired Word.

This entailed two steps, 1) declare the deficient Bible the one sanction by Nicaea, and; 2) find a way of making the former conventional Bible the deficient one. All this would pivot on St. Lucian.

So, let's think about this, if this were a 'put up job' they would need a fall guy, someone on who they could blame the corruption of the conventional Bible, and why it had been accepted as faithful for so long. Enrico Norelli writes,

"Eusebius mentions the martyrdom of Lucian of Antioch at Nicomedia under Maximus Daia on January 7, 312.[8] Rufinus added to his Latin translation of the Ecclesiastical History the apology delivered by Lucian on that occasion; its authenticity is uncertain. Lucian has traditionally been regarded as the inaugurator of the Antiochene exegetical school with its literalist tendency, but in fact that school was begun by Diodorus of Tarsus (see vol. II of this history). **Lucian was a teacher of Arius and many of the latter's followers, who liked to call themselves 'Collucianists.' [co-Lucianists] Lucian seems to have taught a strongly subordinationist Christology, thereby anticipating the Arian doctrine... According to the letter, Lucian was successor to Paul of Samosata;**"[9]

We must remember, we already know Lucian's true thoughts, they were documented at the Council of Antioch and used as a model for that Creed in 341. Further, we also know that at that Council the bishops specifically refuted that they had been influenced by Arius, they were somewhat moderated in their persuasions. We must question now, were these 'Semi-Arians,' or is even that title fair? Further, Lucian is accused of teach a *precursor* to Arianism, not Arianism itself. It is also true that it was subordinationism that was under dispute at Nicaea, a belief many held at the time.

I propose this, all the things appearing in the Antiochian Creed were probably items of debate, why else list them? The Creed itself seems like a moderated concession, 'If you concede this, we will concede everything else.' This means the Trinitarian verse must have existed for it was a subject of debate. To be precise, the message seems to be, "Yes, we concede and affirm the Trinity and its verse, however, it was Athanasius that we object to, and we offer here a truce if only he were to be condemned." And, it is this that, indeed, happened. There are numerous facts such as these the disciples of Tischendorf can't account for.

The linchpin to the discussion is Lucian of Antioch and which 'gospel' he published. Lucian himself has two personas, yet is only one person. It was Lucian that taught the entire school of the Arians, yet, we cannot attribute the whole of their heresy to Lucian. Lucian was also accused of disseminating the most heretical Gospel of all time. This has the ring of truth, he was a student of the heretic Paul of Samosata.

Yet, Lucian apparently recanted and died a saint refusing to recant his faith upon extreme torture. Even St. Chrysostom praised him. This can only mean Lucian taught two doctrines, one is pre-Arian, the other recorded in the Creed of 341. Our entire cause is tied to determining *which Gospel Lucian forged — was it pre-Arian (from his first persona) or Trinitarian (from his second)*?

Modern scholars would have you believe this forgery was our verse at 1 John 5:7, but how can this be? Lucian died in 312, his true doctrine documented in 341 is thoroughly orthodox. Yet, there was no other likely contestant until after WWII when Cerinthus' Gospel was finally made public. At the time, few knew about the alternate heretical 'secret' Gospels. Those who did were purposely keeping it secret. I hope to show that *this* was the Gospel Lucian forged, and that those who determined otherwise probably knew they were falsifying the evidence.

In modern parlance this text is called the *Lucian Recension*. It refers to an entire Bible, not just a verse. 'Recension' is a modern term implying the document is merely a revision of an older document. But it is the phrase "the <u>Gospel</u> that Lucian forged" refers to a Gospel, not an entire Bible, nor even a verse. It was two academics, Westcott & Hort. The timeline of their determination is disconcerting.

Tischendorf only showed that two 'approved' Bibles proved his case, the *Codex Sinaiticus* and the *Codex Vaticanus*. The majority from that period, the *Vetus Latina*, disproved it, so a reason had to be formulated as to why the majority were wrong.

Since the fifteenth century a controversy has been emerging. As the West had been struggling to emerge from the Middle Ages, the East for the most part had been doing quite well, thank you. The Church of the East retained much of the original Christian traditions, as well as the tremendous scholarly accomplishments of the schools of Nisibis and Edessa.

Yet, a tragedy was emerging in the East. As Islam took over, Christianity was subjected to the same Arian forces it had confronted in the early Church. Refugees moving to the West brought with them the Greek 'Byzantine' Bible. In many of those Bibles the verse was either missing or penciled in. Considered much superior to the Vulgate (particularly by Protestants), Erasmus and Robert Estienne (Stephens) began translating it into Latin. Out of this re-emerged the debate, was the verse authentic or not?

This discrepancy further fueled the Protestant vs Catholic debate. It also allowed the Protestants to claim an authenticity the Catholics did not have. The question became, which tradition was right? The 'vulgar' text of the Catholic Church which retained the verse, or the 'scholarly' text of the Eastern Church? Was it possible that the Eastern Church wasn't so 'orthodox' after all? Or, was it the West that was in error? How do we account for all this?

Clearly the East knew about the verse or they could not have 'penciled' it in. And weren't they subject to Islam who certainly controlled how books were printed? But to many moderns the elimination of the verse proved the Church was properly 'unitarian,' a more heterodox, more marketable doctrine.

But these 'assumptions' were based upon a series of more basic assumptions. The implication is this: *either the Orthodox were actually anti-trinitarian and had the verse removed, or they made-up the doctrine and had the verse inserted at a later date.* These assumptions are clearly impossible:

1. That a method had to be devised to ascertain which strain of the Bible was authentic, those with the verse, or those without. Normally, one would think, the winner would be the side with the most copies *at that time in history.* But this did not sit well with English scholars such as Westcott & Hort on who the final decision rested. They believed in a model where the original would be few and pristine, and the copies would be many, amateurish and of a later date (the *Vetus Latina*). This theory also conveniently allowed them to dismiss all the later Latin texts. Their theory that a logarithmically increasing number proved a certain perversion of the original had occurred. Therefore, *to be in the majority would prove inauthenticity, a theory they would have to invert at the point the numbers worked to their advantage.*

2. To prove their logarithmic model, Westcott & Hort would have to find a scapegoat to account for these 'fraudulent' Bibles. It was this they assumed to be *Lucian's of Antioch "**Gospel** that **Lucian forged**"*. Mind you, they never found such a text, they only assumed it because there were no other contestants… or were there? The decision was made: the "*Gospel* that Lucian forged" was the *Textus Receptus*, the basis of the King James Bible, now considered based upon the Lucian Recension.

The result today is our 'revised' Bibles, Bibles conforming to what Orthodox Bishop Porphiry had concluded was clearly of Arian authorship. In these revised Bibles these verses are either entirely removed or marked with an asterisk (such as at the end of Mark) warning of an inauthenticity, contesting the authority they once had. This makes once accepted core doctrines questionable, it also opens the door, if nearly sanctions, a gnostic interpretation.

The warning "the Gospels which Lucian forged," is found in the ancient *Gelasian Decree* by Pope Gelasius I (492–496). It says specifically '*Gospel*.' One must step back and grasp what is going on here. We are to believe that Lucian, someone considered a martyr and saint of the Church, had also deceived the Church and produced a Bible "to be avoided by Catholics."

Over time a prejudice formed around those with an allegiance to Bibles such as the King James Bible. Further still, it opened the door for a near closet industry in publishing competing, often dubious, translations of the Bible. Often the publishing of these Bibles has been conveniently coincidental with the 'discovery' of other confirming Gnostic manuscripts. It was this that directly gave rise to a legitimization of Gnostic theology within the Church as scholars tried to remain faithful to the most 'inerrant' text.

The problem was Lucian *was* both a pre-Arian and a saint. So, which Lucian published the text?

WESTCOTT AND HORT — THE HERMETICAL CONNECTION

By itself the Codex *Sinaiticus* was not enough to prove Tischendorf's case. That challenge was taken up by the two Anglican clergymen, Brooke Foss Westcott and Fenton John Anthony Hort. It was they who tipped the scales—they were not dispassionate observers.

> "He [Westcott] and I are going to edit a Greek text of the New Testament some two or three years hence, if possible. Lachmann and Tischendorf will supply rich materials, but not nearly enough; and we hope to do a good deal with Oriental versions. Our object is to supply clergymen generally, schools, etc., with a portable Greek text which shall not be disfigured with Byzantine corruptions."[10]
>
> — FENTON JOHN ANTHONY HORT

"Byzantine corruptions," although used inaccurately here, specifically refers to our verse in question. In other words, their enterprise was weighted from the start. Before they began they had already assumed a corruption of the text. Based upon what? Tischendorf? If so, they were begging the question from the start, assuming to be true that which they hoped to prove. Is it not more likely that Westcott & Hort were already committed to a tradition, and it was to this 'Arian' tradition of Newton and Cudworth they held their loyalties?

Brooke Foss Westcott, was born near Birmingham in 1825. An aspiring academic he obtained a degree from Trinity College with double-first honours. Then getting honors in Greek, he eventually became bishop of Durham. Quoting the 1911 Encyclopedia Britannica, "He studied assiduously The Sacred Books of the East, and earnestly contended that no systematic view of Christianity could afford to ignore the philosophy of other religions. The outside world was wont to regard him as a mystic; and the mystical, or sacramental, view of life enters, it is true, very largely into his teaching. ***He had in this respect many points of similarity with the Cambridge Platonists of the 17th century...***"[11]

As a mentor, Westcott took on Hort as a student. Accounts say Westcott's research began in 1853, at that time he would have been only 28 and hardly an expert. Therefore, it is more reasonable that the heart of their research as reported elsewhere was from 1870 to 1881. These dates are more coincidental with the emergence of Gnostic texts, something that would later be orchestrated. It was this period that Westcott & Hort concentrated on 'revising' the New Testament, after which they made public the text of the their New Testament. It is commonly considered "one of the greatest achievements of English Biblical criticism."

So as not to do an injustice to the their theory, I will present the exact words as found in their introduction to their Greek 'revised' Text. The introduction is difficult to find as it has been replaced in most versions today. It is here that the *Lucian Recension* theory is first advanced and the *Textus Recptus*, the basis of the Authorized King James Version, is condemned. Notice how the words "there can be little doubt" are used to cover up for scanty evidence. They wantonly ignore the just prior discovery of Bishop Thomas Burgess of the Antiochian Creed based upon Lucian's writings, leading the reader to believe their solution is common sense. Notice also their continuous condemnation of the School of Antioch, the source of the 341 Creed. Is this not something true experts would have addressed honestly?

RECENSION THEORY (from the introduction to their version of the Greek Bible)

"§190. The final process was apparently completed by 350 or thereabouts. At what date between 250 and 350 the first process took place, it is impossible to say with confidence; and even for conjecture the materials are scanty. There can be little doubt that during the long respite from persecution enjoyed by the Church in the latter half of the third century multiplication of copies would be promoted by the increase of converts and new security of religious use, and confusion of texts by more frequent intercourse of churches. Such a state of things would at least render textual revision desirable; and a desire for it might easily arise in a place where a critical spirit was alive. The harmony between the characteristics of the Syrian revision and the well known temper of the Antiochian school of critical theology in the fourth century, at least on its weaker side, is obvious; and Lucianus the reputed founder of the school, himself educated at Edessa, lived in the latter part of the third century, and suffered martyrdom in 312. Of known names his [Lucian] has a better claim than any other to be associated with the early Syrian revision; and the conjecture derives some little support from a passage of Jerome, which is not itself discredited by the precariousness of modern theories which have been suggested by it. When he says in his preface to the Gospels "*Praetermitto eos codices quos a Luciano et Hesychio nuncupatos paucorum hominum adserit perversa contentio,*" ["*those volumes which bear the names of Lucianus and Hesychius, and are upheld by the perverse contentiousness of a few men*"] he must have had in view some definite text or texts of the Gospels or the New Testament generally, appealed to by some definite set or sets of men as deriving authority from names honoured by them. Jerome's antagonism to Antiochian theology would readily explain his language, if some Antiochian Father had quoted in controversy a passage of the New Testament according to the text familiar to him, had been accused of falsifying Scripture, and had then claimed for his text the sanction of Lucianus. Whether however Lucianus took a leading part in the earlier stage of the Syrian revision or not, it may be assigned with more probability either to his generation or to that which immediately followed than to any other; and no critical results are affected by the presence or absence of his name...

[continuing at §248] he adds in obscure language that "they had neither been allowed to make corrections (*emendare*) after the Seventy in the Old Testament, nor profited by making corrections in the New Testament". The latter quotation, enigmatic as it is, distinctly implies the existence of copies of the New Testament or the Gospels bearing in some way the names of Lucianus and Hesychius, and supposed to have in some way undergone correction; and likewise associates the same names with some analogous treatment of the LXX. As they appear in company with Origen's name in a similar connexion in the first quotation, Hug supposed that Hesychius had made a recension of both Testaments for Alexandria, Lucianus for Antioch, and Origen for Palestine... As we have already observed (§§ 185, 190), the Syrian text must have been due to a revision which was in fact a recension, and which may with fair probability be assigned to the time when Lucianus taught at Antioch."[12]

Westcott & Hort are both contending that the verse was made up after Nicaea, yet existed before in the writings of Lucian, neither of which they have evidence of... unless of course they are getting it from the Creed of 341. Notice here, what Westcott & Hort refer here to as *the perverse contentiousness [volumes] of a few men* they have already assumed these volumes to be the conventional Bible—*not the volumes by the School of Cerinthus!*

So, the question becomes, 'Is it possible that a person who "studied assiduously The Sacred Books of the East" had no familiarity with 'the Gospel that Cerinthus wrote'? Both Milton's and Newton's writings were based upon them. Even Irenæus describes them—they were the main source of the very mysticism Westcott ascribes to. Certainly he must have read Cudworth. Did he have no knowledge of the other emerging Gnostic texts, all of which could have been claimants to the throne? What about the Creed based upon Lucian's writing that is listed as having wide impact? If he was familiar with any of this, well then, we have a conspiracy.

So, their theory proceeds, blaming a 'tempting' passage that "an unusual number of scribes" would be fooled 'independently' by:

"57. Except where some one particular corruption was so obvious and tempting that an unusual number of scribes might fall into it independently, a few documents are not, by reason of their mere paucity, appreciably less likely to be right than a multitude opposed to them. As soon as the numbers of a minority exceed what can be explained by accidental coincidence, so that their agreement in error, if it be error, can only be explained on genealogical grounds, we have thereby passed beyond purely numerical relations, and the necessity of examining the genealogy of both minority and majority has become apparent. A theoretical presumption indeed remains that a majority of extant documents is more likely to represent a majority of ancestral documents at each stage of transmission than *vice versa*. But the presumption is too minute to weigh against the smallest tangible evidence of other kinds. Experience verifies what might have been anticipated from the incalculable and fortuitous complexity of the causes here at work. At each stage of transmission the number of copies made from each MS depends on extraneous conditions, and varies irregularly from zero upwards: and when further the infinite variability of chances of preservation to a future age is taken into account, every ground for expecting *a priori* any sort of correspondence of numerical proportion between existing documents and their less numerous ancestors in any one age falls to the ground. This is true even in the absence of mixture; and mixture, as will be shown presently, does but multiply the uncertainty."[13]

— WESTCOTT & HORT

This paragraph seemingly solves both of the above problems... *seemingly*. The first quote specifies the problem—the simple numbers of the majority obliterates that of their preferred. Further, at this point there is no way of determining which are earlier. So they must imagine a scenario that flips the advantage. They associate the majority text with the hypothetical text of Lucian's 'perverse' gospel. They liken it to a virus that proliferates exponentially.

So, are we to believe that fake texts individually hand-written texts can proliferate exponentially, but the 'official' text written by scribes and sponsored by the Empire cannot? The solution is simple. Between rulers Constantine and Julian the Apostate most texts had been destroyed or worn out because of age. The Arians tried to finesse a switch, and the people wouldn't have it, *so they made their own*. Westcott & Hort never considered that Lucian's 'perverse' text could be referring to something entirely different... or did they?

To accomplish the this the Arians needed to legitimize their version of the Bible. In the year 332, or there about, Constantine sent a request to Eusebius of Caesarea to produce 50 volumes of the 'corrected' New Testament as 'determined' by the Council of Nicaea. Eusebius of Caesarea (the historian) has the resources for he has inherited the famous library and scriptorium of Pamphilus of Caesarea, he being his disciple. This dating merges into one of the time periods when Athanasius was exiled. The library is speculated to have over 30,000 manuscripts, and a theological school, the center of Christian scholarship in the third century. 30,000 manuscripts is an immense number for this point in time. Can they prove it didn't have a copy of Cerinthus' gospel?

Constantine is quoted in a letter to Eusebius:

"I have thought it expedient to instruct your Prudence to order fifty copies of the sacred Scriptures, the provision and use of which you know to be most needful for the instruction of the Church, to be written on prepared parchment in a legible manner, and in a convenient, portable form, by professional transcribers thoroughly practised in their art."

— EMPEROR CONSTANTINE LETTER TO EUSEBIUS

Eusebius of Caesarea responds:

"Such were the emperor's commands, which were followed by the immediate execution of the work itself, which we sent him in magnificent and elaborately bound volumes of a threefold and fourfold form."

But all these people either have Arian sympathies or are Arians themselves! Even Constantine, by witness of his baptism, is conceding to them. Within three years Constantine would condemn Athanasius and exile him, the very person who we are told prevailed at the Council! So why are we to believe that the text Eusebius of Caesarea produced was one approved by Athanasius? And this is precisely what Tischendorf says he has found in the codices *Vaticanus* and *Sinaiticus*, 'bound volumes of a threefold and fourfold form.' As proof of this he points towards the 'Eusebian markings', invented by him, within the text. This, Westcott & Hort acknowledge in the introduction to their book:

"About 332 Constantine directed Eusebius to have fifty easily legible copies of the complete Scriptures executed by skilful calligraphers for the use of the churches in his newly founded capital. We learn nothing of the texts or the contents of these "sumptuously prepared volumes" (*Eus. Vit. Const.* IV 37):

but if the contained books corresponded with Eusebius's own list of a few years earlier (*H.E.* III 25), none of our present MSS can well have been of the number. The incident illustrates however a need which would arise on a smaller scale in many places, as new and splendid churches came to be built under the Christian Empire after the great persecution: and the four extant copies are doubtless casual examples of a numerous class of MSS, derived from various origins though brought into existence in the first instance by similar circumstances. These four are the *Codex Vaticanus* (B), containing the whole New Testament except the later chapters of Hebrews, the Pastoral Epistles, Philemon, and the Apocalypse; the *Codex Sinaiticus* (ℵ), containing all the books entire;"[14]

They would have us believe that it was the Council that produced the Canon of Scripture. But Eusebius' canon is not the only surviving canon, it is not by itself authoritative. The *Muratorian Canon*, perhaps the oldest known, lists most of the same books of the New Testament. It existed from about 170. Also, from about that same time is the canon provided by *Irenæus*. Again, substantially the same. So, why elevate Eusebius' canon to being *the* canon? To make their text appear more sanctioned? We must ask, is this scholarship *or collusion! Are they not fudging all the facts?*

All this hangs on Westcott & Hort's Lucian Recension theory. T. Böhm writes in the *Dictionary of Early Christian Literature*:

"an effort has been made to discover a Lucianic recension of the LXX and the NT Koine, which formed the basis of the *textus receptus*. But, for one thing, the criteria are unclear for determining how this recension could have been made by Lucian (the relationship to the Hexapla is also unclear). For another, what is regarded as typical of Lucian can be seen prior to Lucian (Philo, Josephus, Clement Alex., papyri of the 1st and 2nd c., etc.). The effort to find a Lucianic recension must be regarded as a failure."[15]

Quoting the respected scholar and Anglican Dean, John William Burgon, seemingly agrees with this analysis:

"The fact is that **B** [*Vaticanus*] and ℵ [*Sinaiticus*] were the products of the school of philosophy and teaching which found its vent in Semi-Arian or Homoean opinions. The proof of this position is somewhat difficult to give, but when the nature of the question and the producible amount of evidence are taken into consideration, is nevertheless quite satisfactory. In the first place, according to the verdict of all critics the date of these two MSS coincides with the period when Semi-Arianism or some other form of Arianism were in the ascendant in the East, and to all outward appearance swayed the Universal Church. **In the last years of his rule, Constantine was under the domination of the Arianizing faction; and the reign of Constantius II over all the provinces in the Roman Empire that spoke Greek, during which encouragement was given to the great heretical schools of the time, completed the two central decades of the fourth century. It is a circumstance that cannot fail to give rise to suspicion that the *Vatican* and *Sinaitic* MSS had their origin under a predominant influence of such evil fame.**"[16]

So, we can dismiss entirely the confusing matter of counting text, dividing them into recensions and versions. If the entire arguments rests on the genealogical theory, the genealogy of their text is demonstrably Arian. Without an early 'pristine' text, the case completely falls apart.

If Lucian didn't produce the Byzantine text, or at least produced another heretical 'perverse' text, what *was that text*? How do we address this problem, something Dean Burgon and Cardinal Newman were incapable of solving? By showing that the condemned text produced by Lucian was not the Byzantine Majority text at all, it was an entirely different text! The most heretical text ever written was the secret *Apocryphon of John*.

The *Gelasian Decree* lists "the Gospel which Lucian forged' as 'apocryphal,' a gospel, not an entire Bible. Also:

BOOK II, CHAP. 3.—Though Philostorgius extols Arius to the skies for impugning the Divinity of the Son, yet he asserts that the latter is involved in the most absurd errors, because he everywhere affirms that God cannot be known, or comprehended, or conceived by the human mind; and not only by men, (which perhaps were an evil more easy to endure), but also not even by His own only-begotten Son. And he asserts that not only Arius, but also a large body of his followers, were carried away into this absurd error at the same time. For with the exception of Secundus and Theonas, and the disciples of the martyr Lucian, namely Leontius, Antonius, and Eusebius of Nicomedia, the rest of the impious band of heretics adopted this opinion.

— PHILOSTORGIUS, *EPITOME OF HISTORY*

The implication here is that whatever doctrine Arius was pushing, even Philostorgius, a semi-Arian, found reprehensible. The semi-Arians were not in fact against the Trinity in principle, only that *Logos* was an eternal part of it, a dispute seemingly resolved in 341. While Philostorgius impugns many, some of the followers of Lucian such as Eusebius of Nicomedia, he gives a pass. This is consistent with the records of 341 also.

Imagine, if you will, that Lucian, originally a disciple of Paul of Samosata, was once a publisher of a corrupt gospel, and that gospel was indeed a corruption of Christian theology. Or, you can imagine that Lucian published it and used it as a teaching device with honest intentions. Perhaps rejecting Paul of Samosata he even used the text as an example of Paul's heresy to instruct his class. This is still a practice to this day. This means that any reference to it could have easily been merely a way of referring to the *Apocryphon of John* without further impugning Lucian, now regarded as a saint, and avoiding speaking of the text itself. Without clear answers, condemning Lucian is simply rash, unfair, and uncharitable.

Let's recap a bit. We now have a Gnostic false gospel of John written by Cerinthus. It prodded the real St. John to write a Gospel to refute it. We later have Arius attacking the Council of Nicaea, yet presenting a heretical doctrine documented in his *Thalia*. We have shown that his *Thalia* has many points of contact with the *Apocryphon of John*. It has also been shown that there is a history of this document from the time of Paul of Samosata all the way through to the Cathars of the thirteenth century and beyond. Later we see evidence of this very same text emerging in the late sixteenth century before the Enlightenment where it is quoted again. Yet, now that the text has finally emerged to the light of day, we see it represented as the true, lost, authentic theology of the Church! All this with the stamp of approval by scholars with a suspicious allegiance. All this *at the very time when secret Gnostic texts were beginning to be circulated in Europe.*

---

1. Cudworth, Ralph, *The true intellectual system of the universe*: 1617-1688; Birch, Thomas, 1705-1766 p.429

2. Descartes, René. *The Philosophical Writings of Descartes*. Translated by John Cottingham et al., I, 113, Cambridge University Press, 1985. [from a paper by 'Descartes and Scholasticism: An Analysis,' Brien Brockbank]

3. Budge, E. A. Wallis (1983) [1910]. *Egyptian Language: Easy Lessons in Egyptian Hieroglyphics*. Mineola, NY: Dover. p. 15

4. Yates, Dame Frances A. *Giordano Bruno and the Hermetic Tradition*, Univ. of Chicago. 1964

5. Cudworth, Ralph, The true intellectual system of the universe: 1617-1688; Birch, Thomas, 1705-1766, p.319-20

6. Cudworth, Ralph, The true intellectual system of the universe: 1617-1688; Birch, Thomas, 1705-1766 p.429

7. Cudworth, Ralph, The true intellectual system of the universe: 1617-1688; Birch, Thomas, 1705-1766 p.429

8. Hist. eccl. 9.6.3

9. Moreschini, Claudio, and Norelli, Enrico. *Early Christian Greek and Latin literature: a literary history*. Hendrickson, 2005. p. 312

10. Hort, Arthur. *Life and Letters of Fenton John Anthony Hort*, Vol. I, Macmillan & Co., 1896, p.250 https://www.jstor.org/stable/3140075

11. Chisholm, Hugh, ed. *The Encyclopædia britannica: a dictionary of arts, sciences, literature and general information*. Vol. 29. At the University press, 1911.—article 'Brooke Foss Westcott'

12. Westcott, Brooke Foss, and Fenton John Anthony Hort, eds. *The New Testament in the original Greek: The text revised*. Vol. 2. Macmillan, 1881.

13. Westcott, Brooke Foss, and Fenton John Anthony Hort, eds. *The New Testament in the original Greek: The text revised*. Vol. 2. Macmillan, 1881. p.45

14. Westcott, Brooke Foss, and Fenton John Anthony Hort, eds. *The New Testament in the original Greek: The text revised*. Vol. 2. Macmillan, 1881.

15. Döpp, Siegmar, and Wilhelm Geerlings, eds. *Dictionary of Early Christian Literature*. Crossroad Publishing, 2000. pp. 388-389

16. Burgon, Dean John William and Miller, Edward. *The Traditional Text of the Holy Gospels*. p.161

FREEMASONRY AND NAPOLEON'S SOPHISTS
THEIR REAL AGENDA

"Have we digressed in what precedes from the psychology of crowds? Assuredly not. If we desire to understand the ideas and beliefs that are germinating today in the masses, and will spring up tomorrow, it is necessary to know how the ground has been prepared. The instruction given the youth of a country allows of a knowledge of what that country will one day be. The education accorded the present generation justifies the most gloomy previsions. It is in part by instruction and education that the mind of the masses is improved or deteriorated. It was necessary in consequence to show how this mind has been fashioned by the system in vogue, and how the mass of the indifferent and the neutral has become progressively an army of the discontented ready to obey all the suggestions of utopians and rhetoricians. It is in the schoolroom that socialists and anarchists are found nowadays, and that the way is being paved for the approaching period of decadence for the Latin [school system] peoples."[1]

— GUSTAVE LE BON, *PSYCHOLOGIE DES FOULES* (1895)

THE THEOLOGY OF DESPAIR

In order to see what is truly going on we must step back in time a bit and bring another strain forward. It is the strain of Napoleon's Sophesians.

It was in the late 1700s that Deism was making its greatest strides, "Deism being the belief that while God may have created the world, He was never in the world".[2] Newton, while technically not a deist himself, paved the way. If the Church did nothing it would be looking at its own obsolescence. Not understanding the nature of the forces against it, most attempts to resist only furthered the cause of the Adversary.

The modern Christian solution came by way of the author Jean-Jacques Rousseau (1712-1778) in his *Creed of the Savoyard Priest*. It speaks of a Catholic priest who, loving the Church, must now continue his piety in the face of disbelief. The sentiments echo those of Descartes:

"My perplexity was increased by the fact that I had been brought up in a church which decides everything and permits no doubts, so that having rejected one article of faith I was forced to reject the rest; as I could not accept absurd decisions, I was deprived of those which were not absurd. When I was told to believe everything, I could believe nothing, and I knew not where to stop, I consulted the philosophers, I searched their books and examined their various theories; I found them all alike proud, assertive dogmatic, professing, even in their so-called scepticism, to know everything, proving nothing, scoffing at each other. This last trait which was common to all of them, struck me as the only point in which they were right. Braggarts in attack, they are weaklings in defence. Weigh their arguments, they are all destructive; count their voices, every one speaks for himself; they are only agreed in arguing with each other. I could find no way out of my uncertainty by listening to them."[3]

— *EMILE* (ON EDUCATION), JEAN-JACQUES ROUSSEAU

It is upon this sentiment the modern Church was born, keeping up appearances. It might prolong the inevitable, but it was only a matter of time before belief would no longer be a requisite.

And so here we find the formula for the modern Church, structure minus belief, ship minus cargo. Here we find the murmurings of the bloody and the bloodless revolutions, the French, the Russian, the Spanish and many revolutions to follow, the executed priests, the raped nuns, corpses paraded through the streets, all in pursuit of *liberté, égalité, fraternité*. This is not to say that revolutions at times aren't necessary. It is to say that hubris always clouds common sense when we become gods.

The modern onslaught of disbelief has been ruthless. Many if not most schools, universities, HR departments, political systems and the like are stacked against us. What is left for us to do?

I am not so foolish as to believe that everyone before had a perfect faith, or even perfect motives, but I do believe most everyone once knew the Adversary. The average person once had a certain integrity, a strength of commitment. It is the absence of these that reveals the modern—in disavowing Adversary, he targets his rebellion on the idiosyncrasies and missteps of the good, often braggarts purposely using confusion to advance a cause they haven't figured out for themselves.

One thing must be realized, the person in the pew often has more belief than the person in the pulpit for the person in the pulpit has confronted Rousseau's dilemma. In today's world it is unavoidable. Yet, seldom has the preacher come up with the right answer, he is too afraid. Out of despair he once searched for God. He then went on to get a degree granted by people who probably were less sincere than he. Finding that not enough he entered seminary all the while still searching. He was cultivating the belief of the Savoyard Priest, the modern *pharmakon*. The reason you can know this is seldom are people ordained these days if they don't pass the test.

Somewhere along the way he has succumbed, his financial and educational aspirations along with his debt will not allow him to walk away. So, he soldiers on. The prestige of an academic hood appeals more than the pants of the carpenter. Without ever intending to be a philosopher the modern has become an Idealist, he has compromised his sincerity all away. While we may think there is a way around this, there is not. Even the non-denominational self-ordained is in the same boat, his way out being a certain willed-ignorance, something Logos never intended.

WHILE ROUSSEAU WAS NOT FRENCH, it was the French who were most intrigued by his predicament. We can have freedom, or, we can have truth, but seldom can we have both without compromise. It is here they fell under a spell. Misunderstandings that began at the Councils of Nicaea, have metastasized. Protestants began to regard Rome as 'the whore of Babylon.' Catholics regarded Protestants as 'heretics.' Both regarded Jews as 'Christ killers.' Blaming God for their failings, deism became a way out. Once they found deism was not, unlimited freedom became their pursuit.

The inevitable result was the triumph of Arianism (what they called Modernism), a heterodoxy compatible with any other religion. Many began envisioning a world without Christianity at all, the Gnostic 'Unity' based upon some nebulous, undefinable spirituality. This attitude spread throughout Europe, but it met its critical mass in France. Rousseau expresses this malaise, invoking once again the quote by which this book began:

> "An ancient tradition passed out of Egypt into Greece, that some god [Thoth], who was an enemy to the repose of mankind, was the inventor of the sciences. What must the Egyptians, among whom the sciences first arose, have thought of them? And they beheld, near at hand, the sources from which they sprang. In fact, whether we turn to the annals of the world, or eke out with philosophical investigations the uncertain chronicles of history, we shall not find for human knowledge an origin answering to the idea we are pleased to entertain of it at present. Astronomy was born of superstition, eloquence of ambition, hatred, falsehood and flattery; geometry of avarice; physics of an idle curiosity; and even moral philosophy of human pride. Thus the arts and sciences owe their birth to our vices; we should be less doubtful of their advantages, if they had sprung from our virtues."[4]

— JEAN-JACQUES ROUSSEAU, *THE SOCIAL CONTRACT*

Inspired by the American Revolution, the French were not to be outdone… they were to leave no stone unturned. Divide and conquer, pit one side against the other, religion would be belittled, the Deist would conquer.

The first focus was on crippling the Catholic Church. Replacing religion would be the Cult of Reason. To this cult nothing was immune. There was no end to the persecution, property was destroyed, rites and practices forbidden, people raped and murdered, all in hubris.

Finding the Church's devotion to the cycles of the seasons crucial to the traditional faith, the calendar would be reformulated in worship of 'science.' Churches like Notre Dame were seized, altars desecrated, often adorned with semi-naked women as the Goddess 'Liberté,' an effigy of which would one day stand ironically in New York's harbor as a symbol of religious freedom. Thousands of Catholics were killed. Before long the world would see the invasion of Rome and the Pope fleeing for safety.[5]

It was the perverse Marquis de Sade that inspired much of the Revolution, free sex became part of the cause. As part of this war, he wrote books advocating the most obnoxious of sexual practices including child rape. Legend has it that it was the publication of *Les 120 Journées de Sodome,* written from his jail cell, that ultimately triggered the Storming of the Bastille.

The devastation of the Revolution saw a quick rise to power by Napoleon.

"Napoleon had a marvellous insight into the psychology of the masses of the country over which he reigned, but he, at times, completely misunderstood the psychology of crowds belonging to other nationalities; and it is because he thus misunderstood it that he engaged in Spain, and notably in Russia, in conflicts in which his power received blows which were destined within a brief space of time to ruin it."

— GUSTAVE LE BON

Among the first things Napoleon did was return the Church to the Catholics, although it would no longer be a state religion. He also reestablished the traditional calendar. His true aspirations, however, were kept close.

CHAMPOLLION'S REAL AGENDA

Napoleon has been accused of being a despot, but he was the despot France needed. He hid his true aspirations, they were in league with the new Arians:

"I saw the way to achieve all my dreams... I would found a religion, I saw myself marching on the way to Asia, mounted on an elephant, a turban on my head, and in my hand a new Koran that I would have composed to suit my needs. In my enterprises I would have combined the experiences of the two worlds, exploiting the realm of all history for my own profit."[6]

— NAPOLEON BONAPARTE

Confirming Napoleon's true spiritual loyalties:

"In the name of Allah the merciful... People of Egypt, you will have been told that I come as an enemy of Islam. This is a lie... I have come to restore your rights and punish those who oppress you... I worship God more than your oppressors, I respect Mohammed his prophet and the holy Koran... The French are also true Moslems, The proof of this can be seen the fact that they have marched against Rome and destroyed the throne of the Pope, who constantly incited the Christians to make war on all Moslems..."[7]

— NAPOLEON BONAPARTE

Napoleon's Egyptian Campaign (1798-1801) was ostensibly to ensure

French free trade, but in many ways it was the inevitable application of the Cult of Reason. Began ostensibly as an operation to save Egypt from its invaders, it was in reality an invasion itself designed to find evidence to back up Napoleon's theories, that Egypt was the true cradle of civilization. That what lay hidden underneath all wisdom were the seeds of Thoth. Of the some 32,000 troops, 10,000 of which would never return to France, 167 were 'scientists' publicly called *savants,* but were secretly members of the *Order Sacré des Sophisiens.*[8]

Napoleon's invasion was a huge exploration in search of lost wisdom, the ancient germ from which all religions evolved. Little by little the savants collected artifacts, examined them, copied them, made artistic renditions, and ultimately procured many for shipment back to France. Proof of Napoleon's true intentions is the amount of attention he gave to this enterprise, and how little attention he gave to the well-being of his troops. Realizing that Napoleon was disturbing Englands foreign trade, its navy stepped in, easily won the day, and seized much of the bounty, including the precious *Rosetta Stone.*

The story of the *Rosetta Stone* has always been a sort of false flag. Not only has its contribution to unraveling the hieroglyphs been overstated, it didn't even supply the critical 'word' as claimed. The key decipherer, François Champollion, never went to Egypt under that cause, nor did he have first-hand access to the Stone. It's probable the whole story was a diversion designed to distract from Napoleon's true prized possession, the *Dendera Zodiac.* It was by this he would prove Christianity a false religion by claiming the Judeo-Christian calendar had been falsified.

Simply returning to France would risk revealing Napoleon's true intentions and the fact that the disaster that could have been prevented. The taking of Egypt was at the price of numerous mal-equiped troops loosing their lives. Poking a stick in the eye of the greatest navy in the world would not faire any better. To coverup the failure, by 1802 Napoleon's administration had destroyed most of the documents pertaining to the Campaign, and the real reason for his defeat by England. However, the savants needed time to establish a secret underground by which pipelines from their Egyptian archaeological bases could move artifacts and research back to France. It was here where Oliver Cromwell's secret underground, Freemasonry, could be appropriated as the conduit of secret wisdom. Much of this would be conducted through the *Institut d'Egypte* in Cairo. It would all be led by Napoleon's *Sophesians,* a term derived from Plato's 'sophist,' one who knows but doesn't understand.

The intent was to give an archaeological foundation for Napoleon's new spirituality. At the core would be recovering Hermeticism, and re-establishing the crucial links between Hermes and Thoth impugned by Casaubon.

Initially, Champollion's research actually moved against Napoleon's designs. In fact at one point he was offered ordination as a Cardinal by the Catholic Church for thwarting these very designs. Yet, before his death Champollion would supply the crucial evidence needed to wed Egyptian mysticism to Greek philosophy, all backed up by the knowledge gained from the Egyptian Campaign. It is true, while Champollion did strike the death knell of Athanasius Kircher's phoney Egypt-sophistry, he later gave it new life under a seldom reported different guise.

Napoleon's secret religious aspirations were similar to Kircher and Cudworth, a marriage of Hermes and Thoth, the very gnosticism that evolved from Cerinthus' gospel. But how do you rediscover what is not there? You either fabricate or misrepresent it:

"...the Hermetica turned out to be a treasure trove of mystery knowledge for the Sophisians, who freely borrowed elements from these writings [the *Corpus Hermeticum*] and adjusted their contents as they deemed fit for their rituals. This approach should not necessarily be dismissed as the work of amateurs, because it was only in 1822, when the ink of the last entries in the *Golden Book* was hardly dry, that Jean-François Champollion presented his groundbreaking method for deciphering Egyptian hieroglyphics and unlocking the secrets of genuine Egyptian inscriptions and papyri... it needs to be kept in mind that both Champollion and the Sophisians sprang from the same Napoleonic scholarly milieu that was originally spawned by the *Institut d'Egypte* in Cairo."[9]

— DARIUS SPIETH, *NAPOLEON'S SORCERERS*

The purpose of this was to re-legitimize an event that never happened. Almost from the beginning Neoplatonism had imagined a secret encounter by Plato with Egyptian mysticism. It was from this Plato was to have been instructed by Egyptian priests in the Occult arts:

"It has been asserted, that it was in Egypt that Plato acquired his opinions concerning the origin of the world, and learnt the doctrines of, transmigration, and the immortality of the soul: but it is more probable that he learned the latter doctrine from Socrates, and the former from Pythagoras. It is not likely that Plato, in the habit of a merchant, could have gained access to the sacred mysteries of Egypt; for we shall after-wards see, in the case of Pythagoras, that the Egyptian priests were so unwilling to communicate their secrets to strangers, that even a royal mandate was scarcely sufficient, in a single instance, to procure this indulgence."[10]

— WILLIAM ENFIELD

The *Golden Book*, now in the Bibliothèque Nationale in Paris, was the secret guide to rituals and symbolism of the Sophesians. Based upon Eyptianisms, it became a tool in ritualizing and propagandizing the Neoplatonic philosophy, just as Iamblicus had done, a model for future Freemasonry.

The entirety of this fiasco is on display in the legend of the *Rosetta Stone*. While the Sophesians initially were the discoverers, it ultimately became the property of the British. In negotiations between the two, France chose to keep the *Dendera Zodiac* instead. With the Rosetta Stone in England, a competition of sorts mounted between the emerging novice François Champollion and the experienced, highly regarded physicist Thomas Young, the very person who corrected Isaac Newton's Light Theory. While that dispute raged and made all the headlines, a secret agenda was being conducted by the French to delegitimize the Church by using the Zodiac to prove the Bible's chronology was false.

The story is a bit complicated. It is usually presented as a battle solely between Young and Champollion. However, Young was substantially more trained in languages than Champollion who was mainly self-taught, having some aid from Coptic priests. When he did eventually turn to academia, he became *l'enfant terrible*, where the petulance of his young age shown through. His professor Silvestre de Sacy at one point warned Young that Champollion was constantly taking credit for other people's ideas. But Champollion, through his brother, had connections to Napoleon. In this François was able to avoid military service and dedicate his life to his 'sophesian' ambitions.

Champollion's father owned a book store where his son acquired an interest in Egyptian hieroglyphs. He would later claim for himself the accolades given to Athanasius Kircher by proving him wrong. It is not a stretch of the imagination to suppose that Champollion gained this obsession through reading *Oedipus Aegyptiacus,* it perhaps being part of his father's inventory. How else do we explain not only his familiarity with Kircher's hieroglyphic theories, but also his interest in the secrets of Hermeticism?

Young was convinced there was no possible way of accurately reading the 'demotic' script on the *Rosetta Stone,* there was no known source for the root words. Champollion decided he could figure out the root words by using the names of places and landmarks of Egyptian geography. Champollion did have some success at this. Yet, this alone was not enough to give him the notoriety he sought. What was needed was a break-though.

At one point Champollion was literally put under arrest. Trying to straddle both sides of the French political climate, he got caught running afoul of governmental power. His sentence was that he return to his boyhood home, Figeac, where he would stay out of trouble by salvaging the remains of his father's bookstore and becoming a school teacher. But fortune hit…

Legend holds that while employed as a teacher of the young, waiting to be tried for treason, Champollion 'swooned' with a vision that incapacitated him for days. Emerging from this, he dashed off the now famous letter to M. Bon-Joseph Dacier, unlocking the secret to translating Egyptian hieroglyphs. But many complained the letter left few clues how to replicate the procedure, leaving researchers guessing. The consensus today is the 'rebus principle' came to Champollion in a debilitating dream.

So, what did he discover in the remote village of Figeac that could not be found in the universities? I believe it was this.

Perhaps, the educated elite missed something the average child knew. The rebus principle had become a bit of a fad in France. As an entertaining aid to teaching school children, the rebus principle was appearing in numerous reading primers. Very much like the "👁—❤—NY" bumper stickers we often see, the rebus principle was a simple code whereby children could phonetically combine pictures with letters to learn to read. Coincidentally, Champollion realized Egyptian Hieroglyphs were using the same method—it was a solution so simple it is a wonder nobody had figured it out… and why it was kept a secret.

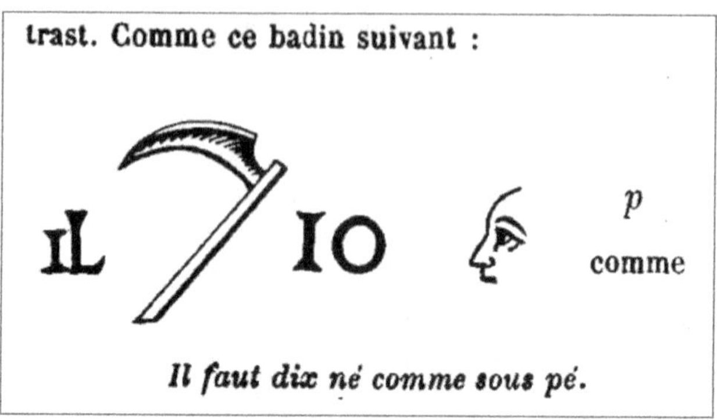

An illustration from Les Bigarurres du Seigneur des Accords *(1866)
that promoted the 'rebus' principle in French schools popular since
the 16ᵗʰ century.*

According to eminent Egyptologist Sir Wallis Budge, Champollion was not the savant of modern legend. Initially Champollion believed that the underlying language of Egyptian was actually Chinese. Failing in proving that, Champollion died without ever completing his hieroglyphic dictionary. It was completed by his brother and other people and has since fell into disuse because of the theory's limitations. The legend of Champollion is largely a fabrication. Sounding as a dig against Champollion, Sir Wallis Budge of the British Museum wrote:

"It will probably be admitted by all that the compiler of an *Egyptian Hieroglyphic Dictionary* should know at first hand every collection of Egyptian monuments and papyri in the world, that he should have visited every great Museum on the Continent and in Egypt, England and America, and copied, or collated with printed editions, every hieroglyphic, hieratic and demotic text of importance, that he should know well the histories of written by classical writers, and the works of the Arab geographers, and Coptic in all its dialects, and that he should have had at his disposal unlimited time, in short that he should have been able to devote his whole life to the making of his Egyptian Dictionary."

— SIR WALLIS BUDGE, *EGYPTIAN HIEROGLYPHIC
DICTIONARY*

Today the Egyptian hieroglyphic system still remains a bit of a mystery. Rather than being the secret container of Egyptian Thothic mysticism, most legitimate researchers find them to be inventory and sales slips from a time when Egypt was an ancient economic power. Much of the legends promoted by the likes of Kircher and the *Hieroglyphs of Horapollo* were made up, having been obtained by clairvoyance. Once believed to be an ancient book from the fifth century, the *Hieroglyphs of Horapollo* is now known to be a book fabricated during the early Renaissance.

Yet, there is an odd tale connected with this all. One of Napoleon's aspirations was to prove the Bible corrupt by using the *Dendera Zodiac* to date the creation of the Earth. If it could be proved that the Zodiac was a representation of the sky, say, 10,000 years before Christ, the Bible would be proved in error.[11]

THE FACT IS, the first hieroglyphs Champollion decoded did not come from the Rosetta Stone as recorded. It was from the Dendera Zodiac. The actual Zodiac is immense and weighs several tons. Removing it to Paris was beyond nineteenth century French technology, much as building the Panama Canal would later be. To do so would mean leaving a major portion behind, the part critical to Champollion.

What did make it to Paris was only an artist's rendition of the missing part. It was this portion Champollion used to crack the code… but it too was a fraud. The rendition was made by known Sophesian, Vivent Denon, and showed a cartouche near the feet of a goddess originally attached to the Zodiac. From that cartouche Champollion found the hieroglyphic interpretation of the Greek word 'autocrat,' thus dating the Zodiac to the first century BC. This foiled Napoleon's aspirations at proving the age of the Earth.[12]

Years later, just before his death, Champollion finally made it to Egypt. One of the main places he went to was Dendera, to see the piece of the Zodiac left behind. Examining this he noticed that very cartouche was blank, the word 'autocrat' was added in by the artist, who more than likely was Denon. Champollion had decoded the work of a fellow Frenchman.

SO, the question becomes, who actually discovered the key to cracking Egyptian hieroglyphs? Who knew enough to commit the fraud? It wasn't Champollion, he had yet to go to Egypt, he had been set up.[13]

Nineteenth century French diagram of the Dendera Zodiac. (public domain)

What it comes down to is this: undaunted by Isaac Casaubon's determination that the Hermetical texts were a fraud, like Cudworth and the Cambridge Platonists, Champollion would take up the challenge, perhaps in an effort to recover his self esteem. He would need to go to Egypt himself to learn to dress and 'walk like an Egyptian,' which he did.

What was needed was an alternate path to re-legitimize Hermeticism. The Rosetta Stone became one of the stories presented for public consumption, to detract from the failures of Napoleon's Egyptian Campaign. What was needed was a means of undermining the Church, Napoleon was smart enough to understand this. Yet in true masonic fashion, to the French Council of State he would say:

"By becoming a Mussulman that I obtained a footing in Egypt. By becoming an Ultramontane that I won over the Italian priests, and had I to govern a nation of Jews I would rebuild Solomon's temple."[14]

— NAPOLEON BONAPARTE

And it is upon Thoth that he would re-build Solomon's Temple. To Napoleon, religion was nothing more than crowd control. Once the rebirth of Arianism was set in motion, even Napoleon's exile could not stop it.

Underneath, the Sophesian agenda was to rehabilitate the ancient heresy, what they believed was the true foundation of religion. Champollion first moved his focus from the Rosetta Stone towards finding pharaoh 'Thutmoses.' Critical to deciphering the acclaimed cartouche, is that the symbol of an *ibis* be representative of the god *Thoth*. But why an ibis? One reason is the long phallic-like beak. It might appear he grabbed this out of thin air. He didn't... the similarity is intentional.

Champollion's rendition of Thutmoses from the Letter to Dacier *some say it actually reads 'djerty' (public domain)*

The cults of both Dionysius and Hermes are both Bacchanalian, they worshipped phallic symbols, particularly 'hermai.' The stone *monuments* spread around the countryside had 'ibis-like' phalluses. Finding such Hermetic-like evidences in the ancient city Khemenu, Champollion believed he had found the city of Thoth. Therefore the name was changed from *Khemenu* to *Hermopolis*.

While this alone may have been enough to convince Champollion that the two gods Thoth and Hermes represented the same philosophy, he knew it would take more than that to convince academia. Champollion expressed his feelings on discovering 'Thoth' in a Letter written while finally in Egypt:

"The rising sun of the 23rd found us in Dakké, the ancient Pselcis, Ψελχις,. I ran to the temple, and the first hieroglyphic inscription which fell before my eyes told me that I was in a holy place dedicated to Thoth, Lord of Pselk: I thus increased my map of Nubia with a new hieroglyphic name of city, and today I could publish a map of Nubia with the ancient names in sacred characters... The Dakké monument has a double interest. From a mythological point of view, it provides infinitely precious material for understanding the nature and attributions of the divine being that the Egyptians worshiped under the name of Thoth (the twice the size of Hermes; a series of bas-reliefs offered me, in a way, all the transfigurations of this god. I found him there first (what must have been) in connection with Har-hat (the great Hermes Trismegistus), his primordial form, and of whom he, Thoth, is only the last transformation, that is to say his incarnation on earth following Amon-Ra and Mouth incarnated in Osiris and Isis. Thoth goes back to the celestial Hermes (Har-hat), divine wisdom, the Spirit of God, passing through the forms…"[15]

— JEAN-FRANÇOIS CHAMPOLLION 'LE JEUNE'

Champollion began to see Thoth-Hermes everywhere. His imagination ran wild. Hieroglyphs of all shapes and forms surrounded by glyphs that barely could be read, all symbolized Thoth. Even a late night musician entering Champollion's tent represented 'Thoth':

"During the evening, while I was playing a game of chess, we brought into our tent a Nubian with a magnificent face, his hair done like the Pharaohs in certain bas-reliefs, his hair divided into an infinity of locks, twisted into corkscrew and forming a sort of wig with a curve exactly like that of ancient Egyptian hairstyles. His features, full of gentleness and nobility, recalled those of the Rhamses on the neighboring monuments. Dressed in a long blue robe covered with a white cloak, this 'Barabra,' a native of the island of Argo near Dongola, had no beard and seemed very young to us. It was a rhapsode: also he held in his hand a lyre of perfectly ancient shape, and whose sound box resembled the shell of the turtle, of which it is said that Thoth-Hermes composed the first lyre invented. The new Orpheus sat down in the midst of us, and was invited to give us proofs of his talent. As soon as he had tuned his instrument, he played a few savage airs in very lively time."[16]

— JEAN FRANÇOIS CHAMPOLLION

The book Champollion himself never finished was his on hieroglyphs. The book he did actually finish is seldom mentioned, *The Egyptian Pantheon*. It is evidence of all this. It is filled with numerous artist renditions of Egyptian hieroglyphs, most of which Champollion captioned as representing the god Thoth in his many guises, even a baboon. In one even the head of a hawk now represented Thoth. From that book:

Thoth as the the god-headed hawk from Champollion's Egyptian
Pantheon (public domain)

THOTH TRISMEGISTUS

THE FIRST HERMES, HERMES THRICE GREATEST

"It is obvious, by examining the monuments which has just been quoted, that *the god-headed hawk* shares all the attributions of the Egyptian Hermes to *the head of Ibis*; And if we also consider that the educated or purified characters always face the Hiéracocephale, it becomes certain that this divinity is superior to the *Ibiocephalus* Hermes; And this supremacy, like this analogy of functions, are very naturally explained by the fact that the Egyptians recognized *two* Hermes among their deities.[17]

We might ask, from what ancient authority did Champollion, or anyone else for that matter, find to equate Thoth with Hermes? The clue is in his *The Egyptian Pantheon,* as Champollion continues:

> **"This important distinction was positively expressed in the work of Manetho,** written by order of Ptolemy Philadelphe. This Egyptian high priest spoke there of THOTH THE FIRST HERMES (θὼθ ὁ πρῶτος Ἑρμῆς), which, before the Cataclysm [Flood], had inscribed on steles, in hieroglyphs and in sacred language, the principles of knowledge, and thus composed the first sacred books, which were translated, after the cataclysm, in *hiérographic* (hieratic) and in the common language, by the *son of Agathodœmon (Δεύτερος Ἑρμῆς)* THE SECOND HERMES father of Tat. **This passage of Manetho confirms what I had already deduced from monuments alone, the existence of two Hermes.** This same distinction is expressly established in *hermetic* books, which, despite the haired judgments that certain modern criticisms have carried out, nonetheless contain a mass of purely Egyptian traditions and constantly agree with the monuments."[18]

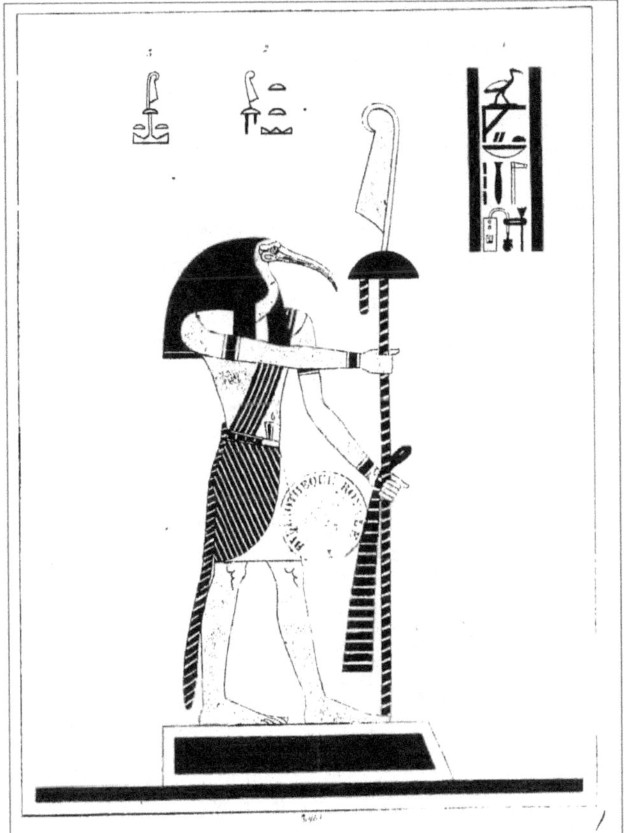

Thoth as the ibis headed Psychopompe from Champollion's Egyptian Pantheon (public domain)

So, like Cudworth, Champollion is getting this from Manetho, a third century BC priest and historian. It is speculated that his name means 'Truth of Thoth.' It is from Manetho's *History of Egypt* that these researchers have been able to tentatively corroborate their Egyptian histories. But it is from this sole testimony that Champollion was able to equate Thoth with Hermes, by his own admission. That this was problematic, it was already considered dubious in the first century as testified by the Jewish historian Josephus. The sketchy history of Manetho is acknowledged in the book *Manetho*, translation and commentary by W.G. Waddell.

THE LIFE OF MANETHO: Traditions and Conjectures.

"Our knowledge of Manetho is for the most part meagre and uncertain; but three statements of great probability may be made. They concern his native place, his priesthood at Heliopolis, and his activity in the introduction of the cult of Serapis.

The name Manetho (Μανέθω, often written Μανέθων) has been explained as meaning "Truth of Thoth", and a certain priest under Dynasty XIX is described as "First Priest of the Truth of Thoth". According to Dr. Černy "Manetho" is from the Coptic ⲘⲀⲚⲈϨⲦⲞ "groom" (ⲘⲀⲚⲈ "herdsman", and ϨⲦⲞ "horse"); but the word does not seem to occur elsewhere as a proper name. In regard to the date of Manetho, Syncellus in one passage gives us the information that he lived later than Berossos: elsewhere he puts Manetho as "almost contemporary with Berossos, or a little later".[19]

— W. G. WADDELL

Most important is whether Champollion's connection of Hermes to Thoth is valid. The 'proof' is entirely contained in a letter as follows:

LETTER OF MANETHO OF SEBENNYTUS TO PTOLEMY PHILADELPHUS.

To the great King Ptolemy Philadelphus Augustus. Greeting to my lord Ptolemy from Manetho, high-priest and scribe of the sacred shrines of Egypt, born at Sebennytus and dwelling at Heliopolis. It is my duty, almighty king, to reflect upon all such matters as you may desire me to investigate. So, as you are making researches concerning the future of the universe, in obedience to your command I shall place before you the Sacred Books which I have studied, written by your forefather, Hermes Trismegistus. Farewell, I pray, my lord King.

Waddell adds:

"Such is his account of the translation of the books written by the second Hermes. Thereafter Manetho tells also of five Egyptian tribes which formed thirty dynasties . . ."

Waddell later comments on the authenticity of that letter:

THE BOOK OF SOTHIS (Appendix IV)

"The Book of Sothis or *The Sôthic Cycle* is transmitted through Syncellus alone. In the opinion of Syncellus, this *Sôthis-Book* was dedicated by Manetho to Ptolemy Philadelphus. The king wished to learn the future of the universe,

and Manetho accordingly sent to him "sacred books" based upon inscriptions which had been written down by Thôth, the first Hermês, in hieratic script, had been interpreted after the Flood by Agatho-daemôn, son of the second Hermês and father of Tat, and had been deposited in the sanctuaries of the temples of Egypt. **The letter which purports to have accompanied the "sacred books" is undoubtedly a forgery**; but the *Sôthis-Book* is significant for the textual transmission of Manetho."[20]

Now I am not saying that ancient records such as of Manetho are not useful to historians such as determining chronologies. What I am saying is that the notion of establishing some proto-model for Christian theology and philosophy, or even unlocking the key to its own secret wisdom, from scant, oddball sources like these is preposterous. We've seen this over and over again, the rehabilitation of some dubious, misinterpreted legend is given more weight than it deserves, and from that academic volumes are written claiming that by this one or two discoveries all tradition must be rewritten.

Like the disciples of Tischendorf, the proclamations of the elite are not to be contested. They alone have access to the real truth… except now they don't. Libraries have been opened up, knowledge is all over the internet. While their beliefs are only relevant to people predisposed that way, it seduces a public starved for a sense of identity and thirsty for secret wisdom. The purpose is clear, and it is the same as Cerinthus'.

THE MISREPRESENTATION OF EGYPTIAN JUSTICE

Religion is nothing without a teaching, what we call a doctrine. Embedded in the doctrine called *Logos* is a principle called *Non-Contradiction*, 'A thing cannot *be* and *not be* the same thing at the same time under the same aspect.' Put more simply, *contradictories cannot both be true.* It was once a core doctrine in Catholic scholastic thought.

Yet, is it any wonder that the coptologists would find the exact opposite in their reading of these ancient hieroglyphs? Think about this (and this might be their greatest slander), nearly 2000 years of Christian history and, researchers don't find just a missing date, or simple place-name was wrong. No, they find that the core of Truth is exactly opposite of what everyone thought! And it is all proved by the Egyptian God Thoth.

Looking at one of the hieroglyphs depicting Thoth and the Scales of Justice, they envisioned a sort of karmic scheme of redemption. They envisioned the scene as representing the final accounting of one's life before what they called the 'Hall of the Two-truths.' It was their version of the Last Judgement. There, the judged person's fate hung in the balance. The guardian was Thoth. On one side was one's heart, the other one's spirit (represented by a feather). Unlike an accounting for one's sins as in Christianity, it was interpreted that the judged must know a secret declaration of innocence formula to pass. It was believed to be a based upon one's deniability for one's actions before God—if one knew the paradoxical 'two-fold' nature of truth, that faith and reason were irreconcilable, then one could prove unaccountable for their actions. How could you be accountable if Truth is unknowable? In other words, the savants saw in these hieroglyphs what they wanted to see, a vindication of gnostic thought.[21]

Thoth supervising the Balance Scales of Justice, in the Hall of the Two Truths, a questionable interpretation — public domain

It was once thought that all Gnosticism grew out of 'dualism,' the cosmic fight of good against evil. Going back to even Zoroaster, the so-called Persian inventor of the doctrine, time and time again the theory has been proved false, if for no other reason it is impractical. It is doubtful Zoroaster himself ever held such a doctrine, dualism was never the key ingredient to second century Gnosticism. In fact, dualism in some form or another is a necessary ingredient to almost every philosophy. If not, how would Man ever distinguish himself from anything else?

Neither did the ancient Egyptians have such system a dualistic sense of truth. To them truth was simple, it was whatever kept their society running smoothly. In essence truth (*Maat*) was 'don't make waves.' They envisioned the afterlife as a frozen stability, a stasis, a sort of frozen permanence from which the blessed could watch the day-to-day life of their offspring. Truth was to live in emulation of this. The change of everyday life was seen as an imperfection. To be balanced in one's life was as close as you could come in the real world. This was represented by the balance scale and the weighing of one's heart.

This is why the Egyptian burial chambers were filled with static possessions of one's prior life. In the afterlife one could contemplate all that he had and lived, perhaps fleeing as a bird now and then to check on your relatives. To them right and wrong was a product of change. As perfection was a change-less permanence, eternity was a frozen motionless existence. Not having a well-thought out system of reason, balance is what served their society best.

"The conception of Maat expresses the Egyptian belief that the universe is changeless and that all apparent opposites must, therefore, hold each other in equilibrium. Such a belief has definite consequences in the field of moral philosophy. It puts a premium on whatever exists with a semblance of permanence. It excludes ideals of progress, utopias of any kind, revolutions, or any other radical changes in existing conditions. It allows a man "to strive after every excellence until there be no fault in his nature," but that implies, as we have seen, harmony with the established order, the latter not taken in any vague and general way but quite specifically as that which exists with seeming permanence. In this way the belief in a static universe enhances, for instance, the significance of established authority; hence correct behavior towards one's superiors possessed for the Egyptians a significance which we may circumscribe, but which we cannot comprehend."[22]

— HENRI FRANKFORT

This history of Gnosticism is visibly corrupt on every level. Even their Egyptian ideal has been misrepresented. The core of Idealism, progressivism, was not an ideal the ancient Egyptian could ever conceive. This means that Modernism was never 'modern,' it was always a reversion to the barbaric pre-Socratic society.

Few if any common people have the time and resources to challenge what the academics teach. It is Hermeticism that became their idea of 'science.' It was designed from the beginning to support an elitist Arian mythology, a totalitarian system of thought itself. Yet, it would be the pipelines established by Napoleon that would feed the twentieth century corruption of Christian thought.

---

1. Le Bon, Gustave. *The Crowd: a study of the popular mind by Gustave Le Bon.*(Psychologie des Foules) 1895
2. Unknown author
3. Rousseau, Jean-Jacques. *Emile, or On Education* (*Émile, ou De l'éducation*) 1762 English, D.C. Heath & Co. 1888
4. Rousseau, Jean-Jacques. 'The Social Contract,' *A Discourse on the Moral Effects of the Arts and Sciences* (*Discours sur les sciences et les arts*). 1750 — p.140
5. It was modeled after the old Persian calendar, weeks having ten days, months thirty. However, in a sort of irony, the Persian based clock of 60 minutes to the hour, twelve hours for both night and day, was replaced with a decimal based clock. It was all a precursor to our metric system.
6. Strathern, Paul. *Napoleon in Egypt*, (New York: Bantam Books, 2008) p.6
7. Strathern, Paul. *Napoleon in Egypt*, Bantam Books, New York. 2008
8. Spieth, Darius. *Napoleon's Sorcerers: The Sophisians*, University of Delaware Press, 2007
9. Spieth, Darius. *Napoleon's Sorcerers: The Sophisians*, University of Delaware Press, 2007 — p.74
10. Enfield, *The History of Philosophy*, p.116
11. Buchwald, Jed Z., and Diane Greco Josefowicz. *The riddle of the Rosetta: how an English polymath and a French polyglot discovered the meaning of Egyptian hieroglyphs.* Princeton University Press, 2020.
12. Buchwald, Jed Z., and Diane Greco Josefowicz. *The riddle of the Rosetta: how an English polymath and a French polyglot discovered the meaning of Egyptian hieroglyphs.* Princeton University Press, 2020.
13. Buchwald & Josefowicz, *The Zodiac of Paris: How an Improbable Controversy over an Ancient Egyptian Artifact Provoked a Modern Debate between Religion and Science*, Princeton University Press, 2010
14. Le Bon, Gustave. *The Crowd: a study of the popular mind by Gustave Le Bon.*(Psychologie des Foules) 1895
15. Autran, Charles. "Bibliothèque égyptologique. Tome XXXI. Lettres et journaux de Champollion recueillis et annotés par H. Hartleben.—Tome deuxième. Lettres et journaux écrits pendant le voyage en Egypte. Paris-Leroux 1909." *Sphinx: revue critique embrassant le domaine entier de l'égyptologie* 14, no. 1 (1910) — Ombos, le 14 février, à 2 heures. p.225
16. Autran, Charles. "Bibliothèque égyptologique. Tome XXXI. Lettres et journaux de Champollion recueillis et annotés par H. Hartleben.—Tome deuxième. Lettres et journaux écrits pendant le voyage en Egypte. Paris-Leroux 1909." *Sphinx: revue critique embrassant le domaine entier de l'égyptologie* 14, no. 1 1910, p.194
17. Champollion, Jean François 'the Young.' *Egyptian Pantheon, collection of mythological characters from ancient Egypt*, (Pantheon Egyptien. collection des personnages mythologiques de l'ancienne égypte, d'après les monuments avec un texte explicatif par M. J, F. Champollion le Jeune, et les figures d'apres les dessins de M. L, J. J. Dubois) figures after the drawings of M. L, J. J. Dubois
18. Champollion, Jean François 'the Young.' *Egyptian Pantheon, collection of mythological characters from ancient Egypt*, (Pantheon Egyptien. collection des personnages mythologiques de l'ancienne égypte, d'après les monuments avec un texte explicatif par M. J,

F. Champollion le Jeune, et les figures d'apres les dessins de M. L, J. J. Dubois) figures after the drawings of M. L, J. J. Dubois

19. *Manetho*: *History of Egypt*, W. G. Waddell trans, Harvard University Press, p.ix
20. *Manetho*: *History of Egypt*, W. G. Waddell trans, Harvard University Press, p. xxvii
21. Faulkner, Raymond, Goelet, Ogden, Andrews, Carol. *The Egyptian Book of the Dead: The Book of Going Forth by Day the Complete Papyrus of Ani*, Spell 125A
22. Frankfort, Henri. *Ancient Egyptian Religion*, Columbia University Press, New York 1948

CHAPTER EIGHTEEN

THE STORY OF A GREAT CONSPIRACY

THE DREYFUS AFFAIR REVISITED

"A short time ago there came into my hands an English novel of Catholic origin, recommended by the Bishop of London, with the title *When It Was Dark*. It gave a clever and, as it seems to me, a convincing picture of such a possibility and its consequences. The novel, which is supposed to relate to the present day, tells how a conspiracy of enemies of the figure of Christ and of the Christian faith succeed in arranging for a sepulchre to be discovered in Jerusalem. In this sepulchre is an inscription, in which Joseph of Arimathaea confesses that for reasons of piety he secretly removed the body of Christ from its grave on the third day after its entombment and buried it in this spot. The resurrection of Christ and his divine nature are by this means disposed of, and the result of this archaeological discovery is a convulsion in European civilisation and an extraordinary increase in all crimes and acts of violence, which only ceases when the forgers' plot has been revealed."[1]

— SIGMOND FREUD

A FORGER'S PLOT REVEALED

Ostensibly the *Dreyfus Affair* (1894—1906) was about a young Jewish French military officer, Alfred Dreyfus, who was 'set-up' by a Catholic superior officer, Charles Marie Ferdinand Walsin Esterhazy. The incident began when a slip of paper (*bordereau*) containing French military secrets was discovered in the waste basket of a German military attaché. Found by a French spy acting as a cleaning lady, subsequent investigations determined the author was Dreyfus. His supporters, called *Dreyfusards,* insisted he was innocent and that it was a case of antisemitic entrapment designed to humiliate French Jews, orchestrated by Esterhazy. The event triggered an international outcry, many later believing it was the first step towards the Holocaust. Dreyfus was found guilty, court-martialed, and exiled for years to a remote 'devil's' island, only later to be returned and eventually exonerated. Most historians agree it was a trap.

But why entrap Dreyfus? By most accounts he was a loyal, dedicated officer. There were also numerous other Jews in the French military who never made such claims. If being Jewish was unremarkable, what singled Dreyfus out? The 'affair' had international implications, too, far beyond what could be explained by a simple human rights affair. Esterhazy, initially denying accusations, eventually admitted that it was a set-up, yet, also insisted he acted nobly under orders in the service of France. He claimed that one day he would tell the real story, yet later claimed if he did he would be killed. His later autobiography said little that justified his claim.

I have done an immense amount of research on this and am convinced there are underlying layers to this story. Let me assure the reader, the conventional surface story is correct, Dreyfus was set-up. But, there is an underlying story that has never been told. I believe the affair did purposely distract from that story, it was a crucial episode in the creation of the modern Church.

In reality the late nineteenth century '*Affaire*' was much more. It was a continuation of a coup begun by Napoleon, to undermine the French monarchy and Catholic French state. Part of the purpose was to use the controversy to further the separation between the Catholic Church and French Republican State. By laicizing the government, it would be a step towards Socialism. To do this would mean going up against the Catholic Church which was still linked to the European monarchies. This itself is easy to prove, however I think there is more.

To establish socialism the Republicans would have to prevent the re-establishment of the French Catholic monarchy. An element of this plan was to exploit newly found Gnostic documents in an effort to discredit the Catholic Church and its theology, thus losing the sympathies of the French people. The process began here set stage for the future collapse of the Catholic Church at Vatican II when the same documents re-emerged. Not contesting their authenticity, the Church was forced to tacitly incorporate them.

There is a remarkable set of coincidences that cannot be explained by the conventional story. Imagine, if you will, you are Dreyfus. You face a long exile to a place one notch up from hell. Who do you want on your legal team as fellow *Dreyfusards*? How would you go about impressing the court of your innocence, dedication, and that you had no interest in affairs other than your assigned 'military' duty? Certainly you would want a good lawyer. Perhaps also a financier. But would you want several people that were out to prove Christianity was a fraud? Would you want several radical politicians interested in toppling the present political balance, people that held the former monarchy in contempt? More than one person was a Biblical archaeologist or had connections to the authentication or sale in ancient artifacts. Several were prominent atheists and Freemasons.

MODERN FREEMASONRY, like the Unitarians, is the inheritor of the faith of Newton, the Arians. The goal of both was to promote the unitarian 'one God' common to all religions. Unlike the Royal Society who were using reductionism to erode faith in reality, French Freemasonry could use Egyptian mysticism and ritualizations to intrigue the mind. What was once a means for Cromwell's partisans to propagate political theories, became a stealthy *Sophesian* means of secretly spreading hermetic mysticism. It also provided a conduit for secretly getting documents out of Egypt to European museums and Gnostic libraries. This fit the needs of emerging French republicans intent on preventing the return of the monarchy. Like Napoleon before, discrediting the Church meant gaining power.[2]

The very nature of a secret society means that it is not possible to access all the information one would like, however a vast amount of evidence is not hidden at all. What prevents the average person from seeing through the muddle is the outrageousness of the affair. Its claims of setting the stage for the Holocaust prevents most from asking obvious questions, and making obvious connections. Much of it can be easily looked up with the proper roadmap. In fact, the main evidence was a bestselling book disguised as fiction, although we find modern version of that book itself censored.

The Dreyfus Affair is crucial in our understanding of history. Most today regard it as either inconsequential or as a revealing display of antisemitism, but nothing more. Yet, in its day the Affair gave pause to most every government on earth, it consistently made the headlines capturing the attention of almost everyone.

This, too, makes one question the conventional story. If we were to remove the Affair itself from the headlines, and just concentrate on underlying coincidences, another story emerges. We find a curious conjunction of notorious parties not explained by the mere conviction to Dreyfus' innocence. We see a meeting point between a party bent on delegitimizing Christianity, and socialist politicians hungry for power who would like nothing better than delegitimizing the Catholic Monarchy. The Affair provided the necessary cover for the French Freemasons, the inheritors of the *Sophesian* past, to prevent the return of the Catholic monarchy leveraged on 'evidence' that the traditional Bible was deficient, and that the Traditions of the Church were corrupt. Behind this was the planned reveal of the secret Gnostic texts, the most important being the *Apocryphon of John*.

I assure the reader that I am not wrong in this, but in order to convince you we will take a somewhat tedious look at all the evidence. This will require a rather serpentine (sic) path.

To be entirely clear about what I intend to show I will state what I believe to be true at the outset. There are literally hundreds of books about 'the Affair', but none provide a satisfactory explanation. My explanation will be based upon a lesser known account testified by freelance Paris correspondent Chris Healy in his book *Confessions of a Journalist* (1904) who interviewed the important parties involved immediately after the Affair. I will fill in other documentable facts. Again, it is critical to understand this event. It amounts to this:

The predominantly Catholic General Staff of the French military were attempting a *coup d'etate* to re-install the Catholic French monarchy under Henri d'Orléans. Supplanted by the French Revolution, Catholic France had been controlled since by factions, mainly the remains of Napoleon Bonaparte's Empire and the French Republicans. This was all part of a broader conspiracy set in motion by Napoleon to spread his own invented religion, and undermine the Catholic state. A critical part of this plan was the dissolution of the Italian Papal States, leading to the forming of the Italian Republic.

With the collapse of its power and the Vatican itself under threat of being seized, the Pope fled to France for safety. France would have provided a suitable refuge for the Catholic Church, Avignon having once been the French Vatican when the anti-popes ruled, the former center of the Church in the fourteenth century. All the buildings and infrastructure still existed then as they do to this day. Transferring power would have been possible if the circumstances allowed. Partially standing in the way of re-constituting Catholic France was that Avignon had a very large Jewish population, a controversy could tip the scales.

Chris Healy records the true motive behind the Affair:

"At one time the General [military] Staff had the idea of pushing his claims to the French throne. In this they were secretly upheld by the great religious Orders, who had more to gain from a son of St. Louis than from a Republic or a Bonaparte. Philippe d'Orléans, the present claimant to the French crown, had lost all support in France by his wild debauchery in earlier days and by his plentiful lack of wit. On the other side was his cousin, Henri d'Orléans, a man of marked intellectuality and daring initiative, who from the beginning of his public career had vividly appealed to the popular imagination as no son of St. Louis had done since the days when young Égalite had fought with the Republican armies under Dumouriez against Brunswick and other invaders of his country. His exploits as an explorer had gained him the gold medal of the French Geographical Society, the highest reward of a cold, learned body of men, whose deliberations were unruffled by any political breeze. His success in Abyssinia recalled the fabulous exploits of his ancestor, Prince Jean de Bourbon, who is said to have penetrated the fastnesses of Ethiopia and Shoa long before Henri Quatre had planted his standard at the Louvre. If he had been the representative of the elder branch of the Bourbons, he would have been a dangerous opponent for supreme power in the Republic. As it was, Prince Henri was admired by hosts of Frenchmen to whom Philippe d'Orléans was anathema, and he was admitted to the secret councils of the Inner Cabinet, who ruled the War Office... **It was a grave infraction of military regulations for these high military chiefs to admit a pékin (a civilian) to their councils; but when the pékin was no less a person than a Prince of the dispossessed royal house of France, the infraction became treason to the Republic.**"[3]

— CHRIS HEALY, JOURNALIST

In other words, to proceed with the re-installation of the monarchy would be to face the charge of treason. But how was the plot uncovered? It was Dreyfus working as a spy himself. The legitimate remains of the Catholic monarchy were meeting with the French military. It was partially this that Esterhazy could not reveal.

The Republicans were essentially a consortium comprised largely of Freemasons, Christian agnostics, and non-practicing Jews. Their desire was to entirely laicize the French government completely separating the Catholic Church from the French State, the model for future 'free' separations of Church and State. These forces combined with elements of the supporting press is what Esterhazy called the '*Syndicate*'. They also formed the basis of

Dreyfus' legal team. Many, if not most, ascribed to the emerging 'Christ is a myth' ideology instigated by Ernest Renan.

Dreyfus was not a simple artillery officer as most accounts record. Like Esterhazy, he was a member of the French Intelligence Service, called the *Second Bureau,* the French version of the CIA. Dreyfus himself testifies of this in his own autobiography *Five Years of My Life*:

> "During my engagement I prepared myself for the *École Superieure de Guerre* [War School for Staff Officers], where I was received the 20th of April, 1890; the next day, April 21, I was married. I left the École Superieure de Guerre in 1892 with the degree "very good," and the brevet of Staff Officer. My rank number on leaving the École entitled me to be detailed as stagiaire [probationer] on the General Staff of the army. I took service in the *Second Bureau* of the General Staff on the 1st of January, 1893."[4]

— ALFRED DREYFUS

While Esterhazy's sympathies were with the Catholics, Dreyfus' were with the Republicans. This put them at cross purposes. It also means Dreyfus would have to be frozen so that he could not reveal his espionage before the coup was complete.

Esterhazy, a superior intelligence officer, had been trained in the *amorceur* system, a technique of planting idiosyncratic evidence on suspects so that potential spies could be tracked and outed. "Then there is the *amorceur* system — creating pretended spies, whose business is to sell false information, and endeavour to find out the real spies who are selling the military secrets of the country."[5] Therefore, under orders, Esterhazy would have been asked to investigate someone in his own circle, Dreyfus.

Dreyfus was a lower senior officer, but had great aspirations to attaining high rank if not becoming overall General of the Military. This would not even be thinkable if there were a real climate of anti-semitism. While most such officers in his position confined themselves to their assigned tasks, Dreyfus' aspirations encouraged him to reach beyond his authority. In this, Dreyfus happened upon the aforementioned coup. This put Dreyfus' and Esterhazy's loyalties at odds, each considering the other as a potential traitor. Exposing Dreyfus could lead to exposing the Republican network of information dissemination, thus allowing the coup to move forward.

The placing of the *Bordereau* in the German Embassy was just this. While it was *discovered* by Esterhazy and perhaps planted by him, the note itself has been claimed to be written by Dreyfus and Emile Zola, a bizarre way of checkmating Dreyfus. By claiming antisemitism, the Syndicate turned a liability into an asset, a tremendous opportunity to create a fiasco, distracting from their true motives of crippling the Church and exposing the coup.

None of this would be possible if the Syndicate didn't have a pipeline for transporting Egyptian artifacts to Europe. Consider this: you have a pre-established information conduit, created and inspired by Napoleon's ideologies. It is a proven means for transferring artifacts from the *French Archaeological Mission* in Egypt to French academic institutions such as the *National Museum*. From there you could disseminate them throughout Europe, such as Berlin. To do this you would need not only an archaeologist in a position of authority at the French National Museum, but also someone with great financial resources, *and* someone to coordinate with the Dreyfus Affair—all this they had in one person, Salomon Reinach.

While Healy doesn't say so, these Republicans, with numerous Masonic connections, found themselves in an opportune moment to discredit the Catholics and win the sympathies of the average person. They could do this by both proving that Jesus was a phoney, and proving the Catholics were antisemitic. Yet, this oddly aligned with the prophet of their cult, Ernest Renan, who regarded Christ's divinity as phoney, *and* was an authentic antisemitic. The Syndicate would have to untangle this mess and turn their liabilities against their enemies.

I must emphasize this: the very document in question here is the secret *Apocryphon of John*, the very essence of heresy. It was this that would have been regarded as precious, as essential to the cause of the Syndicate and the future of atheism. They had strong forces on their side and they were determined not to fail… and those sympathetic to their cause had the document.

WHEN IT WAS DARK…

The famous author Oscar Wilde found himself in the middle of all this. As he was in communication with both sides he found himself in a position to settle the matter. In the process, I believe he threatened to out them all (via Zola's writing), thus forcing them into a sort of 'plea deal.' Healy specifically says that Wilde was one of the few who knew everything, and was working both sides.

I believe the deal was essentially this: Esterhazy admits to planting the *Bordereau* in such a way that he could later retract. This would allow Dreyfus to be freed and re-tried in exchange for silence on the matter of treason. The retraction would allow Esterhazy to save face, but it also meant his side of the story could never be told. It would also risk him being sentenced to jail himself. The second trial against Dreyfus would be just for show, Esterhazy's testimonies would be irrelevant.

On the other side, the threat against the Church by the exposing of the Gnostic documents would be tabled for a more opportune time. This would be in trade for the Monarchy relinquishing their claims to power.

Whether Esterhazy entirely had knowledge of this deal I doubt. I do believe, however, he had a side deal with Wilde. This all would have went very smooth except Esterhazy sensed he was being set up. As protection for his life he threatened to reveal all. The deal would smuggle him to England and given the opportunity to publish his side of the story through Wilde's publisher, Leonard Smithers or some other associate. Once in England, Esterhazy realized that to publish his tell-all would put his life back in danger, he was checkmated.

I know this all sounds fantastic, but let's examine the evidence.

Just after the Dreyfus Affair the bestselling novel *When It Was Dark: The Story of a Great Conspiracy* (1903) was written by Cyril Ranger-Gull under the pseudonym, Guy Thorne. The book was a fiction about how a secret 'syndicate' of *Jewish financiers* and *agnostic archaeological forgers* could falsify evidence disproving Christ's divinity. The title is derived from the phrase in the Gospel of John, 20:1, "when it was yet dark," when Mary Magdalene discovers the empty tomb. It was published by Greening & Co. of London, publishers of Washington Irving, Lord Alfred Nelson, the Scarlet Pimpernel, *books about Oscar Wilde,* and other notables (this fact is itself hidden from most accounts). It is a clear move upwards from Gull's past association with Leonard Smithers, a publisher of pornography. The book is out of character with Gull's past efforts which were primarily cheap spy novels. The fact that Gull could produce a best-seller makes one wonder if Wilde had his hand in that, too.

When It Was Dark: the Story of a Great Conspiracy is a story where a Jewish financier, an adherent to the 'Christ is a myth theory,' aligns himself with an atheist biblical scholar/archeologist to discovers evidence that Christ is a myth. They find a burial tomb with an inscription stating that Joseph of Arimathea had hid the body there, near Jerusalem. This discovery fractures the moral state of the world plunging it into anarchy, that is until the evidence is proved a hoax.

The book becomes the *Da Vinci Code* of its era. Even the Bishop of London, Rt. Hon., Dr. Arthur Winnington-Ingram, heralds the book as one of the most important books ever written in a sermon he gives at Westminster Abbey. This is echoed by the Bishop of Exeter, the Dean of Durham, Field Marshall Montgomery, and others. Many later compare the story to the Piltdown Man hoax, the faking of an ancient pre-historic man's remains, possibly by Fr. Teilhard de Chardin.[6]

The curious thing is that Thorne's book is prefaced with a photograph of a real burial stone on which the hoax is supposedly based. This 'stunt' would make sense today when best sellers can recoup the money in guaranteed sales, but before *When It Was Dark* no other book had sold enough to be considered a best seller. No such "bomb shell" sales were heard of. Authors back then barely made enough money to survive, much less the extravagance and work of creating a fake burial stone. Even with the popularity of the book, Gull/Thorne died near broke.

The fake burial monument from the tomb of Christ depicted in *When It Was Dark (public domain)*

So, why would Thorne go through the trouble of creating a fake burial monument, photograph it, and then stick it in the front of his book? Remember, this was over one hundred years ago, at a time when faking such a photograph would have been easily detected. Somebody put a lot of effort into a person of Gull's reputation.

At the time, many reading *When It Was Dark* actually considered the photograph authentic. It convinced many that the story was a fictionalization of a real story. Therefore, assuming that the book was a tell-all is not unique. Many reputable people thought the same. Granting this, what was the most likely event? How would Gull obtain this secret knowledge? Does he know of a real plot to undermine Christianity? Actual tangible evidence? Did he know that real archaeologists were being financed by agnostic Jewish financiers, and he wanted to prepare the public so they would look upon it with suspicion?

Partial evidence is Zola himself, the very person who triggered the 'deal.' Zola was an untalented author who regularly wrote cheesy newspaper articles typically despised by the French, but popular in England. The whole crisis was busted open when he published an article called '*J'accuse*' — however, Healy says he didn't have the talent to write it nor the credibility. This means it had to have been essentially written by Oscar Wilde, and intended for a British audience. It was Guy Thorne, who admits in his biography of Oscar Wilde, that he was in constant contact with Wilde at the time of the *Affaire*. Further, *it was Esterhazy who stayed at Thorne's house at the time of his writing When It Was Dark!*

"It was to the chambers in the Strand that I shared with a friend that Major Esterhazy came one night hurriedly and in secret, when he fled from Paris during the last trial of Dreyfus. All Europe was asking for his whereabouts, and only myself, my stable companion ... knew the truth. I can see him now sitting in our book-lined room with haunted hawk-like eyes, the whiskers and moustache (shaven for his flight) sprouting in a grey stubble upon his face while he spoke in low nervous tones which cut curiously into the deep bourdon note of the Strand as it mounted to our windows:"[7]

— GUY THORNE, AUTHOR OF *WHEN IT WAS DARK*

If we assume that it took Esterhazy six months or so to get situated in England, and we know it takes at least a year to typeset and publish a book if not longer, and it is also known Thorne was writing at least one other book at the time, then this leaves a window of about two years or so for Thorne and Esterhazy to collaborate. No one can honestly hold that they did not discuss the Affair. This would put Esterhazy right where he would need to be pass the story to Thorne.

Like others in Thorne's circle of friends, all had dubious careers before Dreyfus. Many had documented connections to the Affair, some speculating that it was the group of Smithers who coordinated Esterhazy's escape.[8] Further, there seems to be an epiphany amongst the group of Smithers about this time, some becoming Catholic. Gull himself rose to a prominence he didn't have before. He even wrote a book professing his commitment to the Christian faith. Is this not incredible?

Émile Zola, on January 13, 1898, published his article *J'Accuse* which began turning public sympathies towards Dreyfus. Later that year, on September 1, Esterhazy fled from France, via Brussels, to England. He then, through interviews with Rachel Beer, confessed to being the culprit involved in setting up Dreyfus, which she published in an article September. By 1903 *When It Was Dark* was in the booksellers, the discovery of the *Apocryphon of John* was being kept secret, Salomon Reinach was publishing books intimating its discovery. Yet, Rachel Beer's lawyer later admits in a letter to the French court that the she had no authority to publish the article that led to Esterhazy's conviction, supplying the necessary alibi.

If you follow the money back from Dreyfus, you will find the Jewish Reinach family. They were financiers, art collectors, and archaeologists. They also were leading the 'Christ was a myth' movement in France. Salomon Reinach was an archaeologist, considered an expert in authenticating artifacts, and had published several books on the history of art, largely photographs and diagrams of ancient archeological finds. A lot of the pictures in his book show burial monuments and figures. His brother Joseph was a leading Freemason and also an expert in authenticating ancient artifacts. The two brothers also considered themselves expert translators of ancient codices. They also got involved in a second 'affair' when they controversially authenticated the Glozel archaeological find, something most authorities thought was a fraud.

The Reinachs befriended Dreyfus who was related through marriage. Salomon was also Dreyfus' friend and a primary financial supporter of his defense. At that time the French progressive Republicans saw themselves as either atheists or deists. Therefore non-practicing Jews considered Republicans as allies sharing similar beliefs, that the Church was the real enemy of the people. It is demonstrable that Salomon Reinach had knowledge of the recently discovered finds in Egypt, knowledge of the coup, Freemasonic connections, and was within the high ranks of French National Museum. He is also documented contesting the authenticity of 1 John 5:7. These coincidences give him the precise motive and opportunity.

FRANCE IN NINETEENTH CENTURY EUROPE

"The bold forgeries of the Church, and its bogus Trinity Doctrine, continue. One of these forgeries [1 John 5:7-8] was subjected to interpolation of a later date... If these two verses were Authentic, they would be an affirmation of the Doctrine of the Trinity, at a time when the Gospels, and Acts, and St. Paul

ignore it. It was first pointed out in 1516 that these verses were an interpola-
tion, for they do not appear in the best manuscripts down to the 15th century.
The Roman Church refused to bow to the evidence... The Congregation of the
Index, on January 13, 1897, with the approbation of Pope Leo XIII, forbade
any question of the authenticity of the text relating to the 'Three Heavenly
Witnesses.'"[9]

— SALOMON REINACH, *ORPHEUS*

Is it not interesting that while many if not most Christians will not admit to
our cause, the probable ring-leader of all this does? The friction between
Christian and Jewish relations goes back to the Passion of Christ, the controversy is two thousand years old. Its volatility means that it is rarely brought up
anymore, it is reason enough to disguise 'affairs'. Yet, without this understanding nothing about the Dreyfus Affair nor Vatican II will make sense. The
two affairs are connected.

Once a year, just before Easter, Christians commemorate the Crucifixion
of Christ. In the Good Friday liturgy exists several 'markers' that make the
story unique. Included in these markers are things like, a critical feast just
before Passover, salvation hanging in the balance, three simultaneous crucifix-
ions, the parading and mocking of the main victim through the streets, a twist
in fate where the innocent is condemned and the condemned found innocent,
the casting of lots, blood money, and others. The problem is many of these
very same markers are recorded in the original Book of Esther as documented
by Josephus, particularly in the execution of Haman. There is also an
unspoken Jewish tradition of equating Haman with Christ in Purim sermons.
The problem is both occurrences are considered singular, only once occurring
events. Before the Crucifixion of Jesus, there are no other documented cases
of anyone being killed on a Cross.

It would not take too much to see that these two stories were perhaps
different versions of the same event told from opposite points of view. And
this is exactly what anthropologist Sir James George Frazer (*The Golden
Bough*) did. It would mean that the Book of Esther, thought to be written
around 400 BC (not considered canonical in Judaism but considered canonical
by Christians) was of the wrong date, or at least had been tampered with.
Christians couldn't admit to it because it meant their Bibles had an error. Jews
could not admit to it for it would put them in the trap set by Frazer, that they
had been ritually murdering people for centuries. Frazer saw this as a way of
not only discrediting Christianity, but accusing Judaism of being a continua-

tion of an ancient human sacrificial cult, something there was no evidence of. This is important because it would be exactly this that would be laid at the feet of the Pope prior to Vatican II by the once Dreyfusard, Jules Isaac.

Explaining these coincidences is problematic. Often at the very same time Jews celebrated Purim where the book of Esther is acted out, Christian's celebrated Good Friday when the Crucifixion of Christ was acted out. The result is that Christians historically often believed that the Jews were mocking their holiest of days. Conversely, Jews could point to the Christian Good Friday liturgy and claim the same. Few wanted to face the fact that both could be alternate versions of the same event. If so, the Book of Esther could be legitimately claimed as a 'Fifth Testimony.'

The result of this was old prejudices emerged, such as the beliefs that Jews were 'Christ Killers,' and that Jews were using Christian blood as a *pharmakon* in their Purim cookies. On the other hand, Jews could point to the barbaric practices of the Spanish Inquisition. Needless to say, European tensions were rising at the time of Dreyfus, misconceptions would inevitably lead to Nazi Germany.

What most accounts won't tell you is that the Dreyfus Affair had its roots in a prior 'affair,' called the Tisza-Eszlár affair (1882). An account was published by Emil Reich in a journal called The *Nineteenth Century*, volume 40:

"Of the numerous trials to that effect in recent times, the most gigantic was that of the alleged murder of Esther Solymossy by the Jews of Tisza-Eszlár, a village in Central Hungary, in 1881. In that ghastly case the young son of the Jewish butcher of the village declared before the judge, and in the presence of his father, that he had seen through the keyhole a number of other Jews, were slaughtering Esther, and letting her blood run into a receptacle used for religious rites. The trial lasted for nearly two years, and kept all Hungary, nay Europe, in a state of ever-growing intense excitement. The Jews were acquitted in all the three instances permitted by Hungarian law; but I must add, and from personal knowledge too, that the number of persons other than Jews believing in the innocence of the Tisza-Eszlár Jews was, and probably still is, exceedingly small, although the innocence of the Jews was established beyond the shadow of a doubt...."[10]

Accused of murdering and beheading Solymossy, and later ditching her body in a river, the suspect, a Rabbi, was later declared innocent when it was determined that the body was somebody else's. The Solymossy trial lasted years. There were crowd inspired protests and demonstrations all through Europe.

Much of Christian Europe was not convinced of the accused's innocence, to them it was the re-emergence of the Blood Libel. Similar to the Dreyfus affair, it was believed the verdict had been boughten by the Jewish banking industry. This led to antisemitic politician Gysl Istoczy starting a campaign to evict the Jews from Europe. It was he who started the National Antisemitic Party, the forerunner of the Nazi Party.

While this all seems incredible, there is more. Jules Isaac, the very person who met with two Popes after WWII in an effort to dispel animosities over all this, lived in the very same city as the Dreyfus Affair, Rennes. In his early twenties, the Affair affected Isaac greatly. It was he who later presented his research to Pope John XXIII at Vatican II, that the Catholic Church was teaching contempt of the Jews in its Good Friday liturgies, based upon the above misconceptions. While advocates of Vatican II like presenting this Council as all 'peace and love,' the reality is it hides a seamy core.

Much of this was leveraged as sort of a threat, that Isaac had proof the that the Church had falsified its theology from the beginning... that Christ Himself was a copycat, a mere shadow of the 'Teacher of Righteousness' found in the Qumran Dead Sea Scrolls.

"What is certain, what is universally acknowledged, and what seems, moreover, to imply in the messianic reputation of the departed Teacher, is the fact that for the members of the "New Covenant," the condition of salvation is no less than the faith in the Teacher of Righteousness."[11]

— JULES ISAAC, AT VATICAN II, *THE TEACHING OF CONTEMPT*

And:

"'In John 1:4—5, we read: In him [the Word of God] was life, and the life was the light of men. The light shines in the darkness, and the darkness has not overcome it.' Father Daniélou comments: 'Now this is nothing else but the *leitmotif* of Qumran... The Gospel of John is constructed on the theme of the conflict between light and darkness.'"[12]

— JULES ISAAC, AT VATICAN II, *THE TEACHING OF CONTEMPT*

I believe these contentions could have only had their roots in the 19th century discovery of the secret *Apocryphon of John*. The evidence in the Dead Sea Scrolls simply are too ambiguous without prior evidence. To Isaac, the evidence he presented to the Pope, Christianity was merely an invention of the Gnostic 'Essene" Qumran community, the authors of the Dead Sea Scrolls. These were beliefs held before the Scrolls were discovered, and not sufficiently substantiated by Renan's 'Essenes' theory alone. The motive was to turn the words of St. John against themselves, something not indicated by any 'public' evidence.

Isaac's co-revolutionary and mentor in social Marxism, Charles Péguy stated, "This [Dreyfus] affair finished, we begin the rest of the social revolution."[13] In some ways Péguy could be considered the prototype for the Socialist Church to come. Roughly 60 years from the Dreyfus Affair, Isaac would go to Rome and present his case. At one point Isaac himself indicated that he regarded the capitulations of Vatican II as retribution for the Dreyfus Affair. Could proving that St. John was a Gnostic have been the *leitmotif* of the Dreyfus Affair?

The French Republic gained its credibility from building the Suez Canal. Much of it was funded by the Reinachs who profited greatly. Looking for another similar opportunity, they decided to build the Panama Canal. The Republicans engineered it, the Jewish Reinach family financed it. But, France was no where near up to the task. Their engineering (led by the modernist Eiffel) fell short, their industries could not produce the machinery, their medical system could not handle the resulting malaria of the work force. All this required more and more money to be sunk into the project. Eventually France and the Reinachs had sunk so much into it that they had to abandon the project to the United States.

The result was a huge scandal. It required the common people of France (mostly Catholics) to bail everyone out. Some considered this coalition of Freemasons, Republicans, and Jews as *la colonie étrangère* (the colony of strangers), foreign occupiers of their government.[14] For the selling of one Canal bond alone, the Reinach family pocketed over 6 million francs in 1888.

"The Dreyfus case was begotten by the Panama scandal, and the first persons who made the name of Dreyfus, and Jews in general, a byword and a reproach in France were the Jewish speculators on the Paris Bourse, who robbed the French investor of fifty-five and a half millions sterling, and drove poor Ferdinand de Lesseps, le grand Français, for example, to a dishonourable grave. Consequently, when General Mercier committed the amazing folly of announcing, before any inquiry had been made, that a Jewish officer had betrayed France, there was an echoing roar from the Garonne to the Rhone. 'Of course! Is he not a Jew? To betray is his trade.' The thousands of peasants and small shopkeepers who had lost their whole savings in the Panama swindle classed all Jews alike as a nation which had begun by betraying the Son of God, and had kept their hands in ever since by betraying the sons of men."[15]

— CHRIS HEALY

Similarly, Healy records the condition of the French Catholic Church in the words of M. Huysmans:

"France is a lost country, and there is little hope for it. The priests, politicians, and literary men of to-day are sowing folly at such a speed that we shall want at least two generations to repair their blunders. Look at the clergy! They cannot see that the Faubourg St. Germain is dead as a political force; they don't try to reach the people, because that would interfere with their elegant bavardage in aristocratic salons. If the people are irreligious, it is because the priests do not do their duties as ministers of Christ. They drive the people away from the churches. The workman to-day is brought into contact with the Church on three occasions — baptism, marriage, and deaths— and each time money is demanded from him. Then look at our great Orders! They are great only in name. Where are the great thinkers, orators, world leaders, among the Jesuits, the Dominicans, Franciscans, and Benedictines? *Ils n'existent pas!* That the Church survives their mediocrity and stupidity is to me a standing miracle — a proof of her divinity. There is but one thing which can save the Church and give it new life and vigour: If God in His wisdom would but allow us to be persecuted, then we might restore the ancient grandeur and glory of the Catholic Faith."[16]

The general belief was that the alliance of 'strangers' was purposely exploiting the Canal fiasco to bankrupt the common people. Just before the time of Dreyfus, France had been on the verge of electing the charismatic General Boulanger (General Revenge) as Prime Minister, who would have been sympathetic to the Monarchist faction. The Syndicate then inserted themselves into the arena. It was recorded in *French Freemasonry under the Third Republic.*

"But on January 13, 1898, Zola enters the "affair" by publishing his letter "J'Accuse" in *l'Aurore*, the paper of Clemenceau; Zola accused anti-Semetic officers in the army of having forged the evidence against Dreyfus and claimed that certain anti-Semetic papers used the Dreyfus case for political capital. Zola was tried for libel and forced to leave France, but his statements were supported by **Clemenceau**, by **Brothers Joseph Reinach** and **Yves Guyot**."[17]

"For the Mason, an important result of the Dreyfus affair was the fact that, by drawing together the republicans, it had improved the prospects for the enactment of laic legislation. During and after the crisis the Left organized more effectively to attain power and to push for reforms...In June, 1901, the Committee for Republican Reforms, by calling a congress of the Radical-Socialists, took the first step toward the organization of the Radical-Socialist party."[18]

In other words, Freemasonry was functioning as a spy agency. The leaders in the above quote are precisely the same as claimed by Esterhazy as leaders of the Syndicate. "To those who united with the **Clemenceaus**, the **Reinachs** and the **Yves Guyots** to cover me with insults, for which they were moreover firmly resolved never to give me reason under any pretext..."[19] Guyot was a radical left-wing anti-clerical economist. Likewise, Clemenceau was a left wing journalist and politician. As an anti-clerical he literally invented the radical version of 'separation of Church and State.'

The result was the public began to mock the Church. Anatole (of) France, also a friend of Dreyfus, wrote a book called *Penguin Island*. It is a critique of the Catholic Church likening its parishioners to Penguins who accidentally get baptised and their resulting exploits. The main part of the book is dedicated to Anatole's view of the Dreyfus affair. The book won a Nobel Prize, but is also considered one of the most heretical books ever written, making it to the Catholic Church's index of forbidden books. Just reading it at one time risked getting ex-communicated.

Today, the principal 'villain' is considered to be Esterhazy. A semi-devout Catholic, he later admitted to setting up Dreyfus. At the end of the trial he is smuggled out of France for safe-keeping in England. His intention is to publish the real story, what he calls a "bomb shell," predicting it will sell thousands. Once in England and is given a chance to tell the real story he would be exonerated. Right before he is to leave a co-conspirator of his is assassinated while in prison. Esterhazy then states he is prohibited from telling the real story because he considered it his insurance policy. He apparently reneges on his publishing deal, years later publishing *Les dessous de l'affaire Dreyfus* (*The underside of the Dreyfus Affair*) by a French Publisher. Esterhazy specifically claims the Dreyfus Affair was a setup, and his actions were for an unstated noble cause. It is a rather confusing account, never really gives an explanation, but only testifies that Esterhazy's real story was never allowed to be heard and that he has been treated unfairly. It never attempts to explain any of the above as if he had negotiated his silence. It ends with this:

> "All laws ceased to exist for me. – Arrested in unworthy conditions, with revolting brutality, victim of searches whose sole aim was to take away the documents that were feared to be in my hands, I am finally, after 31 days of arbitrary detention, subject of a dismissal order... I am alone, abandoned by everyone, having for me only the glorious memories of the illustrious soldiers whose name I bear and whose services rendered to the country are forgotten..."[20]

— ESTERHAZY

Yet, a book was published through the associates of Oscar Wilde. It is now known that it was Wilde who 'spilled the beans' with secret information that led to Dreyfus' acquittal, and suspiciously allowed Esterhazy to flee France. Did the Syndicate actually intend to fake the Burial Stone? I doubt it. But I do believe the book was intended to point to the real plot to destroy Christianity. The fake picture of the tomb was a warning pointing to the *Apocryphon of John*.

---

1. Freud, Sigmond. *Group Psychology and the Analysis of the Ego*, James Strachey trans. WW Norton & Company, 1975
2. Watson, J. M. Roberts. *The Mythology of the Secret Societies*, Sribner, 1972
3. Healy, Chris. *Confessions of a Journalist*, Chatto & Windus, 1904
4. Dreyfus, Alfred. *Five Years of My Life*, G. Newnes, 1901. p.2
5. Healy, Chris. *Confessions of a Journalist*, Chatto & Windus, 1904
6. Wilkinson, David '*Guy Thorne*': C. Ranger Gull—Edwardian Tabloid Novelist and His Unseemly Brotherhood, Rivendale Press, 2012, p.194
7. Wilkinson, David. '*Guy Thorne*': C. Ranger Gull—Edwardian Tabloid Novelist and His Unseemly Brotherhood, Rivendale Press, p.116, from, 'The Strand of Twenty Years Ago: Some Personal Reminiscences' in T. P's Weekly, Guy Thorne [C. Ranger Gull] 11 July 1913
8. Maguire, J. Robert. *Ceremonies of Bravery: Oscar Wilde, Carlos Blacker, and the Dreyfus Affair*. Oxford University Press, USA, 2013
9. Reinach, Salomon. Monod, Gabriel, and Alfred Loisy. 'L'«Orpheus» de Ms. Reinach.' *Revue Historique* 102, no. Fasc. 2, 1909, p. 239

10. Knowles, James. The *Nineteenth Century and after*, volume 40, Sampson Low, Marston & Company, London, 1896

11. Isaac, Jules. *The Teaching of Contempt*, Holt, Rinehart and Winston. 1964, p.90 originally published as *L'Enseignement du Mépris,*, Fasquelle Éditeurs. 1962

12. Isaac, Jules. *The Teaching of Contempt*, Holt, Rinehart and Winston. 1964, p.90 originally published as *L'Enseignement du Mépris,*, Fasquelle Éditeurs. 1962

13. Tobias, Norman Cecil. 'Jules Isaac and the Roman Catholic Church advocate for scriptural truth,' 2015, from Jules Isaac, *Expériences de ma vie. Péguy*, Calmann-Lévy, Paris 1960, p.132

14. Tobias, Norman Cecil. 'Jules Isaac and the Roman Catholic Church advocate for scriptural truth,' 2015, from Jules Isaac, *Expériences de ma vie. Péguy*, Calmann-Lévy, Paris 1960, p.36

15. Healy, Chris. *Confessions of a Journalist*, Chatto & Windus, 1904. Chapter XIII, Sidelights on the Dreyfus Affair

16. Healy, Chris. *Confessions of a Journalist*, Chatto & Windus, 1904. p.144

17. Headings, Mildred J. *French Freemasonry under the Third Republic:* The Masons Plan a Laic State, Johns Hopkins Press, 1949, p.131

18. Headings, Mildred J. *French Freemasonry under the Third Republic:* The Masons Plan a Laic State, Johns Hopkins Press, 1949, p.133

19. Esterházy, Marie Charles Ferdinand Walsin. *Les dessous de l'affaire Dreyfus*. Fayard Frères, éditeurs 1898. translated from the French

20. Esterházy, Marie Charles Ferdinand Walsin. *Les dessous de l'affaire Dreyfus*. Fayard Frères, éditeurs 1898. translated from the French

THE SYNDICATE
AS CLAIMED BY ESTERHAZY

Havas Agency — News and Publicity Agency

- World's oldest international news agency with affiliates in London (Reuters) and Berlin (Wolff)
- Still in business, curiously as a both a news and publicity agency, they both report the news and create the news
- Has an odd relationship with French law enforcement in providing information & guiding the arrest of Esterhazy

Mathieu Dreyfus — The First Dreyfusard

- Alfred Dreyfus' older brother and his strongest supporter. Daughter marries son of Joseph Reinach
- Tries to make a deal with the arresting officer Party de Clam. Failing, he contacts Joseph Reinach for support
- Immediately gets in league with anarchist/socialist Bernard Lazare & naturalist Émile Zola

Bernard Lazare — The Second Dreyfusard, Zionist

- Non-practicing Jew, although an atheist he supported the creation of a Jewish state

- First to create the anti-Semitism narrative for the Dreyfus Affair with an article published just before Dreyfus' arrest
- A fan of the Catholic/Modernist Louis Duchesne & his History of the Church. His book is on the Index of banned books, contributed to Pius X writing the encyclical *Against the Modernists*

Joseph Reinach — Financier, Archaeologist, Freemason

- Jewish Brother of archaeologist Salomon Reinach. Also principal sponsor and defender of Alfred Dreyfus.
- Passionately opposed to the Catholic General Boulanger who was vying to re-take the French government
- Intricately connected to the Panama Canal scandal where the failure of French financiers were bailed out by a tax put on largely Catholic middle-class

Salomon Reinach — Agnostic, Archaeologist, Museum Curator

- Jewish Curator of the National Museum. Author of numerous books art and religious, the main theme being that religion (particularly Christianity) is mythology. The brothers had similar interests as archaeologist/Freemason—what one knew, so did the others.
- Had connections throughout Europe and the Middle East whereby he not only surveyed ancient treasure, but also was a dealer. Had early knowledge of recently discovered Gnostic Christian writings.
- A disciple of Ernest Renan. It was Renan's Christ-myth theory that inspired the search for the 5th gospel and the Modernist search for lost Gnostic texts in the Middle East which curiously began around the time of 'Dreyfus'.

Théodore Reinach — Archaeologist, Lawyer, Polymath

- Jewish Brother of Salomon and Joseph. He shared in their interests.
- Like Salomon wrote numerous books on ancient artifacts and translations.
- An expert on Jewish history, he translated Flavius' History of the Jews

Mme. Milescamp — Antiquities Dealer

- Both traded in antiquities and ran a marriage agency. May have been a spy.
- Documented by Esterhazy as who most believed to be the true cause behind the Dreyfus Affair.
- Her name came up at the actual Dreyfus trial where it was mentioned that she somehow was at the center of a misplaced documents scandal.

Rachel (Sassoon) Beer — Journalist and Newspaper Editor

- Actually of Persian-Jewish decent by way of India. Esterhazy suspected she might be the ring leader of the Syndicate.
- As editor-in-chief of the *Observer*, she is credited with publishing Esterhazy's admission of guilt It is upon the Esterhazy admission that all current stories of the Affair rest.
- At trial documented evidence is produced by Esterhazy that she and Rowland Strong fabricated the confession — this is admitted to in her biography

Georges Clemenceau — Radical Left Wing Republican, Radical Atheist

- Founder of the newspaper *Justice*, he wrote for l'*Aurore* during Dreyfus as a strong defender, later publishing a book on the matter.
- 'Fiercely atheist' he is anti-Judeo-Christian and anti-clerical considering himself heir to the French Revolutionists, he fights for the separation of Church and State.
- Once said openly that he was a Buddhist. He was against the idea of Catholic justice. He believed the Dreyfus Affair did more harm to France than the Revolution.

Sébastien Fauré — Anti-Church Anarchist Activist

- As a leader of the libertarian movement he brought them in on the side of Dreyfus
- Founding the newspaper l'*Libertaire* and being anti-Church, judiciary, and military he was the first of the anarchists to side with Dreyfus.

- He was convicted more than once of pedophilia, a fact proven in 2018

Yves Guyot — Radical Left Wing Republican, Freemason

- Anti-clerical he wrote for newspaper, the *Radical* & the *Lantern* in support of leftist reform. A 'scientific materialist.'
- Considered General Boulanger a dictator. Like Clemenceau strongly advocated the separation of Church and State.
- He believed the Dreyfus Affair was galvanizing the right wing. Being a product of Jesuit theology, he considered the Affair a Jesuit plot.

Oscar Wilde — Playwright, Anglo-Catholic Agnostic

- An odd sort of mysterious connection to the Affair, named by Esterhazy as part of the Syndicate. A critical go-between connecting to the Gang of Smithers publications.
- He saw himself as apostle to the faithless, those who 'cannot believe'. Like the Reinach's he was a disciple of Renan who is assumed to be agnostic, but in reality is based on his having claimed to have seen the fifth 'Gnostic' gospel
- Like, Faure, was convicted and jailed for sexual deviancy. He later fled to France and became involved in Esterhazy's final escape to England.

Lord Alfred Douglas — Wilde's Lover

- Homosexual lover of Oscar Wilde
- Emblematic and typical of the outer associates of the syndicate.
- Has an 'epiphany' around 1903, the publishing date of Guy Thorne's *When it was Dark: The Story of a Great Conspiracy*. Disavows his prior life-style—turns strong Catholic

THE GANG OF SMITHERS
LEONARD SMITHERS PUBLISHER, AND THE GANG OF DECADENTS

"It is true enough. There was something strangely bizarre and abnormal about the publisher of books, as curious and abnormal as himself. He had a genuine love of letters, but nothing interested him much save work that had a definite quality of the unhealthy and the grotesque. With a mouth that smiled oddly and eyes that never did, he moves through the memories of that time as a presence rather than a person, passing in and out of the lighted scenes of a play. He amassed a considerable fortune and spent it in uncalculating generosity, an effete and morbid splendour, often generating into the sordid..."

— GUY THORNE

Leonard Smithers — Publisher

- Trained as a lawyer, he became fascinated by rare and pornographic books.
- Publisher of 'obscene modernism'
- Died at age 46 apparently of suicide. His grave was payed for by Lord Alfred Douglas.

Oscar Wilde — Playwright, Anglo-Catholic Agnostic

- Begins life as a highly committed Anglo-Catholic. He looses his faith in college and begins a life of decadence. Spiritual leader of the Gang of Smithers.
- Has numerous books published by Smithers such as *The Ballad of Reading Gaol*, and *The Savoy*. His life-style and arrests make him untouchable by other publishers.
- After being introduced to the writings of the French Ernest Renan, becomes obsessed with the concept of a 'fifth Gospel.' Probably helped organize the rescue of Esterhazy.

Sir Richard Burton — Spy, Explorer, Author

- Considered the first non-Muslim to enter Mecca. He became a master of disguise and revealed to the West before unknown texts and customs.
- Unable to get published by anyone else he was taken on by Smithers. Published *Arabian Nights,* the *Kama Sutra,* and other works.
- Writer of the highly controversial, never published "*Human Sacrifice among the Sephardine or Eastern Jews*", censored to this day.

Aleister Crowley — Satanist, Author, British Spy

- Discovered Kircher's *Oedipus Aegyptiacus* and used it as a window into Hermeticism/Satanism
- Published numerous Occult and Satanists text through Smithers. Along with Mdm. Blavatsky they become the source for the modern Occult.
- Considering himself to be Satan incarnate, he becomes the essential model for 20th century decadence.

Harry Sidney Nichols — Pornographer

- In league with Smithers begins the 'Erotika Biblion Society' — slogan 'Smut is cheap today.'
- Once Smithers is shut down, he flees to Paris publishing by mail-order.
- Eventually dies in America at a mental hospital.

Aubrey Beardsley[1] — Illustrator, Graphic artist

- Begins by illustrating *Le Morte d'Arthur* by Thomas Malory, but shortly thereafter enters the Art Nouveau movement as an artist of decadence.
- Inspired by a relationship with Oscar Wilde, enters into a decadent life style, probably bi-sexual, probably an incestuous relation with his sister.
- At the height of the Dreyfus Affair trials, as sentiment forms against Esterhazy, he converts to Catholicism and forbids Smithers to publish any of his works. **

C. Ranger Gull, aka Guy Thorne — Author

- Writer of numerous insignificant 'fantasy' novels, mostly spy novels published by Smithers. May have been a spy himself. Probably the model for Ian Fleming's Bond novels.
- Esterhazy stays at his house after being smuggled into England. Following this, Gull changes his name to Guy Thorne and writes the very first novel considered a best seller, *When It Was Dark*.
- Following the success of *When It Was Dark*, he abandons his former novels and begins writing books of Faith. He becomes Anglo-Catholic.

**March 7, 1898 — "Jesus is our Lord and Judge — Dear Friend, I implore you to destroy *all* copies of *Lysistrata* and bad drawings … By all that is holy, *all* obscene drawings."[2]

— AUBREY BEARDSLEY

---

1. The graphic art for the Beatles album 'Revolver' was done in his style.
2. In my death agony. — Beardsley, Aubrey. *The Letters of Aubrey Beardsley*. Fairleigh Dickinson Univ. Press. 1970 ISBN 978-0-8386-6884-9

CHAPTER NINETEEN

THE REEMERGENCE OF CERINTHUS' FIFTH GOSPEL

THE DREYFUS AFFAIR CONTINUED

"I have traversed, in all directions, the country of the Gospels; I have visited Jerusalem, Hebron, and Samaria [...] All this history, which at a distance seems to float in the clouds of an unreal world, thus took a form, a solidity, which astonished me. The striking agreement of the texts with the places, the marvellous harmony of the Gospel ideal with the country which served it as a framework, were like a revelation to me. **I had before my eyes a fifth Gospel**, torn, but still legible, and henceforward, through the recitals of Matthew and Mark, in place of an abstract being [...] I saw living and moving an admirable human figure."[1]

— ERNEST RENAN, *THE LIFE OF JESUS* — 1863

In many ways Ernest Renan was a prototype. To him Christ was more remarkable as a man than as a God. For Adolf Hitler, Christ was the quintessential Aryan antisemite. Both believed Jesus to be significant because he had purified himself of his Jewishness. But Renan was also the prototype for future Biblical archeologists who contested Christ's divinity. The Syndicate would like nothing better than to find the archaeological proof predicted by Renan to aid to the triumph of their cause. The problem was that the prototype for Hitler was the political baggage for them.

Therefore, promoting Renan's theory was fraught with dangers. While his

Palestinian expedition blazed the way for future gnostic discoverers, linking too hard to Renan could cause skeptics to question your motives.

The story to follow is similar. Like Renan, it will seem at cross-purposes, but it is not. Christian faith has seemingly been bolstered by discoveries such as the Dead Sea Scrolls made after WWII, however, the purpose was not that. It was to re-define the faith and send it into a different, non-traditional direction. This was to blaze the trail for Cerinthus' gospel by using an orchestrated reveal of documents and falsely interpreted evidence. Understanding this will be crucial to understanding the final chapter.

My present purpose is to give weight to the book *When It Was Dark*, that it truly is a fictionalization of a real story. It was a crucial step in postponing the reveal of Cerinthus' gospel until just following WWII. Underlying all this is something very evil, something much of Christianity has failed to recognize. The modern Church has out of goodwill accepted this new *pharmakon*, but its intention was to undo all the *pharmakon* since Plato, re-launching the barbarisms of the past. You will know this poison not so much by the authenticity of the evidence, but by the trail it has left behind.

Fictionalizations are seldom entirely fiction. They are attempts to tell a true story when circumstances don't allow, or all the facts can't be known or shared. Likewise, my story is not intended to be 100% accurate, it is impossible to know the entire truth, but it will be essentially true in the broader sense. While the details are true, how they fit together is speculation, but the gist of the story must be true. It is not difficult to show that the Dreyfus Affair was a battle for the soul of France, but the many coincidences indicate that it must have also been a crucial battle for the soul of the Church of Christ.

The *Apocryphon of John* is a fake, not because the document itself is fake, or thoughts it represents aren't real, but because it claims to be something it is not, the thoughts of Christ. The same can be said of the documents discovered with it. But this also may be said about something the reader may not expect, the Dead Sea Scrolls. They too have been sold to us as something they are not.

THE DREYFUS AFFAIR was a confrontation between two powerful parties. On one side were the 'strangers' (the Syndicate) made up of Republicans, Freemasons, and non-practicing Jews. While presenting themselves as agnostics, they were a derivative of the new Arians. Their stated object was to free Dreyfus, but their real desire was to politically lay the foundation for a laicized non-Christian state. This they admitted, but doing this would take something of greater scope than just freeing Dreyfus. It would require evidence that the church laity had been doctrinally deceived by the Church. This was all to happen after WWII and fit the Modernist agenda. Vatican II was the attempt to make this all presentable to the laity.[2]

On the other side was the Monarchists backed up by sympathies within the French Military. Still believing in the divine right of Kings, they saw all other governments as pretenders. It is here we face the dilemma presented at the beginning of the book—how do you maintain the divine right of Kings when the Bible on which your authority is based is under contention? The debate over authenticity was never about authenticity alone, it was always married to political power. This was true with Nicaea, true with Napoleon, true with Tischendorf, true with Dreyfus.... and true with Vatican II. The quest for political power was always facilitated by secret agencies.

Dreyfus' best friend was Salomon Reinach who was prominent in Renan's *Christ Myth Theory* movement popularized by the likes of Jules Verne and Anatole France. It arguably began when the French government sponsored Renan and his sister's trip to Palestine to poke around. During the expedition, facing the sudden death of his sister, Renan returned to France to promote the results of his discoveries.

One 'bible' of the new movement was a popular book by William Benjamin Smith *Ecce Deus* (1894). It tried to prove the *Essenes were the real Christians* and that the Gospels were just a fiction based upon Essene legend. This controversial claim was later exploited by Dead Sea Scrolls scholars. The 'Essene' hypothesis is the 'tell' for it consistently appears *prior* to any evidence showing up. It envisions the Essenes as a pre-Christian New-Age cult, proof that Christianity had wandered from its original model. They base this upon a scant two paragraph reference in the writings of Josephus the historian that would be twisted to imply that early Christianity was actually an early socialist cult:

> "Since [the Essenes] are despisers of wealth—their communal stock is aston-ishing—, one cannot find a person among them who has more in terms of possessions. For by a law, those coming into the school must yield up their funds to the order, with the result that in all [their ranks] neither the humilia-tion of poverty nor the superiority of wealth is detectable, but the assets of each one have been mixed in together, as if they were brothers, to create one fund for all."[3]

— JOSEPHUS. *THE JEWISH WAR*

In other words, what they were looking for was evidence that Jesus was in reality a Gnostic monopsychic that the *Apocryphon* had predicted, something on which they could hang their Marxist aspirations. While Dead Sea Scroll researchers for fifty years successfully persuaded the public of this, once the Scrolls were released to the public, neither the text of Josephus nor the archaeological evidence could back up the claim.

Today, when we think of the 'scientist' or the 'academic' we tend to think of the dispassionate observer who looks at the evidence, and then arrives at an objective conclusion. Seldom is this the case. Very often the basis of that conclusion has already been decided.

Before the internet and the democratizing of knowledge, crackpot theories could be advanced by academics without any challenge whatsoever. Hidden from us are the conflicting details—what is left is just the propaganda. Like the latest update to your computer, they are filled with 'shiny objects' all designed to distract from the fact that the update really is fixing gaping holes and mistakes in the operating system. In the past, academic publications could hide their true intentions, and who could challenge them? But now almost anything can be verified.

To think that a tiny 'syndicate' had the power to kneecap the mighty Catholic Church would take a lot of, shall we say, chutzpa, but that is precisely what was the goal. Yet, they were in possession of their Dooms Day device, it was called *Berlin Codex* (8502). It was purchased by Carl Schmidt around 1896 (during the Dreyfus Affair), but certainly must have been discovered before that. Yet, there is much suspicion in that date.

The first is the claim by Renan himself. It was he who claimed to have seen the 'fifth gospel' in 1863! As the authority on which this movement was based, this puts him in a rather precarious position. Either he is lying or the date of discovery is wrong. Could it even be he actually was the one who originally procured it on his expedition to the Middle East?

I believe academics were purposely hiding the fact that this codex was actually Cerinthus' fake gospel. Both the documents discovered just before Dreyfus including Berlin Codex 8502 and the later discovered Gnostic *Nag Hammadi* library contained similar texts, yet the Berlin Codex was kept secret until the discovery of the others. Why? What could possibly be the purpose of orchestrating their discovery, especially coincidental with the Dead Sea Scrolls? I think the reason is obvious, the result *was* the purpose. They were telling us Christianity had been worshipping at the wrong altar for 2000 years, and a 'data dump' might just overwhelm the Church buying time to enact their political agenda before the truth would come out.

Yet, it is clear Salomon Reinach, too, had familiarity with similar Gnostic texts (if not also the Berlin Codex) for he refers to them in his writings. I ask, why should we trust any of these dates? And if the dates are contrived why should we not believe they ALL are being purposely orchestrated?

In 1905, after the controversy of the Dreyfus Affair was over, just after the release of *When it Was Dark*, but long before the 'official' release of the Berlin Codex, Reinach published his book *"Cultes, mythes et religions"* (*Cults, Myths and Religions*). Later, in 1909, he published a general sketch of the history of religions under the title of *"Orpheus; histoire générale des religions"* (*Orpheus; a general history of religions*). Let's look first at the 'fake' inscription on the tomb from the book *When it was Dark*:

I, JOSEPH OF ARIMATHÆA, TOOK THE BODY OF JESUS, THE NAZARENE, FROM THE TOMB WHERE IT WAS FIRST LAID AND HID IT IN THIS PLACE.

I now present Salomon Reinach, One should note the similarity in the claims:

"26. The miracle of Christ's resurrection is related by the Synoptic Writers with irreconcilable discrepancies. **The discovery of the empty tomb is the less credible in that Jesus, if he had been executed, would have been thrown by the Roman soldiers into the common grave of malefactors. The end of Mark's Gospel (xvi. 9-20) is, as we have seen (p. 221), a later addition, which is not found in the best manuscripts. "The tradition followed by the author of the first Gospel is that of the authentic Mark, according to which the principal appearances took place in Galilee; the appearances in Jerusalem on the day of the Resurrection notified by Luke and John are simply ignored."**[4]

— SALOMON REINACH, *ORPHEUS*

The purpose if the same. Reinach clearly believes the Codices *Vaticanus* and *Sinaiticus* are "the best manuscripts" for they leave out the end of Mark's Gospel. This clearly puts him in the Tischendorf camp. This is not in itself such a great claim, but there is more. Notice the date '1886' and the specific attribution to Cerinthus, something supposedly unknown until 1895:

"42. The so-called APOCRYPHAL GOSPELS are of two kinds; the one class, described as dogmatic, relates the whole life of Jesus, after the manner of the

Synoptists; the others, known as legendary, deal only with episodes. The former, which the Fathers of the Church in the third century frequently quote as if they were of equal authority with the canonical writings, were destroyed, no doubt deliberately, because they belonged to schismatic sects. But in **1886** a portion of the **Gospel of St. Peter**, comprising the Passion and Resurrection, was found in a tomb in Egypt. This Gospel was probably identical with that of the **Egyptians**, which the Fathers quoted, and of which they have preserved extracts; it was no doubt written in Egypt, probably at Babylon (ancient Cairo). We have also some, fragments of the **Gospel according to the Hebrews**, the loss of which is especially to be regretted, because it was written for the Judeo-Christian communities of Palestine. *The episode of Jesus and the woman taken in adultery*, which was inserted in St. John's Gospel in the fourth century, was originally in this Gospel. This Gospel should, no doubt, be distinguished from that of the Ebionites (Ebionim, the poor), a Jewish sect anterior to Christianity, which developed a gnostic doctrine. **A contemporary of St. John, Cerinthus, of whom unfortunately we know hardly anything, was supposed to be the author of this Gospel; from a very early period the Gospel of St. John was attributed to him; it was supposed to be a revised version of his Gospel.**

— SALOMON REINACH, *ORPHEUS*

43. The legendary Gospels which have come down to us are expurgated gnostic writings; all that has been left in them are absurdities which are inoffensive to dogma, though singularly repugnant to taste. In the **Gospel of the Childhood, or of St. Thomas**, Jesus is a malicious and vindictive little demon; the miracles of the apocryphal Gospels are worthy of the Arabian frights. The result of the toleration shown by the Church for these legends was that they were widely circulated and translated into every language; literature and art found inspiration in them. Many popular incidents of Gospel history have no authority but that of the apocryphal writers; such are the story of Joachim and Anna, the parents of the Virgin, that of her marriage, of the birth of Jesus in a cave, where he was worshipped by an ox and an ass, of the descent of Jesus into hell, and of the death or trance of the Virgin."[5]

— SALOMON REINACH, *ORPHEUS*

Notice "…it was supposed to be a *revised* version of his Gospel." Reinach, a 'scholar' in this field, gets his timeline wrong (which is clearly known) claiming John's Gospel was written before Cerinthus allowing him to revise it. Either he knows Christian tradition and is misrepresenting it, or he doesn't know Christian tradition which means he must have current, first-hand knowledge of the *Berlin Codex*. This was is forty years before it is made public, confirming that either the codex went through his hands, or that the text was secretly being circulated, or that he is wilfully misrepresenting the facts.

The 'gospel of Cerinthus', as has been shown, is precisely the Secret *Apocryphon of John* found in both the *Berlin Codex* 8502 and the *Nag Hammadi* library. Wikipedia is not the best source of information, but is it too mistaken? "The Gospel of Peter was *recovered* in 1886 by the French archaeologist **Urbain Bouriant** in the modern Egyptian city of Akhmim (60 miles, 97 km) north of Nag Hammadi."[6]

> "The Gospel of Thomas is known to have existed in Greek but, like almost the entire vast literature of gnosticism, was *long believed to have perished with the exception of a few fragments*. In <u>1945</u>, however, it was rediscovered in a Coptic gnostic library near **Naj' Ḥammādī**, Egypt, on the Nile about 125 km (78 miles) northwest of Luxor."[7]

So, we now know *both* text were discovered near Nag Hammadi, one set in 1886, the other in 1945. Bear in mind, subsequent searches for the site didn't reveal the exact location of the find.

However, the Gospel of Thomas here refers to the sayings of Christ and NOT his infancy which exists in more than fragments (discovered in the 1870s). They are entirely different texts! The Gnostic Thomas moderns like to quote is not the one Reinach is referring to, for the one of Christ's infancy is ridiculous for it displays him as a precocious little brat. This means the promotors of such are playing a shell game so as not to expose or risk the out-of-hand rejection of their theories.

What this means is Salomon Reinach more than likely had first-hand knowledge of the *Berlin Codex* or at least some version of the *Apocryphon* from the ambiguous date 1886. The article is cleverly written to make it seem like the extraneous information is just common knowledge among experts. Could anyone deny that Reinach is involved with an orchestrated revision of Christian tradition? What could be the purpose of all this unless they were planning a sort of blackmail?

BERLIN CODEX 8502

Four texts are bound together in the Berlin Codex. All are Greek works in Coptic translations. It contains a fragmentary **Gospel of Mary, Apocryphon of John, The Sophia of Jesus Christ**, and an epitome of the **Acts of Peter**. However, the nature of the discovery is questioned by scholars:

> "The Codex Panopolitanus is far from the only example of an Egyptian Christian "Book of the Dead." The Berlin Codex, which contains the **Gospel of Mary**, the **Apocryphon of John**, the **Sophia of Jesus Christ**, and the **Acts of Peter**, appeared on the antiquities market in 1896. Although the dealer claimed that the book had been found in a wall-niche, the text's first editor, Carl Schmidt, assumed it had been taken from one of Akhmim's cemeteries.[8]
>
> — NICOLA DENZEY LEWIS

So, which is it, a wall niche or a cemetery? Is this provenance we should expect from such a critical text? The Berlin Codex was 'announced' as discovered at Akhmin, Egypt when purchased in 1896. Therefore, to be announced in 1896 means it would have been discovered before 1896, but no date is mentioned, nor the circumstance of its discovery.

Clearly, there was a flurry of activity in the 1880s to discredit the traditional New Testament text. Again, Westcott & Hort published their research in 1881 derived from 'oriental versions.' Again, as before:

> "He [Westcott] and I are going to edit a Greek text of the New Testament some two or three years hence, if possible. Lachmann and Tischendorf will supply rich materials, but not nearly enough; and we hope to do a good deal with **Oriental** versions. Our object is to supply clergymen generally, schools, etc., with a portable Greek text which shall not be disfigured with Byzantine corruptions."[9]

Does this not mean they were all working together? Why the coordination of releases? And why the ambiguity in times and discoveries? Why are different documents given the same name? Why the laxity in standards? Looking at all these efforts together betrays a concerted effort to not only leverage newly found Gnostic texts, but to present the traditional Bible as defective. The purpose can only be to force a doctrinal shift.

Also curious, one of the texts "bound" together within the *Berlin Codex* was the Gospel of Peter (as referred to by Reinach). Yet, records *do* show Peter *was* discovered in 1886, ten years before the *Berlin Codex*. *If Peter is found so must be the rest as they are bound together.* **A bound text cannot be discovered separately.** *Either Reinach knows this, he is not the expert he says he is, or he is being purposely misrepresenting. If he had access to all of the above which he must have to some degree being a curator of the French Museum, is he purposely misrepresenting the text to pave the way for a false scenario?*

The fact of the matter is perhaps something more simple. The state of much science, particularly archaeology, was quite amateurish up to and including the discovery of the Dead Sea Scrolls. There were many initial complaints of the sloppiness of the archaeology. In the 1800s, often the fields of study were invented by the discoverers themselves. This leads to us believing they had an expertise they simply did not have. Researchers read into things what they wanted to see, not what was there. Like we've found with Newton, Galileo and the rest, we should not regard their findings as 'gospel.'

I believe this is evidence that academia, like today, often pretends to have an expertise they simply don't have. The *Apocryphon* would have likely been known across the rebellious schools of religious thought, perhaps even Westcott & Hort. It's all just too much of a coincidence. While we may never conclusively prove this, they likewise can never prove that it wasn't.

If we make the above assumption, which is by no means a stretch, then all these finds began in French researchers hands. The Gospel of Peter was by *French* archaeologist Urbain Bouriant, not by Germans. He delayed publication until 1892, indicating a contrived need to control the narrative. Bouriant was co-founder of the *French Archaeological Mission* to Egypt, stationed at Cairo. In the same year, 1886, Salomon Reinach became curator of the *French National Museum of Antiquities,* as we've shown, he likely had first-hand knowledge of the Berlin Codex. I believe it would be convention that *French* archaeological missions be supervised by the *National Museum of Antiquities,* which means Salomon Reinach would have been involved.

CURIOUS ALSO ARE the Gnostic texts referenced by Reinach and their similarity to the supposedly unknown *Berlin Codex*, and the yet to be discovered *Nag Hammadi* texts:

Berlin Codex 8502	Nag Hammadi	Salomon Reinach mentions
Act of Peter	Act(s) of Peter	Gospel of St. Peter
Gospel of Mary	The Dialogue of the Saviour (Mary)	Hypothetical Mary
Sophia of Jesus Christ	Gospel of Truth	Gospel of the Egyptians
Apocryphon of John	Apocryphon of John	Cerinthus' Gospel of John
	The Gospel of Thomas	The Gospel of Thomas
	Various others	Gospel of the Hebrews

There is an odd symmetry in all this. Recognition of this is not just by me, but experts such a Karen L. King. Often they use just such parallel tables to show how one text authenticates and vindicates the other. If the political agenda to all this were ever in doubt, we need only look to King's own writings:

> "Beginning with the initial discovery of the *Berlin Codex* in 1896, a new phase in the history of the *Secret Revelation [Apocryphon] of John* was inaugurated, one firmly entwined in the identity politics of religion, nationalism, international law, and (post) colonialism of our own times, not to mention the discourses and economics of the university and academy."[10]

> — KAREN L. KING, HARVARD

Is she not claiming the very same coordination, the very same impact on history that we are now claiming? Further, the Berlin Codex was *put up for sale* in 1886, not *initially discovered*. King must know this. Is she not, as the top expert in her field, purposely misrepresenting this? Is this the sloppiness of scholars?

The question is, why did Reinach 'randomly' pick the codices he did? As mentioned, the Gospel of Thomas are actually two entirely different texts, as are Peter's 'Acts' & 'Gospel,' thus clouding the search for which text is which. You could argue that this makes the chart meaningless, *however*, it is also exactly what you would do if you were trying to overwhelm the public with information.

Resources list only that the *Berlin Codex* was bought by Dr. Carl Reinhardt in Cairo, I've not found the precise circumstance of its discovery. Yet, I did find this:

"The reported incident of Mohamed Ali's mother tossing some of the ancient papyrus folios into the fire proved to Western minds that peasants—native Egyptians—could not be trusted with their own antiquities; only enlightened Europeans knew their true value. **The story has a remarkable parallel in Constantin von Tischendorf's "rescuing" of the Codex Sinaiticus from St. Catherine's Monastery in Sinai in 1845.** Tischendorf reports that the monks charged with caring for the precious manuscript tossed papyri leaves into the fire for warmth. The message was clear: native Egyptians could not be trusted to care for their own antiquities, which required "rescuing" by scholars and collectors in the West."[11]

— LEWIS & BLOUNT, *JOURNAL OF BIBLICAL LITERATURE*

How true, but is also curiously similar to the way the disciples of Tischendorf out-of-hand dismissed the *Vetus Latina* as being the work of naïve 'natives.' Are we to believe the same here, is this evidence of racism and elitism—that only 'scholars' are to be trusted with the results?

THE OSCAR WILDE CONNECTION

The following is also speculative: Salomon Reinach had made it a life goal to disprove the Divinity of Christ, that was the purpose of the Renan inspired movement. Yet, conceivably, he once had possession of, or had inside knowledge of the very text that would do that, the secret *Apocryphon of John*.

Further, it is clear from the Dreyfus Affair that there was still a strained relationship between the governments of France and Germany at that time. Evidence of this is the very territory Dreyfus is from, Alsace-Lorraine, a formerly French territory now annexed to Germany as a result of the Franco-Prussian War. In fact, it is the fact that Dreyfus was an Alsatian that led to the belief he was a traitor. Yet, there must have been antiquarian or academic channels, somehow the Codex went from French hands to German.

So, my question is this: *considering this political climate, how does a valuable one-of-a-kind codex, one presumably discovered by a French government affiliated institute in Egypt, go through curators of the French Museum, and then end up in the hands of German officials who are themselves affiliated with the founding of the Nazi Party? Knowing this, was accusing the Catholic Church of Nazi affiliations itself a false-flag to detract from the fact that the party of Renan had provided the very documents that formed the basis of the Nazi religion? And, is it not suspicious that it is kept this very Codex hidden until after WWII?* I ask the reader again to look at the affiliations of the members of the Syndicate, look at the testimony of *Alfred Rosenberg and Origins of the National Socialist Myth.* Is there not something suspicious?

If my scenario is correct, the best way to transfer these rare texts would be through academic/antiquarian collector channels, perhaps utilizing the Republican military. The final custodian was the German Carl Schmidt, a collector of just such Gnostic texts. But the military was under control by General Boulanger, a Catholic and someone who could potentially reinstall the French monarchy, if not become president himself. Indeed, it was Dreyfus himself who was trying to out their coup.

Therefore, Reinach would need someone sympathetic to his cause that he could trust, perhaps a Jewish military person with connections, or a dealer in antiquities (Mme. Milescamp), perhaps even both. To my knowledge no one has yet explained why Mme. Milescamp (an antiquities dealer) was involved in the Affair, and why she was a prime witness at the trial. *Dreyfus, already acknowledged as a spy and an intelligence officer, would fit the bill as he was Alsatian, still had German connections, and spoke fluent German.* He would think it his patriotic duty in support of the French Republic by thwarting a coup. However, if this was discovered by Esterhazy, he would have been prevented from telling the truth, for it would entail making public the very documents he wished to not publicize. A document that contested the very divinity of Christ.

So, what was Esterhazy to do? Once, Esterhazy was tried and appeared to be going to jail, he must figure out how to get the story out without doing more damage than warranted. The plan would be that he be smuggled out of France by the entourage of Oscar Wilde to stay with Guy Thorne. Once there, they would write a fiction as a warning, disguising all the real people as actors in the plot. In this way if the real story ever came out, the public would be prepared and less likely to take it seriously. Esterhazy carried with him 'secret evidence,' it became the first best seller ever, *When It Was Dark.*

HOWEVER, Oscar Wilde has his reasons too. Once a former enthusiast for the Catholic side of the Church of England, he became disturbed by his own homosexual tendencies. It was for this reason that only the disreputable publishing houses often would publish his writings, like Leonard Smithers. Known for cheap popular novels, they were also the publishers of illegal pornography in England. What I call 'the gang of Smithers' were all of the same ilk, and considered Wilde as their spiritual leader. Yet, after the Dreyfus

Affair many had a curious conversion to Catholicism, so many that it forced Smithers out of business. Thorne himself went on to write an apology for Christianity, *I Believe.*

Wilde, too, was intrigued by the prospects of a fifth Gospel:

"Guillot de Saix in his commentary to Le Chant du Cygne [Swan Song], a collection of Wilde's oral tales, states how 'Oscar Wilde se plaisait à dire: "Je suis le treizième apôtre du Christ, et je dois écrire le Cinquième Évangile"' [Oscar Wilde liked to say 'I am the thirteenth disciple of Christ and I am to write the fifth Gospel'].[12]

"When I think about religion at all, I feel as if I would like
to found an order for those who cannot believe:
the Confraternity of the Faithless one might call it..."

> — OSCAR WILDE — *DE PROFUNDIS*

I ask, where did Wilde get such an idea if it were not the *leitmotif* of all this? The way to discover the truth in anything is to resolve the most striking of contradictions—the main contradiction in all this is, why did Oscar Wilde, who was clearly on the side of the Dreyfusards, strike up a friendship with Esterhazy and participate in his escape from France? In *Ceremonies of Bravery,* author J. Robert Maguire records the very words of Salomon Reinach spoken to Wilde's friend Carlos Blacker:

"Blacker had no doubt as to the source of the published information, as he told Salomon Reinach... According to Reinach, in a report of his confidential conversations with Blacker ('he knows everything'), "Blacker confided in four persons: 1- Conybeare of Oxford; 2 - Paton, an Oxford Hellenist resident on Samos; 3 - myself; and 4 - Oscar Wilde."[13]

> — J. ROBERT MAGUIRE, RESEARCHER INTO THE 'AFFAIR'

So, contrary to most published accounts, the two main players in this saga were actually Salomon Reinach and Oscar Wilde, only they were directly connected and knew 'everything.' Curiously...

"Wilde's opinion on the merits and demerits of the famous affaire is worthy of quotation: 'Zola wrote the *bordereau* at the dictation of Dreyfus, and Esterhazy took it round to the German Embassy, and sold it for fifteen francs.'

— CHRIS HEALY, *CONFESSIONS OF A JOURNALIST*

What?!? Were they all working together, or, who set up who? Does not the conventional story all spin in another direction if this is true? *That it was Dreyfus who set up Esterhazy?* Why are we to believe that Dreyfus was even exiled? Very disturbing is that Alfred Dreyfus had his own spies and *knew of the coup d'etat*:

"Mr. X met the Major the next evening with a very grave face.

'Is there anything wrong?' said Esterhazy.

'Well,' replied X, 'I have just left Zola, and he seems very confident. He says that in less than three months Dreyfus will be free, and back at his old post, and that you will be undergoing a sentence of imprisonment for life in a military prison. Why, he claims to know every movement of yours, and of the military party! His spies must be good, if all that he says is true. I don't know myself whether it is correct or not, but he says that there was a meeting of the military cabinet to-day, and that Prince Henri of Orléans was of the party. He then retailed at length all that Esterhazy had informed him the evening before."

— CHRIS HEALY, *CONFESSIONS OF A JOURNALIST*

And what's more is that Esterhazy was also dirty— Healy records that he too was selling hundreds of documents to the Germans and Austrians. Apparently a peace flag was offered to Esterhazy:

"On one of these occasions M. Dreyfus remarked to X: 'We bear no malice against Esterhazy, because we know that, in this matter, he has been but the tool of others. Why does he not confess? If he were to confess, there are those among us who would see that his wife and children did not lack for bread I am told that he has said that he is forced to keep his lips closed, and that he cannot reveal the truth because his wife and children would suffer. If he is sincere, he need have no fear of such a contingency.'"

— CHRIS HEALY, *CONFESSIONS OF A JOURNALIST*

The entire Affair turned on Zola's publishing of a contentious article famously called '*J'Accuse*', but apparently according to Healy, that too was the mastermind of Wilde:

"I now come to an extraordinary announcement which will surprise all those who imagine themselves as familiar with every scene of the *affaire*. The dramatic change in the tide of the affaire which led to the suicide of Colonel Henry was planned by Zola and Oscar Wilde... Nevertheless, Zola tested the information by sending a trusted emissary to the Attaché, and received information which enabled him to force the hands of Cavaignac, who then held the portfolio of the War Department. 'Unless you hold another inquiry,' wrote Zola, 'I shall publish certain documents, copies of which I now send you.' Cavaignac was alarmed, and held his inquiry, when Colonel Henry admitted the fabrication of the incriminating *pièce*, 'Ce canaille de D____,' His suicide, by order, the same evening, caused a world-wide revulsion of feeling in favour of Dreyfus, and the renewed agitation which followed ended in the famous farce of Rennes and the release of Dreyfus. But the successful agitation was all due to the information Oscar Wilde had given."

— CHRIS HEALY, *CONFESSIONS OF A JOURNALIST*

The result of all this subterfuge was a secret meeting in a bar:

"Mention has been made of the extraordinary part played by the late Oscar Wilde in the freeing of Dreyfus by placing Emile Zola in communication with Colonel von Schwarzkoppen. This statement is absolutely true; and what was even stranger was the peculiar meeting that took place one evening in a bar in the Rue St. Honore between Oscar Wilde, Esterhazy, and a Parisian journalist who carried on the campaign against Dreyfus in the English press."

— CHRIS HEALY, *CONFESSIONS OF A JOURNALIST*

I believe the result of this meeting was a conditional resolution to the Affair planned by Wilde. Wilde would use his connections to English publishers to provide a way out. My guess would be that the unnamed journalist who was conducting 'the campaign against Dreyfus' was Rowland Strong, an associate of the Jewish-English newspaper editor and heiress Rachel Beer. The plan would have been this: Esterhazy would make a public confession, that would be later *plausibly denied*. There was incentive on

Beer's part for her paper, *The Observer*, had lost credibility by publishing a false account of the Affair. This 'confession' would return the paper to respectability.

"Meanwhile, in London, Rachel continued negotiations with Arthur Newton, who had offered her Esterhazy's signed confession for an additional one thousand pounds. She was interested in an interview and Newton gave her the fugitive's address in Rotterdam. "It's about time to keep your promise concerning the formal declaration and above all, documents," read her cable to Esterhazy, complete with prepayment for his answer. It seemed a rather incomprehensible move, taking into account Newton's shady character and Esterhazy's notorious lack of credibility, especially given that the second installment of his *Dessous de l'Affaire Dreyfus* had just been reviewed as "even more trashy and unconvincing than the first." But this move may have been less naïve on Rachel's part than it appeared—rather, it was a clever trick to extract a written statement from Esterhazy in order to restore *The Observer's* reputation."[14]

Then came the deniability:

"And I read the document below which I translated at the same time. Here is this translation:

I, Arthur John Edward Newton of 23, Great Marlborough Street Regent Street, in the County of London, Solicitor of the Supreme Court of Judicature in England hereby declare as follows:

1. I was consulted by Commandant Ferdinand Esterhazy in the month of September 1898 and on the 27th day of September 1898 I caused to be issued in the Queen's Bench Division of the High Court of Justice a Writ against the London Observer, of which Mrs. Rachel Beer is the Manageress and Directress, claiming damages on behalf of my client the above named, Ferdinand Esterhazy, for a Libel which had been published in that paper by her Correspondent, Mr. Rowland Strong.

2. Subsequently the action was not proceeded with, as Mrs. Beer paid the sum of five hundred pounds as damages and also paid the costs of the proceedings.

Dated this 26th day of January 1899. Arthur NEWTON."

— *DESSOUS DE L'AFFAIRE DREYFUS*—ESTERHAZY

I Arthur John Edward Newton of 23 Great Marlborough Street Regent Street in the County of London, Solicitor of the Supreme Court of Judicature in England hereby declare as follows –

1. I was consulted by Commandant Ferdinand Esterhazy in the month of September 1898 and on the 27th day of September 1898 I caused to be issued in the Queens Bench Division of the High Court of Justice a Writ against the London Observer, of which Mrs Rachel Beer is the Manageress and Directress claiming damages on behalf of my client the above named Ferdinand Esterhazy for a Libel which had been published in that paper by her Correspondent Mr Roland Strong;

2. Subsequently the action was not proceeded with, as Mrs Beer paid the sum of Five hundred pounds as damages and also paid the Costs of the proceedings

Dated this 26th day of January 1899.

Arthur Newton's actual letter as published by Esterhazy. (public domain)

At this point, however, the negotiated settlement would have only been half fulfilled. Esterhazy would have to find refuge in England, eventually to Guy Thorne's house.

I think we need to pause for a second and ponder this: Esterhazy comes to you and has revealed something extraordinary, something he fears if revealed may cost him is life. After all, he even says it is his insurance policy. Yet, you as an author feel a responsibility to inform the public. So, you write a fiction, but how do you wink to the public clueing them in that it is real?

Certainly you would do it under a pseudonym, but wouldn't you also reveal some odd details that only an insider would know? And, wouldn't those details speak to the core of the plot? The following recollection, or perhaps admission appeared in Wilde's biography:

"Directly "De Profundis" [Wilde's text where he admits his desire to publish a fifth gospel] made its appearance the whole press of England, almost without exception, devoted a large space to its consideration. The sensation the book occasioned was extraordinary and almost without parallel in modern times. An enormous controversy arose about it immediately. Every possible aspect of the book was canvassed and discussed, and, strange as it may seem, a vast amount of venom and bitterness was mingled with the bulk of eulogy. The student of contemporary literature, or perhaps, in view of what I am going to say, it would be better to call it contemporary book publishing, can find no parallel to the interest and excitement this book occasioned, save only in the case of a very different production called "When it was Dark," an over-rated sensational novel by a Mr. "Guy Thorne," whose views excited the various religious parties in the Church of England to a sort of frenzy for and against them... The manuscript of 'De Profundis,' about which he wrote to me very often during the last months of his imprisonment, was handed to me on the day of his release."[15]

— LEONARD CRESSWELL INGLEBY, AUTHOR OF *OSCAR WILDE*

The above comes from the biography of Oscar Wilde, *but the author Leonard Cresswell Ingleby is another pseudonym for Gull/Guy Thorne!* ***The publication of Wilde's 'De Profundis' speaking of a Fifth Gospel, and the publication of Thorne's 'When it Was Dark' revealing a plot to corrupt Christianity was clearly coordinated! Thorne is literally in touch with Wilde on the day of his release.*** *How much more of a 'wink' could anyone want!*

Our story closes with one last utterance—after all this and much more, was Oscar Wilde, ever able to regain his faith? And wouldn't this too be a sign? Clearly, Oscar Wilde before the Affair was filled with doubt. Most assume he was conquered by his lusts, tarnishing his legacy forever. Healy records a different story, leaving us with this touching last scene:

"The last time I saw Wilde he was kneeling in the Church of Nôtre Dame. The sun streamed through the windows, the organ was pealing a majestic chant, and his head was bowed, almost hidden. Perhaps some vision of what his life might have been came to him and scourged his soul anew. I only know that when I left him he was still kneeling before the altar, his face hidden by his hands.[16]

— CHRIS HEALY, *CONFESSIONS OF A JOURNALIST*

1. Renan, Ernest. *Life of Jesus (Vie de Jésus).* Roberts 1863 (the Modern Library, New York, 1927) p. 31
2. To put lipstick on a pig might be more accurate.
3. Josephus. *The Jewish War*, Book II, Chapter 8, 2-3
4. Reinach, Salomon. Monod, Gabriel, and Alfred Loisy. 'L'«Orpheus» de Ms. Reinach.' *Revue Historique* 102, no. Fasc. 2, 1909, p.225
5. Reinach, Salomon. Monod, Gabriel, and Alfred Loisy. 'L'«Orpheus» de Ms. Reinach.' *Revue Historique* 102, no. Fasc. 2, 1909, p.233
6. Bouriant, "Fragments du texte grec du livre d'Énoch et de quelques écrits attribués à saint Pierre" in *Mémoires de la mission archéologique française au Caire* 1892. — From the Wikipedia article
7. *Encyclopedia Britannica* from the article "Gospel of Thomas' https://www.britannica.com/topic/Gospel-of-Thomas
8. Lewis, Nicola Denzey. "Death on the Nile: Egyptian codices, Gnosticism, and Early Christian books of the dead." In *Practicing Gnosis*, Schmidt 1903, attached note—2. Schmidt was correct in his skepticism that a book might have survived nearly two thousand years in a wall-niche; a durable container (as usually found in a grave deposit) is necessary to preserve a book intact.
9. Hort, Arthur. *Life and Letters of Fenton John Anthony Hort,* Vol. I, Macmillan & Co., 1896, p.250 https://www.jstor.org/stable/3140075
10. King, Karen L. *The Secret Revelation of John,* Harvard University Press, p.22
11. Lewis, Nicola Denzey and Blount, Justine Ariel, 'Rethinking the Origins of the Nag Hammadi Codices,' *Journal of Biblical Literature* 133, no. 2, 2014
12. Stevens, Jennifer, *The Historical Jesus and the Literary Imagination* 1860–1920 Chp. 5 — 'The Fifth Gospel of Oscar Wilde'. Guillot de Saix, Le Chant du Cygne: contes parlés d'Oscar Wilde. Recueillis et rédigés par Guillot de Saix, Mercure de France, Paris 1942, p. 95
13. Maguire, J. Robert. *Ceremonies of Bravery: Oscar Wilde, Carlos Blacker, and the Dreyfus Affair.* Oxford University Press, USA, 2013. p.124
14. Negev, Eilat; Koren, Yehuda. *The First Lady of Fleet Street-The Life of Rachel Beer—Crusading Heiress and Newspaper Pioneer,* Random House Publishing, 2012
15. Ingleby, Leonard Cresswell (a pseudonym for GUY THORNE), *Oscar Wilde*, 1907, p. 362
16. Healy, Chris. *Confessions of a Journalist,* Chatto & Windus, 1904. p.137

CHAPTER TWENTY

ALL WE LIKE SHEEP
THE BACKSTORY OF VATICAN II

"Such also is approximately the state of the individual forming part of a psychological crowd. He is no longer conscious of his acts. In his case, as in the case of the hypnotised subject, at the same time that certain faculties are destroyed, others may be brought to a high degree of exaltation. Under the influence of a suggestion, he will undertake the accomplishment of certain acts with irresistible impetuosity. This impetuosity is the more irresistible in the case of crowds than in that of the hypnotised subject, from the fact that, the suggestion being the same for all the individuals of the crowd, it gains in strength by reciprocity... We see, then, that the disappearance of the conscious personality, the predominance of the unconscious personality, the turning by means of suggestion and "contagion of feelings and ideas in an identical direction, the tendency to immediately transform the suggested ideas into acts; these, we see, are the principal characteristics of the individual forming part of a crowd. He is no longer himself, but has become an automaton who has ceased to be guided by his will."[1]

— GUSTAVE LE BON, *PSYCHOLOGIE DES FOULES*

AN OVERVIEW

It should be apparent by now that the ideal of the modern state, the peace-loving 'One', is not the utopia socialism claimed it to be, it is the mob. Philosophy was born in response to the mob. The modern socialist mob has lived up to little that it has promised. As Calhoun has shown it is strained living conditions that leads to the Behavioral Sink, the dystopia. As the ancient Greeks have shown, it was the democratic crowd that led to mob rule. So, why would politicians constantly appeal to the crowd? Why would modern Christianity use the socialist mob as a model for its future theology?

One of the biggest misrepresentations was the question of who killed Christ. The determining moment was when Pilate faced Jesus in the face of the mob. Pilate's full intention was to exonerate Jesus, but he was outplayed by the Pharisees. Pilate's official title included the designation 'Caesar's Friend,' without which he could not rule. If Pilate did not follow the demands of the mob, the Pharisees made it clear that they would report this to Caesar. The result would be Pilate's loss of title. Through clever manipulation, the Pharisees put that title into jeopardy. Right then Christ's fate was sealed—Pilate was out-played. To admit to Jesus' claim as King would mean acknowledging that the Herodian line was a phoney, which it was, thus running afoul of the Empire that established that line. Either way, Pilate loses, it was a Catch-22. The chants, 'Crucify Him, Crucify Him,' tell the entire story, it was the mob that killed Christ.

Similarly, the throne of France was outplayed, too. To do nothing was not an option, to try was treason. The result of the Dreyfus Affair was that Alfred would be set free. He would later finish a distinguished military career in the service of the French Republic. Esterhazy's career would go in the other direction, living out the rest of his life in England. But not every noble act is rewarded by notoriety, nor are they done by noble men. True, the monarchy was prevented from re-establishment, however, if my speculations are correct, the Syndicate did not achieve all their designs either. With their plans of a completely laicized state thwarted, they would have to re-group for a better day. Their main weapon, the secret Gnostic texts, would be rested to appear at a better time. *When It Was Dark* proved its purpose. By tainting public opinion revealing the texts now would have been met with skepticism. A coordinated 'data dump' at a later date would work much better. Until then, the texts were all safe hidden in Berlin, ready to inspire a new 'third' Reich. Would the members of the *Syndicate,* many of who were Jewish, have been so self-sure had they known?

The Dreyfus Affair taught the new Arians a lot. Much better than one witness, three would work much better. These would be the *Berlin Codex*, the *Nag Hammadi Library*, and the yet to be discovered *Dead Sea Scrolls*. There would be a 50 year hiatus, giving plenty of time for Nazi researchers like Otto Rahn to shore up loose ends. Convinced they had discovered the true Church, an all-out Indiana Jones-like quest was launched to ferret out evidence of the new 'Holy Grail,' searching in places like Montségur France, the last Cathar stronghold. Even in defeat, the Nazi ideal moved forward dressed in more humanitarian 'New-Age' garb.

Again, under assault was another Trinitarian phrase, "Go ye therefore, and teach all nations, baptizing them in the name of the Father, and of the Son, and of the Holy Ghost." It was this that would be labelled 'colonialism,' a dirty word to the socialist. To colonize was to civilize, but to socialism, it meant depriving people of their natural culture, something they considered the worst of all sins. It was to steal away people's natural truths.

The 'remedy,' we are told, is naturalism, to encourage cultures to return to their natural state. Yet, as we have seen and are seeing today, this is not a return to the wholesome, but a relaunching of the barbaric. So what are we getting wrong?

To the modern, the solution is to create the socialist state, what Enfield called *Orientalism*. They see knowledge as sort of a trap—to know means you have to judge, to judge means you have to discern 'this is better than that.' It is this basis of what they call 'western thought' that deprives people of their natural culture. To the degree modern Christianity adopts this scheme, is to the same degree it aids the Adversary.

Around in circles we go, what the occult has called the '*ouroboros,*' the snake of eternity eating its own tail. Not believing in God they create new gods, the current being Artificial Intelligence. So where do we get off this train?

The answer has always been with, it is the portion of Plato they all ignore. In amongst their floods of education, their data dumps, their continual pursuit of higher education, their misrepresented evidence, they never noticed that they conceptually understand very little. To conceptually understand anything at all is a talent the AI god will never achieve. Like sophistry, the endless digital cataloging of information will never lead to getting the gist of something. Evidence is worthless if the machine cannot ponder the conclusions.

In an effort to advance their cause, the moderns (the new Arians) have for centuries exposed us to their philosophy, yet never the source of their evidence, the *Apocryphon*. One must ask 'why'? They show us glimpses, such as *Sinaiticus,* but from Arius on down they "hide the whole of their doctrine." This sounds fishy. Could it be that the doctrine itself is not as powerful as the mesmerizing curiosity its absence creates? They seem to know that if they were to reveal the whole of their doctrine that they would give up their power. What we have to realize is there is no whole of their doctrine, it has no conceptual core for it is anti-conceptual from the start. Their philosophy is not a doctrine, it is a spiritual possession.

It has been widely believed that the scientific revolution began with the introduction of the *Corpus Hermeticum* in the fifteenth century.[2] Yet, for anyone having taken time to read the text there just isn't much there that is scientific, much less Christian. This absence of detail has led to the belief that Gnosticism is based upon hidden knowledge. But, how likely is this?

The entire Gnostic enterprise begins to look less and less scientific the more you look. It's a cult looking for self vindication, a way to subvert the masses to their cause. While we usually look at 'scientific revolutions' such the Enlightenment and the Renaissance as 'revolutionary,' we can now see they were subversive—to 'scientifically' dissect reality to the point where nobody has any confidence that it is real. Once having gained power, histories were re-written, prophets created, to be sympathetic to their cause.

While we may never be able to fill in all the hereditary gaps of the secret *Apocryphon of John* through all ages, what IS known to have existed, at least from the twelfth century, is *The Book of the Secret Supper,* also known as *Interrogatio Iohannis.* It is this that began to gain popularity just before the Enlightenment, just as the *Corpus Hermeticum* gained popularity before the Renaissance. All the crucial information is there, it is a redacted version of the *Apocryphon.* Written as a series of question posed by St. John to Christ at the Last Supper, it supports all the basic concepts of Gnosticism, particularly that creation itself is a Satanic unreal construct. In it, Satan assumes the role of Demiurge (second of God), and John the Baptist assumes that of a fraudster giving a false baptism of water in place of the occult 'in the spirit.'

> "And again I asked the Lord, "How is it that the world received the Baptism of John, but Thine is not accepted by all?" The Lord replied to me: "That because their works are evil and they come not to the light. The followers of John marry and are given in marriage, whereas my disciples marry not at all but remain as the angels of God in the heavenly kingdom."[3]

— THE BOOK OF THE SECRET SUPPER

The reason gnostics 'marry not' is it is their effort to thwart creation by thwarting procreation.

TO BE ACCEPTED into the world of Biblical Criticism you must have a sense that the Bible is deficient, that something has been purposely hidden and you are savvy enough to ferret it out. Your thoughts are refined, more informed than the average. You see through the mundane, you are not fooled by the conventional. This 'savvy-ness' allows you to disregard the testimony of the many, you seek only the affirmation of the one or two.

I point out the following not so much because it could be true, but because it will display a double standard. Many texts were authenticated in a less than scientific era. Another case in point is a text sometimes referred to as 'the other Dead Sea Scrolls.' In 1883 Wilhelm Shapira offered for sale a set of Hebrew scroll fragments. The circumstance of their discovery was recorded by Shapira:

> "I am going to surprise you with a notice and a short description of a curious manuscript written in old Hebrew or Phoenician letters upon small strips of embalmed leather and seems to be a short unorthodoxical book of the last speech of Moses in the plain of Moab ... In July 1878 I met several Bedouins in the house of the well-known Sheque Mahmud el Arakat, we came of course to speak of old inscriptions. One Bedouin asserted that the antique brings blessedness to the place where it lays. And begins to tell a history to about the following effect. Several years ago some Arabs had occasion to flee from their enemies & hid them- selves in caves high up in a rock facing the Moujih (the neues Arnon) they discovered there several bundles of very old rugs. Thinking they may contain gold they peeled away a good deal of Cotton or Linen & found only some black charms & threw them away; but one of them took them up & and since having the charms in his tent, he became a wealthy man having sheeps etc".[4]

Considering procuring them, the British Museum turned them over for analysis to Christian David Ginsberg. After three weeks he called in a French authority, Charles Clermont-Ganneau who announced to the public in 1883 that they were a forgery. Shapira was run out of the country, humiliated he eventually committed suicide always believing in the authenticity of his discovery. Today researcher Shlomo Guil considers them authentic.

THE HIPPIES OF THE DEAD SEA

I ask, have you ever been hard-sold a product? You buy a product that is supposed to do all these things, and then you get it home and realize it doesn't. The goal was not to meet your needs, but the needs of the salesman. The Dead Sea Scrolls were the product of a hard-sell. The fine print released over fifty years later promises nothing that was originally advertised. Put simply, the Scrolls were authenticated to backup the claim that the secret *Apocryphon of John* represented the true Church, a claim that is demonstrably false. A clever argument cannot make something true that is not.

In 1950 the top Jewish Scholar in Second Temple Judaism, Solomon Zeitlin, wrote a fifty-eight page article in the *Jewish Quarterly Review* proving the *Dead Sea Scrolls* an "entire hoax". On page fifty he writes, "Professor Albright entitles his article 'Are the *'Ain Feshka* Scrolls a Hoax?':

> "I reiterate that, the Dead Sea Scrolls are a hoax. The title of the book in which the Isaiah Scroll and the Habakkuk Commentary were published should be *The Scrolls of St. Mark's Monastery*. The words *Dead Sea* are a misnomer."[5]

> — SOLOMON ZEITLIN

Now, I for one have no qualms with somebody who makes an honest assessment believing they are authentic, but where have you or anyone else seen the evidence that they are not? Christians at the time of their discovery believed the Dead Sea Scroll insured the authenticity of the Church. Few people noticed that they flipped Church doctrine on its head. The result was the Church celebrating an entirely new, non-traditional, 'socialistic' approach to Christianity. And how would you contest this? All the 'experts' proclaimed it, yet, you couldn't check, they were kept secret until the 1990s. But once made public, the 60s-like, New Age peace & love cult led by the 'Teacher of Righteousness' we were sold, was shown to have virtually no basis in fact. They read into the text what they wanted to see, just as they authenticate the texts that support their doctrines.

The Dead Sea Scrolls authenticity nor their coordinated discovery with other Gnostic texts was apparently never questioned... or perhaps it was, but authenticating them was more politically expedient. The fact that they were proclaimed authentic the very moment the then leftist socialist state of Israel was recognized by the UN made the event a miracle, and never a tip-off. The Scrolls then went on to become a key ingredient for an entire revision of

Christian theology, a revision evidence will show was in the planning since the late 1800s. It was on this that the Council of Vatican II was built in the 1960s. *In almost every case the philosophy came first, the evidence second.* Once found, the legitimate evidence is exaggerated to fit, illegitimate evidence is not owned up to, contrary texts are painted as irrelevant, minority texts elevated to primacy, all orchestrated to confirm their philosophy.

The theological model for Vatican II was that of Fr. Teilhard de Chardin, a paleontologist credited with co-finding the famous Piltdown Man in 1912. The fact that it was proved a hoax less than ten years before Vatican II, and that Teilhard's writings had been condemned, mattered not.[6] Nor that his writings were considered useful by the CIA as propaganda:

"1. Pierre Teilhard de Chardin. Source praised this decased [deceased] Frenchman's philosophical writings and said that they would make a great impression on the Soviet intelligencia if his writings were rendered into their languages. Source stated it was not true that this Jesuit's writings were on the Vatican's Index."

— CIA DOCUMENT — CIA-AERODYNAMIC VOL. 27
(OPERATIONS)_0055

Of what interest has the CIA in religion? Why would it push a known heretical theology out as propaganda? The 'source' listed above was probably Fr. Malachi Martin, a member of the Secretariat of Cardinal Bea of the Vatican. Martin is acknowledged as a 'mole' secret agent converted by George Shuster, a member of Abraham Heschel's entourage who were lobbying the Pope for doctrinal change, particularly in regard to the Jews.[7] All were associates of Jules Isaac, one of the last remnants of the Dreyfus Affair.

It didn't matter that Jules Isaac's New-Age cult of the Essenes, theorized by Renan since the middle 1800s, did not hold up under close examination. It didn't matter that this was all tied to Salomon Reinach's 'Jesus is a myth' school of thought and Cerinthus' false gospel. Proof of this does exist, but have you seen any of it?

All this contributed in a major way to the new direction of Christ's Church. While you can debate philosophy, how do you argue against fabricated and misinterpreted 'tangible evidence'? How do you argue with the experts? You should see it for what it is, a type of voodoo that cares little about legitimacy as it does providing a path for 'a new way of thinking.' It is a Gnostic cult backed up by academic ne'er-do-wells.

Dr. Karen King is a case in point. Beginning her academic career in woman's studies, certainly inspired by the Dead Sea Scrolls, she concentrated her leftist politics on becoming a Biblical scholar. When finding a small, credit-card-sized manuscript claiming to be the *Gospel of Jesus' Wife*, nothing triggered her skepticism. All she saw was opportunity. Now that it has been proved a fraud she is still undaunted. Following the *modus operandi* of her gnostic predecessors, authentic evidence means nothing to them, what matters is the philosophy.

The very same criteria they use to discredit others does not apply to them. Never mind that the Secret *Apocryphon of John* is perhaps one of the most mysogynist texts ever written, it is serves King's 'feminist' academic purpose —to undermine tradition and the western way of thinking. Ariel Sabar in his book *Veritas: A Harvard Professor, A Con Man and the Gospel of Jesus Wife*, comments:

> "Her method was "hermeneutics"— a system of interpretation that encouraged women to claim their rightful place in scripture through against-the-grain readings and imagination. King's predicament was that she called herself a historian. She demanded that people be "accountable" to facts and history, though she herself believed in neither."[8]

Need I tell you that 'hermeneutics' is yet another method derived from Hermes? Mind you, texts knowingly condemned since the second century are advocated by modern Gnostics as representing authentic Christianity. Often the provenance of these texts is terrible, one or two or so are typically leveraged against thousands. Often these are boughten in some market from an unnamed bedouin, found by teenage sheepherders, travel to places unknown, and even documented as having been confused with other texts. In King's case, she got it from a con-artist.

I, myself, have a rare original copy of St. Robert Bellarmine's *Controversies* written specifically against such heresies. An amateur could see it is obviously authentic, it's not the type of thing anyone would even think of forging, or even know to emulate. It has the stamps of custodian libraries since 1615, the condition is right, the ink is right, the paper is right. Yet, if you take it to be authenticated (I have), they won't—it doesn't have the right 'provenance.' Why? Because I own it! Presumably, had a museum presented it, would it be authentic? Clearly, an anonymous bedouin has more credibility than I do. I once took it to the Antiques Road Show. Their entire effort consisted of looking for similar copies on the internet, which of course do not exist. Therefore, they conclude, *"it has no value."* Yet, one oddball Gnostic text makes 5000 Biblical texts obsolete. Tischendorf's Bible, found in a waste basket, warrants the revision of every other Bible in existence. Doctrines, theology, and philosophy hold no weight.

THE FACTS LEADING UP TO VATICAN II

For nearly 2000 years the Jews have been accused of Deicide, but an objective look at the facts cannot come to that conclusion. Even the modernists to follow here all agree, in some form or another it was the mob.

Looking at the events leading up to the Ecumenical Council of Vatican II, one cannot help making comparisons, the question is, 'who committed ecclesiacide'?

The 1890s brought a flurry of Biblical critics, Westcott & Hort in England, the school of Tischendorf in Germany. But there is one we have not discussed, Fr. Marie-Joseph Lagrange was Rome's contribution to the cause. Fr. Lagrange became interested in Modernism at about the very same time Gnostic texts were being discovered in the late 1800s. While we are led to believe this is just coincidence, I believe it all had more to do with the discovery of the *Berlin Codex* whose 'secret' was leaked to academia. What else explains this flurry of activity, the conviction to their cause? I believe this launched a cadre of experts intent on getting ahead of the curve, to cash in on the inevitable downfall of tradition. It would revive the ancient Arianism and contest the authenticity of traditional Western values. As purveyors of a radical new evangel, fame and fortune was all in their future. Even further, it was sexy.

Fr. Lagrange used the Church of St. Stephen's in Jerusalem to found the now famous *École biblique et archéologique française de Jérusalem*, the very institution behind the later discovery of the *Dead Sea Scrolls*. It was also this very same *École biblique* that published the Catholic 'revised' Bible, called the *Jerusalem Bible*. In it, 1 John 5:7 was reduced to "so that there are three witnesses," following the lead of Westcott, Hort, & Tischendorf.

Lagrange founded the *Revue biblique* in 1892, the year the Gnostic *Gospel of Peter* was officially made public. This brought suspicions that Lagrange was a Modernist. The Papal encyclical by Pope Pius X *Pascendi* (*On the Doctrines of the Modernists*) condemning modernism was largely written in response. In 1904 Lagrange wrote *The Historical Method*, which brought about another warning as to his critical methods. By 1912 he was given the order of silence and to cease publication of the *Revue biblique,* much like would later be done to the writings of Fr. Teilhard de Chardin. Considered sort of a holy witness to their cause, upon death Lagrange was buried at St. Stephen's.

The problem lay in an earlier Papal encyclical, *Providentissimus Deus*, published in 1893. While it encouraged the use of history and science in the study of the faith, Lagrange saw it as a green light to incorporate the controversial historical-critical method started by the Griesbach/Tischendorf school. Rome believed that the silencing of Lagrange would put an end to this all… it didn't.

With prior belligerencies begun under Napoleon, the Vatican was almost entirely engaged with self-survival due to the breakup of the Papal States. The approach war brought a change in politics, Mussolini relinquished claims to the Vatican property and allowed the Church some autonomy. These distractions and those as a result of WWII meant underlings were effectively functioning as Pope on certain issues. With Pius XII preoccupied, Cardinal Bea had expanded authority opening the door for the re-habilitation of Lagrange and a calculated revision of Church doctrine and tradition.

It was the Ecumenical Council of Vatican II that to some degree severed the past, and confirmed the modern Church. Pressured by the atrocities of WWII and the fact Jules Isaac was leveraging them against the Church, provided a rationale for unifying all the world's faith under the umbrella of the 'Catholic' (now meaning 'universal' as in a franchise) Church. By proclaiming, '*Let There Be Peace on Earth and Let it Begin with Me*', Rome acquiesced to take some responsibility for those atrocities and claiming it would be the center of a new movement. To this end, all faiths were invited to send representatives to the Council of Vatican II. Jewish participation was particularly encouraged because of charges that the Church was guilty of 'teaching of contempt' for their having killed Christ, a charge specifically levied by Jules Isaac (who had lost family to the Holocaust), and promoted by Heschel and Cardinal Bea.

There are literally hundreds of books trying to explain Vatican II, none of them will tell you the following story. These books miss the simple point: if you provide a rationale for something people are already inclined to believe, people will accept the evidence unquestionably. Leveraging the predisposition of many having contempt for Rome, and others having contempt for Christianity, it would now be taught that it was Rome who had contempt of everyone else, particularly the Jews. This was reason enough for an entire revision of Christian tradition and replacing it with Gnosticism. It was the result of a long line of 'scholars' going back to Renan insisting the authentic Church was Gnostic and the Vatican new-found desire to embrace all faiths.

The method was to exonerate Modernism as represented by theologians such as Lagrange, Pierre Teilhard de Chardin, and Alfred Loisy. Cardinal Bea would have to find a way turning the encyclical *Providentissimus Deus,* originally intended to condemn Loisy (who was eventually excommunicated as a heretic), towards his favor.

The strategy was this: rather than contest the charges of contempt, which were largely fabricated from misreading the word *perfidis*, the Church decided to conditionally admit to them with the purpose of using them as a springboard for a complete revision of the Church. By siding with the Historical Critical Theorists the atrocities of WW II could be linked to ancient Church traditions, tainting those tradition, and paving the way for the new evangel.

In 1930 Augustin Bea, later to become Cardinal Bea, was appointed head of the *Pontifical Biblical Institute.* A disciple of Marie-Joseph Lagrange, Bea began to teach the doctrine amidst charges of Modernism. When Pius XII became Pope in 1939 he had all he could do to keep the Church out of financial ruin, help the Jews during the Holocaust, and dodge claims that he was a Nazi sympathizer. Amidst this, Cardinal Bea became *de facto* Pope.[9]

One of Bea's first agendas was to gain a certain respectability as an orthodox church historian. Foreseeing the dispute he was about to create, Bea needed a method of deprecating one of the Church's most holy days that had become controversial, Good Friday. The reason for this is its Litany included the word '*perfidis*,' meaning 'lack of faith,' which was understood by Jews as 'deceitful.' Jews saw this as a 'teaching of contempt,' when the prayer was only intended to pray for their salvation. Bea believed fixing this discrepancy was not enough. So, to detract from it, a minor Saturday service of blessing candles was elevated to a 'new' phantasmagorical liturgy disguised as an ancient liturgy, the Easter Vigil.

In Europe, hiding from the Nazis, Isaac was coordinating with Modernist Catholic theologians. Using the *perfidis* controversy as a starting point, he brought to bear all the research of his Renan-inspired predecessors. The plan was two-fold, prove the Church was teaching the wrong theology, then liken Christianity to the Nazis. Isaac's book *Jésus et Israël* would be released privately at a conference in Seelisberg, Austria, to prepare their party for the coming confrontation with the Church. It was before the announced discovery of the Dead Sea Scrolls.[10]

Jésus et Israël represented yet another orchestrated take-down of the Catholic Church. While the book was written by a Jew, there is actually very little Jewish about it—it is essentially a re-hashing of Catholic Modernist doctrine leveraged with accusations that the Church was somehow responsible for the Holocaust. Jules Isaac admits his collusion with heretics in the Preface:

"Should I apologize for citing Alfred Loisy here rather than Bultmann or Martin Dibelius? For it is fashionable to refer to German writers rather than French. But Loisy, unjustly forgotten today, had considerable renown among my generation. And in Levroux, the little town in the old province of Berry where I was hidden in the spring of 1944 when I wrote Part III of this book, in which exegesis is given the most extensive treatment, it would have been very hard for me to get hold of the writings of Bultmann or Dibelius. I was only too happy to have at my disposal, thanks to the great kindness of my friend Gustave Monod, the four large commentaries by Father Marie-Joseph Lagrange; they were the solid foundation on which I was able to build this work."[11]

The above quote does not appear in the French edition. While the English edition claims to be a faithful translation of the French, it in fact fudges significantly. The main issue as I see it is, were the Dead Sea Scrolls discovered as advertised, or were they coordinated to promote the Gnostic myth begun by the late 19th century 'Jesus is a myth' school? In the later English edition we find the Gnostic inspiration for Isaac's ideas and proof of their source in Renan.

"It is undeniable, however, that similarities do exist; these have been strongly substantiated by the Dead Sea Scrolls: "The Qumran documents manifest clearly that the primitive Christian Church is rooted, to a depth that no one could have suspected, in the Jewish [Essenian] sect, and borrowed from it a good part of its organization and its rites, its doctrines, ... its mystical and moral ideal."[12]

Yet, the French edition makes no such claim for it is was completed in 1946, before the Scroll's discovery. Yet it does have a suspicious 'guarded' reference to the Dead Sea, even before the Scrolls had been found. The corresponding quote from the French says:

"Dressed in white linen, they led an ascetic and monastic life, far from the world, on the shores of the Dead Sea, subject to severe rules chastity, purity, sobriety, silence, and work."[13]

Again, the 'facts' proceed the evidence. How did they know one would lead to the other? Finding a mystical 'Essene' community was clearly an agenda installed early on. This only makes sense unless they are trying to authenticate Cerinthus' fifth gospel, and this will be their evidence.

Isaac is providing very little theology or evidence of his own. Nor is much based on Jewish tradition, one must look very hard for any Jewish thought at all. He is essentially a mouthpiece for the Modernist Fr. Marie-Joseph Lagrange, by his own admission. Did he just happen upon these texts hiding in the quaint French countryside at the height of the Holocaust, or, was he part of a larger Modernist subversion?

While Bea was moving forward to re-invent the Church, both he and Isaac were coordinating with Rabbi Abraham Heschel, a mutual friend:

"[Christians] correctly understood that I was comparing them to the Nazis. If I had made the statement in a straightforward fashion saying 'you are Nazis,' it would have sounded ridiculous."[14]

— RABBI ABRAHAM HESCHEL

Heschel also advised Bea in "a rabbinic strategy in which an obsolete custom or tradition could be ignored without abrogating the law."[15] Would Heschel make such an offering unless Bea was looking for it? Bea, green-lighted to begin the process of change, eventually revised liturgical rites, paving the way for folksy musical adaptations, burlap banners, and in-the-round Bauhaus architecture. But first, and most importantly, Bea penned a Papal encyclical *Divino Afflante Spiritu*, and attributed it to the Papacy.

The purpose of this encyclical was to rehabilitate Fr. Lagrange's theology, preparing Christianity for the future discoveries of St. Stephen's *École Biblique*. The technique was this: to circumnavigate the charge of *Modernism* levied against Lagrange by Pius X, by appealing to a prior encyclical, *Providentissimus Deus,* intended to guard against dubious scientific methods. The very *condemnation* of Alfred Loisy's heretical theology by Leo XIII was now going to be turned into an *approval* by appealing to the very same encyclical! All of this leveraged on the authority of Lagrange's *École biblique*. Again, look at the quote from Isaac's introduction and realize it was he that delivered the death-blow. It was a clever shell game. From that Encyclical:

"Wherefore the same Pontiff, as he had already praised and approved the **school for biblical studies** [*École biblique*], founded at **St. Stephen's,**

Jerusalem, [Lagrange] by the Master General of the Sacred Order of Preachers - from which, to use his own words, "biblical science itself had received no small advantage, while giving promise of more" — so in the last year of his life he provided yet another way, by which these same studies, so warmly commended in the Encyclical Letter *Providentissimus Deus*, might daily make greater progress and be pursued with the greatest possible security… which contributions may be considered as the complement or fruit of the movement so happily initiated by Leo XIII. And first of all Pius X, wishing "to provide a sure way for the preparation of a copious supply of teachers, who, commended by the seriousness and the integrity of their doctrine, might explain the Sacred Books in Catholic schools… might promote the study of the Bible and all cognate sciences in accordance with the mind of the Catholic Church" he founded the Pontifical Biblical Institute, entrusted to the care of the illustrious Society of Jesus [Jesuits], which he wished endowed "with a superior professorial staff and every facility for biblical research"; he prescribed its laws and rules, professing to follow in this the "salutary and fruitful project" of Leo XIII.

— EXCERPTED FROM *DIVINO AFFLANTE SPIRITU*

Once done, he later went on to tacitly admit that excavations were already on-going and that prior research had been done by people of little skill, perhaps covering for the fact that the attempts of the late 19th century didn't deal the desired results.

… For, apart from anything else, when Our Predecessor published the Encyclical Letter *Providentissimus Deus,* hardly a single place in **Palestine had begun to be explored by means of relevant excavations. Now, however, this kind of investigation is much more frequent and, since more precise methods and technical skill have been developed in the course of actual experience, it gives us information at once more abundant and more accurate.** How much light has been derived from these explorations for the more correct and fuller understanding of the Sacred Books all experts know, as well as all those who devote themselves to these studies."[16]

— EXCERPTED FROM *DIVINO AFFLANTE SPIRITU*

All this is happening at the highest ranks of the Vatican, underlined by Papal encyclicals, in an attempt to keep step with dubious 'scientific' evidence. The question again is, how would Bea know these 'new' finds would support Loisy's theology ahead of time? How would Isaac write about them in his book *Jésus et Israël,* introduce that book at a conference in Seelisberg, Austria, all prior to the documented finding of the Scrolls, something suspiciously announced publicly at the very moment Israel was proclaimed a recognized 'socialist' state by the UN? How do we explain such coincidences? And what about the fact that the CIA was demonstrably involved in all this? The clue is this 'oriental' reference:

"The *Essenes* or *Therapeutæ* were grouped near the birthplace of John, on the eastern shores of the Dead Sea. It was imagined that the chiefs of sects ought to be recluses, having rules and institutions of their own, like the founders of religious orders. The teachers of the young were also at times species of anchorites, somewhat resembling the *gourous* of Brahminism. In fact, might there not in this be a remote influence of the *mounis* of India? Perhaps some of those wandering Buddhist monks who overran the world, as the first Franciscans did in later times..."[17]

— ERNEST RENAN, *LIFE OF JESUS*

Once again we are back to Ammonius Saccas and Iamblicus. I agree, 'imagined' is exactly the right word. How did he know to insert these 'orientalist' philosophies in 1863, and that they would be confirmed at the Dead Sea after WWII? Yet these are the very predictions proved false in the 1990s, fifty years after their discovery.

Understand, no one is saying that there were not early Gnostic groups and that they did not have authentic writings, Cerinthus is proof of that. What I am saying is that Tischendorf's concept that the oldest text dictates doctrine and trumps everything else is foolishness. Look around you, if someone a thousand years from now finds an old Edsel in a garage, does that prove everyone today drives Edsel's? The only thing any ancient document can prove is that some 'one' person believed in one particular doctrine. The discovery of one incident statistically proves nothing.

The fact that the Dead Sea Scrolls never represented a gnostic New Age cult is now commonly accepted. The Qumran cult has been shown to be an ultra-severe morality cult that rejected normal Judaism. This fact was hidden for nearly a half a century. That a pre-Christian, Buddhist cult was predicted nearly one hundred years before is also telling.

The *Berlin Codex* discovered over fifty years before containing the

Gnostic *Apocryphon of John* was coordinated to be released with the discoveries of the Gnostic *Nag Hammadi Library,* no one can deny that. They were found in a cave that could not be found afterwards.[18] Similarly, the discovery of the *Dead Sea Scrolls* has a questionable provenance having travelled throughout the Middle East, possessed by numerous factions, even spending time in New York, only to be authenticated and coordinated with the announcement that Israel was granted statehood.

All this has the suspicious stamp of the CIA. In reality the Seelisberg Conference was quietly promoted by the Catholic Church and the American National Conference of Christians and Jews founded by Everett Clinchy. However, the official itinerary handed out at the Conference listed sponsorship by *The World Brotherhood,* a CIA front sponsored by both Clinchy and Allen Dulles.

The result were two Papal Encyclicals, *Pacem in Terris,* subtitled 'On establishing universal peace in truth, justice, charity and liberty' (1963), and *Nostra Aetate* 'In Our Time' (1965). The first was a critique of modern society listing 173 points of 'social justice,' the second a capitulation proclaiming the legitimacy of all religions.

While both encyclicals sound wonderful to the modern ear, the Catholic Church would not have made such a concession unless it had conceived a new basis of power, and a new basis of faith. If they could not find truth in tradition, they would find it in innovation. It would not be long before Isaac's book was shown to not carry much weight either, the claim of 'teaching of contempt' could not stand up to scrutiny—'lacking faith' was just not the same as *perfidious* contempt. If one looks at popular publications from that time period such as articles in *Look* magazine, it is obvious the intent was to advance world socialism all backed up by what would be called Liberation Theology. The Church had become more useful to the politician than to the one looking for salvation. In many of these articles the very people once silenced as heretics, such as Fr. Teilhard de Chardin, were now portrayed as visionaries and martyrs. The true purpose was transparent—Gnosticism was true, Orthodoxy was the fraud. The theology of the Church was now to be based upon a falsification of Platonic doctrine.

THE END OF THE FINAL CHAPTER

As we have seen from the beginning, philosophy was founded on the idea that ancient barbaric customs, *pharmakon,* needed replacing, it was leading to the hubris of the mob. As we have also seen from the same source, writings themselves are poor representatives of philosophical concepts. To accept the modern school we must reject both of the above. While the majority of scholars today may consider themselves 'platonists,' the fact is both of the quotes at the beginning of this book come from Plato, and they themselves contest the very sophistry we now see. Disregarding doctrine and philosophy is to sever religion from the very thing a religion is meant to do, to teach a moral conformity of mind to reality in the hope of an everlasting life.

What we firmly state is that the orthodox Church was not an invention of the fourth century. It was the falsification of 1 John 5:7 that began and allowed this misrepresentation. Once understood, the evidence everywhere. In this argument numbers matter not, only authenticity does, and that is proven by the authenticity of the 'Three Holy Witnesses.' With the verse in its proper place, John's writings as a rebuttal to Cerinthus simply make more sense as do the events of Nicaea.

We now find ourselves in a peculiar dilemma. We expect to find a Christ that is both authentic and scientific. He must fulfill the demands of our personal frailties yet be more technologically relevant than our cell phones, more entertaining than the best rock concert. The underlying Arian philosophy, universal unity, the monopsyche, is the basis of socialism, and totalitarianism. The Christian doctrine of 'love' has been completely misrepresented as a simplistic compassion, stripped of truth and responsibility. Faith is no longer a faith in something, but faith in faith itself. It all gives the illusion of freedom, but it is not. The goal is the pleroma, the one thought. The doctrine is one of control more than freedom. Society is simply more controllable if we all think the same thing.

What should be 'a tell' is that it always leads to a dystopia, not the promised utopia The monopysche lacks the ability to define 'the moral.' Having a false understanding of what philosophy and truth are, it avoids both like the plague. Never understanding the plight of philosophy, it seeks meaning in a new *pharmakon* based on entertainment and social apps. It has deaf ears to the warnings of Plato, someone it claims to regard as its master. The Church it invents is no more remarkable than anything else.

Therefore, the unity this system seeks avoids the very conceptual understanding of Truth that would give the system meaning. For this reason, it fills this void of meaning by forcing itself onto others, demanding higher and higher allegiances to Unity. The result is it mocks itself as it declares gibberish as poetry, noise as music, slop as art. It does this all the while declaring that which does have beauty and meaning as being too western. In this it produces nothing more than trances, nothing more significant than confusion.

The fact is we've all been duped. Not knowing the source, the magic power of the gnostic has mesmerized our ways as we try to attach meanings to things where no meaning was ever intended. We've assumed a profundity behind their art that was never there. Just as we have been led astray by false evidence, we can now return knowing the true source of their falsities.

While there have been many attempts at solving the dilemma of modern culture, none will work until we see it for what it is: the sophisticated elaboration of a very ancient heresy. What comes to mind is a quote from the movie Patton, "Rommel, you magnificent bastard! I read your book!" It is this we need to do, and hopefully I've given the road map.

It is all a conceptual misunderstanding of the nature of Freewill. True Freedom could never be unlimited permission to do whatever one liked. Freedom can't be promised through propaganda, marketing, or by fulfilling insatiable desires. Nor can it be found in the membership to a moral-less club that abolishes all doctrine, all rules, and all traditions. None of this cultivates the mind, nor promotes understanding. The best it could ever do is promote sophistry, a method by which the trivial trumps the conceptual. Freedom will never rectify that which Truth cannot.

---

1. Le Bon, Gustave. *The Crowd: a study of the popular mind by Gustave Le Bon.*(Psychologie des Foules) 1895
2. Lindberg, David C. *The Beginnings of Western Science*, Univ. of Chicago, 1992
3. Wakefield, Walter L. and Evans, Austin P. *Heresies of the High Middle Ages*, Columbia University, 1969, p.462
4. Guil, Shlomo. *"The Shapira Scroll was an Authentic Dead Sea Scroll"*. Palestine Exploration Quarterly, 2017. p.9
5. Zeitlin, Solomon. *Jewish Quarterly Review*, Vol. XLI, July 1950, No. 1. p.50
6. Admonition:

    "Several works of Fr. Pierre Teilhard de Chardin, some of which were posthumously published, are being edited and are gaining a good deal of success.

    Prescinding from a judgement about those points that concern the positive sciences, it is sufficiently clear that the above-mentioned works abound in such ambiguities and indeed even serious errors, as to offend Catholic doctrine.

    For this reason, the most eminent and most revered Fathers of the Holy Office exhort all Ordinaries as well as the superiors of Religious institutes, rectors of seminaries and presidents of universities, effectively to protect the minds, particularly of the youth, against the dangers presented by the works of Fr. Teilhard de Chardin and of his followers. Given at Rome, from the palace of the Holy Office, on the thirtieth day of June, 1962. – Sebastianus Masala, Notarius – L'Osservatore Romano, July 1, 1962," p.1 https://www.ewtn.com/library/CURIA/CDFTEILH.HTM
7. Kaplan, Edward K. *Spiritual Radical: Abraham Joshua Heschel in America*, Yale Univ. p.243
8. Sabar, Ariel. *Veritas: A Harvard Professor, A Con Man and the Gospel of Jesus Wife*, Anchor, 2020. p.335

9. Kaiser, Robert Blair. *Pope, Council and World*, Macmillan, New York, 1963, p.156-7 Blair was the official news correspondent to Vatican II

10. Isaac refers to the Dead Sea Scroll discovery in the book prior to the date given of their discovery.

11. Isaac, Jules. *Jésus et Israël*, Éditions Albin Michel, 1948. — *Jesus and Israel*, Holt, Rinehart, Winston, English Edition, 1971, p.xxiv

12. Isaac, Jules. *Jesus and Israel*, Holt, Rinehart, Winston, English Edition, 1971, p.83

13. Isaac, Jules, *Jésus et Israël*, (the French edition) p.83

14. Kaplan, Edward K. *Spiritual Radical: Abraham Joshua Heschel in America*, Yale Univ. p.271

15. Kaplan, Edward K. *Spiritual Radical: Abraham Joshua Heschel in America*, Yale Univ. p.242

16. Vatican   —   https://www.vatican.va/content/pius-xii/en/encyclicals/documents/hf_p-xii_enc_30091943_divino-afflante-spiritu.html

17. Renan, Ernest. *Life of Jesus*. Roberts, 1863 (the Modern Library, New York, 1927) p.137

18. Rudolph, Kurt. *Gnosis: The Nature and History of Gnosticism*, A&C Black, 2001, p.35

EPILOGUE

One of the surprising discoveries I made while researching this was a fairly large branch of Christianity influenced by a rather strange idea —that the true Christian Church didn't begin until the late Middle Ages. To them, the Council of Nicaea was not the affirmation of the true Church, it was proof the early Church was not the real Church. The failures of the Council, they believe, led to the collapse of the Roman Empire followed by the inevitable Dark Ages. To them, authentic Christianity only first began with Europe's re-discovery of the Greek Bible, which by then many lacked the verse in question. They, therefore, were locked in a predicament. Not trusting anything before the re-emergence of this Bible as authentic, they had no choice but to regard everything necessary for salvation to be contained therein. It wasn't so much that they wanted there Bible to be infallible, *it had to be infallible as they trusted nothing else.*

I have a deep distrust over this mode of thinking, yet finding your way out is not without peril itself. Imagine yourself to be a math professor and student comes to you asking you to assess her new discovery—is her equation true or false? Only a professor exceeding her in knowledge could ever make such an assessment, but is this not us when we say 'this particular Bible is infallible, and I understand everything therein'? How do we make such a determination without claiming a certain infallibility ourselves? And isn't this a sort of hubris?

It was this very thinking that led to the authentication as 'infallible' a set of verses that are clearly Arian. It was this misplaced expectation of inerrancy that forced them to condemn one version of the Bible for the another *for all time*. It was the same expectation of *Man's* infallible judgment combined with the belief that he is in position to make a once-for-all determination that created the predicament.

Yet, on some level we are all faced with this problem. To 'know' does not mean we can know everything exhaustively, there is a limit. Many things we can know for certain. Some things will always be our best guess. Some we accept on faith. However, to many people (such as the above) the Council was a vain effort to know too much. The Council wouldn't have been held if the people had only trusted in the inerrancy of Scripture, but as has been said, to know without understanding leads to sophistry.

An honest evaluation of the Council of Nicaea reveals none of this sort of thinking. We find three parties, not two. We find Arius, condemned for having a doctrine few understood, yet, he eventually does ask for reconciliation. While conceding he is wrong, he is questioned over his sincerity, and his humility. We find Athanasius, a person condemned more times than Arius for his lack of humility and rash behavior, but primarily because he held a truth many were hesitant to embrace.

I look at the two main parties of Nicaea, and I find their conventional labels inadequate… nor is the conventional story. I don't see two parties at each other's throats, nor do I find doctrinal questions worthy of condemnation. The key word, *homoousios*, was actually avoided as much as possible, perhaps because of its ring of Gnosticism. Yet, the word was forced upon them politically, and they came to a definition that that allowed the faith to heal and move on.

I see not the Council of Nicaea, or even Constantinople as the determining factor. It was St. Lucian, someone the above thinking would condemn, and a Council most have never heard of as the best representation of Christian charity and of what was truly going on—where one party paused, confirmed what they knew, and admitted what they didn't. This very fact that they were willing to approach the dilemma in the way they did, only confirms their holiness. It also confirms that the expectation of inerrant thinking is not without error itself.

I now find the more Jewish approach to Scripture more appealing. Questions over the acceptability, the understanding, the authenticity of a verse may come up, but in the end there is a general acceptance to let scripture be scripture, not everything therein is for us to know. Some things must be preserved for another generation to know. This is the purpose of Tradition. As a wiseman once told me[1]…

"…let God be God."

———————————————

1. Blessed Archimandrite Fr. Anthony Good

APPENDIX TO CHAPTER TWENTY

CONTENTS

FRATERNITÉ MONDIALE
(WORLD BROTHERHOOD)
37, QUAI WILSON, GENÈVE (Suisse)

Table of Contents to the Seelisberg Conference handout showing affiliation with the Fraternité Mondial aka World Brotherhood. Officially it was founded in 1950, but here it appears as a sponsor of the event.

WORLD BROTHERHOOD

Established in 1950 by men and women who believe in a spiritual or moral interpretation of the universe to promote understanding, justice and cooperation among people differing in religion, race, nation, social status or culture

Building for Brotherhood, 43 West 57th Street, New York 19, New York

Tel. MUrray Hill 8-7530   Cable Address: NYWORLDBRO New York

Executive R. istry
70-3287

Co-Chairmen

Arthur H. Compton   Carlos P. Romulo
Paul-Henri Spaak   Konrad Adenauer
Madame Vijaya Lakshmi Pandit

Administrative President
Everett R. Clinchy

Executive Secretary
Margaret Grant

GENERAL ASSEMBLY

Hermann J. Abs, Frankfurt a.M.
F. Albert-Buisson, Paris
Roger Auboin, Basle
Charles E. Beard, Dallas
Marcel Bélaïche, Alger
G. D. Birla, New Delhi
F. Bender, Amsterdam
Pierre Bonvoisin, Bruxelles
Sam Bronfman, Montreal
Baron Collot d'Escury, Amsterdam
Alphonse Dain, Paris
Albert DeSmaele, Bruxelles
Allen W. Dulles, New York
Lady Eaton, Toronto
Abderrahmane Farès, Alger
Ferdinand Friedensburg, Berlin
Ejnar Glashof, København
John D. Hayes, Toronto
Robert Hentsch, Genève
Paul G. Hoffman, Pasadena
Barbara Ward Jackson, London
Rajkumari Amrit Kaur, New Delhi
Guill Konsbruck, Luxembourg
Blair Laing, Toronto
Franz Landertshammer, Wien
Herbert H. Lehman, New York
Trygve Lie, Oslo
Victor Loeb, Bern
Henry R. Luce, New York
H. N. MacCracken, Poughkeepsie
Alfred Mayer, Wiesbaden
Sir Robert Mayer, London
John J. McCloy, New York
George B. McKibbin, Chicago
T. H. McKittrick, New York
George Meany, Washington
Leo Model, New York
Emmanuel Monick, Paris
Ludovico Montini, Roma
Luigi Morandi, Milano
V. V. Nortikar, Banaras
Heinz Nordhoff, Wolfsburg
Per Norlin, Stockholm
Basil O'Connor, New York
Adriano Olivetti, Ivrea
Giulio Pastore, Roma
Warren Lee Pierson, New York
Alfredo Pizzoni, Milano
P. Kodanda Rao, Bangalore
Eberhardt Reinhardt, Zurich
Paul Reynaud, Paris
Eleanor Roosevelt, New York
Ramon del Rosario, Manila
James N. Rosenberg, New York
P. Rossy, Bern
F. J. Th. Rutten, Nijmegen
P. J. S. Serrarens, Luxembourg
M. Raziuddin Siddiqi, Peshawar
Gregg M. Sinclair, Honolulu
Gurbax Singh, New Delhi
Spyros Skouras, New York
Robert A. Solberg, Paris
Hilel Storch, Stockholm
John L. Sullivan, Washington
Vidui A. Tun, Quezon
Kotaro Tanaka, Tokyo
Gaston Tessier, Paris
Norman Thomas, New York
Francisca Tirona-Benitez, Manila
Wilfred Tsukiyama, Honolulu
E. de la Vallée-Poussin, Bruxelles
Prince Wan Waithayakon, Bangkok
Marcus Wallenberg, Stockholm
Juan Williams, Bruxelles
Lars Wirström, Stockholm
Arthur W. Woo, Hong Kong
Sir Zafrulla Khan, Karachi
Umberto Zanotti-Bianco, Roma
Walter A. Zimmerman, Seattle

April 28, 1958

Mr. Allen W. Dulles
Central Intelligence Agency
Washington 25, D. C.

Dear Allen,

As a member of the General Assembly of World Brotherhood you are aware, of course, of the fact that we are a charitable non-profit organization and that our work is supported by funds which we receive from individuals, corporations and foundations. In carrying on correspondence with these various sources of funds our regular letterhead, on which your name appears, is used.

The New York Social Welfare Law requires that we must have the written consent of any person whose name may be used in soliciting funds in the State of New York. The New York Department of Social Welfare interprets this law as meaning that a letter soliciting funds, written on a letterhead carrying the names of individuals, constitutes the use of these names for the purpose of soliciting contributions.

We should therefore appreciate your signing the enclosed Form of Consent and returning it to us in the enclosed envelope at your earliest convenience. Your help is very much appreciated.

Sincerely yours,

Everett

Everett R. Clinchy

ERC:mp
Enclosures

(EXECUTIVE REGISTRY FILE

EUROPEAN DIVISION

European Executive Committee Chairman
Albert De Smaele
Divisional Executive Secretary
Pierre A. Vissaur
Centre International, Geneva, Switzerland

ASIA-PACIFIC DIVISION

Divisional Executive Secretaries
Dr. & Mrs. William A. Shimer
c/o Oo Thein, 340 Maha Bandoola St.
Rangoon, Burma

NORTH AMERICAN DIVISION

United States Executive Committee Chairman
George B. McKibbin
43 West 57th Street, New York
Canadian Executive Secretary
Richard D. Jones
221 Victoria Street, Toronto, Canada

A letter from Dr. Everett Clinchy, Commissioner to the Seelisberg Conference, to Allen Dulles, head of the Central Intelligence Agency (CIA) acknowledging membership.

IV-2686

WORLD BROTHERHOOD

Established in 1950 by men and women who believe in a spiritual or moral interpretation of the universe to promote
understanding, justice and cooperation among people differing in religion, race, nation, social status or culture

Building for Brotherhood, 43 West 57th Street, New York 19, New York

Tel. MUrray Hill 8-7530   Cable Address: NYWORLDBRO New York

SPONSORS

Herman Abs, Frankfurt a. M.
Marcel Beloiche, Alger
G. D. Birla, New Delhi
F. Bender, Amsterdam
Pierre Bonvoisin, Bruxelles
N. Brounshausen, Luxembourg
Samuel Bronfman, Montreal
Jacques Chevallier, Alger
Giovanni Cireolo, Roma
Baron Collot d'Escury, Amsterdam
Sir Stanford Cooper, London
Alphonse Dain, Paris
S. K. Dey, Calcutta
William J. Donovan, New York
James G. Douglas, Dublin
Allen W. Dulles, New York
Lady Eaton, Toronto
Abderrahmane Fares, Alger
Benson Ford, Detroit
Ferdinand Friedensburg, Berlin
Einar Glashof, Kobenhavn
B. Th. W. van Hasselt, den Haag
John D. Hayes, Toronto
Paul G. Hoffman, Pasadena
Rajkumari Amrit Kaur, New Delhi
Gulli Konsbruck, Luxembourg
Heinrich Krumm, Frankfurt a. M.
Herbert H. Lehman, New York
Patrick J. Little, Dublin
Victor Loeb, Berne
Henry R. Luce, New York
H. N. MacCracken, Poughkeepsie
Eugen Margaretha, Wien
Alfred Mayer, Wiesbaden
Sir Robert Mayer, London
John J. McCloy, New York
Walter McKee, Genève
George B. McKibbin, Chicago
T. H. McKittrick, New York
George Meany, Washington
Emmanuel Monick, Paris
Gaston Monnerville, Paris
Ludovico Montini, Roma
Luigi Morandi, Milano
V. V. Narlikar, Banaras
Heinz Nordhoff, Wolfsburg
Per Norlin, Stockholm
Basil O'Connor, New York
Adriano Olivetti, Torino
Vijaya Lakshmi Pandit, New Delhi
Giulio Pastore, Roma
Warren Lee Pierson, New York
Alfredo Pizzoni, Milano
P. Kodanda Rao, Bangalore
Paul Reynaud, Paris
Carlos P. Romulo, Manila
Eleanor Roosevelt, New York
James N. Rosenberg, New York
F. J. Th. Rutten, Nijmegen
P. J. S. Serrarens, Luxembourg
M. Razluddin Siddiqi, Peshawar
Gregg M. Sinclair, Honolulu
Spyros P. Skouras, New York
Albert De Smaele, Bruxelles
Hilal Storch, Stockholm
Roger W. Straus, New York
Vidal A. Tan, Quezon
Gaston Tessier, Paris
Norman Thomas, New York
Francisco Tirana-Benitez, Manila
Cosme de la Torriente, Habana
Vittorio Valletta, Torino
Vittorino Veronese, Roma
Thomas J. Watson, New York
Arthur W. Woo, Hong Kong
Sir Zafrullah Khan, Karachi
Umberto Zanotti-Bianco, Roma
Walter A. Zimmerman, Bangkok

Co-Chairmen
Arthur H. Compton   Carlos P. Romulo
Paul-Henri Spaak   Konrad Adenauer
Madame Vijaya Lakshmi Pandit

Administrative President
Everett R. Clinchy

Executive Secretary
Margaret Grant
Building for Brotherhood
43 West 57th Street, New York

April 8, 1958

The Honorable Allen W. Dulles
Central Intelligence Agency
Washington, D. C.

Dear Allen,

In reviewing the recent activities of World Brotherhood, it has occurred to me that, as one of the founders of this organization, you might be deeply interested in some of the developing potentials for reaching world audiences and for creating constructive relationships among peoples on all continents.

Before describing some of our overseas projects, I should like to point out that each one of them was launched with the conviction that there is a crying need for citizen participation in international and intercultural activities at levels which cannot be successfully exploited through governmental channels alone. Our recent success has strengthened this conviction. We are equally aware, however, that in order to capitalize upon these successes, and to take our work beyong the realm of initial experiment, we must seek out sound advice from those who, like yourself, have had long experience in dealing with the relations of people of many nations, races, beliefs and cultural backgrounds. We also need advice on potential sources of material support to enable World Brotherhood to take advantage of the opportunities opening up.

I

First, in November 1957, as an effort to stimulate thought on problems of brotherhood and international human relations, we, with the cooperation of the Voice of America and the world press, announced an international essay contest on "What World Brotherhood Means to Me". By February 1958 we had received essays from 108 nations and territories —including a number from Iron Curtain countries. The great majority came from "uncommitted" areas such as India, Burma, Ghana, Nigeria, etc. and the contents revealed an almost universal concern with the basic verities of brotherhood. The four winners from Ghana, Burma, Mexico and Denmark, came to New York for two weeks as our guests. After their return, and after our second prizes - 125 copies of "The Family of Man" - had been distributed in fifty countries, we received in the form of

EUROPEAN DIVISION

European Executive Committee Chairman
Albert De Smaele
Divisional Executive Secretary
Pierre A. Visser
Centre International, Geneva,
Switzerland

ASIA-PACIFIC DIVISION

Divisional Executive Secretary
William A. Shimer
Box 3106, Honolulu

NORTH AMERICAN DIVISION

United States Executive Committee Chairman
George B. McKibbin
43 West 57th Street, New York
Divisional Executive Secretary
Richard D. Jones
221 Victoria Street, Toronto, Canada

BIBLIOGRAPHY

Armfield, Rev. H. T. *The Three Witnesses: the Disputed Text in St. John Considerations New and Old*, Samuel Bagster and Sons, London, 1883

Augustine, St. Schaff, Philip. *St. Augustine's City of God and Christian Doctrine.* CCEL, 1890

Augustine, Marcus Dods. From Nicene and Post-Nicene Fathers, First Series, Vol. 2. Edited by Philip Schaff. (Buffalo, NY: Christian Literature Publishing Co., 1887.) Revised and edited for New Advent by Kevin Knight. http://www.newadvent.org/fathers/120105.htm

Augustine, 'Chapter 23.—What Hermes Trismegistus Thought Concerning Idolatry, and from What Source He Knew that the Superstitions of Egypt Were to Be Abolished,' *The City of God*, Philip Schaff,

Athanasius, *On the Councils of Ariminum and Seleucia*

Autran, Charles. 'Bibliothèque égyptologique. Tome XXXI. *Lettres et journaux de Champollion recueillis et annotés par H. Hartleben.*—Tome deuxième. Lettres et journaux écrits pendant le voyage en Egypte. Paris-Leroux 1909.' *Sphinx: revue critique embrassant le domaine entier de l'égyptologie* 14, no. 1 1910

Babiniotis, Georgios, https://johanninecomma.blogspot.com/2020/09/voulgaris-vindicated-by-leading-greek.html

Bakan, David, *Sigmund Freud and the Jewish Mystical Tradition*, Free Association Books, London, 1958/1990

Beatrice, Pier Franco. "The word 'homoousios' from Hellenism to Christianity." *Church History* 71, no. 2, 2002

Bellarmine, Robert. Disputationum De controuersiis christianae fidei (Disputations about Controversies of the Christian Faith). Peter L P Simpson August 2013. 1615. http://books.google.com/books?id=vqJaa8h_teQC&pg=PP22&dq=bellarmini+controversiae&hl=en&sa=X&ei=5ZGvUcO9HtS44APBqoHgAg&ved=0CDkQ6AEwAjgU

Bentley, James. *Secrets of Mount Sinai: the story of the world's oldest Bible--Codex Sinaiticus,* Doubleday & Co. New York, 1986

Bittle. Celestine N., O.F.M. Cap. *Reality and the Mind: Epistemology,* Fallacy of Idealism,, Bruce Pub., Milw. 1936

Browne, Charles Gordon and Swallow, James Edward. *Nicene and Post-Nicene Fathers, Second Series*, Vol. 7. Philip Schaff and Henry Wace ed. (Buffalo, NY: Christian Literature Publishing Co., 1894.) Revised and edited for New Advent by Kevin Knight. http://www.newadvent.org/fathers/310231.htm.

Bruce, Frederick Fyvie. *The Canon of Scripture.* Downers Grove, IL: Intervarsity Press, 1988

Buchwald & Josefowicz, *The Zodiac of Paris: How an Improbable Controversy over an Ancient Egyptian Artifact Provoked a Modern Debate between Religion and Science,* Princeton University Press, 2010

Buchwald, Jed Z., and Diane Greco Josefowicz. *The riddle of the Rosetta: how an English polymath and a French polyglot discovered the meaning of Egyptian hieroglyphs.* Princeton University Press, 2020

Budge, E. A. Wallis. *Egyptian Language: Easy Lessons in Egyptian Hieroglyphics.* Dover, Mineola, NY, 1983 [1910]

Bueno, P., Balbín, R. & Barroso, R. (cur.)'A study of the microscopic residue and organic compounds in grinding tools and jar contents.' El dolmen de Toledo (pp. 235–241). Alcalá de Henares, Spain: Universidad de Alcalá.

Burgess, Thomas. (Bishop of St. David's) *A Vindication of 1 John,v.7, From the Objections of M. Griesbach*, 1756-1837

Burgon, Dean John William and Miller, Edward. *The Traditional Text of the Holy Gospels*

The Catholic Encyclopedia, (Saint Augustine, New York, 1886, p. 51) Portalié, E. 1907. *Life of St. Augustine of Hippo*. New York: Robert Appleton Company. Retrieved March 9, 2023 from New Advent: http://www.newadvent.org/cathen/02084a.htm]

The Catholic Encyclopedia, Havey, F. *'Alogi'*. Robert Appleton New York, Company. 1907 — Retrieved February 25, 2023 from New Advent: http://www.newadvent.org/cathen/01331b.htm

The Catholic Encyclopedia. Havey, F. *'Clement of Alexandria'*. Robert Appleton Company. New York 1908 — Retrieved March 9, 2023 from New Advent: http://www.newadvent.org/cathen/04045a.htm

The Catholic Encyclopedia, Chapman, J. 'Paul of Samosata'. Robert Appleton Company. New York 1911 — Retrieved Jan 20, 2024 from New Advent: http://www.newadvent.org/cathen/11589a.htm

Charinus, Leucius. "The Secret Book of John and Thalia," Academia.edu https://www.academia.edu/44862334/_The_Secret_Book_of_John_and_Thalia_

C.I.A. FOIA Reading Room, https://www.cia.gov/readingroom/

Copenhaver, Brian P. *Hermetica: The Greek Corpus Hermeticum and the Latin Asclepius in a new English translation, with notes and introduction*. Cambridge University Press, 1995.

Couliano, Ioan P, *Eros and Magic in the Renaissance*, Univ. of Chicago, 1987

Burgess, Thomas. *A Vindication of 1 John 5:7, from the Objections of M. Griesbach*, Anglican Bishop of St. David's, 1756-1837

Caldwell, Thomas S. J. (trans.) Marquette University in Milwaukee, WI. The translation comes from the *Codex Fuldensis* (c. A. D. 541-546)

Calhoun, John B. 'Population Density and Social Pathology,' *Scientific American*, Nov. 1970.

Champollion, Jean François 'the Young.' *Egyptian Pantheon, collection of mythological characters from ancient Egypt*, (Pantheon Egyptien. collection des personnages mythologiques de l'ancienne égypte, d'après les monuments avec un texte explicatif par M. J, F. Champollion le Jeune, et les figures d'apres les dessins de M. L, J. J. Dubois) figures after the drawings of M. L, J. J. Dubois

Chisholm, Hugh, ed. The Encyclopædia britannica: a dictionary of arts, sciences, literature and general information. Vol. 29. At the University press, 1911.—article 'Brooke Foss Westcott'

Collins, Derek. *Magic in the ancient Greek world*. John Wiley & Sons, 2008

Crombie, Alistair Cameron. *Robert Grosseteste and the origins of experimental science*. Clarendon Press, 1953

Cudworth, Ralph, *The true intellectual system of the universe*: 1617-1688; Birch, Thomas, 1705-1766

Cumont, Franz. *Astrology and Religion among the Greeks and Romans*. GP Putnam's sons, 1912

Cyril of Alexandria, *Fourth Letter of Cyril to Nestorius*, NPNF2 14:198) — https://www.thegospelcoalition.org/essay/trinitarianism-in-the-early-church/

Dakyns, H. G. trans. *The works of Xenophon*. Vol. 1. Macmillan and Company, 1890

Descartes, René. *The Philosophical Writings of Descartes*. Translated by John Cottingham et al., I, 113, Cambridge University Press, 1985.

Dobson, John Lowry. *Advaita Vedanta and modern science*. Vivekanada Vedanta Society, 1979

Dodd, Charles H. *The Bible and the Greeks*, Hodder & Stoughton, London, 1954

Döpp, Siegmar, and Wilhelm Geerlings, eds. *Dictionary of Early Christian Literature*. Crossroad Publishing, 2000

Dreyfus, Alfred. *Five Years of My Life*, G. Newnes, 1901

Duhem, Pierre. *To save the phenomena: An essay on the idea of physical theory from Plato to Galileo*. University of Chicago Press, 2015

Durant, Will. *Caesar and Christ: The Story of Civilization, Volume III*. Vol. 3. Simon and Schuster, 2011

Derrida, Jacques,, and Johnson, Barbara. "Plato's Pharmacy." *Dissemination. University of Chicago Press, Chicago* (1981): 61-171 from the French translation of the Greek by Léon Robin

Enfield, William. *The History of Philosophy: From the Earliest Times to the Beginning of the Present Century: Drawn Up from Brucker's Historia Critical Philosophiae*. 1839

Elliott, J.K. *Codex Sinaiticus and the Simonides Affair*, Mt. Athos, 1982

Encyclopædia Britannica, Inc. *Article on George Berkeley* 1994-2001

Encyclopedia Britannica from the article "Gospel of Thomas' https://www.britannica.com/topic/Gospel-of-Thomas

Encyclopedia Britannica 1911. Chisholm, Hugh, ed. *The Encyclopædia britannica: a dictionary of arts, sciences, literature and general information*. Vol. 29. At the University press, 1911. — article 'Arius'

Enderbie, Percy. *Cambria Triumphans: Brittain in its Perfect Lustre*, 1661

Epiphanius, Williams, Frank, ed. *The Panarion of Epiphanius of Salamis, Books II and III. De Fide: Second*. Vol. 79. Brill, 2012

Esterházy, Marie Charles Ferdinand Walsin. *Les dessous de l'affaire Dreyfus*. Fayard Frères, éditeurs, 1898

Eucherius, Episcopus Lugdunensis

Eunapius, *Lives of the Philosophers and Sophists* 'Maximus' 1921 (English translation)". https://www.tertullian.org/fathers/eunapius_02_text.htm

Eusebius, Kirsopp Lake. *Eusebius: Ecclesiastical History, Books IV (Loeb Classical Library, No. 153)*. Loeb Classical Library, 1926.

Evans-Wentz, and Yeeling, Walter ed. *The Tibetan book of the dead: Or the after-death experiences on the bardo plane, according to Lama Kazi Dawa-Samdup's English Rendering*. Oxford University Press, 1937. introduction, Carl Jung

Faraone, Christopher. *"Empedocles the sorcerer and his hexametrical pharmaka." Antichthon 53 (2019): 14-32*. translation Kingsley, 1995

Faulkner, Raymond, Goelet, Ogden, Andrews, Carol. *The Egyptian Book of the Dead: The Book of Going Forth by Day the Complete Papyrus of Ani*, Spell 125A

Felt, Brian E. & Butler, Thomas. ed. *Monumenta Bulgarica: A bilingual anthology of Bulgarian texts from the 9th to the 19th Century*. Michigan Slavic Publications, Ann Arbor, 1996

Ferrando, Mike. *The Comma Calmly Considered, Symbolum of Antioch 341 AD*, July 10, 2022 — Found and translated in, 'The Christian Examiner, and Church of Ireland Magazine,' vol 2, 1826, p. 57-58)

Forsberg, Randall Caroline Watson. 'Ritual Cannibalism, A Case Study of Socially Sanctioned Group Violence,' in *Toward a Theory of Peace*. Cornell University Press, 2019, ISBN: 1501744356

Foxe, John. Foxe's book of martyrs. Morgan & Scott, 1899. Chp. 3—'Persecutions Under the Arian Heretics'

Frankfort, Henri. *Ancient Egyptian Religion*, Columbia University Press, New York, 1948

Freud, Sigmond. *Group Psychology and the Analysis of the Ego*, James Strachey trans. WW Norton & Company, 1975

The Gospel Coalition, https://www.thegospelcoalition.org/essay/trinitarianism-in-the-early-church/

Graves, B.M. et al., 'The Death of Socrates', Classical Quarterly, 23, 1973, pp. 25-8 and 'Did Socrates Die of Hemlock Poisoning?', New York State Journal of Medicine, 77.1, Feb., 1977, pp. 254-8, 'Hemlock Poisoning: Twentieth Century Scientific Light Shed on the Death of Socrates,' pp. 156-68 in Boudouris, K.J., ed, The Philosophy of Socrates, International Center for Greek Philosophy and Culture, Athens, 1991

Gibbon, Edward *The Decline and Fall of the Roman Empire*. Strahan & Cadell, London. 1776

Goodrick-Clarke, Nicholas. *The occult roots of Nazism: secret Aryan cults and their influence on Nazi ideology: the Ariosophists of Austria and Germany, 1890-1935*. Tauris Parke, 2005

Graney, Christopher. 'How a Jesuit Astronomer and His Student beat Isaac Newton to a Key Idea by more than 50 Years,' May 2019 — https://www.vaticanobservatory.org/sacred-space-astron omy/how-a-jesuit-astronomer-and-his-student-beat-isaac-newton-to-a-key-idea-by-more-than-50-years/

Guil, Shlomo. "The Shapira Scroll was an Authentic Dead Sea Scroll". *Palestine Exploration Quarterly*. 2017

Guitton, J., *La Philosophie de Newman*, Paris, 1933

Hall, Manly P., and Knapp, J. Augustus. *The Secret Teachings of All Ages: An Encyclopedic outline of Masonic, Hermetic, Qabbalistic and Rosicrucian Symbolical Philosophy*, H.S. Crocker Company, 1928

Harris, R. Baine (ed.) 'Imagery in Plotinus and Indian Thought' in, *Neoplatonism and Indian Thought* (Norfolk, VA, 1982), 129.9 (*Dorrie, op. cit.*, p. 54) The International Society for Neoplatonic Studies

Haydock, George Leo. *The Holy Bible*. E. Dunigan and Brother, 1852

Healy, Chris. *Confessions of a Journalist*, Chatto & Windus, 1904

Headings, Mildred J. *French Freemasonry under the Third Republic*: The Masons Plan a Laic State, Johns Hopkins Press, 1949

Hippolytus, *Haer.* 5.7.8–9 by MacMahon, J.H. Trans. *Ante-Nicene Fathers*, Vol. 5. Edited by Alexander Roberts, James Donaldson, and A. Cleveland Coxe. Christian Literature Publishing Co., Buffalo, NY 1886. — Revised and edited for New Advent by Kevin Knight. http://www.newadvent.org/fathers/050105.htm.

Hort, Arthur. *Life and Letters of Fenton John Anthony Hort*, Vol. I, Macmillan & Co., 1896, p.250 https://www.jstor.org/stable/3140075

Houghton, H.A.G. *Augustine's Text of John. Patristic Citations and Latin Gospel Manuscripts*. Oxford: OUP, 2008. ISBN 978-0-19-954592-6

Huxley, Aldous. *The doors of perception*. London: Chatto and Windus, 1954

Iamblichus, Bulmer-Thomas, Ivor. Robin Waterfield (trans.) *The Theology of Arithmetic: On the Mystical, Mathematical and Cosmological Symbolism of the First Ten Numbers*. Grand Rapids, Michigan: Phanes Press, 1988

Iamblichus, from the https://theosophytrust.org/282-iamblichus web site

Ica, I. Jr. *Mistagogia: Experienta lui Dumnezeu in Orthodoxie* (Sibiu: Deisis, 1998) 184-267. (The Form of God and Vision of the Glory: Some Thoughts on the Anthropomorphite Controversy of 399 AD) https://www.marquette.edu/maqom/morphe.html

Ignatius, Saint, and Polycarp, Saint. *The Apostolic Fathers*. Vol. II. MacMillan, 1890. J.B. Lightfoot

Ingleby, Leonard Cresswell [Guy Thorne], *Oscar Wilde*, 1907, p. 362

Irvin, Jan R. *God's Flesh: Teononácatl — the True History of the Sacred Mushroom*, Logosmedia, 2022

Isaac, Jules. *Jésus et Israël*, Éditions Albin Michel, 1948. — *Jesus and Israel*, Holt, Rinehart, Winston, English Edition, 1971

Isaac, Jules. *The Teaching of Contempt* (*L'Enseignement du Mépris*), Holt, Rinehart and Winston. 1964, Fasquelle Éditeurs. 1962

Isaac, Jules, *Expériences de ma vie. Péguy*, Calmann-Lévy, Paris, 1960

Jesuits letters from missions. *The Jesuit Relations and Allied Documents Travels and Explo-*

rations of the Jesuit Missionaries in New France (*Relations des Jésuites de la Nouvelle-France*) 1610-1791, Vol.1, p.273, translated from the French

Johannes de Sacro-Bosco (John of Holywood) *On the Sphere of the World* (*De sphaera mundi*), 1230

Jones, Robert (trans.), *Philosophic Fire: Unifying the Fragments of HERACLITUS*

Josephus. *The Jewish War*, Book II, Chapter 8, 2-3

Kaiser, Robert Blair. *Pope, Council and World*, Macmillan, New York, 1963

Kaplan, Edward K. *Spiritual Radical: Abraham Joshua Heschel in America*, Yale Univ.

King, Karen L., *The Secret Revelation of John*, Harvard University Press, 2006

Kircheri, Athanasii [Athanasius Kircher], *Ars magna lucis et umbrae*, 1671

Kircheri, Athanasii [Athanasius Kircher], *Oedipus Aegyptiacus*, 1676

Knowles, James. The *Nineteenth Century and after*, volume 40, Sampson Low, Marston & Company, London, 1896

Le Bon, Gustave. *The Crowd: a study of the popular mind.* (*Psychologie des Foules*), T. Fisher Unwin, London, 1896 (1895)

Lewis, C. S., *Miracles*, Macmillan Publishing Co., New York, 1947

Lewis, Nicola Denzey. "Death on the Nile: Egyptian codices, Gnosticism, and Early Christian books of the dead." In *Practicing Gnosis*, Schmidt 1903

Lindberg, David C., *The Beginnings of Western Science*, Univ. of Chicago, 1992

Lindahl JR, Fisher NE, Cooper DJ, Rosen RK, Britton WB, *The varieties of contemplative experience: A mixed-methods study of meditation-related challenges in Western Buddhists*, 2017 PLOS ONE 12(5): e0176239. https://doi.org/10.1371/journal.pone.0176239

Maguire, J. Robert. *Ceremonies of Bravery: Oscar Wilde, Carlos Blacker, and the Dreyfus Affair.* Oxford University Press, USA, 2013

Maluf, Fakhri (Brother Francis). From a *Philosophia Perennis: Course on Scholasticism*, St. Augustine Institute, https://store.catholicism.org/complete-philosophy-mp3-set.html

Manetho: History of Egypt, W. G. Waddell trans, Harvard University Press, 1964

Mansel, Henry Longueville. *The Gnostic Heresies of the first and second centuries, by the late HL Mansel, with a sketch of his work, life, and character, by the earl of Carnarvon.* Ed. by JB Lightfoot. J. Murray, 1875

Martin, David. *A Critical Dissertation Upon the Seventh verse Fifth Chapter of St. John's First Epistle, wherein the authentickness of this text is fully prov'd against the Objections of the modern Arians*, referring to the section on the *Vetus Latina*, William and John Innys, 1719

Maulana, Helmi, and Hadis, Dan. *The Holy Qur'an: text, translation and commentary*, Karya Abdullah Yusuf Ali.

Mercier, Cardinal Désiré. *A manual of modern scholastic philosophy.* *V*ol. 1. K. Paul, Trench, Trubner & Company, Limited, 1916

Milton, John. *A Treatise on Christian Doctrine: Compiled from the Holy Scriptures Alone.* J. Smith, 1825

Milton, John. *The Complete Poetry of John Milton*, ed. John T. Shawcross, Anchor New York, 1971

Milton, John. *Paradise lost*, Peter Parker, 1667

Moreschini, Claudio, and Enrico Norelli. *Early Christian Greek and Latin literature: a literary history.* Hendrickson, 2005

Nazianzen, Gregory. *Orations*, Oration 45-Second Oration on Easter from New Advent, – https://www.newadvent.org/fathers/310245.htm

Negev, Eilat; Koren, Yehuda. *The First Lady of Fleet Street-The Life of Rachel Beer— Crusading Heiress and Newspaper Pioneer*, Random House Publishing, 2012

Newman, John Henry. *Apologia Pro Vita Sua:* Longmans, Green, Reader, and Dyer, 1876

Newman, John Henry. *The Arians of the fourth century.* Longmans, Green, and Company, 1901

Newton, Isaac *Principia* (*Philosophiae naturalis principia mathematica*), Last Edition 'General Scholium.' Apud Guil. & Joh. Innys, Regiæ Societatis [Royal Society], Londini, 1713 & 1726 [the General Scholium only appears in some of the very last editions]

Newton, Isaac. *An historical account of two notable corruptions of scripture: In a letter to a friend.* R. Taylor, and sold by R. Hunter, 1830 — Compiled from the Bishop Horsley's Edition 1785 taken from the authors own hand writing and a letter transcription from Oxford

Nichol, Mark. *75 Contronyms (Words with Contradictory Meanings)* https://www.dailywrit ingtips.com/75-contronyms-words-with-contradictory-meanings/

Nolan, Frederick, *An Inquiry Into the Integrity of the Greek Vulgate, Received Text of the New Testament*, 1815

Nolan, Frederick, *Testimony of the African Church Bible*

Noll, Richard, *The Aryan Christ: the Secret Life of Carl Jung*, Random House, 1997.

Nuttall, Anthony David. *The Alternative Trinity: Gnostic Heresy in Marlowe, Milton, and Blake.* Oxford University Press, 1998

Payne, Philip B.and Canart, Paul. 'The Originality of Text-Critical Symbols in *Codex Vaticanus*', p.106 https://pbpayne.com/wp-admin/Payne2000NovT-Vaticanus_umlauts_1Cor14_34-35.pdf

Pentecostal Theology, https://www.pentecostaltheology.com/johannine-comma-1-john-57-trinity-vs-oneness-debate/

Philostorgius, 'Photius, Patriarch of Constantinople', *Epitome of the Ecclesiastical History of Philostorgius,*. Edward Walford trans https://www.tertullian.org/fathers/philostorgius.htm

Philostorgius, Levenson, David B. "The Palestinian Earthquake of May 363 in, the Syriac Chron-icon Miscellaneum, and the Letter Attributed to Cyril on the Rebuilding of the Jerusalem Temple." *Journal of Late Antiquity* 6, no. 1 (June 24, 2013): 60–83. https://doi.org/10.1353/ jla.2013.0010. p.62

Plato, *Dialogues of Plato: Containing The Apology of Socrates, Crito, Phaedo, and Protagoras.* Colonial Press, 1899. Benjamin Jowett trans.

Plato, *Phædrus,* 244d, 244d-244e — *Dialogues of Plato: Containing The Apology of Socrates, Crito, Phaedo, and Protagoras.* Colonial Press, 1899. Benjamin Jowett trans.

Plato Laert., in *Apologia*, in Enfield, *The History of Philosophy, from the Earliest Periods*, 1839

Plotinus, MacKenna, Stephen, and Page, Bertram Samuel. *The Six Enneads,* Encyclopaedia Britannica, Chicago, 1952

Porphyrius, Russian Orthodox Archimandrite/Bishop, Первое путешествие в Синайский Монастыґ в 1845 году, 1856

Porphyrius, Archimandrite/Bishop. "Proceedings of the Kiev Theological Academy," November, 1865,

Porphyry, MacKenna, Stephen (trans,) 'The Enneads,' *On the Life of Plotinus and the Arrange-ment of his Work from Plotinus*, https://sacred-texts.com/cla/plotenn/enn001.htm

Rahn, Otto. *Crusade against the Grail: The Struggle between the Cathars, the Templars, and the Church of Rome.* Simon and Schuster, 2006 (1933)

Redondi, Pietro. *Galileo Heretic*, Princeton University Press. 1987

Reid, Thomas. Derek R. Brookes ed. *An Inquiry into the Human Mind on the Principles of Common Sense,* 1764. Edinburgh UP. 1997

Reinach, Salomon. Monod, Gabriel, and Alfred Loisy. 'L'«Orpheus» de Ms. Reinach.' *Revue Historique* 102, no. Fasc. 2, 1909

Renan, Ernest. *Life of Jesus* (*Vie de Jésus*). Roberts 1863 (the Modern Library, New York, 1927)

Rinella, Michael A. *Pharmakon: Plato, drug culture, and identity in ancient Athens.* Lexington Books, 2010

Roberts, John M. *The Mythology of the Secret Societies.* Sribner, 1972

Rogers, John. *Newton's Arian Epistemology and the Cosmogony of Paradise Lost,* ELH, Volume

86, Number 1, Spring 2019, pp. 77-106 — (Article) Published by Johns Hopkins University Press

Rousseau, Jean-Jacques. *Emile, or On Education (Émile, ou De l'éducation)* 1762 English, D.C. Heath & Co. 1888

Rousseau, Jean-Jacques. 'The Social Contract,' *A Discourse on the Moral Effects of the Arts and Sciences (Discours sur les sciences et les arts).* 1750

Rubenstein, Richard E. *Aristotle's Children: How Christians, Muslims, and Jews Rediscovered Ancient Wisdom and Illuminated the Middle Ages.* Houghton Mifflin Harcourt, 2004

Rudolph, Kurt. *Gnosis: The Nature and History of Gnosticism* A&C Black, 2001

Sabar, Ariel. *Veritas: A Harvard Professor: A Con Man and the Gospel of Jesus Wife,* Anchor, 2020

Salza, John, *Why Catholics Cannot Be Masons,* TAN Books, 2008

Sass, Louis Arnorsson. *Madness and modernism: Insanity in the light of modern art, literature, and thought.* Basic Books, 1992

Sayers, Dorothy L. *The lost tools of learning.* 1948

Scheiner, Christoph and Locher, Johann Georg. *Disquisitiones Mathematicae de Controversiis et Novitatibus Astronomicis.* 1614

Schneller, Ludwig. *Search on Sinai,* Epworth Press, 1939

Socrates of Constantinople. *Historia ecclesiastica,* VII:32

Socrates Scholasticus, *The Ecclesiastical History of Socrates Scholasticus (Socrates, Historia Ecclesiastica,)*

Sozomen, 'Arius,' 'Recantation to the Emperor Constantine', *Ecclesiastical History,* 2, 27. LPNF, ser. 2, vol. 2, 277. (*Socrates, Historia Ecclesiastica, 1. 26*) http://legalhistorysources.com/ChurchHistory220/LectureTwo/AriusLetter3.htm

Sozomen. 'Athanasius and the Council of Tyre, 335' from *Historia Ecclesiastica,* Chap. XXV. Illegal Deposition of St. Athanasius https://www.earlychurchtexts.com/public/sozomen_on_athanasius_and_the_council_of_tyre.htm

Spieth, Darius. *Napoleon's Sorcerers: The Sophisians,* University of Delaware Press, 2007

Stevens, Jennifer, *The Historical Jesus and the Literary Imagination 1860–1920,* Chp. 5 — 'The Fifth Gospel of Oscar Wilde'. Guillot de Saix, Le Chant du Cygne: contes parlés d'Oscar Wilde. Recueillis et rédigés par Guillot de Saix Mercure, Paris, France, 1942

Strathern, Paul. *Napoleon in Egypt,* Bantam Books, New York. 2008

Travis, George. *Letter to Edward Gibbon author of Decline and Fall of the Roman Empire,* CF and J. Rivington at St. Paul's Churchyard, 1785, — Letter IV to Sir Isaac Newton

Trismegistus, Hermes, and Salaman, Clement. *The Way of Hermes: New Translations of The Corpus Hermeticum and The Definitions of Hermes Trismegistus to Asclepius.* Inner Traditions, 1999

Tertullian, *Against Praxeas,* II—'Ante-Nicene Fathers,' Eerdmans, Grand Rapids, MI. 1971

Tertullian, *Against Praxeas,* II. — https://www.thegospelcoalition.org/essay/trinitarianism-in-the-early-church/

Thorne, Guy [C. Ranger Gull] 'The Strand of Twenty Years Ago: Some Personal Reminiscences' in T. P's Weekly, 11 July 1913

Thorne, Guy. *When It Was Dark,* Greening & Co. of London 1903

Tobias, Norman Cecil. 'Jules Isaac and the Roman Catholic Church advocate for scriptural truth,' 2015

Unitarian Universalist Association website — https://www.uua.org/files/documents/tapestry/uu_history_timeline.pdf

Unger, D. J. 'Ancient Christian writers: Against the heresies.' Paulist Press (1992). *Against Heresies,* St. Irenæus, 3.11.1 *Against Heresies,* St. Irenæus, 3.11.1

Various, *The Early Church Fathers and Other Works*, Wm. B. Eerdmans Pub. Co. 1867 Edinburgh, Scotland

Vasilev, Georgi. *Heresy and the English Reformation: Bogomil-Cathar Influence on Wycliffe, Langland, Tyndale and Milton.* McFarland, 2014

The Vatican, *Divino Afflante Spiritu* — https://www.vatican.va/content/pius-xii/en/encyclicals/documents/hf_p-xii_enc_30091943_divino-afflante-spiritu.html

VETUSLATINA.ORG: *Resources for the Study of the Old Latin Bible*, https://itseeweb.cal.bham.ac.uk/vetuslatina/

Wakefield, Walter L. and Evans, Austin P. *Heresies of the High Middle Ages*, Columbia University, 1969

Watson, J. M. Roberts. *The Mythology of the Secret Societies*, Sribner, 1972

Whitehead, Neil L. 'Carib Cannibalism: the Historical Evidence', quote from *Archivo General de Indias*, Sevilla, 1951

Wiles, Maurice. *Archetypal heresy: Arianism through the centuries.* OUP Oxford, 1996

Wilkinson, David. *'Guy Thorne': C. Ranger Gull—Edwardian Tabloid Novelist and His Unseemly Brotherhood*, Rivendale Press 2012, ISBN 978 904201 20 5

Westcott, Brooke Foss, and Fenton John Anthony Hort, eds. *The New Testament in the original Greek: The text revised.* Macmillan, 1881

Whisker, James B. *The philosophy of Alfred Rosenberg: origins of the national socialist myth.* Noontide, 1990

Williams, Frank, ed. *The Panarion of Epiphanius of Salamis, Books II and III. De Fide: Second.* Vol. 79. Brill, 2012.

Williams, Rowan. *Arius: Heresy and tradition.* Wm. B. Eerdmans Publishing, 2002

Wiseman, Cardinal Nicholas Patrick Stephen. *Essays On Various Subjects*, 'Two Letters on some parts of the Controversy concerning the Genuineness of 1 John v. 7,' Charles Dolman, London, 1853.

Wisse, Frederik. 'The Nag Hammadi Library and the Heresiologists.' *Vigiliae Christianae*, 1971

Yates, Dame Frances A. *Giordano Bruno and the Hermetic Tradition*, Univ. of Chicago 1964

Zeitlin, Solomon. *Jewish Quarterly Review*, Vol. XLI, No. 1. July 1950

INDEX